THE GROWTH ILLUSION

For Margaret and George
Mary
Boru, Joss and Lucy

THE
GROWTH
ILLUSION

HOW ECONOMIC GROWTH HAS
ENRICHED THE FEW,
IMPOVERISHED THE MANY,
AND ENDANGERED THE PLANET

Richard Douthwaite

The Lilliput Press

First published in 1992 by
THE LILLIPUT PRESS LTD
4 Rosemount Terrace, Arbour Hill,
Dublin 7, Ireland
in association with
GREEN BOOKS
Ford House, Hartland, Bideford,
Devon EX39 6EE, England

A CIP record for this title
is available from
The British Library

ISBN 0 946640 87 4
ISBN 0 946640 88 2 (pbk)

Set in Caslon by
Koinonia Ltd of Manchester
Printed in Dublin by
Colour Books of Baldoyle

Contents

Graphs and Illustrations

Acknowledgments

Had it not been written in Ireland, this book would have been quite different. My research for the chapter on the Irish experience of economic growth – which was originally included only because I felt an Irish-published book ought to have one – turned out to be crucial and changed my views fundamentally. However, I doubt if the book could have been written anywhere else anyway. It is the product of a large group of people, not just the author, and a particular set of circumstances; had both these elements not been right, the job could not have been done.

So I owe profound thanks to those who helped the project along. This is their book too. In particular, I would like to thank those who commented on the manuscript at various stages. In Ireland, these were John Bradley of the Economic and Social Research Institute, John Gormley and Paul O'Neill of the Green Party, David Hickey of An Taisce, Douglas McCulloch of the University of Ulster, Susan Farrell, Gillies Macbain, Susan Minish, John McNamara, and Ken Stevens. Tony Whilde and Marianne ten Cate of the Corrib Conservation Centre each read two drafts and then volunteered to help with proof-reading. In England, George and Margaret Douthwaite, Richard Gault, Sandy Irvine and Juliet Solomon read drafts and made valuable contributions.

Those who helped with particular chapters include John Hall, Earl Davis and Margret Fine-Davis, Tom Stark, John Wells, Chris Wermann, Peter Warburton, Libby Lyon, Mary Gorham, Michael Campbell, Lord Stoddart, Alan Kucia, Richard Wilkinson, Karen Nicolaysen, George Teeling Smith, Keith Godfrey, Walter Yellowlees, Eric Millstone, Cecilia Armelin, Gwynne Lyons, Boo Baskin, Paddy Roe, Leonard Nelson, O. P. Steeno, David Barker, Duncan Dormor, Eugene Paykel, Chris Whelan, Mayer Hillman, Jenny Bernard, Lesley Webster, Fr Smith, Paul Everitt, Phil Douthwaite, Helen and Rob Brydges, Jonathan Gershuny, Julian Simon, Nick Sturgeon, Clare Heardman, Fiona Weir, Tracy Heslop, Bob Douthwaite, David McConnell, Fergal O'Gara, Tom Whitty, Wilfred Beckerman, Robert Whelan, William Nordhaus, Malcolm Slesser, Bert de Vries, Jobst Kraus, Paul Hell, Gerd Grozinger, Reinhard Loske, John Adams, David Fleming, Mary Gillick,

Jeremy Wates, Chris and Bríd Smith, Lars Petter Hansen, Tom Cross, Peter Mantle and Ambrose Joyce. For help with the Dutch chapter I owe a debt to Lucas Reijnders who read it in draft and brought it up to date immediately before the book went to press, and to Roefie Hueting, whose ideas influenced the shape of the book as a whole. Besides them, Marius Hummelinck, Dolf Boddeke, Johan Vijfvinkel, Peter van der Toom, Sible Schone, R. S. de Groot and Marijke Vos took considerable time and trouble to help me during my research in the Netherlands. My Indian collaborators included Baba Amte, Vikas Amte, Lucas Babu, Eliazar Rose, Vilasrao Salunke, Daniel Mazgaonkar, Osmond and Yvette Gonsalves, Sujit Patwardhan, Sarojini Nadimpalli, Sharad Joshi, G. Britto, Winin Pereira, A. Jockin, M. D. Nanjundaswami, P. Harischandra, M. V. Pai, R. L. Gupta, Vijay and Saroja Parulkar, Vijay Paranjpye, Prembhai and Ragini Prem, P. K. Salian, Raut Thakaram, and B. V. Parameswara Rao. Contributions to the Irish chapter were made by Peter Shanley, Peter Flanagan, Jeremy Browne (Lord Sligo), Sheila Mulloy and the late Jeff O'Malley. Brendan Minish helped convert my word-processing disks to a format suitable for the typesetter. John Bradley, Mari-aymone Djeribi and Anne Lewis prepared the graphs.

Organizations which were particularly helpful included Trinity College Library, Dublin, Sainsbury's, Friends of the Earth (London), Earthwatch, the Institute of Alcohol Studies, the British Road Federation, the Climate Action Network, the Chemical Industries Association, the Woolwich Building Society, Robert Fleming & Co. Ltd., Greenpeace, and the Centre for Policy Studies.

Finally, I must express my gratitude to Antony Farrell of my Irish publishers, The Lilliput Press, who asked me to write the book in the first place and who, in addition to encouragement, gave me somewhere to stay when I needed to be in Dublin for research. His contribution was crucial. So was that of Séamus Ó Brógáin, my editor, who checked many details and tightened up the text. But the most important contribution of all came from my wife, Mary, who not only put up with relative poverty while the work was being done but supported me every step of what, at times, must have seemed a very long way, particularly as I was permanently preoccupied. To her, my love and thanks.

Foreword

Modern industrial man regards economic growth (or economic development, as it is called when it occurs in the Third World) as synonymous with progress, and thus sacred. It is seen as providing a veritable panacea for all our problems, and signalling the path that we must religiously follow in order to create a material and technological paradise here on Earth. This is the fundamental tenet of what is, in effect, the religion of industrial man, with which we have all been imbued since our earliest childhood: one that underlies all the disciplines into which modern knowledge has been divided – whether it be economics, sociology, physics, or even the reductionistic or mechanistic ecology currently taught in our universities; one too that is fervently promoted by corporations and their political allies throughout the world.

To give credibility to this myth, we increasingly interpret our problems as being of a purely economic nature, and ascribe them to insufficient growth or development, thus identifying human welfare with Pigou's 'economic welfare' and implying that economic growth is the only answer. The World Bank, for example, insists that the goal of the vast and highly destructive schemes which it continues to finance throughout the world is the eradication of poverty. Bilateral aid agencies seek to maintain the same fiction. The principal purpose of USAID, a former Secretary of State told his country's Senate Foreign Affairs committee, is 'to meet the basic needs of poor people in the developing countries'. This is difficult to reconcile with the fact that about 75 per cent of both US and British bilateral aid is 'tied' to the purchase of their technology, in particular power stations, large dams, and other installations which mainly provide services to the urban rich.

The rapid degradation of the world's remaining agricultural lands is also invariably attributed to traditional agricultural practices. Thus USAID, regardless of the fact that such practices have been used sustainably for thousands of years, links the deterioration of the 'soil resource base' in arid lands to mismanagement, arising from the use of 'traditional technology and agricultural practices'. Mrs Thatcher, in her 1989 address to the United Nations General Assembly in New York, blamed what she called 'cut-and-burn' agriculture, and recommended action 'to improve agricultural methods – good husbandry, that ploughs back nourishment into the soil', a rosy picture of modern industrial agriculture.

Malnutrition and famine are also associated primarily with archaic agricultural practices, even though, on the admission of the ex-US Secretary of State for Agriculture Bob Bergland, agriculture in China 'produces nine times as many calories per acre as we do in the United States'. The Food and Agricultural Organization of the United Nations (FAO) even produced a report in 1984 entitled 'Land, Food and People' to show that food availability in the Third World is directly proportionate to the amount of fertilizer used, no mention being made of the diminishing returns on fertilizer use experienced wherever modern agriculture has been introduced.

The FAO cites poverty as another cause of malnutrition and famine. People starve because they do not have the money to buy the food they need, a problem which clearly can be solved only by further economic development. No one points out that, despite the unprecedented economic development of the post-war years, more people than ever before lack the money with which to pay for their food; nor, for that matter, that malnutrition is now a serious problem in the United States of America, the most highly 'developed country' in the world, where upwards of thirty million people are said to be affected.

The population explosion is also ascribed to poverty: poor people's insecurity leads them to produce more children, who can be put to work to earn money for their parents. Rapid economic development will make them rich and provide them with the requisite security, thereby assuring a 'demographic transition' such as has already occurred in the industrial world. Again no one mentions that this transition occurred only once per capita income had reached a level incomparably higher than that which Third World people can ever possibly achieve; nor that in the meantime economic development, by destroying people's families and communities, annihilating their natural environment and forcing them off their land and into the slums, is in fact the greatest source of their present insecurity.

Even global warming is increasingly perceived as an economic problem. The National Academy of Sciences in its recent report, 'Global warming: policy implications', actually suggests that the solution might reside in 'geo-engineering': for instance, siting 50,000 one-square-kilometre mirrors in space so as to reflect heat from the sun away from the earth – the financing of which would obviously require an unprecedented spurt in economic growth or development.

Attacking the myth of economic growth, as Richard Douthwaite has done in this brilliant and highly documented book, is thus a very subversive enterprise – one which must undermine the whole structure of modern knowledge and, one might add, that of modern society itself. For the corporations into which our society is organized cannot continue to expand – as they must to survive – if our ever more daunting problems do not provide them with the appropriate commercial opportunities. The demolition of this myth, however subversive it may be, is of vital importance, for, in reality, economic growth is the main cause of social and environmental destruction and the associated poverty and misery. The living world, ever less capable of absorbing the impact of our activities, will otherwise inevitably become degraded to the point where it can no longer support complex forms of life.

Only when the myth of economic growth has been totally discredited will it be possible to imbue people with the world-view consistent with a less destructive way of life, enabling us to inhabit the beautiful planet we have inherited without systematically destroying it. For this reason Richard Douthwaite's book is of the greatest importance to us all.

EDWARD GOLDSMITH
Richmond, London
January 1992

Introduction

> Anyone who believes exponential growth can go on forever in a finite world is either a madman or an economist. – Kenneth Boulding, economist

In the 1989 elections to the European Parliament the British and Irish Green parties surprised themselves and everybody else by doing remarkably well. On the Sunday after the poll the environmental correspondent of *The Observer*, Geoffrey Lean, wrote an article under the headline, 'Why I did not vote Green' in which he explained that he had not supported the Green Party because its anti-economic growth policies would lead to a slump. Moreover, he claimed, several leading environmentalists who had carefully studied the Greens' manifesto had not voted for it either, for the same reason. Most of those who had voted for the party had not known what it stood for and would not have voted for it if they had.

The following Sunday a writer and television presenter, Michael Ignatieff, wrote a reply in which he said he had read the fine print of the Greens' manifesto and had voted for the party, 'because they have been so right for so long about the size of the problem ... [They] were there before anybody else was ... and deserve electoral reward.' But, he said, being right about the problem was not enough: pragmatic solutions were also required.

Should the fundamentalist, anti-growth Greens win out over the pragmatists, I'm sure to desert them for a party which does welcome the post-modern world. Green fundamentalists persist in thinking of growth as a machine set in motion by the corporate giants to manipulate and satisfy false needs. I don't think the needs satisfied by modern growth are false at all. I like growth because it has brought refrigerators, cars, central heating, summer holidays and decent retirement pensions to working-class people all over the Western world. Future growth should bring these humble goods to the people of the Third World. I am looking for an environmental politics that welcomes rather than condemns these aspirations.

I was amazed a journalist like Lean who had written about environmental problems week after week should have failed to realize that almost all of those problems were created by an economic system which needs to expand continuously if it is not to collapse. It was equally shocking that someone as well informed as Ignatieff should believe that our planet has enough resources to enable the people of the Third World to consume them at Western levels in perpetuity. In fact, in view of the content of the rest of his essay, it was hard to see why he thought they should even try.

Ignatieff described how the better-off of the Western world had tried to escape the consequences of noise, traffic pollution and urban decay by moving to 'the house with the garden on the quiet street', leaving behind the poor 'who can't buy their way out of the city smog for a weekend, can't move away from the street where lorries shake the windows and deposit the black silt of the exhaust on the sills.' But the would-be escapers had found that there was no longer anywhere to run to: 'We pollute the skies flying towards the unspoiled and the untamed and when we land, we discover the pollution got to the beach before we did.' And so, instead of trying to flee, people were turning to fight and starting to vote Green.

The purpose of this book is to explain to Lean, Ignatieff and the millions who share their views exactly why economic growth is the cause of our environmental problems and why its continuation, even if we take steps to limit pollution, cannot be part of the cure. In fact humankind has already overloaded the earth's restorative mechanisms and we urgently need to cut back our consumption of its resources.

I found this a difficult book to write. Everyone in the West is brought up to think the future will be richer materially than the present and this pattern of thought is very hard to break. When I examined my own attitudes I found that emotionally I shared Ignatieff and Lean's belief that growth makes things better while at the same time I knew intellectually that it did not.

In fact I only realized what my hidden beliefs were when I read Hazel Henderson's brisk and blunt statement in her *Politics of the Solar Age* (1981) that, since everything humankind does involves consuming some of the earth's resources, there is a limit to the amount of human activity that can be built on top of a finite resource base. Since this dashed my hopes that it would be possible to find a way in which the economy could continue to grow indefinitely by substituting intellectual or artistic strivings for damaging production-oriented ones, Henderson's judgment seemed too harsh, too final, and I looked frantically for a way out. Her comment was all the harder to accept because it was not discussed at all but delivered as if it were entirely self-evident.

The reason I was upset at the thought that growth might not be able to continue was that, like most other people, I thought the process was, on balance, beneficial. But where was the evidence? In 1921 R. H. Tawney introduced his book *The Acquisitive Society* by pointing out: 'It is a commonplace that the characteristic virtue of Englishmen is their power of sustained practical activity, and their characteristic vice a reluctance to test the quality of that activity by reference to principles.' J. K. Galbraith picked up Tawney's thought in the 1960s and extended it to everyone. 'One of the generally amiable idiosyncrasies of man is his ability to expend a great deal of effort without much enquiry as to why' he wrote in his widely read essay 'Economics and the quality of life'[1] before moving on to explain that since no-one in advanced countries ever asked what society was trying to achieve, people were unaware that there was any need for choice about how resources were used.

As a result of this tendency to avoid measuring performance against objectives, very few people have assessed whether the assumed benefits of growth are being delivered. All a careful search of the literature turned up were several discussions of the potentially harmful side-effects of growth written in the sixties and seventies, notably by E. J. Mishan,[2] and these were largely theoretical, with little discussion of the facts. This dearth of inquiry is strange since dozens of economic historians have written papers discussing the extent to which the Industrial Revolution improved the lot of workers in Britain in the last century. In fact, if one were paranoid it would be easy to think that it was the result of a conspiracy to stop researchers critically analysing growth. In Orwell's *Nineteen Eighty-Four*, the state rewrites the history books to conceal the attractiveness of the past. Our present masters are more subtle: they change the basis on which the statistics are collected and thus make long-term comparisons impossible. Anyone who doubts this should try comparing tables in two issues of the official British *Annual Abstract of Statistics* with a forty-year gap between them.

Successful public speakers have a rule: 'Tell the audience what you are going to say, then say it and then tell them what you've said.' I intend following that approach here. What I hope this book will show is that economic growth has made life considerably worse for people in Britain since 1955 and that, even if growth was beneficial at one stage in human history, it is now downright damaging. Further attempts to grow will do so much harm that any benefits the expansion might bring will be outweighed many times over. Even the hope of further growth is harmful, because it lulls us into accepting changes like the continued rise in the world's population which, in a no-growth world, must be seen as disastrous. Equally importantly, the prospect of growth has enabled us to escape doing anything about the poor by telling them that things will get better for them if they just hang on. The promise of jam for all tomorrow has eased our consciences about the unequal division of bread today.

So why do we persist in trying to grow if we are getting damaging results from almost every investment we make? One answer I suggest is that our measure of progress is so defective that it is still giving us favourable signals. Another is that the groups that make the investments that generate growth are getting good returns – although at the expense of everyone else. And thirdly, many of the negative effects of growth have yet to reveal themselves, particularly those connected with the environment. But the real reason we have not stopped growing is that our economic system would collapse if we did – exactly as Lean said – and so I spend a lot of time suggesting a path out of this doomed-if-we-do, doomed-if-we-don't situation.

Rather than striving to achieve rapid growth – the creation of ever-larger bundles of an unspecified selection of goods and services – I propose that we set ourselves specific targets and measure our success in terms of our progress towards them. This involves a radical change in the way we approach economic management. At present most Western governments pride themselves on leaving decisions to the market, believing that they ought to direct their national economies to the least possible extent. These governments believe that it is for the consumer to say, through his or her expenditure, what should be produced, by whom and how, because both maximum personal freedom and greater economic efficiency lie in that direction. Unfortunately, however, this argument breaks down beyond a certain point because there are many things that only collective action can bring about.

It is the job of political parties to lay before the electorate alternative views on the direction society – and consequently the economy – should take. Once we have chosen between their proposals at the ballot box, the resulting government should legislate accordingly, leaving the markets to work out the fine details, not the overall direction. At present, however, none of the major parties – in Britain, the United States, or Ireland – does this because they are unaware, as Galbraith said, that there is any alternative to the road we are on. Bar the Greens, all parties have accepted growth as the national goal and believe that decisions made in the market are the best way of speeding it along. If this type of thinking continues, our future will be one that none of us has sanctioned and very few desire.

Many of this book's conclusions would have surprised me when I set out to write it. All my life everyone has agreed that growth creates jobs and I found it difficult to overcome this conditioning and accept that, because the process depends on the introduction of labour-saving technology, growth actually destroys them. Once I had made the mental switch, however, I could not see why making it had taken me so long. Several other reluctant discoveries also turn conventional economic wisdom on its head; for example, I argue that inflation is frequently beneficial, and that growth makes it inescapable for governments to increase the proportion of national income they spend on providing public services.

Because the book breaks new ground and comes to radical, unconventional conclusions, I urge readers to take the time to move steadily through it from beginning to end. Approached in this way, it may change the way they think about the world.

Growth has been non-controversial as a national objective because in theory the extra resources it creates have been available to give the Right its profits and the Left the means to improve social welfare. However, I hope that by the time they turn the last page, people from all parts of the political spectrum will feel that the setting of replacement objectives is an urgent necessity. I also hope they will be convinced about what those objectives should be.

1
Quality or Quantity?

The Senior Tutor had seen change coming. He blamed science for re-establishing the mirage of truth, and still more the pseudomorph subjects like anthropology and economics whose adepts substituted inapplicable statistics for the ineptness of their insights. – Tom Sharpe, *Porterhouse Blue* (1974)

When we hear politicians talking about 'raising the standard of living through sustainable economic growth' most of us are happy to treat it as just another meaningless platitude. Nobody, after all, would expect them to promise to cut our standards of living or claim that the economic growth they are proposing to bring about will last a few years and then disappear, leaving us in a worse mess than before.

But we ignore the formulation at our peril. By using it our leaders are capitalizing on a confusion most of us share about the link between 'the standard of living' and another phrase, one they use less often: 'the quality of life'. On the face of it these two expressions mean exactly the same thing. In fact they do not. 'Standard of living' is a technical term that means 'the per capita rate of consumption of purchased goods and services' which, in turn, given our economic system, inescapably means 'the rate at which we will use up the earth's limited resources'. But spelling things out in this way would make the politicians' proposals sound so profligate that it is never, ever done.

And what does 'quality of life' mean? In the early 1970s researchers[1] from the British Social Science Research Council (SSRC) asked carefully selected samples of 1,500 people exactly that question three times in the space of five years. 'There has been a lot of discussion about the quality of life recently,' they said to their interviewees each time. 'What do you think are the important things which go to make it up?' The answers they got were fascinating. In a society that was regularly condemned for its materialism, non-material factors such as a good home life and a contented outlook were rated as important by more people than were such things as the quantity of consumer goods they had. Of the replies that can be put into one category or the other, 71 per cent were about things that have little or nothing to do with cash. The results of the most recent survey, that of 1975, are set out below. Because the respondents could give more than one answer if they wished, the total does not add up to 100 per cent.

Definition of the quality of life	%
Family and home life	23
General contentment	19
Money and prices	18
Living standards, consumption	17
Social values	16
Personal beliefs, religion	11
Social relationships	10
Housing	10
Health	10
Work	9
Freedom of all kinds	7
Leisure, holidays, travel	6
Natural environment	4
Education and culture	4
Comparison with past and other countries	4
Possession of consumer goods	3
Pressures of life	3
Worries, mental health	2
Negative statements	2
Altruistic statements	2
Equality and justice	2
Other	3
Don't know	10

The most interesting thing about these results is not that people said that consumption was only one factor in determining the quality of their lives but that anybody should be surprised that they did so. At the beginning of this century a survey that produced such results would have seemed quite banal. In those days even economists accepted that economic factors were only one element in determining what they called 'happiness' or 'satisfaction'. Later, wanting to make economics seem more scientific, the profession began to talk about 'welfare' instead (a term introduced by a Cambridge University professor, Arthur Pigou, who used it in 1920 in the title of his book, *The Economics of Welfare*). Seventy years later, after doing little else but considering ways of improving welfare by increasing consumption, most economists find the interviewees' commonsense views somewhat shocking.

The roots of their surprise feed on Pigou's book. Whereas Jeremy Bentham, the social philosopher best known for a phrase he borrowed, 'the greatest happiness of the greatest number', held that the welfare of society was the sum of all the satisfactions of all the individuals in that society, Pigou ignored those satisfactions that could not be measured in cash terms and confined his analysis to what he called 'economic welfare'. This he defined as 'that part of social welfare that can be brought directly or indirectly into relation with the measuring rod of money.' For Pigou, the amount of economic welfare was proportional to the size of the national income, although he put in the important condition that everything else had to remain the same, particularly the way in which national income was distributed. 'Provided the dividend [his term for income] accruing to the poor is not diminished, increases in the size of the aggregate national dividend, if they occur in isolation without anything else whatever happening, must involve increases in economic welfare.'

Pigou's careful caveats have, of course, been forgotten. Unless they make a conscious effort to do so, most people, like most economists, no longer recall that economic welfare is merely a part of total welfare and that we can only say unequivocally that a rise in national income has improved the national welfare if no-one has been made worse off. For almost all of us a rise in national income means a rise in national welfare, full stop, and, as a result, the terms 'standard of living' and 'quality of life' are bound to be confused. Even when I was half way through this book and – on an intellectual level – certainly knew better, I found I had to make a deliberate effort to stop using the phrases interchangeably in conversation. So effective has our indoctrination been that it is hard to accept the notion that a higher standard of living might, in some circumstances, be a bad thing. With this in mind, I use 'a higher level of production and consumption' rather than 'a higher standard of living' wherever possible for the rest of this book.

If we think in terms of the factors identified by the SSRC surveys, it is easy to envisage circumstances in which a rise in the volume of production (in other words, economic growth) could diminish national welfare (in other words, the quality of life). For example, higher rates of production at work could affect relationships at home and cause far more unhappiness than could ever be cured by higher wages. The extra production could also increase atmospheric pollution and cause sickness and misery for thousands of people who could never be compensated adequately from the proceeds of the additional output, even if a way could be found to do so. And just because a country is producing more goods does not necessarily mean that its people get to enjoy them: the new production (and an increased share of the old) might be exported to pay off financiers overseas or be used for investment in new factories and roads, things that bring scarcely anyone any pleasure.

With examples like these in mind, a Dutch economist, Roefie Hueting, has argued for the past twenty years that people in developed countries might be better off if they produced less. Hueting[2] thinks that at least seven factors play a role in determining the quality of life, only one of which is equivalent to Pigou's 'economic welfare'. These are:

1. The quantity of goods and services produced and consumed.
2. The quality of the environment people enjoy, including space, energy, natural resources and plant and animal species.
3. The fraction of their time available for leisure
4. How fairly – or unfairly – the available income is distributed.
5. How good or bad working conditions are.
6. How easy it is to get a job. 'Supporting oneself by one's own work is one of the essential aspects of existence and the absence of a possibility of doing so means in all probability a considerable loss of welfare.'
7. The safety of our future. 'Man derives part of the meaning of existence from the company of others. These include in any case his children and grandchildren. The prospect of a safer future is therefore a normal human need and the dimming of this prospect has a negative effect on welfare.'

If we add to Hueting's list the additional factors suggested by the SSRC survey we come up with at least twelve things that have a claim to be considered in any computation of whether people are better off because of economic growth or indeed any other changes in society. These additional factors might be summarized as:

8. How healthy we are.
9. The level of cultural activity, the standard of education and the ease of access to it.
10. The quality of the housing available.
11. The chance to develop a satisfactory religious or spiritual life.
12. The strength of one's family, home and community ties.

The immediate thing to notice about all twelve factors is that, with the exception of factor 1, they cannot be measured in cash terms. Indeed some of them cannot be measured scientifically at all. This has meant that they have been ignored by economists, who, in their efforts to turn their subject into a scientific discipline, have preferred to have nothing to do with those areas of life that might involve them in making 'value judgments'. This is the real reason for the scarcity of research on the overall effects of economic growth on non-monetary aspects of human welfare I mentioned in the Introduction.

What evidence there is, however, suggests that growth has not improved the quality of life or, if it has, that the improvement has been marginal. For example, the SSRC survey showed that people in Britain believed that their quality of life was declining. Interviewees were asked how their level of consumption had changed over the previous five years, and almost unanimously they said that it had gone up and they expected it to continue to do so in the next five years. Yet when they were asked to rate the quality of life at the time of the survey on a scale from 0 to 10 and to say what they thought it had been five years previously and what it would be in five years' time, their verdict was almost unanimous: the quality of life was going down. Britain, they said, rated 8 five years ago, was 7.2 now (in 1975) and would be 6 by 1980 if things carried on as they were.

The SSRC research programme was axed in 1976 in an effort to save £100,000. In 1977, however, two researchers in Dublin, Earl Davis and Margret Fine-Davis, got funds from the European Commission to ask 2,000 people in each of eight EC countries (Britain, France, Germany, Italy, Ireland, Denmark, Belgium and the Netherlands) a barrage of questions about their lives.[3] Perhaps the key question they asked was, 'Taking everything into account, how satisfied are you with your life in general?' and from the piles of answers they found that the best predictor of whether people would say they were content was whether or not they were happy with their health. They also found that there was a close correlation between the way people felt about their health and their actual health as determined by a doctor. Other factors had a bearing on life satisfaction too, of course. There were statistically significant links between how people felt about their housing and the neighbourhood in which they lived. Married people tended to be more satisfied than those who were single, widowed or divorced.

But, surprisingly, income did not matter, at least not in France, the Netherlands and Britain, and it was only the seventh or eighth most important predictor in Italy, Ireland and Denmark. Only in Germany, where it was number three, and Belgium, number four, did it seem to have any direct bearing on how people felt about their lives.

Since this study, research into the factors that determine the quality of life has been badly neglected.[4] Governments have been left with only the rate of growth to tell them how well, or badly, they are doing. Yet respected economists have been pointing out for years that the rate of growth is a very poor guide to anything at all. Growth only measures changes in 'gross national product' – the sum of the sale value of all the traded goods and services produced in a country during a year – and this is a very odd animal indeed. For example, since GNP only includes the value of things that are bought and sold, the vast array of activities outside the monetarized part of the economy is ignored entirely. The preparation value of meals eaten at home is excluded, while meals eaten at a restaurant are put in; do-it-yourself repairs to the car are out, garage repairs in; caring for Granny at home is out, nursing-home care is in.

In fact the more self-sufficient people are, the lower their GNP will appear to be at a given level of consumption. British visitors to rural Ireland are often amazed at how well-off the locals seem in spite of lower wages, higher taxes and higher prices in the shops. The mystery is explained by the fact that many of the sparkling new bungalows have been built on family land by the owners and their friends: only the materials and specialist jobs cost money. Many of these people cut their own fuel and grow their own vegetables too, but the value of these and of the house construction is, quite properly, left off their income tax returns. Naturally the Irish national income statisticians adjust their data in an attempt to correct for these non-monetary activities, but all the signs are that they do not correct by nearly enough, particularly as they have an extensive black economy to allow for as well. Michael Heaney, a community development worker on the Inishowen peninsula in Co. Donegal, says that official visitors are always surprised by how prosperous his area seems. 'If you just look at the figures in Dublin or Brussels you would certainly write Inishowen off as a hopeless case,' he says. 'We have 50 per cent unemployment, a high dependency ratio and a very peripheral location. But it's not like that at all. A fair bit of the income isn't declared. If you are a farmer and do a bit of fishing on the side you can make quite a good living.'

Since country people can be more self-sufficient than anyone in a town can manage to be, differing degrees of urbanization can throw up false results. So too can changes over time: if, between one generation and the next, families stop baking their own bread, making their own jam, keeping a pig or sewing their own clothes, some part of the gains in GNP that seem to have been made during the period have to be written off. The changes involved when GNP increases can make statistical comparisons unreliable. It is therefore very dangerous to use GNP as a proxy for even level-of-consumption data – to say nothing of the quality of life – when comparing one country with another. All GNP reveals is the size of the legal monetarized sector, not an economy's true size.

Since GNP only measures things which are bought and sold for cash, it ignores clean air, pure water, silence and natural beauty, self-respect and the value of relationships between people – all of which are central to the quality of life. Of late, economists have been hoping to rectify some of these omissions by learning to calculate, for example, how much more a house is worth if it does not have a motorway at the bottom of the garden, but the day will never dawn when GNP figures can be adjusted to take them all into account.

Some surprising things included in GNP can distort it so much that the year-to-year comparisons required for growth calculations become utterly unreliable unless major corrections are made. One is taxes. If a government imposes consumption taxes such as excise duties or VAT, these will pump up the GNP figure making the nation appear to be richer and to be growing faster while the people might actually be worse off. Only if one uses 'GNP at factor cost' figures can one avoid being led astray. A second distortion is that depreciation is included in GNP. This is logical enough since machines have to be made to replace existing ones and, as GNP includes all traded goods and services, the value of the replacement ones has to be there. But nobody believes that the more rapidly we write down our productive assets the richer we are, and we consequently have to strip depreciation out of GNP to get a more meaningful figure. If we strip out both taxes and depreciation we are left with a figure the statisticians call 'net national product at factor cost' (NNP) but this is rarely used in public discussions on the growth rate and, since it shares all GNP's other defects, it is little better as a guide to the level of national well-being.

One type of depreciation excluded from GNP (and NNP) calculations would reduce the published figures for many countries substantially. At present, no adjustment is made for the extent to which a country's natural resources – its minerals, fossil fuels, forests, or soils – are sold off or used up in the production of the goods that the GNP figure represents. Someone who played a large part in the development of national income accounting, Richard Stone, explained why this was in his book, *National Income and Expenditure* (1944), which has been reprinted again and again for the benefit of generations of undergraduates:

Goods and services have no value in themselves. We do not pay nature for accumulating large deposits of coal in the earth, or for stimulating the growth of pearls inside oysters or for creating the human brain. When we speak, therefore, of the value of a good or of a service we mean the price we have to pay to induce human beings to bring forth these products for the enjoyment and enrichment of the community: the price we have to pay to induce, let us say, the miner to dig coal out, the owner of capital to finance the necessary equipment, the owner of the land to allow his field to be dug up. Coal underground is worth nothing, *per se*; nor, for that matter is the pearl in the oyster or the latent ability of the poet or scientist.

This attitude – that the fruits of nature are free goods – goes back to the early days of economics as a discipline. It is a product of the period immediately after the Middle Ages, when the development of improved pumps so that deeper mines could be dug, and of better transport so that more distant territories could be exploited, made the earth's resources seem unlimited. The only shortage was of people to develop them (hence, among other things, the slave trade). It is only recently that economists have begun to realize that concentrating on the flow of income and ignoring what is happening to the national stock of wealth is dangerous. As *The Economist* put it in 1989, 'a country that cut down all its trees, sold them as wood chips and gambled the money away playing tiddly-winks would appear from its national accounts to have got richer in terms of GNP per person'.

The change in attitude among economists was preceded by the publication in 1977 of a book, *Nature's Price*, by two Dutch non-economists – a journalist, Walter van Dieren, and the former managing director of one of Unilever's animal food companies, Marius Hummelinck – who thought that if a cash value was put on nature's gifts, industrial society might be shocked into halting its destruction of them. Another twelve years had to pass before this concept was taken up by the profession. In 1989 David Pearce suggested in a report (published as *Blueprint for a Green Economy*) commissioned by the British government that national accounts should try to measure changes in the stock of environmental and natural resources and should allow for welfare lost through pollution. It will probably take as long again for the corrections to be made.

Another distortion in the GNP figure is the inclusion of exports, which are never consumed in the country that makes them. Some Third World countries are showing reasonable GNP growth as a result of higher exports but, because the earnings from them are used to pay interest on foreign debt, their people are becoming worse off.

If we exclude exports from GNP in order to get an idea of welfare, we ought to include imports, some of which we get to enjoy. But only some. Many imports are investment goods such as machine tools which go to increase, not just maintain, the national productive potential. Many home-produced goods fall into this category as well, of course, and the proportion of imports and home production being invested can vary widely from country to country (net investment was 43 per cent in Singapore in 1985 while in North Yemen it was –15 per cent) and within a country from year to year (in Britain the figure has been as high as 23 per cent and as low as 14 per cent since 1948). As a result the raw GNP figure is again a very unreliable guide to how much is actually left for personal consumption. A similar correction needs to be made for defence which varies quite widely from country to country, soaking up anything from 1.8 per cent of GNP (Ireland) to 27.1 per cent (Israel).

When we have stripped down GNP and made huge corrections for the depletion of natural resources and for items which, because they are inputs rather than outputs, never get used for people's welfare or enjoyment, what have we left? The answer is a whole rag-bag of goods and services. Some of the goods in our rag-bag are genuinely valuable, like food, and others are possibly harmful, like pornography. Economists are not ashamed that their measure is so unselective. On the contrary, they are proud that it is value-free. 'Who are we to say what people should buy?' they say. 'Consumers freely chose this set of purchases to maximize their individual satisfaction and, the more goods they are able to purchase, the greater that satisfaction.'

But is it? And was the consumers' choice free? Growth is a dynamic process, and after it has happened, the world is a different place. It is easy – and valid – for one person to say that, as things stand, if he had a car he would be better off because it would be quicker and pleasanter than walking to the bus through the wind and rain. But the process of giving a car to that person and to everyone else who wants one changes the situation so drastically that it is not possible to say whether, after the process has been completed, the community as a whole will be better off and the new car owners will get the benefits they thought they would. The increase in traffic might lengthen journey times to such an extent that the new car owners take longer to get to work than they did before. Other people's journey times will almost certainly go up as a result of congestion and the total time the community spends travelling to work could increase. Bus frequencies will probably be cut and fares raised for lack of demand. Thus, even though GNP will increase because of the extra spending on transport, it is possible – even probable – that the country as a whole will be worse off in welfare terms and that many people will be running their cars largely out of necessity because of the way things have developed and not because they like doing so.

Similarly, if the process of growth alters the distribution of income in a country – and particularly if it makes it less equitable – we cannot say, as Pigou stressed, that just because overall consumption is higher, overall well-being has gone up. Even if everybody's income goes up equally, living standards need not improve because the increased spending power could be exhausted bidding up the prices of those consumer goods whose supply cannot be increased sufficiently to match the demand. These could be cottages in the country, membership of smart clubs, access to fashionable schools or fishing rights on the River Tweed. The old analogy that if everybody sitting in a theatre stands up to get a better view, nobody gets any advantage applies exactly to this case. And if there are some people who cannot stand up because their income has not increased to the same extent as everybody else's – pensioners and the unemployed, perhaps – their view will become considerably worse. Even though they may have a little more money than before, they will not be able to afford to maintain their former position.

The reason we are emotionally attached to growth and why we find it so hard to say it should stop is that everybody feels that if they had a little bit more of something they would be better off. What we fail to realize is that what is possible for one person is probably not possible for all and if everybody gets a little bit more it may alter or destroy not only the expected benefits but also those that people enjoyed before the change. Until a few years ago the Algarve was a pleasant holiday destination, accessible only to a few. Now it appears in every package tour catalogue and hotels have been built where almond groves once stood. The region has been completely altered, some would say for the worse, and many of the people who once spent springtime there have found somewhere more distant to go instead. Perhaps the Algarve provides more consumer satisfaction now because economic growth has enabled more people to go there but it is not offering the same product that it did. Because the place and the clientele have changed, objective comparisons are impossible. Without making value judgments we cannot say whether growth has made things better or worse.

Many of the purchases consumers make out of the fraction of GNP left to them are made out of necessity rather than from choice. If the number of flights from an airport increases, the people living near the runway might have to buy sound-deadening double-glazed windows in order to be able to live normal lives. Both the increased number of flights and the new windows will register as an increase in GNP, but the windows are a forced expenditure and will not increase anyone's well-being – indeed they will not even restore the situation to what it was beforehand.

Because the world is so complex it is very difficult to say what proportion of the purchases people make is truly voluntary, truly discretionary. If people have to buy a smart suit or drive a new car to maintain their position in the pecking order, rather than because they actually enjoy having them, these are involuntary purchases. The key word is 'maintain'. Any expenditure that has to be made in an attempt to keep things as they are, like the sound-reducing windows, is essentially involuntary and does not increase well-being. The spending on cleaning up after the *Exxon Valdez* oil spill in Alaska falls into this category: it has appeared in the US national income statistics as an increase in GNP, but no-one would claim it was done out of choice or that anyone got pleasure from it.

There is strong evidence that the proportion of involuntary expenditure consumers have to make out of the fraction of national income that trickles down to them rises sharply as that income goes up. Two eminent economists, William Nordhaus and James Tobin,[5] have even gone so far as to suggest that because a consumer's wants can be influenced by the producer – through advertising, for example – it might be that 'productive activity does no better than satisfy the wants which it generates,' creating no net gain in the level of human satisfaction. Unfortunately, having raised this hare, they followed it no further in their subsequent work. However, it is certainly true that, to paraphrase one of Northcote Parkinson's famous laws, needs expand to fill the income available. How else can we explain the fact that, although per capita incomes in the Hamburg area are more than three times those in Ireland, people living there do not seem to be significantly better off in terms of the amount of discretionary spending they are able to undertake?

The growth of involuntary consumption as incomes rise is the reason why people find it so hard to cut back and to live on an income that, after allowing for inflation, once served them quite well. It is not so much that they have grown accustomed to a higher standard of living but rather that the old systems that made a more frugal life possible have disappeared. In 1989, in response to a letter complaining that there were too many chi-chi boutiques in Bath but not a single shop where you could buy a few assorted nails and screws in a brown paper bag, *The Sunday Times* sent a reporter shopping for a tap washer, a sink plug and a lavatory chain in Birmingham. 'You won't get them in the city centre,' she was told in one store, 'you need a specialist shop.' In fact she found them at her fourth attempt. In Bath, the only way to renew a tap washer proved to be to buy a complete new set of taps. So when the Green Party points out that in future we shall have to manage on less, it should also point out that facilities like old-style ironmongers will have to be provided to make it possible. Just as growth changes everything, contraction will do so too. Nobody should feel that the future will consist of living on less in today's world.

Several attempts have been made to devise new indices that rectify some of GNP's defects as a measure of economic welfare, although no-one has got anywhere close to building one that measures human welfare as a whole. Tobin, who went on to win a Nobel Prize, and Nordhaus, whose views on the greenhouse effect we will discuss later, produced one of the first attempts in 1972.[6] The pair realized that Pigou's claim that the level of GNP was closely correlated with the level of economic welfare was looking increasingly shaky and that, as several generations of economists had happily made this claim their own, the profession was in danger of falling into disrepute. Accordingly, they set out to prove the claim was still valid by constructing a better index of economic welfare which they called their 'measure of economic welfare' (MEW), an indicator they hoped no-one would ever need to use if they succeeded in proving that GNP did the job just as well.

Their starting point was the recognition that while GNP was a measure of production, what the ordinary citizen was interested in was his or her level of consumption. They eliminated from the GNP total for each year between 1929 and 1965 not just everything that the public did not actually consume but also everything which could be considered 'regrettable necessities' – such as the cost of travel to work, police services, national defence, sewage disposal and road maintenance. Then they made further deductions for health and educational expenditure, which they treated as capital investments, and for the 'disamenities' endured by people who have to live and work in cities, treating the higher wages they earn there not as benefits but as compensation for the conditions they are forced to bear. To the residual annual figures they then added sums to allow for the benefits provided each year by the national capital stock (which now included education and health), for the leisure that people enjoy and also for the things like housework that they make or do for themselves.

Nordhaus and Tobin were happy with the results of their calculations. Over the 36-year period they examined, per capita NNP grew at 1.7 per cent

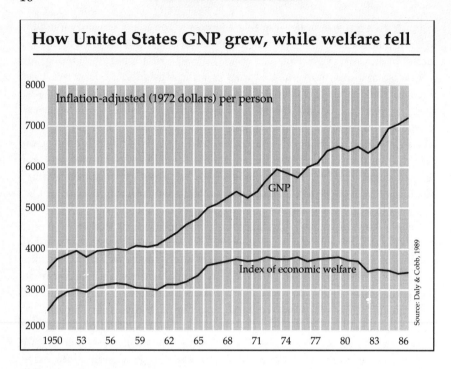

How United States GNP grew, while welfare fell

Figure 1.1 Although US national income per person more than doubled between 1950 and 1986, the sustainable welfare of its people scarcely rose at all and may now be declining.

a year and per capita MEW at 1.1 per cent. 'The progress indicated by conventional national accounts is not just a myth that evaporates when a welfare-oriented measure is substituted,' they crowed, mission accomplished.

But other people were not so enthusiastic, pointing out, as Herman Daly and John Cobb do in their book *For the Common Good* (1990), that 'the relatively close association' between growth of per capita GNP and MEW disappears when the Nordhaus and Tobin findings are examined for anything shorter than the 1929-65 span. Between 1935 and 1945, for example, per capita GNP rose by almost 90 per cent while per capita MEW went up by only 13 per cent. Similarly, between 1947 and 1965 GNP went up by 48 per cent but MEW by only 7.5 per cent. And even these small MEW increases are suspect: if we drop the Nordhaus and Tobin assumption that the productivity (and hence the value) of housework went up by the same amount as the productivity of paid labour, we find that MEW grew by only 2 per cent between 1947 and 1965.

'With their own figures, Nordhaus and Tobin have shed doubt on the thesis that national income accounts serve as a good proxy measure of economic welfare,' Daly and Cobb comment before going on to construct their own index, which attempts to remedy what they see as Nordhaus and Tobin's failings. While basically similar in approach, the Daly and Cobb index allows for the destruction of natural resources. It also updates the allowances that Nordhaus and Tobin made to compensate for all forms of pollution, bringing them more into line with recent findings about its extent and seriousness. Their other changes include the deletion of any estimated value for leisure and the dropping of 'human capital' – the capital value of health and education – from the national capital figure and thus from the flow of annual benefits. But perhaps the most important difference between the two approaches is that Daly and Cobb were not out to demonstrate that GNP is an approximation of economic welfare and that GNP growth is therefore a Good Thing.

Although the results they get are far and away the best estimates we have of whether our system is really increasing economic welfare, Daly and Cobb present them with some diffidence. 'There are many questions one could raise about whether human beings become better off as a result of increased consumption ... Our calculus of economic well-being has failed to take into account the fact that happiness is apparently correlated with relative rather than absolute levels of wealth or consumption. Having more is less important than having more than the "Joneses" yet in the absence of any way to quantify this sense of relative well-being we have ignored this important finding in our index.' They also point out that they have been forced to estimate quantities that are inherently unmeasurable.

Even allowing for these qualifications, the fact that the Daly and Cobb index shows that economic welfare in the United States rose to a peak in 1969, remained on a plateau for eleven years and then began to fall is worrying because this was a period in which GNP per head went up by 35 per cent and consumption of fossil fuels increased by around 17 per cent. Perhaps, to use a phrase of Roefie Hueting's, the lighthouse on which we have been taking our bearings was built in the wrong place.

In summary, all we can say about GNP is that it is a measure of the volume of trading going on in a country which has no necessary relation to the quality of life. Because so much changes when it increases – attitudes, income distribution, the level of noise and pollution, and indeed the whole economic system – it is impossible to say from first principles whether the results of growth will be good or bad. While we as individuals might feel better off if we had more, society as a whole may not benefit.

But if theory will not answer the question 'Is growth good?' history may. In the next eight chapters we look at the effects economic growth has had on the lives and happiness of ordinary people in Britain over the past two hundred years.

2

Why Capitalism Needs Growth

I put for a generall inclination of all mankind a perpetuall and restlesse desire of power after power, that ceaseth only in death. And the cause of this is not always that a man hopes for more intensive delight than he has already attained to; or that he be not content with moderate power: but that he cannot assure the power and the means to live well which he hath at present without the acquisition of more. – Thomas Hobbes, *Leviathan* (1651)

If a country's national income is as poor a measure of its people's well-being as the last chapter suggested, why does every industrialized country judge not just its government's success but its national vigour on the basis of the size of its annual increase in GNP? Why are national leaders never content with moderate rates of growth and constantly striving to speed up the process?

It is not the results of growth that are important to the people who make it happen. What matters is the process itself; and the more of that process there is, the better politicians and business people like it. Growth means change. More rapid growth means even more change; more change means more market opportunities to be turned into profits. And more profits are not only the system's motivating force but the source of the financial resources needed for it to grow faster still. For a company director, corporate growth creates a virtuous circle with increased profits leading to increased investment leading to more growth, more profit and more investment still. For his ally, the politician, national growth means more tax revenues to spend and more influence in the world.

But it is not just that firms like growth because it makes them more profitable: they positively need it if they are to survive. A fundamental part of the modern capitalist system is the payment of interest on borrowed money. If someone borrows £10,000 at 10 per cent interest, there are only two ways in which they can find the extra £1,000 they will owe twelve months later. One is by taking the money out of their salary or savings: in other words, impoverishing themselves. The other is by investing in some business enterprise which will give at least a 10 per cent return so that they can pay the interest from its profits. But where do the profits come from?

Profits can only be made in three ways, although combinations of these are common. Growth is one method. When an economy grows, incomes increase and profits can come from those extra incomes without anyone having to be made worse off. (This is why we pay such attention to the growth of GNP. Despite its faults in other directions, the amount by which GNP increases from year to year is a measure of the potential for profit in an economy.)

The second way of making profits applies if there is little or no growth. In this case a new business must win orders previously filled by other firms: in other words, some or all of its profits will be made at the expense of someone else. This is of course the fundamental reason why the Roman Catholic Church condemned usury until as late as 1830 and why Islam still does. In economies that were growing only very slowly, if at all, as was the case in Europe until the Agricultural Revolution and in the Muslim countries until oil was found this century, no-one could pay interest on borrowings except at their own expense or that of others. As both courses were undesirable, it made sense for society, through religion, to ban an unproductive, harmful practice.

The third way of securing profits to fund interest payments is by inflation. Let us suppose that most businesses in a country find that their profits have fallen because sales have not increased by as much as was expected or because interest rates on their borrowings have gone up. No managing director likes having to report to shareholders that the ratio of profit to turnover has fallen and firms will want to restore their margins by putting prices up. In a closed economy, one that does not trade overseas, they will be able to do this because most of their competitors will be in the same situation and will be putting prices up too. And so inflation will take place. In a more open economy, however, companies have less freedom to raise prices as they risk losing business to foreign competitors who do not need to raise their prices as they are not experiencing the same profits squeeze. Consequently, only firms minimally exposed to outside competition will be able to push prices up by as much as they need: the rest will have to put up with lower profits to some degree.

So what happens in Britain or Ireland if the economy does not grow? In both countries, new investment is taking place each year: Britain devotes around 20 per cent of its GNP each year to increasing – not just maintaining – its capital stock, which is the national collection of machines, factories, roads, houses and so on. In Ireland, the equivalent figure is 19 per cent a year. If there is no growth, it means that huge sums – in Britain almost £60,000 million in 1987 – have been spent without generating any return.*

The immediate effect is on industry. Firms that have borrowed from their banks or shareholders to expand find that they have not earned anything extra to pay the additional interest or dividend they are committed to pay and that, because of international competition, they cannot restore their margins by inflating their prices. The extra interest payments have to be met out of existing profits, which are consequently reduced, leaving less available for investment from retained earnings the next year. But less investment is needed anyway, since each business has underused capacity created by the current year's unproductive investment. So investment programmes for next year are cut back, causing job losses among builders, machinery suppliers, architects, lawyers and financiers. Naturally, the newly unemployed have less to spend with the businesses that supply them and chain stores, travel agents and garages are forced to make lay-offs too. And so we enter a downward spiral, with no growth leading to an actual depression, not just a year or two of marking time. In our present economic system, the choice is between growth and collapse, not growth and stability. No wonder people want growth so badly.

This was the reason that the former British Prime Minister, Edward Heath, once said 'the alternative to expansion is not an England of quiet market towns linked only by trains puffing slowly and peacefully through green meadows. The alternative is slums, dangerous roads, old factories, cramped schools, and stunted lives.'

For governments, the effects of no-growth are equally bad. Since business profits fall sharply, the amount of tax collected from companies drops. Then overtime falls and lay-offs start, cutting the amount the state collects in income tax while pushing social security payments up. Finally, there are the second-round effects, like lower VAT receipts because the unemployed and people on reduced incomes do not buy so many luxury goods. And if the government has itself been borrowing to fund its capital spending programme (or even current expenditure), it will have increased interest payments to make, compounding its problems further.

A government caught in this position can cut its spending to keep its budget in balance but this will exacerbate the depression. An alternative is to borrow money to pump into the economy to keep demand up and prevent the slump becoming too bad. However, this strategy cannot be continued for more than two or three years without the national debt burden

---

* It is, of course, possible for a firm to show a profit on its capital investment without generating higher sales by achieving higher labour productivity. However, since it has to shed its surplus workers to achieve this profit, its surplus is made at the workers' expense and that of the rest of the economy, which is taxed to enable the state to pay the redundant workers' dole. We will explore the consequences of this later.

becoming cripplingly high. Successive Irish governments found this out the hard way between 1975 and 1985 when they tried to eliminate unemployment entirely and then, after 1979, to shield the country from the worldwide recession caused by OPEC's oil price increase. Ireland's foreign borrowings jumped from £4 to £2,269 a head during this period as a result.

It is easy to see why businesses and governments constantly strive to create growth, since the alternative is debt, depression, unemployment and commercial disaster. They are obeying the growth imperative, a force that has largely shaped the past 240 years, leading to the construction of empires, two world wars and the creation of the European Economic Community, among much else. More recently this imperative has endangered the planet environmentally and has generated such an orgy of financial speculation that the savings of millions of people are almost certain to be lost.

EXPAND OR DIE

The growth imperative works on Darwinian principles: it ensures that only the fastest-growing businesses and nations survive. And just as evolutionary survival is due to the possession of more appropriate genes, the key to commercial growth is the adoption of more appropriate technology. In a Third-World village, the growth potential of traditional technology is exhausted. In his book *Transforming Traditional Agriculture* (1964), Theodore Schultz quotes from a study made by David Hopper in a village in India in the mid-1950s:

An observer in Senapur cannot help but be impressed with the way the village uses its physical resources. The age-old techniques have been refined and sharpened by countless years of experience, and each generation seems to have had its experimenters who added a bit here and changed a practice there and thus improved the community lore. Rotations, tillage and cultivation practices, seed rates, irrigation techniques, and the ability of the blacksmith and the potter to work under handicaps of little power and inferior materials, all attest to a cultural heritage that is richly endowed with empirical wisdom.

Hopper made careful measurements of the time and the amount of land each farmer devoted to a particular crop and compared these with the relative produce prices. He concluded that the villagers could not improve their economic output by switching the proportions around. 'Are the people of Senapur realizing the full economic potential of their physical resources?' he asks. 'From the point of view of the villagers, the answer must be "Yes" for in general each man comes close to doing the best he can with his knowledge and cultural background.'

Hopper also calculated that the return on any additional capital investment made by the villagers would be low – around 3 per cent – regardless of whether it was spent on land, on bullocks or on extending the irrigated area, so long as they remained within the confines of their traditional technology. From this we can conclude that the farmers have carried on investing until they reached the point where they would rather consume the investment funds this year than have 3 per cent more to consume next year. After all, the future is uncertain and next year they might be dead, so they might as well live a little better now, especially as the extra from investing would make so little difference anyway. (In economic jargon, the villagers' investment stops when the rate of return drops to equal their rate of time preference.)

The point of a new technology is that it enables an item to be made or grown with a different, lower-cost selection of the factors of production (land, labour, energy, capital) than was possible previously. Because costs are lower per item produced, profits can be made, at least until everybody adopts the same method and competition causes prices to fall. When Hopper visited Senapur, a field was irrigated by yoking two oxen to a rope tied to a big leather bucket down a well. During the past thirty years, however, electrical or diesel pumps have been introduced to the village. Although it required very much more capital to buy them in the first place and a regular input of energy from the outside world, the new pumps displaced the oxen and the men who drove them. The first farmers to go over to the new ways found that they were able to irrigate a larger area than in the past and that consequently they could either get higher yields of some of their existing crops or put a bigger area under water-demanding ones like rice, which tend to earn a higher return than crops that can be grown almost anywhere.

So the pioneer farmers increased their production and altered the relative amounts of the crops they grew. For a while, prices remained unaffected and they enjoyed good profits. However, as more and more pumps were installed, output increased significantly and prices began to fall, reducing the income of those farmers who had failed to adopt the new irrigation method. This group suffered another setback too: the new power pumps meant that more water could be extracted and from greater depths than previously possible, so the water table around the village dropped. Naturally, the old-style farmers deepened their wells and lengthened their ropes but because their oxen had further to haul, they were unable to raise as much water as they used to. In short, these farmers found themselves caught in a rather neat, but nasty, pincer movement: they could not produce as much as before because they had less irrigation water and the market price for their reduced output had fallen. Moreover, if they tried to install pumps to catch up with their neighbours they would not get as much profit as the pioneers did, because of the price fall. Indeed the traditional farmers' situation might have deteriorated to such an extent that they would be unable to service the loans on their pumps, even supposing they were able to arrange them.

Here is the growth imperative at work: once change begins to take place, no-one has the option of not adapting to it. Anyone who doggedly continues in the traditional way will be wiped out, just like an old man I saw on my last visit to India. He was standing beside his one-room shack in a remote part of Tamil Nadu waiting for his neighbours to bring him their leather irrigation buckets to repair. But now that power pumps had arrived nobody was coming any more and beside each well in the surrounding fields was a freshly dug pile of earth, a sign that the hole had been deepened recently and that fierce competition for water was going on.

This sort of technological struggle is taking place all around the world. At an environmental conference in Skibbereen, Co. Cork, in 1989, Eugene Hayes, who runs training courses for young farmers on behalf of the Irish government's agricultural development agency, Teagasc, said that he thought that very few of his trainees would be able to make a life on the land. 'I haven't told them so,' he said, 'but they've left it three years too late. Technology represents a carrot and a stick and for those who go for it first, there is success. For those who are slow to move there is a fight for survival because the increased production due to new methods drives prices down and makes it financially impossible for people using the old ways to continue to do so. They can only go on making sacrifices for so long.'

The growth imperative applies equally harshly in industry where it forces manufacturers to adopt the latest, lower-cost methods or go to the wall. The best-known and most exhaustively studied example is that of the improved spinning methods introduced to the British cotton industry at the start of the Industrial Revolution. In the thirty years from 1780, this transformed a small, struggling, part-time occupation for rural people that was unable to compete with Indian imports into an industrial sector that provided 8 per cent of GNP and 40 per cent of Britain's exports in 1812. The price of yarn fell dramatically from 38s (£1.90) per pound in 1786 to 6s 9d (34p) in 1807; and although part of this reduction was due to a fall in raw cotton prices, itself the result of Whitney's invention of an improved gin, those who did not take a spinning jenny into their home to replace their spinning wheel could not continue in business. Moreover, once changes in the industry had started they led to others so that by 1812, spinning could only be carried out economically in factories where water or steam power was available, and the number of home workers began to decline. Ten years later the power loom arrived and independent home weavers were forced from the trade – and into great poverty – by relentless downward pressure on their earnings. In her account of this period in her book *The First Industrial Revolution* (1965), Phyllis Deane writes:

Britain was first in the field with the new machines and with cheaper, finer cottons and was therefore able to reap the innovator's profits. By the time her rivals had followed her lead, prices had fallen to more competitive levels and the boom profits had been won. The initial lead ... meant that the country ... could go on getting higher-than-average profits for a considerable time, simply because it was enjoying larger economies of scale and could go on supplying its products at keener prices.

Among Britain's rivals were Indian hand-weavers who made such fine quality cloth that Parliament banned imports of their printed calico in 1700 to give domestic producers a chance. Between 1797 and 1813, a further impediment was put in the Indians' way – the duty on white calico was raised from 18 per cent to 71 per cent. Later, to speed the expansion of the English mills, India's British rulers cut the import duty on Lancashire cottons to 2·5 per cent at a time when the duty on Indian cloth consumed in India was 17 per cent. They also imposed a tax on household spinning wheels.

Somehow, however, traditional Indian producers have managed to survive and the battle between them and highly mechanized mills – in Bombay, this time – is still going on. In 1989 V. P. Singh's incoming government, worried by increasing unemployment, made noises about assisting the hand-loom sector, but even had its period in office been rather longer there is very little doubt that the outcome would have been the same. Only tourists and committed followers of Mahatma Gandhi are today prepared to wear *khadi*, the local name for hand-spun and hand-woven cloth. When I watched the weavers do their traditional dance in Rudrur, a village in Andhra Pradesh, one night in 1988, they had not woven anything for over eight years.

In Ireland and Scotland too the march of technology is irresistible and only a few hand-looms remain. One-third of Irish tweed is produced by Magee's of Donegal, which uses modern German looms for the bulk of its production, changing them every five years to keep up with the latest developments. The company also employs thirty home weavers working by hand on simple, traditional looms to produce the fabric for their men's jackets which – for marketing reasons rather than social concern or sentiment – are always made from hand-woven cloth. Scotland's Harris tweed has an identical marketing strategy.

Every industry provides dozens of similar examples of battles between new technology and older methods in which the old-style producers lose market share and are eventually driven out of business. No quarter is ever given: advanced firms never limit their output to allow older methods to survive except on a token basis within their own organizations to enable them to talk about tradition in their advertisements. Innovators always seek increased markets for their output because this not only maximizes their profits but also increases their chances of survival. Once an innovation appears, no firm can be sure of being able to continue to produce as it did before for more than a limited time, no matter where it is in the world. No society is safe either since the technologies it chooses – or is forced by competitive pressures to adopt – will determine the future relationships between the people who make it up.

IMPERIALISM: TRADE AT THE POINT OF A GUN

In the past, even military might has been used to compel countries wanting to protect their producers or to preserve their society to open up to competition. Britain imposed the Anglo-Turkish Commercial Convention on the Ottoman Empire in 1838 and repeated the process with Persia in 1841. The first of these actions had particularly serious consequences: by 1881 the Turkish state was bankrupt, although the empire was allowed to stay largely intact for a third of a century more, because the European powers were reluctant to compete too fiercely for its territory in case this led to war.

In the end of course it did, or, more accurately, it provided the spark for one that would have broken out anyway. The growth of nationalism and Turkey's financial problems provoked two revolts in the Balkans in 1875 and 1878. During the second of these, Russia helped Serbia to become independent and the Austro-Hungarian Empire took over Serbia's neighbour, Bosnia-Herzegovina. When the Austrian Archduke Franz Ferdinand was shot by a Serb in Bosnia-Herzegovina in 1914 and the Austrians and their German allies decided that Serbia should be punished, Russia felt it could not stand aside and allow its protégé to be invaded. It called on Britain and France to honour their obligations under a treaty designed to contain Germany, and the First World War began.

The effects of other commercial interventions by capitalist states have been just as far-reaching. The most flagrant case of a country being opened up as a market against its rulers' wishes is that of Japan. For over two hundred years the country had deliberately isolated itself by restricting the size of ships that its people were permitted to build, refusing food, water and fuel to foreign vessels and trading only through the Dutch, who were confined to an island in Nagasaki Bay and allowed onto the Japanese mainland only once a year. 'The policy of the shogunate was to maintain a static society,' says Richard Storry in his *History of Modern Japan* (1960), describing how travel within the country was deliberately restricted, to the extent that the use of boats was banned at one river crossing so that everyone had to wade across, except for a few important travellers, who were carried.

Nevertheless Japanese scholars kept a close eye on the progress of science and technology in the West after 1719, when the eighth shogun had been shown an astronomical telescope and realized how important it could be for

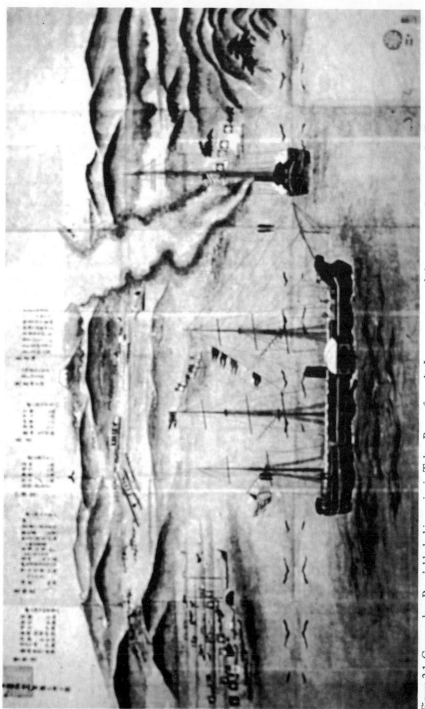

Figure 2.1 Commodore Perry's black ships arrive in Tokyo Bay to force the Japanese to open their economy to international trade.

calculating the calendar; previously anyone found studying Western culture had been imprisoned or killed. In 1811, the magnificently named Institute for the Investigation of Barbarian Books was set up to translate foreign works. But Japan was not allowed the luxury of settling for itself whether it should adopt or adapt Western methods: the United States decided it would force it to do so. 'From the late eighteenth century onwards there was a new wave of Western expansion in the Far East,' writes Pat Barr in his book *The Coming of the Barbarians* (1967). 'The wealthy nations of the world were seeking new outlets for the goods which their new industrial skills could produce; Japan was known to be a relatively prosperous nation – a completely untapped market. The end of her seclusion was inevitable. It was mainly a question of who got there first.'

On 8 July 1853 Commodore Matthew Perry's squadron sailed into Tokyo Bay. After several days, during which the Americans made every attempt to overawe the Japanese with their military might and their technology – troops paraded daily and a model steam railway on which people could ride was set up – a meeting was held with representatives of the shogun. Perry told them that the American president wanted to make a treaty with Japan so that trade could flourish across the Pacific and then Japan would grow great and prosperous in its own right. He would return again with more ships in the spring for an answer.

Diaries and letters written by the Americans at the time show that they were well aware that they were about to change an apparently idyllic society irrevocably. The shogun's advisers realized it too, and were divided over whether they should attempt to repel the foreigners by force or accept the inevitable. The latter group won and in 1858 a commercial treaty was signed, by which time the Japanese had already started an iron and ship-building firm in Mito. Ten years later the country had built its first railway entirely from its own resources. Did the Americans ever feel that they should have left well alone?

Like Japan, China tried to avoid trading links with the outside world. As Tsui Chi says in his *Short History of Chinese Civilisation* (1947), 'the Chinese mind is naturally conservative and respectful of tradition; suspicious of innovation. And with their huge productive land and their modest standard of living the majority were able to live in perfect contentment, working the land by the ancient traditions and producing simple but beautiful goods without the use of machines. They had no desire to trade with the foreigner nor to learn his methods.' In 1793, when King George III of England sent Lord Macartney to request that Macao (now Aomen) and Canton (Guangzhou) cease to be the only ports open to foreign vessels and that three more ports be opened up, the Manchu emperor, Qian Long, rejected the suggestion, replying: 'As your ambassador can see for himself, we possess all things. I set no value on objects strange or ingenious and have no use for your country's manufactures.'

Another attempt was made by Lord Amherst in 1816. However, he high-handedly landed at a port closed to foreigners in the north of the country because it was closer to Beijing and was consequently refused an audience with the emperor, although this may also have had something to do with his refusal to kowtow.

In spite of these rebuffs, unofficial trade with China began. British ships laden with opium produced by the East India Company would anchor in the estuary of the Pearl (Zhujiang) River between Macao and what is now Hong Kong and smugglers' boats would come out to them under cover of darkness. The smugglers paid for the opium in silver, and it is estimated that 1,270 tonnes of coins were removed from the Chinese economy in 1838 alone. A drain on this scale could not be ignored, particularly as the people found it hard to get enough silver currency to pay their taxes, and the emperor decided to make opium smoking a capital offence, giving his citizens a year to break the habit. Lin Zexu, governor of two central provinces, decided that he could not eradicate the problem there unless the supply was cut off at source and he went south to the Pearl estuary, where he ordered defences and look-out posts to be built along the shore. Then he wrote to the British consul in Canton, demanding that all the opium owned by the British merchants be handed over within three days.

When this demand was rejected, Lin blockaded the houses used by the British in the part of the port where they were allowed to stay for six months of each year. When it became clear that he intended to starve them into submission, the merchants capitulated and over a thousand tonnes of opium was delivered to him, which he destroyed on the beach, flushing the remains into the sea. Lin then wrote to the emperor suggesting that in future, Westerners trading in opium should be hanged, although he made it clear that normal trading was welcome in the provinces for which he was responsible. However, when British seamen killed a Chinese man in a brawl a little later and the consul refused to hand over the culprits, Lin banned all foreign trade until the matter was settled. This was too much for the British and in 1840 they sent not just the customary gunboat but fifteen, with 15,000 troops on board.

The outcome was that Canton, Amoy (Xiamen) and Shanghai were captured and when Nanjing came under the British guns, the Chinese court panicked and accepted an unequal treaty which not only opened four more ports to foreigners but meant that the British were paid $6 million to cover the cost of the war and $9 million for the loss of their opium and the dislocation of trade.

In 1856 the Second Opium War broke out, again over a trivial incident. Again more ports were opened and massive reparations were paid. Tsui Chi describes the result:

The huge sums of money that had to be squeezed from the groaning people as indemnities to the wealthy Europeans brought the Empire to the verge of bankruptcy. Through the low customs duty and preferential tariffs accorded in the treaties to the industrial nations of the West, foreign machine-made goods poured into China, and not only ousted native goods but effectively prevented the development of a national industry ... The most grievous of all the consequences was that the Chinese lost all faith in themselves and their nation; they relaxed their endeavours at reform and development; they were over-impressed by the scientific inventions and war machinery of the Westerners that they began to despise their own ancient civilization and servilely to imitate the foreigners.

MATERIALS AS WELL AS MARKETS

During the second half of the nineteenth century, a change began to take place in the relationship of the industrialized countries with the rest of the world. Although manufacturers still needed wider and wider markets to keep their profits buoyant, they increasingly began to look abroad for their raw materials too, and with the development of the railway and the steamship it became possible to ship not just high-value luxuries and precious metals but bulk commodities from almost anywhere on the globe. Plundering missions, like those of the Spanish in the New World, the Portuguese and later others in Africa and the East India Company in India, were converted to a more formalized system necessary to keep the 'mother-country' supplied with raw materials.

As part of this change the East India Company was abolished in 1858, discredited by the 'Indian Mutiny' the year before; its armies and officials were transferred to the Crown. 'It was deprived of its powers which had been wielded for two centuries with such merciless despotism ... the public conscience of the nation was awakened by the spectacle of a structure of tyranny and wrong far exceeding in atrocity and extent anything that had ever been known in the history of the human race,' wrote an American author, C. Edwards Lester, in *The Glory and Shame of England* (1864). An English merchant agreed,[1] saying that the company had obtained local goods 'by every conceivable form of roguery ... fines, imprisonment, floggings, forcing bonds upon them etc.' The company's indigo trade was typical: peasants in Bihar and Bengal were made to grow the crop at loss-making prices for fear of imprisonment, and forced labour was also used for its processing.

A more subtle form of exploitation began, which was later attacked by the Indian economist Dadabhai Naoroji in *Poverty and UnBritish Rule in India* (1901). Naoroji pointed out that increasing amounts of tax revenue were being taken out of his country to cover India's share of the maintenance costs of the British army and navy throughout the world, the pensions of expatriate government officers and railway staff, and the huge debt incurred in building the railway system. He calculated that this drain had been £3 million a year at the beginning of the 1800s and was over £30 million by 1900, a sum equivalent to £1,600 million today. 'Even an ocean, if it lost water every day which never returned to it, would be dried up in time. Under similar conditions, even wealthy England would soon be reduced to poverty,' he wrote. 'The former rulers were like butchers hacking here and there but the English with their scientific scalpel cut to the very heart … and soon the plaster of the high talk of civilization, progress and what-not covers up the wound.'

In Africa the need for supplies as well as markets brought about the scramble for territory among the European powers during the 1880s and 1890s. Until that time, apart from some settlement by the Dutch and the English in the far south and the French in the far north, European colonization had been largely limited to a few trading and slaving posts at the mouths of the greater rivers. Although the slave trade is estimated to have killed a hundred million people and destroyed native societies over much of Africa, it was not banned internationally until 1884. However, the American explorer H. M. Stanley realized the true potential of the continent several years earlier. 'There are forty millions of people beyond the gateway of the Congo and the cotton-spinners of Manchester are waiting to clothe them. Birmingham foundries are glowing with red metal that will presently be made into ironwork for them and the trinkets that shall adorn those dusky bosoms,' he told a meeting of British businessmen in 1872.

Other countries had spotted Africa's potential too and by the end of the century France had secured 4 million square miles, Britain 3 million and Germany, Portugal, Belgium and Italy about 900,000 each. Only two countries – Liberia and Ethiopia, just 4 per cent of a continent the same size as the United States, Australia, India and China put together – were not incorporated into the supply and marketing system of a major power. Ghana (the Gold Coast), which had been a source of gold and slaves since the Portuguese built the first coastal fort there in 1482, became a British colony in 1874 even though a parliamentary commission had recommended withdrawal from the forts only nine years before on the grounds that there was no point in keeping them since Britain had banned the Atlantic slave trade in 1807. The reason for the sudden change of heart was that indigenous entrepreneurs had turned to producing palm oil and palm kernels which the mechanized factories of Europe needed for lubrication and the manufacture of soap and candles. The country was one of the world's top five rubber producers by 1890 and that same year cocoa production started.

One of the first acts of the imperial power in many of the new colonies was to impose a hut tax or a head tax since this broke down local self-sufficiency and started the process of monetarizing their economies. It also had the effect of forcing the people to come to work for the new overlords or to produce something to sell to them. Ghana fiercely resisted the hut tax when attempts were made to impose one in 1852. As a result, revenue had to be raised largely from import duties instead and this meant that the colony's administrators were doubly reluctant to encourage the development of indigenous industry: not only would local firms supplant British products but import duties would drop.

The years from 1860 to 1914 have been called the period of 'neo-mercantilism' because each industrial country sought to form a large, self-sufficient trading unit to which it supplied manufactured goods and from which it obtained foodstuffs and raw materials. In 1864 C. Edwards Lester wrote this analysis of British policy from an American perspective:

Yes, England preaches to us Free Trade which means for us to buy everything from her and she take nothing from us in return but breadstuffs, provisions and raw materials for manufacture ... That has always been her policy towards all nations, especially us. Her power and importance – now all reduced down to her balance in exchange – gold. All countries owe her money, we most of all. She makes money by taking the raw material from other nations, manufacturing and selling it back, and in both cases to a considerable extent, fixing the price herself ... She knew that she could not rule the world by her arms but by her manufactures. She has, therefore, always endeavored to suppress the development of manufactures in other nations ... England always drained everyone of her customers of their gold and thus held what she is struggling to keep, the balance of exchanges in her favor.

A crucial plank of mercantilist doctrine was to prevent gold leaking from one economic system to another. Accordingly, each rival colonial system erected tariff barriers against the others; Germany in 1879, France in 1892 and finally Britain with the introduction of 'imperial preference' in 1897. But Germany, the most populous European power as a result of Bismarck's assembly of previously independent states and by 1913 the most economically powerful, had come rather late to the territory-grabbing game and was unhappy with what it had got. The French historian Marc Ferro puts it this way:

Following English and French examples, Germany was in turn converted to overseas expansion, either for new markets or for cheap raw materials. But the world had already been conquered and partitioned; there was no 'place in the sun' for Germany and her immense economic power remained concentrated on a relatively small national territory, her field of expansion narrowly circumscribed by her rivals' positions. The vast demands of a maturing economy could not be met although the economy was itself fully competitive, nor did she have a financial base on the same scale as her economic power. England felt threatened ... Anglo German rivalry became a public matter, orchestrated and fomented by press and cinema. Some statesmen in both countries sought accord but the two countries were pushed by the logic of imperialism.[3]

Thus it was the need for growth that brought about the First World War.

3

Ill Fares the Land

A people may be too rich because it is the tendency of the commercial, and more especially of the manufacturing system, to collect wealth rather than diffuse it. Great capitalists become like pike in a fish pond who devour the weaker fish and it is certain that the poverty of one part of the people seems to increase in the same ratio as the riches of another. – Robert Southey, Poet Laureate (1829)

What had Europe's quest for profits and growth brought about apart from the colonization and exploitation of much of the world, the destruction of many traditional ways of life and the First World War in which almost nine million soldiers died? In particular, were the British any better off? Had their quality of life improved as a result of 150 years of effort? And if it had, could those gains not have been accomplished in other, more direct, less destructive ways?

Economic growth is a very indirect way of improving anything apart from the balance sheets of the companies responsible. Companies and entrepreneurs make decisions on whether or not to invest according to the likely profitability of their projects *to them*. For over two hundred years, provided they did not break the laws devised and developed by members of their own property-owning class, business people have had no responsibility to consider how their ventures would affect anyone or anything else. In the period up to the First World War it was not thought morally objectionable for a factory to, say, install power-looms and displace several hundred hand-weavers so long as this was profitable. In fact the social consequences of investment have not been much of a consideration since.

The intellectual underpinning for this cavalier attitude to one's fellows goes back at least to 1704, when Bernard de Mandeville, a Dutch doctor living in England, celebrated his mastery of the English language by writing a long piece of doggerel originally entitled *The Grumbling Hives or Knaves Turned Honest* and later *The Fable of the Bees*. In this he argued that civilization was the result of human vices and that self-interest resulted in public good:

> Vast numbers thronged the fruitful hive,
> Yet those vast numbers made 'em thrive,

Millions endeavouring to supply
Each other's lust and vanity.

...

Thus every part was full of vice,
Yet the whole mass a paradise.

After numerous complaints about the level of sin, Heaven turns the knaves honest. As a result, none of the bees has any motive to continue work and the hive ceases to thrive.

English intellectuals were appalled by the immorality of this tale and one of the motives for Adam Smith's first book, *The Theory of Moral Sentiments* (1759), was to debunk it. The force of de Mandeville's arguments was irresistible, however, and although Smith delayed publishing his next book, *The Wealth of Nations* (1776), for several years in a vain effort to come to some other conclusion, he was finally forced to write that if each individual pursued his own advantage he was 'led by an invisible hand to promote an end which was no part of his intention,' and as a result did more to promote the interests of society than if he had deliberately set out to do so. Smith's ideas about the division of labour can also be traced back to de Mandeville's verse.

In spite of Smith's misgivings about endorsing a shallow excuse for selfishness and greed, his 'invisible hand' theory governs our thought about commercial behaviour today and lies at the root of most of our economic and environmental problems. The rationale behind the theory is that a newcomer has to have a cheaper or better product to elbow his way into a market against well-established competition. Consequently, the general good will be served in the long run by allowing competition and new entrants in every trade and industry since doing so provides a way for more efficient people and methods to come to the fore.

This argument might be true if markets worked perfectly, which they do not, and if entrepreneurs were required to pay the full costs of the resources they use or spoil, which they are not. Many of the innovations in the period up to 1914 – and since – have involved the substitution of energy from fossil fuels for human or animal power. The price of fossil fuels was (and is) set at the cost of getting them out of the ground, which is about as sensible as valuing the money one withdraws from the bank at the cost of the bus fare to go and get it. It ignores the fact that reserves are finite and need to be shared with future generations and that the fuels themselves cause serious pollution which imposes a cost on us all. As a result, fossil fuel energy has been seriously underpriced and we have used too much of it, damaging not only the livelihoods of people using low-energy methods of production but also the biosphere and the resources base of future generations.

The only way to ensure that society makes a net gain from technical innovations is to require the gainers to compensate the losers for everything they have lost and also to pay to restore the environmental damage they have done. Unless this happens, we can never be sure that one group is not enriching itself at the expense of another because it has better access to capital, enjoys monopoly powers, exploits its workers, pollutes the environment or cheats unsophisticated customers.

Modern democratic societies are beginning to introduce mechanisms by which winners compensate losers but current models are still very imperfect and often give developers the wrong signals about whether or not they should proceed. The dole, for example, is potentially a way of transferring some of the benefits of technical change from the firms that profit by it to those who suffer and lose their jobs. As things stand, however, the taxes to pay unemployment benefits are raised from the general population, not merely from innovating firms, and monetary payments, however high, cannot compensate the unemployed for their dispiriting idleness, as we will see later. Similarly, no business pays for the environmental damage it routinely does as part of its production processes – although this situation will change with the introduction and sale of pollution permits which are being considered by almost every industrialized country in the world.

Where there is no adequate mechanism for compensating the losers, growth can result in widespread impoverishment and a decline in the quality of life. Between 1750 and 1850, according to Deane and Cole's *British Economic Growth* (1967), the output per head in Britain doubled, growing most quickly between 1800 and 1850. However, the quality of life for the vast majority of the British people got steadily worse at least until the 1840s as a result of the changes taking place. One reason for this is that the Deane and Cole figure seriously overestimates the actual increase in production, because it includes the gain in the monetarized part of the economy and ignores the production that was lost when people became unable to grow or gather much for themselves after being forced from the countryside and into the towns. The other reason is that much of the extra production resulting from the changes in technology was either re-invested or went to the landed gentry and to the middle class. Eric Hobsbawm describes the process in *Industry and Empire* (1969):

The British aristocracy and gentry were very little affected by industrialization except for the better. Their rents were swelled with the demand for farm produce, the expansion of the cities (whose soil they owned) and of mines, forges and railways (which were situated on their estates) … The successful middle-class and those who aspired to emulate them were satisfied. Not so the labouring poor – in the nature of things the majority – whose traditional world and way of life the Industrial Revolution destroyed without automatically substituting anything else.

Some idea of the harmonious, prosperous world that was destroyed in the quest for growth is given by Daniel Defoe in his *Tour through the Whole*

Island of Great Britain, an account of thirteen journeys made around England, Scotland and Wales between 1723 and 1725. Defoe was well satisfied with what he saw: 'If novelty pleases, here is the present state of the country described, the improvement, as well as in culture, as in commerce, the increase of people, and employment for them. Also, here you have an account of the increase of buildings, as well in great cities and towns, as in new seats and dwellings of the nobility and gentry; also the increase in wealth, in many eminent particulars,' he wrote in his preface, and not once in over 600 pages did he find cause to mention poverty. Similarly, Richard Gough's *The History of Myddle,* an account of life in a Shropshire village written between 1700 and 1706, gives no impression of general hardship, although he describes the lives and problems of all his neighbours.

A century later, however, between 1822 and 1826, William Cobbett made his *Rural Rides* and was appalled by the social destruction and concentration of economic power that he saw going on. On a ride through the Cotswolds in September 1826 he comes to the village of Withington:

Here in this once populous village you see all the indubitable marks of most melancholy decay. There are several lanes crossing each other which must have been streets formerly. There is a large open place where the principal streets meet. There are, against this open place, two large, old roomy houses with gateways into back parts of them ... These were manifestly considerable inns and, in this open place markets or fairs or both used to be held. I asked two men who were threshing in a barn how long it was since their public house was put down or dropped. They told me about sixteen years. One of these men, who was about fifty years of age, could remember three public houses, one of which was called an inn ...

Withington is very prettily situated; it was, and not very long ago, a gay and happy place; but it now presents a picture of shabbiness scarcely to be equalled. Here are the yet visible remains of two gentlemen's houses. Great farmers have supplied their place, as to inhabiting; and, I dare say, that some tax-eater, or some blaspheming Jew, or some more base and wicked loan-mongering robber is now the owner of the land; aye, and all these people are his slaves as completely, and more to their wrong, than the blacks are the slaves of the planters in Jamaica, the farmers here acting, in fact, in a capacity corresponding with that of the negro-drivers there.

A part, and perhaps a considerable part, of the decay and misery of this place is owing to the use of machinery and to the monopolizing in the manufacture of blankets of which fabric the town of Witney was the centre and from which town the wool used to be sent round to and the yarn, or warp, come back from, all these Cotswold villages and quite a part of Wiltshire. This work is all now gone and so the women and the girls are a 'surplus *popalashon, mon*', and are, of course, to be dealt with by the 'Emigration Committee' of the 'Collective Wisdom.' There were, only a few years ago, above thirty blanket manufacturers at Witney: twenty five of these have been swallowed up by the five that now have all the manufacture in their hands. And all this has been done by that system of fictitious money which has conveyed property from the hands of the many into the hands of the few.

As at Withington, most of the changes Cobbett saw and deplored were the result of successful attempts by the rich to adopt new industrial and agricultural technologies and thereby achieve growth at the expense of the rest of the population. There was no compensation mechanism since only the rich had a voice in Parliament: men had to own freehold land with a rateable value of £2 a year to qualify to vote, and MPs had to have a land rental income of £600 a year if they came from the shires or £300 a year if they came from boroughs. Some idea of how much money this represented in the early 1800s can be gained from the fact that the cost of running a carriage, complete with horses, coachmen and footmen was about £200 a year while a good workman working fourteen hours a day was hard pressed to take home 25 to 30p a week. Even after the 1832 Reform Act the income rules for MPs stayed in force and property qualifications meant that less than one-fourteenth of the population could vote.

In Defoe's day most agricultural land was still in open fields, with families holding the right to farm various scattered strips although some compact farms had been built up in a few places after 1660 by purchasing, renting and exchanging strips and then fencing or walling the resulting block off from the rest. But these farms had been assembled by agreement, a slow, tedious process that did not suit entrepreneurs wanting to try out improved animal breeds and a four-crop rotation, techniques that could not be used in the open fields. So these gentlemen began introducing Private Members' Bills in Parliament to enforce enclosures. Between 1760 and 1820, according to Hobsbawm, half of Huntingdonshire, Leicestershire and Northamptonshire was enclosed, more than two-fifths of Bedfordshire and Rutland, over a third of Lincolnshire, Oxford and the East Riding of Yorkshire and a quarter or more of Berkshire, Buckinghamshire, Middlesex, Norfolk, Nottingham, Warwick and Wiltshire.

Only families allocated twenty-five acres or more during an enclosure were generally able to hang onto their holdings because of the high legal costs involved (the list of parliamentary officials who had to be paid ran from the Speaker and his secretary down to two doorkeepers, four messengers and various clerks) and the expense of hedging or walling off their new farm. In any case, farms of less than twenty-five acres were often not viable under the new system because their owners no longer had access to the common and woodland, which had also been carved up. But at least families unable to afford to keep their land got some cash for what they lost; the real victims of enclosures were those who made their living from the commons and had no rights to space in the open fields. Cobbett visited Horton Heath in Hampshire in 1807 and 1808. It consisted of 150 acres and was surrounded by thirty cottages, each with its own garden. The heath provided the cottagers with grazing for their animals, rabbits to eat and wood for their fires. Cobbett noted the names of the cottagers and counted their children, cows, calves, pigs, geese, ducks, fruit trees and beehives. So intensively was the common used that he claimed the output from it was equivalent to that from 200 acres of enclosed land, indicating, if he was correct, that enclosure might actually have reduced agricultural output.

When commons like Horton Heath were enclosed, the cottagers were forced to become labourers on their richer neighbours' enclosed farms or to leave the area and move into the cities. On a journey from Highclere near Newbury to Hambledon in Hampshire in November 1822, Cobbett passed through village after village in which all that remained was a large number of small paddocks in which the cottagers' houses had once stood and huge churches, four times too large for their parishes' present populations.

Agricultural wages fell sharply as a result of the number of displaced cottagers seeking employment. Cobbett describes visiting the break-up sale of a farm near Reigate in 1825. He noted that although the farmer had fitted out a room as a parlour, complete with carpet and bell-pull, and equipped himself with a mahogany table, fine chairs, a decanter, glasses and a dinner set 'in the true stock-jobber style,' much of the house seemed in a state of disuse, including the big oak table at which the farmer and his men had at one time taken their meals together.

Why, Cobbett asks, had the farm's agricultural labourers – perhaps ten or fifteen men – its boys and maids ceased to live and eat with the family? Because, he answers himself, even though a large number of people can live and be boarded in a house for much less per head than two or three people living separately, wages had fallen so much that it was cheaper for the farmer to pay them in cash and force them to manage for themselves.

Therefore [the farm] became almost untenanted; the labourers retreated to hovels called cottages and instead of board and lodging they got money; so little of it as to enable the employer to drink wine; but then, that he might not reduce them to quite starvation they were enabled to come to him in the king's name and demand food as paupers ... The blame belongs to the infernal stock-jobbing system. There was no reason to expect that farmers would not endeavour to keep pace, in point of show and luxury, with fund holders and with all the tribes that war and taxes created. Farmers were not the authors of the mischief; and now they are compelled to shut the labourers out of their houses and to pinch them in their wages in order to be able to pay their own taxes.

Cobbett's mention of the labourers demanding food as paupers and of the high level of taxes is a reference to the notorious Speenhamland system, the second ingenious method by which the less well-off were compelled to subsidize the rich. It started innocently enough when the Berkshire magistrates met in Speenhamland near Newbury in May 1795 and decided that, in view of the widespread distress among rural labourers in the county, they would top up their wages out of the rates. Unfortunately this meant that ratepayers who were too poor to employ labourers were in effect subsidizing their neighbours who were rich enough to do so by making wages up to a more reasonable level. Although many of these smaller landowners were consequently forced to sell up, the system spread throughout most of the south of England. The only areas it did not reach were those where wages were kept above the Speenhamland minimum because of the availability of alternative work in the textile mills or the mines.

A third ploy used by the landowning rich to improve their lot was the Corn Law of 1815, which prevented the import of grain unless the price rose above £4 a bushel. Ostensibly this law was passed for the best of reasons: to stop farmers going bankrupt as many had done the previous year when Continental imports became possible again with the ending of the Napoleonic Wars. During the twenty years of fighting rents had naturally risen to reflect the profits that grain growers were able to make but when foreign supplies became available again and prices dropped, many farmers found themselves unable to continue to pay them, particularly as they also had to pay high rates because of Speenhamland. Even freehold farmers got into trouble because they still had interest payments to make on money borrowed to pay the cost of enclosing their land. Although these justifications were put forward at the time, the law was immediately and correctly seen as an attempt by landowning interests to benefit from the growing urban population and it continued to cause controversy until it was repealed in 1846.

Jean-Charles Sismondi, one of the lesser-known fathers of economics, travelled around England a few years before Cobbett and was so upset by what he saw that he rejected the idea that the 'invisible hand' could be relied on to turn everything to good – an argument he had previously supported in a book – and called on the government to intervene to slow the rate of industrialization and prevent the imbalance between rich and poor getting worse. In 1819, when the slump that followed the Napoleonic Wars was at its height with the labour market still glutted with ex-soldiers and sailors and prices in steep decline, he wrote that achieving the maximum level of production did not necessarily mean the achievement of the greatest happiness of the people. The problem of distribution was more important than any other economic problem and it would be better to have a lower level of production if it were more fairly distributed.

Sismondi also argued that capital was, by its nature, obliged to seek continual increase and that the workers' spending power was necessarily inadequate to purchase everything they themselves produced, especially in view of the introduction of machinery, because of the payments that had to be made for capital. He advocated a return to the independent producer, small farmer and artisan.

Malthus, on the other hand, rejected the idea of a fairer distribution of land and wealth, because he felt that the benefits accruing to the privileged few outweighed the disadvantages to the underprivileged many. 'By securing to a portion of society the necessary leisure for the progress of the arts and sciences, it must be allowed that a check to the increase in cultivation confers on society a most signal benefit.' He thought that attempts such as Speenhamland to better the lot of the lower classes were futile, since those being helped would only breed more children, and poverty would reappear. 'It makes little difference ... whether that state of demand and supply which occasions an insufficiency of wages to the whole of the labouring classes be produced prematurely by a bad structure of society and an unfavourable distribution of wealth or necessarily by the comparative exhaustion of the soil. The labourer feels the difficulty in the same degree, and it must have nearly the same results, from whatever cause it arises ...'

But when conditions reached their worst, around the middle of the century, the tide of opinion began to run against the Malthusian position. Dr J. P. Kay, commissioned by the Senate of Cambridge University to compare the living conditions of the poorer classes throughout Europe, reported[1] in 1850 that 'a low standard of living always tends to stimulate improvident marriages, to unduly increase the numbers of the population and to engender pauperism, vice, degradation and misery.' He was appalled by country people's housing conditions in England and Wales, particularly as all ages and both sexes had to share a common bed. 'The crowding of the cottages has of late been growing worse and worse. The promiscuous mingling of the sexes in the bedrooms has been increasing very much.' His study concluded that, at a time when Britain was undoubtedly the leading industrial country in the world, 'the poor of England are more depressed, more pauperized, more numerous in comparison with the other classes, more irreligious and very much worse educated than the poor of any other European nation, solely excepting Russia, Turkey, South Italy, Portugal and Spain'. It was a shocking turnabout from the time, just seventy years earlier, when Arthur Young, one of the chief popularizers of the new agricultural methods, could write: 'When you are engaged in this political tour [of France], finish it by seeing England, and I will show you a set of peasants well-clothed, well-nourished, and tolerably drunken from superfluity, well-lodged and at their ease; and yet amongst them not one in a thousand has either land or cattle.'[2]

The land grab by the rich was remarkably successful, however, from their point of view, as C. Edwards Lester explained in 1864:

In 1688, while England had a population of only 5.5m., 170,000 of them were landowners and in 1786 the number rose to 250,000. In 1861, with a population of over 20m., England had but 30,766 landowners; thus, with five times the population she had only one-sixth as many landowners, making a disproportion in a little less than two centuries of nearly thirty to one. The baleful results of such a system on the independence and prosperity of the agricultural class must be apparent at a single thought. The yeomanry, of whom England could once proudly boast as the bone and sinew of a free state, have been, especially in the last twenty years, driven in increasing numbers into other and less healthful pursuits or to distant lands; while the great mass of tenants and farm laborers are brought into subjection to the will of the lord of the soil who can turn them from their holdings at his pleasure.[3]

Hobsbawm confirms this concentration:

The political and social structure of Britain was controlled by landlords, and what is more, by a rather small group of perhaps 4,000 people who between them owned something like four-sevenths of the cultivated land, which they let to a quarter of a million farmers who in turn employed – I take 1851 as a convenient date – about a million and a quarter labourers, shepherds and so on. Such a degree of concentrated landownership was unparalleled in other industrial countries.[4]

Forced from the countryside either directly by enclosures or indirectly by the low wages that enclosures caused, the newly created poor faced a bleak future in the rapidly growing towns and cities. Their working hours were very much longer and more intensive than anything most of them had experienced before. In the country, working hours had been governed by the season and the weather and craftspeople had generally taken Mondays off: now there were no such restrictions, and workers had to perform at the pace of a powered machine rather than their own. Urban housing conditions, water supplies and sanitation were appalling, with the result that disease was rife. Moreover, everything these workers needed had to be bought for cash: the economy had become fully monetarized as far as they were concerned. No longer could they go out on the heath to collect wood for the fire or catch a rabbit for the pot, and the network of friends and relatives on whom they could call for assistance had generally been lost.

Life expectancy figures show clearly the effect of going blindly for growth and letting the 'invisible hand' take care of the hindmost. Even in 1871 a new-born child could not be expected to live for as long as one born during the reign of Elizabeth I. However, death rates per thousand of population are very difficult to compare because, if the age breakdown of two populations differs, the place with the younger population ought to have the lower death rate, simply because fewer people can be expected to die of old age in any given year. Nevertheless, something of the full horror of urban conditions in the middle of the nineteenth century can be gleaned from the fact that in Liverpool in the 1840s the death rate was 39.2 per thousand. This is equivalent to the death rate today in a population consisting entirely of 65 to 74-year-old men. In Liverpool, the average age was very much lower – probably well under thirty.

In theory, of course, life expectancies should have increased rather than fallen because the periodic localized shortages and famines that had caused many deaths in pre-industrial Britain were now avoidable since the building of the canals and railways enabled food to be brought in from other areas. But theory and practice are not necessarily the same thing in a society that believes in the supremacy of the market, as the Irish potato famine so clearly showed.

A FALSE DATUM

But of course we know about the hardships of the urban poor. Because Britain's towns and cities were shaped in the mid-1800s and many buildings constructed then are still in use, we feel we know the period well, particularly as we have read so much about it. We know about women and children as young as five working naked in the mines, crawling through the seams pulling tubs of coal. We know of the excessive hours demanded of mill workers in hot, humid conditions and the respiratory diseases they frequently caught as a result. From Dickens we know about the baby farms and the workhouses; from Mayhew we know about crime, drunkenness and prostitution. And because things are many times better now in the Western world, we feel that humanity is making progress and that economic growth is doing us good.

We are getting the wrong impression. The reason I have spent so much time on detailing the social destruction caused by the first century of the Industrial Revolution is to be able to argue now that if we measure our progress from 1850 or 1860 we are using a false datum: we are picking a period as our starting-point in which living conditions for most people were worse than they had been for centuries and when the degree of exploitation and relative poverty was greater than it had ever been in Britain in historic times. Moreover, since this period of hardship was created by the growth process, we must not give that process credit for partially restoring what it had first taken away.

The problem we have with selecting any period other than some time in the nineteenth century to measure our progress against is that in spite of Chaucer, Shakespeare, Fielding and many other writers, we have very little idea of what daily life was like in the Britain that the Industrial Revolution destroyed. While the composite mental picture we draw from *The Canterbury Tales*, *The Merry Wives of Windsor* and *Tom Jones* is probably one of unsophisticated fun, we also remember things like the Black Death and chamberpots being emptied from upstairs windows, suspect that things were really pretty bad for most people, and are happy that we live today.

Our conceptual difficulties are compounded by a shortage of data. Almost the only figures we have for the period between 1650 and 1750 are Gregory King's 1688 calculations[5] that 2,795,000 people – just over half of the 5.5 million population of England at the time – were living in poverty. King's marvellous phrase for poverty was 'decreasing the wealth of the king-dom' because he claimed that out of an average income of £10 10s 0d (£10.50) each year, the poor spent 4s 6d (23p) more than they earned – an amount which scarcely seems profligate. Whole classes fell into this catego-ry – labouring people and out-servants (1.275 million), cottagers and pau-pers (1.3 million), soldiers and seamen and their families (220,000) and vagrants (30,000): in other words, all the hewers of wood and drawers of water for the rest of society, whose income averaged £67 a head. King's results are hardly surprising as in every economy élites organize things so that they have plenty of servants on the borderline of poverty to look after them. The really significant thing about his figures is that only 51 per cent of the population in 1688 was considered to be poor, very much less than the 86.9 per cent which Hobsbawm categorizes as 'struggling and poor' as late as 1890.

Even though we can never know exactly how much worse the search for growth made life for the majority of the British people in the worst years of the Industrial Revolution, it is generally accepted that after 1850 things began to improve. Mitchell and Deane's calculations,[6] for example, found that real wages began to go up after 1857. But why was this? Was growth at last starting to benefit the many rather than the few?

The answer is a categoric no. The years between 1850 and 1914 during which living conditions for ordinary people improved most were those in which per capita national income did not rise. Estimates by E. H. Phelps Brown and P. E. Hart[7] show that there was no growth at all in national income during the Great Depression between 1873 and 1887 and that profits were stagnant for even longer: they reached £355 million in 1874 and, apart from two years when they equalled or inched above it, did not reach that level again until 1894. And yet, even though wages fell in some of those years, prices fell so much faster that people lucky enough to stay in work became appreciably better off. This phenomenon of living standards rising as growth retreats will be encountered again in the next chapter.

INCREASING POWER OF THE TOWNS

The improvement in living standards started in the 1850s for three reasons. One was that money wages began to go up because the flow of new labour from the countryside and from Ireland slowed down both absolutely and in relation to the numbers already employed in manufacturing and mining. After 1851 more people lived in urban areas than rural ones so that even if the percentage of the rural population fleeing the land each year had stayed constant rather than dropping, the influx to the towns, in proportion to the number of people already there, would have fallen and wages would have had a chance to move up.

The second thing that increased wages was the fact that over nine million people – half of them Irish – emigrated from Britain and Ireland between 1837 and 1886, a huge number when we consider that the average population of the British Isles between those dates was 32 million. Since the flow consisted almost entirely of the young and active, the effect on the labour market must have been enormous.

The third factor was the repeal of the Corn Law in 1846, itself a sign of the shift in the urban-rural population balance. The amount of imported wheat was allowed to rise from 11 per cent of total consumption between 1841 and 1850 to 31 per cent of a much larger volume in the next decade. Food consumption grew rapidly as a result of the lower prices, as the following table, from Michael Mulhall's *Fifty Years of National Progress 1837-1887* (1887) shows:

Increase in food consumption per head during the great depression, 1873-87

	Meat (lb)	Wheat (lb)	Sugar (lb)	Tea (oz)
1837-40	66	255	18	19
1841-50	72	260	20	24
1851-60	81	301	29	35
1861-70	91	321	41	51
1871-80	96	325	60	67
1881-86	106	356	70	75

The most significant effect of the repeal of the Corn Law, however, was delayed until 1872, when home agricultural output actually began to fall as a result of a flood of food imports. From 1874, the United States provided at least half of Britain's wheat, and by 1900 only 12 per cent was home-grown. Meat producers were affected too: the development of refrigeration enabled the first Argentine beef to be sold in Europe in 1877 and New Zealand mutton arrived on the English market in 1882.

Just as had happened in 1814, farm rents failed to adjust to reflect the problems in British agriculture and tenant farmers were badly hit. Mulhall writes, 'The combined value of grain and meat produced yearly is less now [1886/7] than it was 40 years ago but rent and taxes have increased 36 per cent thus causing the margin in favour of farmers to diminish in an alarming degree.' He then prints a table showing that net farm incomes averaged £64.2 million annually between 1861 and 1870 but had dropped to £27.9 million by 1886, rents having risen from £61.2 million to £65.1 million and taxes and tithes from £15.3 million to £25.4 million over the same period. 'Thus the farmer's margin is now only half what it was in the earlier years of the present reign, being reduced to eleven shillings [55p] per acre.'

Inescapably, the sharp fall in farm incomes cut the demand for industrial goods from the agricultural sector and was a major factor in tipping the economy into recession. The flight from the land accelerated, with the agricultural labour force falling by 27 per cent from an average of 3.3 million in the 1860s to 2.4 million in the early 1880s – in previous decades the fall had been 10 per cent or less. By 1886, one million men were without work in Britain as a whole and two years later the word 'unemployment' entered the Oxford Dictionary for the first time.

No-one realized that the collapse in agriculture was responsible for a major part of industry's problems and influential industrialists even welcomed the imports that were destroying their domestic customers' purchasing power because the foreign food was around half the price of the home product thus enabling them to reduce wages. Manufacturers certainly needed to make reductions somewhere: their prices fell steadily after 1873 until, by 1896, many were at their lowest level for 200 years. Mulhall comments:

There was an increase of wages averaging 50 per cent from 1840 to 1880 but since the latter year much of the advance has been lost. Wages are nominally as high now [1886/7] as in 1880 but the number of men working full-time is less. After making all deductions we find the working man earns 20 or 25 per cent more than in 1840 and the prices of necessaries have mostly fallen. These advantages are counterbalanced by the rise in rent for whereas house-property in 1840 averaged a value of £30 per inhabitant, it now stands at £75, a proof that rents have risen exactly 150 per cent.

Mulhall concludes his survey of national progress by pointing out that 15 per cent of the population lived in houses valued at over £20 a year in 1886 compared with only 5 per cent in 1840; that 10 million people in the working classes had savings accounts and had been saving an average of 14 shillings (70p) a year each since 1875 and that returns from the Probate Court showed that 31 per cent of the population were then dying 'beyond reach of want', compared with only 17 per cent fifty years earlier. However, much was still wrong. 'It is to be lamented that the enormous increase in wealth since 1840 has not been accompanied by a greater attention to the wants of a suffering humanity' he writes after deploring a lack of hospital beds, the slums in the cities and the rising rates of suicide and divorce.

Not all parts of the economy were affected equally by the Great Depression. In some industries – coal and pig iron production, for example

– output continued to grow but at a much reduced rate in comparison with earlier periods. The fall-off in domestic demand might not have had such a long-lasting effect if interest rates had been able to fall to match the lower rates of profit. However, just as the failure of rents to fall had twice caused distress in farming, now unrealistically high interest rates – kept aloft by the rates of return that could be had in the Empire and elsewhere overseas – paralysed British industry. The flow of funds out of the country was so massive (£100 million in 1890 alone, equivalent to over £5,000 million today) that, in the early 1880s, of the £5,800 million worth of securities quoted on the London Stock Exchange, only £64 million represented investments in British industry. It was only after Baring Brothers' bank almost collapsed in 1890 because of its involvement in an Argentine railway that people began to grow more cautious about investing money overseas. As a result, interest rates halved, dropping from 4 per cent to 2 per cent, and the domestic economy began to recover.

THE MIDDLE CLASS SUBSIDIZE THE RICH

In their book on the economics of British imperialism, *Mammon and the Pursuit of Empire* (1989), two American academics, Lance Davis and Robert Huttenback show that until 1885 returns from investing in countries under British control were at least 25 per cent higher than from similar projects at home. However, the best returns went to the first people to introduce a technique in any territory and, when competitors started up later on, the rate of profit began to fall. They also show that while the cost of maintaining the Empire was largely carried by the middle class through higher taxes (Britain's per capita defence expenditure was twice that of France or Germany), the main group to benefit from investing overseas was the ruling élite. 'Imperialism can best be viewed as a mechanism for transferring income from the middle to the upper classes' they conclude.

As very little new domestic investment took place until after 1890, it was inevitable that Britain would fall behind other industrial countries technologically. In any case the need for innovation was blunted because the lower wages removed much of the incentive to install labour-saving equipment. Output per miner actually began falling in the 1880s and the level of mechanization in the industry fell behind that in Germany or the United States. 'There seemed to be no limit to the population reservoir both from within old-established mining families and from without, to supply the manpower for the pits; over 1,100,000 were thus employed in 1913,' writes Sidney Pollard, in *Development of the British Economy 1914-1950* (1962). Pollard also gives many examples of the effects of the lack of investment:

While blast furnaces hardly changed in this country, abroad new building and replacement constantly enlarged their size and raised their efficiency, and the same could be said of the steel furnaces and converters. Britain adopted the cheaper basic processes only very slowly; the final change-over even from puddled iron took place long after it had been completed elsewhere. In the introduction of special alloy steels, which formed one of the most important fields of innovation in the early twentieth century, Britain made her share of the discoveries but fell behind in their adoption.

Since they could not grow by expanding their sales or by adopting new technologies, British firms sought to grow by acquisition, a method that came into its own again a century later for exactly the same reasons. The period from 1880 to 1914 is notable for the number of industrial mergers. Imperial Tobacco, a combine of thirteen firms, began in this period, as did British Oil and Cake Mills (seventeen firms), Distillers, Associated Portland Cement, J & P Coats (nineteen firms) and many other well-known names.

Once business conditions improved as a result of the fall in interest rates, the improvement in living conditions ceased. Prices began to rise again in 1896 and, as Keynes noted in *The Economic Consequences of the Peace*, the wealthy were allowed to appropriate a large part of the benefits of the resumed growth, with the result that the Edwardian period became known as *La Belle Époque*, a period of highly conspicuous consumption by the well-to-do. By 1913, 0.85 per cent of the population – 170,000 people – owned 65.5 per cent of the capital in the country, while at the other extreme 87.4 per cent owned only 8.5 per cent between them. The consequences of this polarization of wealth were revealed in 1917 when every young man was examined for military service. 10 per cent were found to be totally unfit, 31.5 per cent had marked disabilities, 22 per cent had partial disabilities and only just over one-third were in satisfactory shape.

It seems very doubtful that economic growth brought any real benefits to the majority of British people in the period up to 1914, particularly as a study of the purchasing power of builders' wages by Phelps Brown and Hopkins[8] shows that the prosperity such workers enjoyed between 1400 and 1500 as a result of the redistribution of economic power by the Black Death was not achieved again until 1870. Naturally there were some changes for the better, such as the technical ability to eliminate local famines through the development of better transport systems. But whether the reduction in the death rate from starvation outweighed the increase in deaths from contagious diseases in the expanding towns cannot be calculated for lack of data.

What can be said with certainty is that those changes that did benefit the majority of people were generally the result either of improved medical knowledge or of legislation to control growth rather than growth itself. For example, social reforms seem to have followed each extension of voting

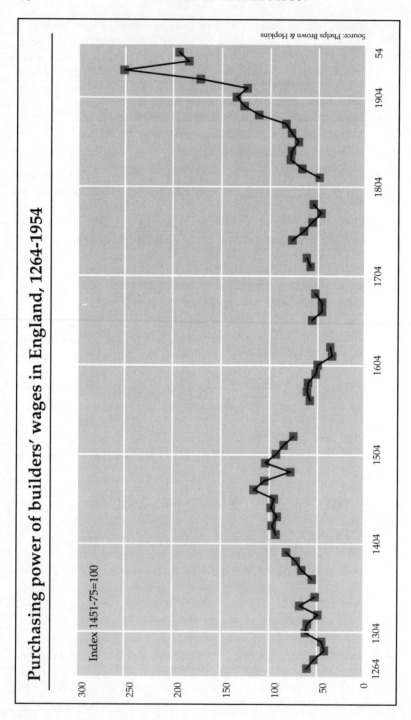

Figure 3.1 Purchasing power of builders' wages in England

rights much more closely than each expansion of national wealth. After the Reform Act of 1832, which increased the proportion of the adult population able to vote from 5 to 7.1 per cent, laws were passed regulating factory conditions (1833), school buildings (1833) and local government (1835), and prohibiting the employment of women and boys under ten in the mines (1842 – although the law was ignored in some coalfields for several years). After the 1867 Reform Act, which extended the vote to 16.4 per cent of adults, elementary education was reorganized and expanded (1870) and the sewers were improved (1871-2).

Even if we cannot overcome the prejudices created by our acceptance of a false datum and feel that the British people were materially better off in 1914 than in Defoe's day, we have to decide just how much of the improvement was due to the exploitation of people overseas or the use of resources on a non-sustainable basis. Since we are trying to assess the benefits of growth alone, the effects of reaping windfall profits at the expense of the environment or as a result of impoverishing others must be eliminated, and once this has been done, any remaining gain could only be very small, if indeed it is positive at all. A third correction is required too: some allowance has to be made for the fact that a high proportion of the population fell from their former status as independent craftspeople, farmers and cottagers to membership of the proletariat, people without property with nothing to sell but their labour. But how do we value their former status in monetary or consumption terms? How much better diet, clothing, rented housing and education would they have needed to have had in 1914 to compensate for its loss? These questions are unanswerable.

My feeling is that if the people of the world could have been asked in 1714 whether they wanted things to stay as they were or (given perfect foreknowledge) they would like to live two centuries later, they might well have opted for the latter. But such a choice would probably have been determined by reasons more closely connected with the increasing emphasis being placed in 1914 on the worth and rights of the individual than anything material that growth had brought about.

This change in society's values was a product of the growth process. While an individual in a stationary society can improve his or her lot, it is impossible for a whole class to do so except as a result of a major redistribution of economic power, such as that brought about by the Black Death. To avoid constant attempts at revolution, most stationary societies seek to legitimize the status quo by suggesting that it was ordained from on high: the old Deo Gratia/Divine Right claims of the British monarchy and the Hindu belief that we are what we are in this life because of our performance in the last are examples of this. Only when the idea of growth makes it seem possible to improve the living conditions of the poor does it become intolerable that they should continue to live in an unsatisfactory way.

So the answer to the question we set ourselves – could the benefits of growth have been achieved in any other way? – is no. Growth gave us the feeling that social progress is possible, and this attitude could not have been implanted without growth taking place. True, humankind had evolved other concepts of progress before economic growth came along: in art, knowledge, civilization and in political freedom, for example. But even as late as 1830 the historian Lord Macaulay had to argue that material progress was taking place. In answer to Southey's claim in his *Colloquies on Society* (1829) that people had been better off in Sir Thomas More's time, 300 years earlier, Macaulay wrote:

History is full of the signs of this natural progress of society. We see in almost every part of the annals of mankind how the industry of individuals, struggling up against wars, taxes, famines, conflagrations, mischievous prohibitions and more mischievous protection creates faster than governments can squander and repairs whatever invaders can destroy. We see the wealth of nations increasing and all the arts of life approaching nearer and nearer to perfection in spite of the grossest corruption and the wildest profusion on the part of rulers.[9]

Pollard argues in *The Idea of Progress* (1968) that, as far as social progress is concerned, the Great Exhibition of 1851 was the turning point in public attitudes.

And when, from the middle of the 19th Century, it became possible in Britain and in the USA and soon elsewhere also to make some of the products and benefits of the new system of production available to the great mass of the producing classes, both opposing schools of thought took this to be a confirmation of their idea of progress: for the bourgeois, a confirmation that what was good for him could at last be shown to be good for the country as a whole; for the proletarian, his first small victory, the first step upon an advance which would ultimately usher in his chapter in the story of the upward march of man.

But the idea that growth itself is progress or is necessary for progress is a dangerous illusion which the better-off have been only too keen to propagate: as we have seen, there was an inverse relationship between social progress and growth in the eighteenth and nineteenth centuries, with ordinary people gaining most when growth was checked or slowed. In the chapters that follow we will see that this pattern has continued right up to the present day.

4

The Benefits of War and Depression

If, in the interests of a supposed stability, a halt is to be called to the process of raising real incomes, it is an issue which should be squarely presented to those who are most affected by it. It is all very well for the dilettante economists of wealthy universities, their tables groaning beneath a sufficiency of the good things of this world, their garages furnished with private means of transport, to say, 'Food is cheap enough. Charabancs are vulgar. The railways are admirable. We have enough of plenty. Let us safeguard security.' It is for the millions to whom a slice of bacon more or less, or a bus ride to the sea, still matter, to make a decision. – Lionel Robbins, *The Great Depression* (1934)

Although British national income did not grow in cash terms during the whole of the period between the wars, the common people became much better off. Their lot also improved during the wars themselves when the forces of capitalism were closely controlled, and again later as a result of the fiercely redistributive taxes imposed by the 1945 Labour government. On the other hand, whenever business conditions improved briefly only the rich gained. In other words, there was an exact repeat of the phenomenon in the second half of the nineteenth century when, as we have just seen, conditions improved for those who managed to hang onto their jobs during the Great Depression and then fell back to some extent once growth resumed.

The First World War brought about a massive shift in income from the rich to the poor. Some of this was achieved through the taxation system. In 1913, for example, income tax was 1s 2d (6p) in the pound with an additional 6p in supertax on incomes above £5,000. During the war, however, income tax trebled and supertax went up to 6s (30p) on the highest incomes – rates that would have been unthinkable a year or two earlier but which subsequent governments have been able to maintain or increase. In their *British Political Facts* (1975), David Butler and Anne Sloman calculate that a bachelor earning £10,000 a year would have had £9,249 left after paying tax in 1913. In 1922, however, he would have been left with only £5,672, even though his purchasing power had been cut to one-third by inflation.

The combined effect of tax increases and price rises was to reduce the number of high income earners by two-thirds. Although 5,000 people had

pre-tax incomes above £10,000 in 1914 and 9,200 in 1925, if one corrects
for the changes in taxes and the decline in purchasing power, as A. L.
Bowley did in his book *Has Poverty Diminished?* (1925), the number of
those who had £10,000 to spend or save after tax in 1914 was 4,000 and
only 1,300 reached the equivalent figure in 1925 when they needed to earn
£30,000 gross to maintain the same purchasing power.

Besides cutting the rich down, the war built the poor up: it eroded the
differences in wages between the skilled and the unskilled and made more
jobs available. Although wages were controlled for most of its duration and
did not keep up with prices, family incomes rose in real terms because more
people were at work and the work itself was more regular. In addition,
whenever the authorities sanctioned wage increases they frequently gave a
flat-rate rise to everybody, thus providing unskilled workers with a bigger
proportionate increase than their skilled colleagues. By 1920 a labourer's
wages were three times what they had been in 1914, an increase roughly in
line with the rise in the cost of food, while a skilled worker got only 2.3
times as much per hour as before the war.

The demobilization of the four million men in the armed forces and the
redeployment of a million munitions workers at the end of the war was
accomplished with a speed and ease that surprised everyone. Although
30,000 men left the forces each day during January 1919, 'it is a striking fact
that, in twelve months, the economic system absorbed nearly twice as many
people as were unemployed on the average during the bad years of the Great
Depression 1931-32' wrote an economist, A. S. J. Baster, in *The Little Less*
(1947), a book he hoped would help with planning for the future after the
Second World War. By 1920 there was even an acute labour shortage in
most parts of the country, created in part by the reduction of the working
day from nine to eight hours with no loss of pay. This reduction was the
result of a trade union campaign based on scientific studies of industrial
fatigue and meant that 46 or 48 hours, rather than 54, became the standard
working week, a figure that (if overtime is included) many unskilled workers
put in to this day.

Pent-up demand also played a part in the creation of jobs for the returning troops. As Baster says,

The story of how motor-cars were turned out instead of howitzers, cash-registers
instead of gun-sights, beer engines instead of aeroplane motors, dyestuffs, rayon and
fertilizers instead of explosives and poison gas makes the classical process of beating
swords into ploughshares sound archaic and amateurish indeed ... Businessmen discovered that, to begin with, there was an insatiable public demand for almost everything. Industrialists wanted new buildings put up and worn-out machinery replaced.
Railway companies wanted quantities of new rolling stock and years of deferred
maintenance made good, and traders wanted to re-build their stocks. Private cus-

tomers wanted new houses, motor-cars, clothes and all the things they had been deprived of in the war. The significant thing is that in most cases the pressure of accumulated demand was matched by accumulated money savings built up deliberately against the time of rehabilitation or accumulated willy-nilly by the normally improvident for want of a spending outlet during war-time.

As a result of the high demand, wholesale prices began to go up in early 1919 and by April the following year they were 30 per cent above their level when the war ended. But after the boom came a dramatic collapse and between January 1921 and May 1922 the cost of living halved. The cause of the crash was exports – or rather the lack of them, as sales abroad in 1921 were only half what they had been in 1913 – simply because many of the traditional markets for cotton and coal had been taken over by other suppliers during the war while other former customers, especially in Europe, were too impoverished to buy.

The employers made great efforts to cut wages to match the falling prices and 7.6 million workers had to accept pay cuts in 1922 and a further 7.6 million in 1923. Overall, however, the drop in pay was only 32 per cent against the 50 per cent fall in the cost of living, so everybody who managed to stay in work during this period came out much better off.

Even those who lost their jobs were better off, or better off at least than they would have been had they become unemployed before the war. This was as a result of the introduction of the national insurance scheme by Lloyd George's government in 1911; and by March 1921 a dole of 18s (90p) a week was being paid to 15 per cent of the insured labour force, a figure that rose to 17 per cent as the year wore on. Since the benefit had been calculated on the supposition that the average rate of unemployment would be 4 per cent – as it had been up to 1914 – the contributions quickly ran out and a significant chunk of the incomes of the wealthier part of the community, the taxpayers, started finding its way to the poor.

According to Phelps Brown and Hart[1] the net result of these changes was that the share of national income going to wage-earners rose from 36.6 per cent in 1913 to 41.9 per cent in 1924, and much of this extra went to the less well-paid. In terms of gross (pre-tax) pay, however, those on salaries did even better and salaries and wages, which together made up 55 per cent of national income in 1913, took 66.7 per cent in 1924. This 21 per cent increase in purchasing power at the expense of the property-owning classes is staggering, especially as national income in real terms actually fell between the two years.

The answer to Bowley's question, 'Has poverty diminished?' was an almost unqualified yes. His survey of five towns – Reading, Northampton, Bolton, Warrington and Stanley in 1924 – showed that poverty had only increased in the last, a mining town in Co. Durham, because of the collapse of coal exports. Elsewhere, the proportion of families which had been in poverty in 1913 had dropped by 80 per cent and even in Stanley, which had been the richest of the five in 1913, this proportion had only risen from 6 to 7.5 per cent.

THE RICH STRIKE BACK

Of course the rich – or at least that proportion of the rich who had their assets denominated in cash – tried to snatch some of their losses back. Although there was no way that they could undo the worldwide inflation the war had caused they could at least insist that their pounds buy the same amount of gold and dollars as they had done before the war. So, hiding its real motives behind phrases often used on similar occasions since – 'moral obligation to our creditors' and 'making for economic stability' – the City of London pressed the Treasury and the Bank of England for sterling to be restored to its pre-war exchange rate of $4.8666 to the pound, a level that required British prices to be cut by between ten and fifteen per cent if export competitiveness was to be maintained. (Or, to put it another way, the banks, the main holders of sterling cash, wanted their money to be worth 10 to 15 per cent more at the expense of everyone else in the community.) Churchill, the Chancellor of the Exchequer, was warned of the 'quasi-catastrophic' effects this would have on industry, of 'unlimited unemployment, immense losses and ruin,' but in spite of his own misgivings he went ahead on 28 April 1925 with a course that *The Economist* described over forty years later as 'unrelievedly bad'.

Any gains the bankers made as a result of this return to the gold standard at the pre-war level were at the expense of two groups. Those who lost their jobs obviously suffered, and Churchill's move reversed the steady decline in the unemployment figures that had been taking place since 1922; the other victims were the owners of businesses, whose profits dropped 11 per cent the following year. But the lower prices that the new exchange rate required benefited everybody else, because, while their wages fell slightly, their cost of living fell even more. Prices in fact continued to drift down until 1933 and weekly wage rates followed them so tardily that by the time the cost of living moved up again in 1935, the average employee was 16 per cent better off.

This steady shift of national income from rich to poor began to create new domestic markets to replace the traditional export trades – coal, cotton and shipbuilding – that the revaluation of the currency had hit so hard. Housing completions, less than 30,000 a year in 1920, shot up to 174,000 in 1925 and continued to climb, to reach 350,000 by 1935, with the result that over four million houses were built between the wars. 'But even more strik-ing than this quantitative success was the improvement over the same period in the quality of the general level of housing conditions,' wrote Mark Abrams in his book for the Fabian Society, *The Condition of the British People* (1945). The national electricity grid was started and work on it absorbed 100,000 men at the height of the depression in 1931. Ford built its plant at Dagenham in the early thirties and employed 15,000 workers from the start. Hoover arrived from Canada at around the same time and drove imported vacuum cleaners from the market.

So, although national income in real terms was below its 1913 level for every year except two up to 1934, most people's incomes – even those of the unemployed – got significantly better, so much so in fact that an unem-ployed man with a family was better off in the thirties than a fully employed unskilled labourer in 1913.[2]

But when growth began again after 1934, real wages began to slip back and average real earnings dropped 2 per cent between that year and 1938. Who were the beneficiaries? The recipients of profits, of course, who saw their share of national income rise from 23.9 to 26.2 per cent – an increase of almost a tenth. Even so it is estimated that annual real wages went up by 30 per cent between 1913 and 1938 and Abrams suggests that the effective rise in per capita consumption was in the region of 50 per cent if one con-siders that the working week was cut by 10 per cent in 1919 and that most families had fewer dependants. He points out that there was a redistribution of wealth as well as income during the period. In 1913, 170,000 people – less than 1 per cent of the 18,745,000 people aged 25 and over at the time – owned 65.4 per cent of the wealth; by 1936, the top 1 per cent owned 55.7 per cent.

The Second World War brought about a further redistribution of income in favour of the less well-off, and for much the same reasons: wage differen-tials were eroded, the demand for labour was high, profits were controlled and taxes were highly progressive. Between 1938 and 1943, according to Abrams, salaries went up by 24 per cent but wages increased by 64 per cent and in mid-1944 average earnings were 82 per cent above the 1938 figure, largely because of the amount of overtime. Although a lot of the additional earnings went to pay taxes, which collected three times as much revenue as before the war, there was a real gain in purchasing power since the prices of basic commodities such as food were rigidly controlled. However, because there was little in the shops that was unrationed on which the extra income could be spent, savings went up eightfold.

In a careful assessment of the effects of the war and the immediate after-math on income distribution, Allan Cartter, an American economist, in *The Redistribution of Incomes in Post-war Britain* (1955), concludes: 'The redistribution has been substantial, amounting to 13.1 per cent of national income in 1948-49, which seems to represent the high water mark.' In *The Levelling of Incomes since 1938* (1951) Dudley Seers agrees: 'Since pre-war, the net effects of income, tax and price movements were all egalitarian', adding that 1949 saw a 'clear reversal of the previous consistent tendency for wage earners to gain at the expense of property incomes'.

Although both these comments were made in the early fifties, they were not premature. Detailed figures published by Tom Stark of the University of Ulster in a Fabian pamphlet *Income and Wealth in the 1980s* (1990) show that the poorer half of the population got only 23.7 per cent of the national income before tax in 1949 and that their share dropped to 22.1 per cent in 1959. There was, however, an improvement in the sixties and by the mid seventies the proportion was up to 24.3 per cent. It then dropped back and fell below the 1949 figure, reaching 22.7 per cent by 1984/5 for reasons we shall discuss in the next chapter.

1949 also marked a temporary end to radical attempts at social engineering in Britain. For the following thirty years, both major parties were content to leave the system broadly as they found it. This was because, after they discovered the apparent wonders of economic growth in the mid-fifties, both agreed that the argument over how the national cake was to be divided was essentially sterile; what really mattered was the best and quickest way of enlarging it. Growth, with its promise of more for everybody, largely defused the capitalist-socialist ideological struggle. Instead, 'Butskellism' (the broadly similar economic and social policies pioneered by R. A. Butler, Conservative Chancellor of the Exchequer from 1951 to 1956 and then Home Secretary, and Hugh Gaitskell, Chancellor of the Exchequer in 1950 and later leader of the Labour Party) flourished, long after its inventors had moved or passed on. Commenting on the lack of any significant differences between the two major parties in *The Other Revolution* (1979), Arianna Stassinopoulos wrote:

If we apply any of the tests by which socialism can be measured – the level of public expenditure, the proportion of the working population employed by public authorities, the size and privileges of the bureaucracy, the degree of intervention by the state in economic and other matters, the incidence of taxation – we find that the most recent Conservative governments have in practice been just as 'socialist' as the Labour ones.

In effect, British politics became almost exclusively about increasing production: vision and values were forgotten. As Jimmy Porter commented in John Osborne's play *Look Back in Anger* (1956), 'There aren't any good, brave causes left any more.'

5

Mrs Thatcher and the
Struggle Against Inflation

If I were to characterize the past decade, the most remarkable thing was the generation of a global consensus that market forces and economic efficiency were the best way to achieve the kind of growth which is the best antidote to poverty. – Barber Conable, President of the World Bank (January 1990)

The election of a Conservative government under Margaret Thatcher in 1979 brought to a close the thirty-year period of near-consensus on how the British economy should be run. For the new Prime Minister, leaving everything to growth and collective bargaining was not enough. The richest half of the community she represented felt that progress towards greater equality had gone too far, even though the distribution of both income and wealth had not shifted against it for a generation. Striving for harmony was out; readiness for confrontation was in – as, indeed, it had to be: conflict was inescapable if she was to reverse trends towards greater state involvement in the distribution of income and the safeguarding of the interests of the poor that had been running, with the odd hiccup, since 1851.

Two factors produced this radical about-turn in Conservative Party policies. One was that after the experience of the three-day week caused by the miners' strike in 1972, there was a feeling that Britain had become ungovernable by the old consensus methods. The other was the worldwide period of high inflation in the early 1970s. Until then, public attitudes to a moderate level of inflation were in general so relaxed that the city editor of the *Sunday Telegraph* could write on 28 April 1963: 'The great social justification to my mind of a mildly inflationary economy is that a society in which borrowers do better than lenders of money is fundamentally more attractive than when the reverse is true.' The writer was Nigel Lawson, who, as Chancellor of the Exchequer, played a large part in the attack on inflation and in the consequent creation of an unattractive society.

The average rate of inflation in Britain between 1954 and 1968 was 3.2 per cent so when it soared to 15.9 per cent in 1974 and 24.2 per cent in 1975, it was scarcely surprising that people began to feel much less relaxed about it. There were several reasons for the more rapid rate. One was that a massive increase in the US balance of payments deficit in 1970/1 had unleashed a flow of dollars on the world. This caused booms in most of the main industrial countries where the expansions were helped along by the fact that many of them were holding elections at the time and governments needed to encourage the voters. Another reason for the inflation was that the era of fixed exchange rates, which began with the Bretton Woods agreement in 1944, had finally broken down in March 1973 and, now that countries were allowing their exchange rates to float, they felt that they did not need to control their expenditure quite as carefully as in the past.

In Britain this period became known as the 'Barber Boom' after the Chancellor of the Exchequer who announced an ill-fated 'dash for growth' in his 1972 Budget. 'We now have a rare opportunity to secure a sustained and faster rate of economic expansion over a considerable period of years,' he said as he increased the budget deficit and cut taxes by £1,200 million at a time when inflation was already running at 7 per cent. Yet in a normal year, even with this level of inflation, the effects of pumping so much extra money into the economy might have been fairly limited; Barber's mistake was to do it while simultaneously freeing the banks from the controls on lending under which they had functioned since the war. The result was that loans to the private sector soared to £6,430 million in 1972, 345 per cent up on the year before, providing the fuel for rapid price increases.

The general boom in the industrialized world caused acute shortages of some basic materials including foodstuffs. Manufacturing costs and the cost of living went up and wages responded by rising more quickly than at any time in the previous fifteen years. The inflationary spiral was given a further twist in October 1973 when OPEC doubled oil prices and then doubled them again two months later. Since oil is, in differing degrees, an ingredient in everything produced and consumed in industrialized countries, a massive, multi-stage inflation had to be carried out to allow their economies to adjust to the increases. In the first stage, manufacturers put up prices according to the amount of oil they were using directly. Then they raised them again to pass on the increased prices of the things they bought. A third stage followed, in which firms accommodated second-stage rises – and so it went on, with several rounds of price increases, each smaller than the last, spread over two or three years, until the effect of a huge rise in the cost of a basic ingredient in the productive process had worked itself through.

When the dust had settled in 1977, with the British bank rate back down from its maximum of 15 per cent to the 5 per cent it had been in 1971, everyone was pleasantly surprised by how quickly the world's economies had returned to their pre-crisis condition, particularly in view of the pessimistic predictions made when the crisis broke. However, one powerful economic force had been badly hit – the bankers – and they resolved that they would never get themselves into a similar position again.

The bankers' problem had been entirely of their own making. After Barber lifted the controls on their lending, many of the 'fringe' banks had greatly expanded their loans to property developers. As a result, far too much building work went ahead and property values collapsed. One bank, London and County Securities, which had taken deposits direct from the public, found that it could no longer raise funds on the money markets, and when other small banks were found to be in a similar position, there was a clear danger of panic – particularly after the National Westminster Bank took the unprecedented step of announcing that its own position was sound. Because many people subscribe to the principle that one should never believe anything until it is officially denied, the statement really sounded the alarm.

The situation became so serious at Christmas 1973 that the Bank of England was forced to compel the clearing banks to lend enough to the fringe banks to prevent their collapse, which would have brought the whole financial structure down. The government also ended a freeze on commercial rents imposed by the previous Labour government after it had been warned that the accounts of some clearing banks might otherwise have to be qualified by their auditors. Had this happened it would inevitably have led to questions about the clearers' solvency with dire consequences for the City's status as an international banking centre and for the exchange rate of the pound.

The lifting of the rent freeze encouraged buyers back into the property market, and after March 1975 the crisis had passed its peak. But it was a very close-run thing, especially as the Bankhaus Herstatt had been forced to close in Germany and the Franklin National Bank narrowly escaped the same fate in New York. As David Smith, economics correspondent of *The Times*, puts it in *The Rise and Fall of Monetarism* (1987), 'a world-wide monetary binge had brought the international financial system within a whisker of collapse. The system survived, but only just. The case for prudent monetary control was stronger than ever.'

Consequently, when oil prices tripled in the first half of 1979 as a result of a very cold winter and of production cuts in Iran in the wake of its revolution, the bankers were ready. They had plenty of arguments with which to persuade politicians not to undertake another monetary expansion big enough to allow the world to adjust to the higher energy prices via inflation again. They feared a rapid inflation because, if one took place, their capital might not grow as rapidly as their loans and they would have to raise outside equity to stay within the law, thus diluting their own holdings. Just as in 1925, when British banks forced sterling to return to the gold standard to restore the value of their capital, world bankers advocated putting national economies on the rack to suit their own interests.

So it was that on 6 October 1979, in response to bank pressure, the US Federal Reserve announced that it was going to use interest rates to control an inflation that was then running at 13.3 per cent, up from 9 per cent the previous year. The announcement immediately pushed the prime lending rate up to 15 per cent – it had also been 9 per cent the previous year – and it peaked at 21.5 per cent in December 1980. Not surprisingly, American GNP growth which had been 5 per cent in 1978 plummeted to minus 3 per cent in 1982 before starting to rise again. Britain adopted similar policies, raising the Bank Rate by 3 per cent to an unprecedented 17 per cent in November 1979 and 1 million jobs in manufacturing industry were lost in consequence. Unemployment rose from 1.25 million in 1979 to almost 4 million by 1984. (This figure is disputed, but is correct if consistent methods of counting are used. See the graph on page 127.) The world economy went so deeply into depression that oil prices fell back below their 1978 level in real terms and British retail price inflation, which had not fallen below 8 per cent in the whole of the seventies, was brought down to 5 per cent.

Besides the memory of a financial near-collapse, the main asset the banks had in persuading the politicians to take such drastic action on their behalf was the public perception that inflation was harmful. The popular prejudice was based on highly coloured accounts of the German hyperinflation in the wake of the First World War in which people were said to have needed wheelbarrows to carry their money when they went out shopping. It had strengthened during the fifties and sixties, when the main economic problem governments had faced had been keeping the British inflation rate in step with rates in other countries so that the pound's fixed exchange rate could be maintained. The whole postwar period seemed to have been an endless series of inflation-induced balance-of-payments crises cured by cutting state spending, imposing pay pauses and import controls, and restricting the outflow of capital and the use of hire purchase.

The idea that inflation was bad got a further boost when the raw material shortages and the OPEC action of the early seventies accelerated the rate of price increases considerably above anything known since the war. A torrent of books and articles on both sides of the Atlantic condemned the process out of hand. *Inflation – A World-Wide Disaster* (1973) was the dispassionate title of a book by an economist who had previously worked for the IMF and the World Bank, Irving Friedman. 'Inflation is the key postwar economic problem,' Aubrey Jones wrote as the first line in his *The New Inflation*, which also appeared in 1973. 'Inflation is now the key problem of our age,' the blurb on P. J. Curwen's *Inflation* (1976) agreed.

Friedman's onslaught on his subject is typical of the genre: all allegation and no evidence. Not one of the assertions he makes in the following extract is supported by data:

The effects of persistent inflation are devastating on all kinds of societies. None is immune. To accept the persistent rising trends as inevitable is to accept the inevitability of the devastating effects – devastating because they attack and erode the fundamentals on which any organized society rests, irrespective of political and social ideology and structures. The ills of such inflation fall most heavily on the poorest but the great majority of people are increasingly harmed in many different ways. Among its victims are national objectives of satisfactory levels of growth, employment and income distribution.

The single exception to this tide of unreason that I have been able to trace is a slim study *The New Inflation, its Causes, Effects and Cures* (1972) by G. L. Bach, a professor at Stanford University. It devotes twenty-eight pages – about a quarter of its length – to establishing from first principles what the effect of an inflation should be on output, incomes, wealth, households, business and international trade. Bach finds that elderly people with few debts and holding a relatively high proportion of their wealth in fixed value assets lose, while young families, generally heavily in debt as a result of house purchase, gain. He argues that since the Second World War inflation had caused a massive shift in purchasing power from households, as major net savers, to the federal government and to businesses, but that, as the government is the agent for everybody, taxpayers have been the major beneficiaries of this flow: without inflation, the tax take would have to have been higher. There is no evidence that inflation has any effect on growth or employment. 'The effects [of inflation] appear to be less drastic than is often claimed,' Bach concludes.

Although there was little apart from Bach's lone voice to suggest otherwise, economists had not in fact reached a consensus that inflation was bad. As my old professor, Richard Lipsey, put it in an essay, 'After monetarism',[1] in 1984, 'opinions range from the view that the costs are trivial to the view that the costs are enormous and include an eroding of the social fabric.' Yet the profession completely failed to make its divergences of opinion known. While the job of an economist amounts to no more than advising on the allocation of scarce resources between competing ends, no economist of note went on record in 1980 as suggesting that the conquest of inflation might be unworthy of the level of resources being devoted to it. This was a shameful failure. True, 364 economists did sign an open letter to *The Times* in March 1981 saying that the Conservatives' monetary policies would 'deepen the depression, erode the industrial base of our economy and threaten its social and political stability.' However, this was in response to a budget that had reduced demand by the equivalent of 7 per cent of GNP at a time when industry had already shrunk by 17.5 per cent and unemployment was rising by 100,000 a month. It did not discuss the pros and cons of fighting inflation and there was no serious discussion of the subject later. As a result, both the Conservative and Labour parties came to accept that inflation threatened both economic growth and the national social fabric and that strong measures should therefore be taken to keep it under tight control. Neither party stopped to ask what the cost of such measures might be and whether the price was worth paying.

Margaret Thatcher was unaffected by the spate of publications attacking inflation. Her mind was already made up: as early as 1968 she had made a speech to the Conservative Party conference suggesting that the money supply be controlled to moderate it. In 1974 she worked closely with Sir Keith Joseph to set up the Centre for Policy Studies, one of whose objectives was to propagate anti-inflation, monetarist views. So it was no surprise that on 15 September 1975, during her first visit to the United States as party leader, she should make two speeches which set out her views on the question in some detail. The speeches were published by the Centre for Policy Studies[2] in book form in 1977 and make fascinating reading, not only because she gave full warning of all the economic and social changes she subsequently tried to make but also because she provided references to the authorities from whom she drew. In doing so, however, she showed herself to be bizarrely prescient: no fewer than eleven of the twenty-nine references are to books and newspaper articles that were not published, and in most cases not written, at the time she made her speeches. (Presumably a CPS researcher inserted the fake references when the speeches were being prepared for publication to make her views seem more authoritative.) One of the sources she anticipated was a then-unpublished book by her economic guru in Chicago, Milton Friedman, who subsequently visited London several times to conduct seminars on monetarism for civil servants.

In both her speeches, Mrs Thatcher argued that the high levels of income tax required by the welfare state had been a major source of inflationary pressure because they had led to higher pay settlements. Businesses had been unable to pass the full cost of these settlements on to their customers and, consequently, their profits had fallen for two decades and they had been unable to invest as much as they had done previously. (This was nonsense: the proportion of GDP invested the previous year had been the highest since 1945 and was probably the highest in history.) 'It appears, as a natural consequence, that our underlying rate of economic growth has stopped improving after thirty years of modest but perceptible acceleration,' she said.

Savers and retired people had already suffered severely from inflation and 'negative real profits' threatened the life assurance and pensions institutions 'who are in a position where it becomes more and more difficult to plan and guarantee the flow of future income they have promised their beneficiaries.' In addition, private employers were having to spend enormous sums topping up pension funds. After quoting Keynes – 'There is no surer means of over-turning the existing basis of society than to debauch the currency' – she went on to say, 'It has taken us a long time to realize as a nation that unless we elevate the reduction of inflation to a first priority, moral values, our social and political institutions and the very fabric of our society will fall apart.' After she became Prime Minister in 1979, she acted on this belief: the reduction of inflation took precedence over all else.

Despite the references she quoted, there was little factual basis to support Mrs Thatcher's views. If savers suffer from inflation it is mainly because they have to pay income tax on the gross interest received, with no allowance for the amount they need to earn to keep their capital intact. Their problem has therefore more to do with the tax system than with rising prices. Only one group of savers suffered as a result of the steady inflation that took place between the mid-1950s and the end of the 1960s: retired people living on fixed incomes from annuities. However, the gradual erosion of their personal purchasing power was buffered by their state pensions, which rose with the cost of living, and there was little serious hardship.

For workers, inflation had been largely neutral: wages and salaries had kept in close step with prices as a result of the pay bargaining process. Indeed two left-wing economists, Francis Green and Bob Sutcliffe, denounced anti-inflation policies as 'anti-working class' in their book *The Profit System* (1987). For companies, inflation had been good because it had eroded the consequences of bad investment decisions. It had also allowed firms to make creeping adjustments in wage differentials: workers with skills in short supply had their real wages raised gradually while those in declining areas of business, workers who would never have agreed to take less money in cash terms, had received increases of less than the inflation rate. This process had signalled to existing and potential workers that perhaps they should look for a better-paid job, enabling the declining sector to shrink gracefully. In short, mild inflation had created a forgiving business environment.

But the facts did not matter because Mrs Thatcher's support came from wealthy people and financial institutions for whom controlling demand – and hence inflation – by limiting the money supply was infinitely preferable to achieving the same end by raising taxes, a substantial fraction of which they would have had to pay. The higher interest rates that monetarist poli-cies demand also suited many of her supporters, those who had money to lend. As J. K. Galbraith puts it,[3] 'monetary policy is not socially neutral ... A restrictive monetary policy is in sharp contrast with a restrictive fiscal policy which, relying as it does on increased personal and corporate income taxes, adversely affects the rich.'

In trying to suppress inflation Mrs Thatcher was dealing with a force she did not understand. Inflation is an important economic balancing mechanism because if the rate of inflation (say 4 per cent) plus the rate of GNP growth in real terms (say 3 per cent) is equal to the rate of interest (say 7 per cent), the division of national income between borrowers and lenders stays constant. This is because when the money rate of growth equals the rate of interest the income of both groups rises in proportion to the way it was distributed the previous year. The graph below, which charts the balance between the growth of GNP in money terms and the rate of interest from 1949 to 1987, shows that from 1955 to 1970 the shares that borrowers and lenders took of the proceeds of the growth process were broadly in step with each other – some years, borrowers did well, because the economy grew rapidly and/or inflation was high; in other years, they suffered because the

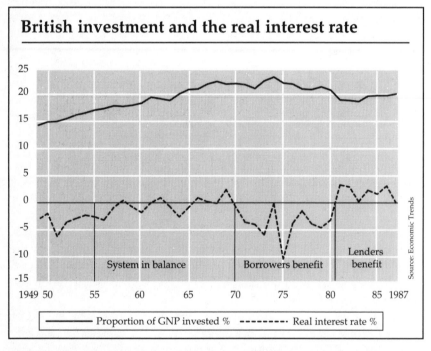

Figure 5.1 The real interest rate (the broken line, which shows the long-term interest rate corrected for both growth and inflation) hovered around zero between 1957 and 1969 indicating that borrowers and lenders shared out the proceeds of growth fairly evenly. When Mrs Thatcher came to power, however, borrowers continuously lost ground to lenders. The upper line, which shows the proportion of GNP invested each year, falls after 1973 because firms invested more heavily in other EC countries and also because after 1980, the high real interest rates made investment in productive projects in Britain unattractive.

combined effect of inflation and growth did not increase their income enough to pay their additional interest charges. Taking one year with another, though, what they gained on the swings they lost on the roundabouts and borrowers' and lenders' incomes kept the same broad relationship with each other.

As trades unions used the pay bargaining process to keep wages in step with both inflation and productivity gains during this period, all three groups in the economy – borrowers, lenders and workers – received not equal shares of the new wealth but shares equivalent to the proportion they had been taking before. There was no significant change in each group's relative income.

A nicely balanced system like this does not arise by chance: there has to be a balancing mechanism. This is what inflation provides, although few people recognize it does so. It works in two ways. I argued in chapter 2 that if almost all companies in an industry find their profit margins dropping below accepted levels as a result of higher interest charges, increased wages or more costly raw materials they will try to raise their prices, and, in the absence of foreign competition, they will succeed. The inflation caused by their action cuts the real cost of the money the firms borrow (or, to put it another way, the lenders' share), the real wages of their employees and the real prices they pay to their suppliers. The effect of these cuts is to raise the firms' margins.

On the other hand, if corporate profits rise above their accepted level, firms will increase their investment, as shown by the second line on the graph. This line, which represents the change in the proportion of national income invested, tends to move up whenever companies' share of national income grows and falls whenever they get less. When firms increase their rate of investment, the demand for labour generally increases as well, which tends to push wages up and thus, potentially, increase the share of national income that goes to employees. The higher demand for capital may also push up interest rates, increasing the lenders' national income share. And when the factories created with the additional investment come into production, the increased supply will tend to push prices down, also increasing the relative national income shares of the non-firm sectors.

In other words, we have a balancing mechanism that generates inflation whenever it acts. When corporate profits are down, firms push their prices up to compensate. When corporate profits are up, increased investment pushes up the price of labour and possibly of land and capital as well. But for this mechanism to work, governments must have a sufficiently relaxed attitude to inflation to allow it to take place. If they interfere excessively, as Mrs Thatcher's three governments did, one or more of the main groups in the economy – borrowers, lenders and labour – inescapably suffers.

Because of Mrs Thatcher's views, inflation was prevented from sharing out the proceeds of the growth process between borrower and lender after 1979. Real interest rates (rates corrected to allow for inflation) were positive for her entire period in office whereas between 1949 and 1979, they were positive only exceptionally. As a result, there was a very significant shift in wealth in favour of the better-off – exactly what Mrs Thatcher wanted – with the top two per cent of the nation amassing as many new assets as did the bottom 50 per cent. A table adapted from Labour MP Gordon Brown's well-researched survey of the Thatcher years, *Where There is Greed* (1989), shows this clearly:

Marketable wealth of individuals at 1989 prices

	1979	1989	Rise	% Share of total rise
Top 1%	£380,000	£572,000	£193,000	17
Next 1%	£148,000	£236,000	£88,000	7
Bottom 50%	£3,130	£4,170	£1,590	24

Brown also says that the wealthiest 1 per cent increased their landholdings between 1976 and 1984 from 52 per cent to 64 per cent of the nation's area and that they owned 53 per cent of company shares.

The emasculation of inflation also meant that there was a big increase in the national level of indebtedness – indeed, much of the rise in wealth shown in the table above was in the form of paper claims against people or companies. One of John Major's economic advisers, Sarah Hogg, then economics correspondent of *The Sunday Telegraph*, wrote in 1989, 'In 1980, the personal sector – ordinary individuals and very small businesses – was £12bn. in the black; by last year [1988] it was £14bn. in the red.' She added that the rate of savings had fallen too. 'In 1980 we spent only 86 per cent of our disposable incomes. By last year we were spending almost 96 per cent'. Her figures are supported by a survey of 1,785 households published by the Policy Studies Institute in 1990 which shows that the volume of personal credit advanced by banks, building societies and finance houses doubled in the 1980s and that a tenth of all households had difficulty repaying a loan during 1989. Significantly, it was those under thirty who were most likely to be in debt – exactly the group that Bach suggested an inflation would help.

Company debt soared too as firms were forced to borrow to cover the higher interest payments they had to make. Annual net corporate borrowings from the banks rose from £547 million in 1975 to £6,356 million in 1980 when the Bank of England's minimum lending rate reached 17 per cent and growth was –2 per cent. The level then fell to £1,618 million in 1983 as growth resumed – it almost reached 4 per cent – and interest rates

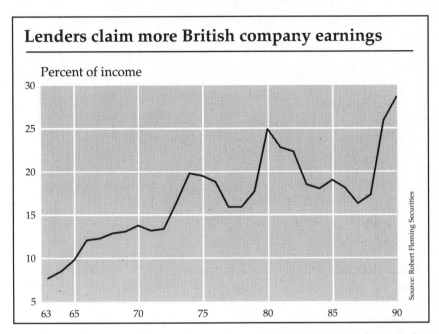

Lenders claim more British company earnings

Percent of income

Source: Robert Fleming Securities

Figure 5.2 From just over 7 per cent in 1963 to almost 30 per cent in 1990, lenders have taken an increasingly large share of the earnings of British companies.

fell so that it became possible to make profits again. Distress borrowing rose again in 1988/9 when interest rates were pushed up quickly from 9 to 15 per cent. This increased the proportion of company income that had to be devoted to interest payments to the crisis level of almost 30 per cent, as the chart shows.

Ironically, the struggle after 1979 to limit inflation by raising interest rates created a problem for the policy's instigators, the financial institutions, because it created a gulf between the amount money could earn if invested in a typical productive project and the rate of interest the entrepreneurs behind those projects were being asked to pay. Moreover, because the interest rate rise had produced a recession, very few of the institutions' domestic customers wanted to borrow anyway, except, as we have just seen, to pay their interest bills or to stave off collapse. The banks' problem of what to do with their funds was compounded because, as a result of the oil price rise, most OPEC countries had more money than they knew what to do with, having moved from having a small balance of payments deficit of $700 million in 1978 to a surplus of $100,000 million in 1980. Much of this money had been put in British and American banks on deposit.

To find a home for the OPEC cash as well as their own, bankers literally packed their suitcases and flew to the Third World. During a meeting of the Inter-American Development Bank in Madrid in 1981 senior bank officers queued up to offer funds to the man in charge of Mexico's borrowing as he lounged in an armchair at his hotel. A year later Mexico had borrowed so much that no-one was prepared to lend it more to repay old debts as they became due. It threatened to default, alerting the world to the crisis the banks had created.

The bankers offered money to potential Third World borrowers at a price based on the London interbank offered rate (LIBOR) plus 1 per cent. This meant that, if world interest rates increased, the rate of interest payable by the borrowing country did as well. It was a lazy man's way of doing business because it made it impossible for borrowers to calculate the return they had to get from the projects for which they wanted the loans and the risk they were running by taking the loans on. However, the bankers thought their interests would be secure whatever happened to their borrowers' projects and rarely investigated them thoroughly. What mattered was that their profits in the current year would be satisfactorily increased by the fixed margin they creamed off the top of the loan as a charge for agreeing to grant it. As for the future – well, as one banker, Walter Wriston, said at the time, countries don't go bankrupt, do they?

A factor that added to the banks' dangerous complacency was that they had done some Third World lending to recycle Middle Eastern funds after the 1973 oil price shock. These had generally worked out well, largely because the prices of the commodities exported by the borrowers had increased at an annual rate which exceeded the rate of interest being charged. In other words, there was no overall change in the relative wealth of borrower and lender throughout the period. The debt/export ratio had stayed constant and there was a net inflow of funds to most developing countries.

In the early 1980s, however, the deliberate contraction of demand in the United States and the EC caused commodity prices to plunge while the interest rates the producing countries had to pay were kept high. Consequently, rather than the wealth of both parties increasing in step, as had happened previously, money – or rather, claims on money – flowed from borrower to lender each year between 1981 and 1986 at a rate equivalent to interest at 20 per cent. As a debt doubles every 3.5 years at an interest rate of 20 per cent, the inevitable result was that these countries' ratio of debt to GNP tripled by 1987, although almost no new money was lent.

After the debt crisis became public in 1982 the value of the banks' Third World loans was gradually written down, involving them in showing huge losses. At the time of writing, however, debtor countries have still not been released from their obligation to pay the full amount due, although some have been able to buy up some of their debt at a big discount on the secondary market where it was sold by smaller banks anxious to get cash for a very doubtful asset.

Besides lending to the Third World, the banks indulged in many other dangerous practices to keep their depositors' money profitably occupied. One of these, treasury management, has become particularly important, and as a result the most prestigious positions in many banks are no longer held by loan officers but by the staff who use unlendable funds to speculate on changes in interest and exchange rates. This is done on a huge scale. One tiny bank by world standards – Allied Irish – claims that it does 1 per cent of all the dealing in dollars that goes on throughout the world. Only a fraction of the dollars it buys and sells are destined for customers who want to use them for trade: most of the activity is pure speculation, or 'taking positions' as the bank delicately puts it. The most worrying feature of this practice is that the banks are playing in a zero-sum game in which one bank can make a profit only to the extent that other banks – or national governments supporting their currencies – make a loss. There is no benefit at all to ordinary men and women who ultimately pay the cost of their activities.

Another result of the high interest rates in the eighties was that the only loans the banks were generally able to make were to firms in distress, or highly speculative ones, chiefly in non-productive projects. A record $100,000 million was lent by American banks for management and leveraged buy-outs in 1988 while the British paid out over £6,400 million in 1989, up from almost nothing at the start of the decade. So desperate were banks on both sides of the Atlantic to place their funds that they were prepared to put up 85 per cent of the cost of buying a company, even though that amount often was far more than the tangible value of its assets. A few years previously the same institutions had wisely limited themselves to advancing only 50 per cent of the cost of a buy-out and had demanded twice the interest rate margin to cover the risk.

Not unexpectedly, many buy-out loans turned sour. So too did many loans to the property sector for ventures which could only be successful if there was a continuing rise in real estate prices. Total bank lending to property companies in Britain as a proportion of total commercial loans went up by half between 1985 and 1989, reaching almost 12.5 per cent. When the boom broke in mid-1989, £52,000 million was outstanding, of which a fifth had gone sour a year later. The biggest speculative property loan of all was the £6,000 million – or more – that the world's banks pledged to the Channel Tunnel. The omens here are not good: a specialist who assessed the project on behalf of a major British bank told me he was unhappy about the traffic forecast but that his opinion had been ignored.

One socially damaging way developed by the banks for using otherwise unlendable funds was to put them into mortgages, a field an older generation of bankers had shunned because hard-won experience had taught them it was unsafe to borrow short to lend long. The fact that there were insufficient prospective borrowers to take all the money they wanted to place while still meeting safe lending criteria did not daunt the new men – they just lowered the criteria, forcing the traditional lenders in this area, the building societies, to follow suit. So while in 1979 the building societies made 95 per cent of all new housing loans, by 1989 their share had dropped to only 71 per cent.

Before the banks moved in to confront them, building societies had rationed their mortgage funds by making potential borrowers save with them for a number of years before they would even entertain a loan application. In addition, mortgages were limited to 95 per cent of the purchase price and could not exceed 2.5 times the husband's income plus half his wife's annual earnings, as it was expected that she would stop work if she became pregnant. A further restriction was that borrowers could expect to wait at least six months for the money once their application was approved.

Oddly, these tiresome restrictions had big advantages for borrowers. One was that mortgages were cheaper than any other loan available, which was why people were prepared to wait to get them. In addition, the delays limited the flow of funds onto the property market, so that house prices actually fell relative to the cost of living from the mid-fifties onwards. The combination of low-cost loans and cheap housing meant that in 1976 the average house-buying family had to devote only 24 per cent of the husband's gross income to paying the mortgage.

The banks destroyed this cosy world. They entered the market by making their mortgages immediately available and by undercutting the building societies' interest rates, particularly on larger loans. The building societies were forced to speed up their service to compete; in particular, they had to stop requiring people to save with them for a period before getting a loan, thus killing off their flow of compulsory low-cost deposits from future borrowers. To make up this loss they had to offer higher interest rates to other types of saver and put up their mortgage rates to compensate.

By the end of the adjustment process the mortgage rate offered both by banks and building societies was between 1 and 1.5 per cent above the banks' base rate compared with being roughly equal to it beforehand. However, a couple who shopped around could get a 100 per cent mortgage for up to three times their joint income – more or less twice the amount they would have been able to borrow previously. Young professionals, whose incomes could be expected to rise rapidly, could even get four times their earnings.

The availability of bank money had little effect on the housing market until economic conditions began to improve in the mid-eighties, but then it drove prices very much higher. The price of the average house soared from £38,121 in 1986 to £62,159 in 1989, although average earnings only rose from £10,790 to £14,014 in the same period. As a result, the ratio of house prices to average earnings, 3.30 in 1985, reached 4.44 in 1989. No extra houses were built because bank mortgages were available: the private sector completed one eighth fewer houses between 1981 and 1987 than between 1971 and 1977. Instead, the additional sums received by housebuilders went to the land-owners who sold them the sites. A typical building plot in southeast England which would have cost £6,846 in 1980 was £40,264 when the market peaked in 1988, according to the Inland Revenue.

Who benefited from the increased competition in the mortgage market and the higher prices it caused, besides the

NICKI, HERE'S THE £400,000 YOU ASKED TO BORROW.

She's doing quite well for herself is Nicki. So when she asked to borrow £400,000 it was no problem. Abbey National will lend you over £1 million if you can keep your half of the bargain.

At 10.1% gross, equivalent to an APR of 10.6% for endowment and pension mortgages, and 10.8% for repayment mortgages, you will find the interest rate as competitive as the house-buying market.

If you want to move as quickly as Derek and Nicki, call in at your local branch.

ABBEY NATIONAL

ABBEY NATIONAL BUILDING SOCIETY, MORTGAGE SERVICES DEPARTMENT, 201 GRAFTON GATE EAST, MILTON KEYNES MK9 1AN. Full written details are available from address above.

Figure 5.3 A building society's response to bank competition

landowners? Elderly people who sold a large family house to buy something smaller; middle-aged sons and daughters when their deceased parents' house came to be sold; and the banks themselves. Inflating house prices by relaxing lending constraints is the best method imaginable to cream off the public's disposable income, as few people under sixty fail to buy the most expensive property they can afford.

And who lost? House buyers generally because they had to get themselves more deeply in debt and pay over a higher proportion of their income for housing than at any time since records began. In the first quarter of 1990, with mortgage rates at 15.25 per cent, the average house-buying family was paying a staggering 45.8 per cent of its main earner's pre-tax income to meet its mortgage obligations, almost twice the proportion fourteen years before. In fact the net effect of the banks' move was to shift income and capital away from people of family-rearing age to couples who had largely completed raising their families and to the retired, the same groups that were the main beneficiaries of the higher interest rates.

Banks were not the only ones to have made risky, unproductive investments because of high interest rates. Businesses had to do so too. Two competing satellite broadcasting systems, Sky and BSB, spent well over £1,000 million each before the threat of an imminent recession forced them to amalgamate, sums so large that no-one would have tried to raise them for such speculative ventures a few years previously. On a smaller scale, but also demonstrating the frivolous nature of projects into which people ploughed money during this period, was a British lottery, Golden Grid, into which Irish investors sank, and lost, £22 million in 1989. Almost simultaneously a share offering in Paris and London raised $2,000 million for the establishment of a Disneyworld in northern France.

One way the wealthy found to generate a high interest return on their cash was through the privatization of Britain's nationalized industries. At one time serious investors would have turned up their noses at the thought of buying shares in public utilities (as most of the sell-offs were) because the profit they would be able to make on their capital was bound to be closely regulated. While Mrs Thatcher was in office, however, people with money on their hands looked at things differently. One reason was that the price they paid for the assets they bought from the public was adjusted downwards every time interest rates rose to give them the right rate of return. Another was that they felt they had a Prime Minister who would not clamp down at all hard on profits. The most important reason of all, however, was that they had few investment alternatives and none in industries with such stable demand.

But back to the banks. The problem for all lenders, and one the banks have not yet recognized in spite of the Third World debt crisis, is that if inflation is removed as the mechanism that reduces the claims of lenders when these become unsupportable, another, harsher mechanism comes into play. This is default; and at the time of writing it threatens to bring the banks to disaster: after all, it was only by pretending that loans nobody could reasonably have expected to be repaid were still good that most of the leading British and American banks saved themselves from collapse after Mexico threatened to default in 1982: some of them had lost twice their shareholders' capital, an occurrence that should have forced them to close their doors. Today the credit ratings of most of the world's major banks are much lower than when the debt crisis broke, and few will survive when all their pigeons in property lending, leveraged buy-outs and currency speculation come home to roost. If this happens – and I believe it is imminent – those with savings in banks, building societies and pension funds will lose almost everything in a financial disaster of such proportions as to make 1929 seem like a hiccup. The closure of the Bank of Credit and Commerce International (BCCI) in 1991 is a sign of things to come: this bank embarked on its fraudulent course only after it had made such huge losses in its foreign exchange dealings that it seemed unlikely it could ever recover.

Only in one sense can it be said that Mrs Thatcher's high interest rate policies were a success: they led to a huge growth in the financial services sector. In 1979 banking, finance and insurance contributed 11.5 per cent of GDP while a decade later the figure was almost 20 per cent, not far short of the 22.5 per cent contributed by the whole of manufacturing industry. Over a million extra people found jobs in the sector between 1979 and 1989, the year the boom broke; employment rose from 1,647,000 to 2,675,000. Towards the end of the period one graduate in every ten was being recruited by accountancy companies to join a £2,000 million a year profession. But what did this expansion achieve beyond an increase in the GNP figures? It is difficult to avoid the conclusion that it was largely parasitic as it brought so few benefits to anyone not directly involved. Indeed it is a prime example of the growing inefficiency of a growth-led economy in which paper profits are more important than tangible gains.

Of course, more direct methods were used to switch resources to the better-off besides high interest rates and low inflation. Taxes were one. The introduction of the poll tax, which required a person to pay the same amount as everyone else in his or her local government area, regardless of income or wealth, was the most blatant example. Perhaps more serious,

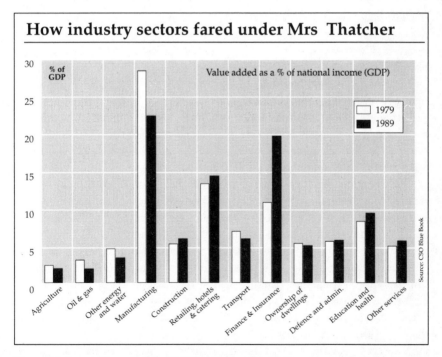

How industry sectors fared under Mrs Thatcher

Source: CSO Blue Book

Figure 5.4 A parasitic part of the British economy, financial services nearly doubled in size under Mrs Thatcher's three governments until it almost equalled manufacturing in importance.

however, was the reduction of the top rate of income tax from 83 per cent (plus 15 per cent on investment income) to 60 per cent almost as soon as Mrs Thatcher came into office and then to 40 per cent in 1988. After he had announced this latter reduction, the then Chancellor, Nigel Lawson, was asked if his budget marked the end of the use of taxation as an instrument for the redistribution of wealth. 'I hope so,' he replied. 'I hope we are in for a new era in this country.' The justification for the move was the encouragement of entrepreneurship and thus of economic growth.

Gordon Brown estimates[4] that between 1979 and 1989, the top 10 per cent of taxpayers enjoyed 55 per cent of the tax cuts, saving them £50,200 million, while the bottom 10 per cent shared £900 million. Capital gains and inheritance taxes and the tax take from small businesses were eased too.

The most remarkable change in the eleven year period, however, was the gap which opened up between the wages of high-paid and low-paid employees. From the time records began in 1886 to 1979, the lowest-paid 10 per cent of male manual workers always earned between 67 and 71 per cent of the national median wage. By April 1990, however, the proportion had dropped to 63 per cent. The most highly paid 10 per cent of men, on the other hand, received between 157 per cent and 161 per cent of the median wage from 1968 to 1979. By 1990, according to the official *New Earnings Survey*, it was 181 per cent. Put another way, the best-paid group received 47.4 per cent more money in real terms in 1990 than in 1979 bringing their salaries up to a minimum of £29,578. The worst-paid group, by contrast, all earned less than £7,249, just 2.9 per cent more in real terms than when Mrs Thatcher took office.

Anyone earning less than two-thirds of the median wage is regarded by the Council of Europe as below the 'decency threshold'. In 1979, 38.1 per cent of the British work force was below the threshold; in 1987 the figure was 45.8 per cent: a total of 9,430,000 adults.

Commenting on these changes in *The Independent on Sunday*, A. B. Atkinson, a professor at the London School of Economics, said that there had been a shift in values, and pay had become much more market-oriented and less constrained by accepted customs and differentials. 'There has also been a large structural change. Manufacturing has been in decline and services have grown rapidly. In services, there are well-paid jobs at the top of fast-growing sectors like banking and insurance and badly-paid jobs for cleaners and porters.' He also suggested that the abolition of wages councils and the weakening of trade unions had contributed to the relative decline in the pay of the worst-paid group.

Another factor that shifted purchasing power away from the less well-off was the growth of unemployment, which increased from 4 per cent of the work force in 1979 to over 11 per cent in 1986, and then dropped back to 6 per cent in 1990 before it turned upwards again. Although people from all walks of life became unemployed, the elderly and the unskilled suffered most, the latter not only because they had no scope to step down a rung on the skills ladder to make themselves more employable but also because of the continuous reduction in the number of manual jobs as a result of labour-saving technologies.

Measures taken by Mrs Thatcher ensured that the long-term unemployed were considerably worse off than they had been before they lost their jobs. She abolished pay-related unemployment benefit in 1982 and raised the number of contributions required to receive unemployment benefit from one year to two in 1988. Research at the London School of Economics[5] showed that as a result the average unemployed person was £151.84 a year worse off in real terms in 1989 than ten years previously and that the benefit level for a single person had fallen by almost 20 per cent in relation to earnings. At least one unemployed person in eight was £10 a week worse off, the study said. By contrast, people at the top end of the labour market who became redundant generally received a generous golden handshake.

The cumulative effect of these changes was to raise the number of families receiving social security benefits by two-thirds between 1979 and 1987, according to a 1990 report by the Institute of Fiscal Studies. Almost two million families were below the supplementary benefit line in 1987, despite the fact that this was intended to be a level below which no-one should fall. Moreover, those people on benefit were much further behind the rest of the population than they had been in 1979, because benefit rates had not increased as rapidly as average earnings. 'There are more people on low incomes, more people on the minimum safety net benefit and, indeed, more people with incomes below the minimum benefit level,' the report said.

The number of children living in poverty rose from 17 per cent in 1979 to 28 per cent eleven years later. Three million lived at or below the supplementary benefit level, according to Jonathan Bradshaw, a professor at York University and the author of a report sponsored by UNICEF, *Child Poverty and Deprivation in the UK* published in late 1990. 'Children have borne the brunt of the changes in the economic conditions, demographic structure and social policies of the United Kingdom,' he said at the launch of the report. 'Inequalities in children's lives have increased. The lives of children in a two-parent family living in owner-occupied housing in the south of England served by good public services have improved. By contrast, the lives of children in an unemployed or single-parent family, living in rented accommodation, in the inner city, with deteriorating health, education and social services have got worse.'

At 8.4 per thousand live births, Bradshaw added, infant mortality was higher in Britain than in several other European countries. The trend for children to get taller from generation to generation had stopped after the seventies; children from families where the father was unemployed or on benefit were significantly shorter than those from more affluent homes.

'The pursuit of equality is a mirage,' Mrs Thatcher told the Institute of Socio-Economic Studies in New York in 1975. 'Far more desirable and more practicable than the pursuit of equality is the pursuit of equality of opportunity. Opportunity means nothing unless it includes the right to be unequal.' The title of her speech? 'Let Our Children Grow Tall.'

6

Ned Ludd Was Right

These machines were ... an advantage inasmuch as they superseded the necessity of employing a number of workingmen who, in consequence, were left to starve. By the adoption of one species of frame in particular, one man performed the work of many and the superfluous labourers were thrown out of employment. Yet it is to be observed that the work thus executed was inferior in quality; not marketable at home and merely hurried over with a view to exportation ...

The rejected workmen, in the blindness of their ignorance, instead of rejoicing at these improvements in arts so beneficial to mankind, conceived themselves sacrificed to improvements in mechanism. In the foolishness of their hearts, they imagined that the maintenance and well-doing of the industrious poor were objects of greater consequence than the enrichment of a few individuals. – Lord Byron in his maiden speech in the House of Lords (12 February 1812)

In common with generations of English schoolchildren, I was taught to sneer at the Luddites, the destitute working men who destroyed stocking-knitting machines and lace-frames in Nottinghamshire and the surrounding counties in 1811 and 1812 before Lord Liverpool's government suppressed their protests by hanging or transporting their alleged leaders. My teacher explained that the workers' distress had been caused mainly by the sharp rise in food prices during the Napoleonic War. The Luddite idea that the introduction of machinery destroyed jobs was, of course, ridiculous: we only had to look at all the machinery used today (the early 1950s), and yet there was full employment. Luddites were misguided men who had blocked progress.

It is only recently that I have been able to exorcize this early indoctrination and have come to realize that Ned Ludd – the pseudonym adopted by the machine-breakers' unknown leader – was right: mechanization does destroy jobs. Indeed, it is not the Luddites who were misguided: we are, for rejecting people's observations and experiences over fifteen hundred years. The Roman historian Suetonius describes how, when a mechanical engineer offered to carry some heavy columns to the Capitol cheaply using a labour-saving device, the emperor Vespasian 'gave no mean reward for his invention

but refused to make use of it saying: You must let me feed my poor commons.' In *An Unfinished History of the World* (1979), the right-wing historian
Hugh Thomas (who unaccountably attributes this remark to an emperor,
Diocletian, who had not been born when Suetonius was alive) suggests that
the attitude it displays was the prime reason the Roman Empire did not
industrialize. 'The Emperor could not conceive that the population might
be better fed than through back-breaking work,' he comments with disdain.

Until the Industrial Revolution got fully into its stride, anyone who
invented a labour-saving machine was likely to be given a hard time. The
medieval crafts guilds had strict rules governing the methods their members
could use, and workshops had to be open to the street so that inspectors and
the public could see that these were obeyed. Guilds also fixed the hours of
work, prohibiting production on Sundays and holidays and also after dark
(on the grounds that poor light would affect the workmanship). They determined 'fair' prices, set quality standards, prevented outside goods being sold
in their towns except on special fair days, controlled entry to their crafts,
and generally limited competition. If a guild member was able to purchase
raw materials at a bargain price, he was expected to share his good fortune
with his fellow-members.

Hugh Thomas tells the story of a Nottinghamshire curate, William Lee,
who invented a machine for knitting socks in 1589, apparently because the
woman he was courting spent more time on her knitting than with him.
The Crown discouraged him from taking the invention any further, and,
when armed rioters beset his house, he had to flee to Paris, where he died of
grief. John Kay, inventor of the flying shuttle, which doubled a weaver's output when it was introduced in the 1730s, also had to flee to Paris for safety
but managed to survive the experience. Even the water-wheel was suspect
during this period, although it had been in use since Roman times. The
eighteenth-century French philosopher, Montesquieu, criticized it for
'depriving labourers of their work'. And when Joseph-Marie Jacquard, who
had invented a loom that allowed designs to be woven into the fabric rather
than being embroidered on later by hand, was sent for by Napoleon in 1803
he was not sure if he was to be rewarded or arrested.

Thus the views of those who took part in the Luddite riots were the conventional ones of their time, and Adam Smith's idea that the 'invisible hand'
would ensure that the adoption of the new techniques would turn out to be
beneficial was the real revolutionary teaching. Although the Luddites
refrained from harming 'any living thing' until twelve of them were shot by
soldiers at the instigation of a factory owner, the disturbances were extremely serious. Twelve thousand troops had to be sent to the affected areas, more
than Britain was deploying at the time in the Peninsular War. The rioters
received widespread public support, in part because the machine-made

goods were inferior to hand-made ones, and the soldiers had little enthusi-asm for their task. Officers sometimes refused to enter a building without a magistrate's warrant, even though they could hear machinery being smashed inside. Thomas believes that Lord Liverpool's attitude was crucial: 'Doubtless, if the governments of the early industrial age had wished, or had been forced, to please the workers, the factory movement and the industrial revolution would have been brought to an end.'

Smith's ideas won the day because they suited the interests of the ruling class perfectly and were easily understood. Indeed, in many points they merely reflected what people were already thinking. As Joseph Schumpeter writes,[1] 'he disliked whatever went beyond plain commonsense. He never moved above the heads of even the dullest readers ... And it was Adam Smith's good fortune that he was thoroughly in sympathy with the humours of his time. He advocated the things that were in the offing, and he made his analysis serve them.'

David Ricardo, another founding father of economics, was not so easily understood – Galbraith[2] calls him 'a man of superb clarity of mind and terri-ble obscurity of prose.' Consequently, he was readily ignored when he wrote anything inconvenient, as he did in his *Principles of Political Economy and Taxation* (1817), just five years after the Luddites had been put down. He pointed out that if an improved stocking machine enabled one man to do the work of four and the demand for socks only doubled, it was inevitable that some workers would lose their jobs. The working class was therefore right in thinking that the use of machinery was generally detrimental to its interests. However, investment in machinery should not be restricted because the thwarted capital would move to other countries and create employment there.

But if machines really do destroy jobs and not just permit us to spend our time in more pleasurable or more productive ways, how have we been able to think otherwise for so long? Haven't innovating firms generally had the best employment-creation records? The answer is yes, they have, but they have only managed to achieve this by destroying jobs elsewhere. Until the end of the 1960s, elsewhere was usually overseas: industrial countries were able to maintain full employment by destroying the livelihoods of Third World craftspeople. We have already seen how the British-controlled gov-ernment of India imposed taxes on hand-looms and tariffs on cloth to favour Lancashire textile producers, and how increasing amounts of tax rev-enue were taken out of India during the nineteenth century to pay for the maintenance of the British army and navy and for the pensions of Britons who had worked there. The whole *raison d'être* of the Empire was to provide cash flows and orders for manufactured goods to maintain prosperity and employment at home.

The flow of work and wealth from overseas enabled Britain and the other European powers to provide jobs for those people that continuous agricultural changes were displacing from the land. It also meant that the underemployment or unemployment the growth process created was conveniently out of sight, in countries where it could be attributed to the idleness or stupidity of the natives. Today, however, only two major industrial countries, Germany and Japan, still have a substantial financial inflow, and it is this that has enabled them to maintain high levels of employment. On the other hand, Britain and the United States, which have seen their domestic unemployment rates climb steadily, have been running trade deficits. America's unemployment rate would be considerably worse if it had not had such a large inflow of loans from overseas, a flow that turned it from the world's biggest net creditor in 1983 into a net debtor country that owed foreigners an estimated $60,000 million by 1985.

Having eaten away the Third World, the capitalist system is now beginning to destroy prosperity in the countries that gave it birth. The American Dream has already turned sour, breaking a 200-year run in which each generation could confidently expect to live better than their predecessors, to move into better-paying jobs as they got older and to see their children flying even higher still. Of course there was the odd bad patch during those twenty decades; but from the end of the Second World War to the early 1970s every year brought higher wages, more leisure, and a greater stock of material possessions, a phenomenon that supposedly demonstrated the superiority of capitalism and free enterprise over communism and state intervention.

But in 1973 the steady increase in average real wages on which the dream was based went sharply into reverse. Pay rates have fallen ever since, dropping almost as rapidly as they went up. By 1989, according to the Bureau of Labor Statistics, they were 20 per cent below the peak. As a result, the number of people considered by the Bureau of Census to be in poverty rose from 23 million in 1973 to 35.3 million a decade later. Had millions of women refused to go out to work to compensate for the decline in their men's wages (the number of female workers rose from 16.6 million to 27.3 million between 1973 and 1986) the poverty figures might have become worse still. As it was, even with all the extra female earners, by 1982 families' median real income had declined by 10 per cent. Family incomes have gone up a   little since, and the number considered in poverty has consequently gone down, but there was no sign while this book was being written that the trend to lower real wages had been reversed. As a result of the trend, the after-tax income of the top 1 per cent of households rose 122 per cent in real terms between 1977 and 1988, giving them almost as much purchasing power as the bottom 40 per cent combined.

But why did American wages get steadily lower? It was not that the US

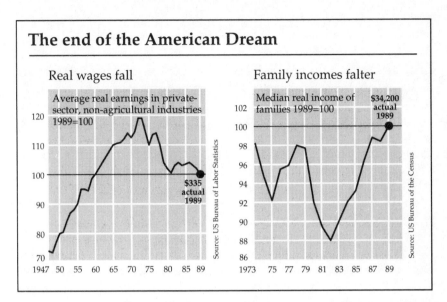

The end of the American Dream

Figure 6.1 Average weekly earnings have been falling in the United States since the early 1970s. The only reason family incomes increased slightly was that more women went out to work.

economy had permanently ceased to grow (although it is in recession at the time of writing). Far from it: GNP rose by an average of 2.65 per cent and the number in employment by 2 per cent each year between 1973 and 1988. Rather it was that a system that boasts of its efficiency had become progressively less efficient, using ever more resources, especially fossil energy, to achieve less and less, because of the distortions produced by the growth process itself. One of the distortions was that new technologies made people redundant without the economy having anything else equivalent for them to do, just as Ned Ludd feared was happening in 1812. Only low-paid, low-skilled jobs were available.

We need to build a simple economic model to see what had gone wrong. Suppose there is a country called Erewhon that has half its workers in its combined industrial and agro-industrial sector and the rest in its services sector, which takes in both private and state employees. The essential difference between the two sectors is that it is very difficult to increase the productivity of workers in the services sector – a teacher can look after only so many children, a nurse after so many patients – but in Erewhon's agriculture and industry, technological improvements are coming along all the time and each worker produces more every year.

Another feature Erewhon shares with many real countries is that there is a limit to the amount of food and industrial goods its people can consume: they can drive only one car at a time, watch one television or eat one meal.

And, as Erewhon is a wealthy country, most of its citizens are already consuming as much of these goods as they feel they want to. What's more, even
their demand for additional services is more or less satisfied: servants can be
a nuisance and destroy one's privacy, and it is only necessary to consult one
doctor unless things have gone rather seriously wrong. Consequently, it
would take an appreciable fall in service prices to induce Erewhonians to
consume many more. In fact the only things they really want are more posi-
tional goods, like membership of the smartest golf club or ownership of the
finest country estate. The pursuit of these things serves to spur them along,
but no matter how well their country does economically, they will always be
in limited supply.

So what happens if, over a decade or so, Erewhon's industry doubles its
productivity? As there is no unsatisfied demand for food or merchandise
from the home market, producers will attempt to expand their sales overseas. But how is Erewhon to be paid for its exports? It does not need extra
supplies of foreign goods; its market is already glutted, and if it takes them it
will put its domestic producers out of business. Only if it is prepared to use
its overseas earnings to buy up companies or other investments abroad, as
Japan has extensively done, can it continue to export without creating
unemployment at home. Alternatively, individual producers can cut their
prices in an effort to increase their companies' sales at the expense of competitors at home, but this again would lead to a loss of jobs, with the forces
of competition determining where the redundancies fall. Only if the industrial sector can double its sales will it be able to avoid shedding staff, and if
it has to export to achieve the doubling, that might lead to the loss of jobs
elsewhere in the economy. In these conditions, a rise in productivity in
Erewhon will almost inevitably lead to people being put out of work.

So the next question has to be, where are the redundant workers to go?
They have only two options: to remain unemployed (which, as Erewhon has
a system of state unemployment relief, we can regard as becoming members
of a special category of state employees that provides no services in return
for its pay) or to join the service sector proper and bid down the rates of pay
there until everyone seeking work is taken on or wages fall to a level so little
better than unemployment pay that the mutual undercutting stops.

This latter outcome seems to be very close to what has actually happened
in the United States. In their 1986 report to the Joint Economic Committee
of Congress entitled *The Great American Jobs Machine*, economics professors
Bennett Harrison and Barry Bluestone investigated the wages and quality of
the new jobs the United States was able to create in such great numbers
from the early sixties until the beginning of the present recession. 'Were we
becoming a nation of low-wage hamburger flippers, nurse's aides, janitors
and security guards as the mass media sometimes reported?' they ask. 'The

demise of high-wage manufacturing jobs in cities like Detroit and Youngstown, combined with the proliferation of McDonald's and K-Marts in virtually every town provided an image of the American economy as a new low-wage bastion.' What is their answer? In a later book, *The Great U-Turn* (1990), they write:

During the first half of the 1980s the U.S. economy continued to churn out new jobs at about the same rapid pace as during the previous decade, but we discovered that a majority of the jobs created after 1979 were of dubious quality when measured by the annual earnings they offered. America was surely creating more than just hamburger flippers and security guards but nearly three out of five (58%) of the net new jobs created between 1979 and 1984 paid $7,400 or less a year (in 1984 dollars). In contrast, less than one in five of the additional jobs generated between 1963 and 1979 had paid such low wages.

National economies only benefit from technologies that save labour if there are expanding sectors in which those made redundant can be re-employed. It makes no economic sense to sack people and keep them idle, unless it is part of a crude and inhuman attempt at wage control. On the other hand, sacking workers can make a great deal of sense to an individual company as a way to cut costs and increase profits. Consequently, circumstances frequently arise in which the interests of the nation and those of the entrepreneur are diametrically opposed.

Mainstream economics does not recognize that these conflicts can happen, because it still believes in Adam Smith's 'invisible hand'. Yet Smith's contention was not true when he made it and is even less true now in a resource-constrained world. There is not, and there never has been, any economic mechanism that ensures that if I devise a labour-saving technique that puts hundreds of thousands of people out of work and gives jobs to just a few, everybody everywhere will ultimately benefit. The only thing that determines whether I introduce my technique is my decision whether it will provide me with a personal gain. I am not required to consider how the introduction will affect the livelihoods of other people. More powerfully, if I do develop scruples, the growth imperative forbids me to delay introducing my technique because if I do not innovate someone else will, reaping the pioneer's profits, and unless I follow suit I will be driven out of business. What a shame Smith did not remain true to his instinctive opposition to de Mandeville's ideas! Lord Liverpool's reaction to the riots might have been very different and, if Hugh Thomas is right, the Industrial Revolution might not have taken place.

Growth in fact produces jobs in exactly the way a chain letter produces money. 'If you work as hard and innovate as fast as we do,' the high-employment countries tell the rest of the world, 'you too will have our booming, profitable companies and our low rates of unemployment in a few years' time.' What no-one points out is that the chain-letter principle cannot make *everyone* rich. Only those with their names near the top of the list come away with jobs or a profit, made at the expense of those below. But the rich countries have exhausted the resources of the countries below them which no longer have any jobs or money to send up the chain, particularly as the international banks refuse to lend to them any more. Consequently, the only way that the industrialized countries can keep the present game going is to play against each other, concentrating jobs and generating poverty within the borders of their own lands.

SUPPORTING THE UNEMPLOYED

If they are to survive, people displaced by technological change from the productive parts of the economy like manufacturing and agriculture still need the food, clothes and shelter made by the sectors that sacked them. Moreover, they need as much of these goods as the rest of the population if they are not to become an underclass. In other words, the sectors that made them redundant still have to provide for them, unless they are banished overseas in the way that the Irish economy has dealt with its surplus labour in the years since the Famine. If they stay at home, all that has to be settled is at what level the productive sectors will support the ex-employees and what services, if any, they will supply in return.

Anyone displaced from a productive sector needs to have an amount equivalent to their former pay transferred to them if their real income is not to be reduced. There are two ways this can be brought about. One is by way of the price cuts that are likely to follow an increase in productivity: if industrial prices come down by the full amount of the wages of the people it dismisses, the rest of the economy will automatically save enough money to be able to take the redundant workers on. However, such deep price cuts are most unlikely, because the new technology will probably not generate sufficient savings: some of the money previously spent on wages will have to go to pay for capital equipment instead. In these circumstances the state will step in and enforce a further transfer by imposing taxes to enable it to sup-port re-dundant workers not absorbed by the service sector and stuck in limbo on the dole.

In practice, both transfer methods – taxation and price cuts – will be used: industrial and agricultural prices will fall in comparison with wages, and taxes will rise as a proportion of GNP. In practice too the taxes will be levied on the whole economy, forcing the sectors which did not displace labour to charge the ones that did higher prices or fees so that they can col-lect funds to pass on to the government. And sure enough there is *prima*

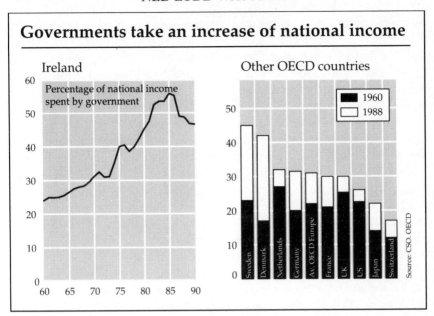

Figure 6.2 The proportion of national income Western European governments had to spend to maintain standards was forced up by distortions created by the growth process. The increase in Ireland was especially large.

facie evidence that this is happening: in all western countries the proportion of GNP collected by the government has grown as economic growth has taken place, as the graph above shows.

By imposing taxes on the whole economy to support labour displaced by one sector of it, governments throughout the world have re-created the Speenhamland system in forms which are probably more destructive than the Berkshire magistrates' version which Cobbett so trenchantly attacked. Twentieth-century Speenhamland distorts economic life because the taxes it entails increase the prices of the products or services of the non-growing sectors, and consequently people use less of them by substituting industrial products instead. For example, many town councils have found that, as a result of higher income and social security taxes, the costs of keeping streets clean with brooms and barrows have gone steadily up. They naturally look around for ways to become more 'efficient' and buy mechanical sweepers from the industrial sector to hold their work force and wage bills down. This puts more people on the dole and drives social security taxes up another notch. In short, because of a distorting tax system, the cycle of higher paper wages, mechanization and the destruction of jobs is self-reinforcing.

Not unnaturally, this habit of making everyone pay higher taxes to support those put out of work by companies gaining or retaining their competitive edge has not been popular, though few people have understood exactly what was going on. A widespread aversion has developed – and not just among those on the Right – to the steady increase in taxes and state power that has seemed an inescapable accompaniment of the growth process. Determined efforts were made in the United States under Reagan and in Britain under Thatcher to resist the trend. As with inflation, however, neither leader understood the underlying cause of the problem they were attempting to tackle, and consequently botched the job.

The problem was not just that technology was making more and more people unemployed and that social security costs were being forced up; it was also that those employed in the state sector naturally wanted their wages to keep up with those earned by their neighbours working in areas in which technology enables productivity to rise. This required the proportion of national income absorbed by state services to go up sharply. To understand why this was so, consider a national education service in which, for simplicity, teachers' salaries comprise the entire costs. If the service has the same number of teachers after real wages have doubled in the growth sector as it had before, and if its teachers' wages have kept up, the real cost of education will have doubled and the proportion of GNP it consumes will have risen substantially as a result of the growth elsewhere. (The actual rise in the proportion of GNP that education takes depends on the relative sizes of the growth sector and of the education service before and after the growth has taken place. However, the only way education could have continued to absorb the same proportion of GNP before and after the growth is if it was able to increase its productivity at the same pace as the growth sector.)

Mrs Thatcher was not alone in trying to hold state expenditure to a fixed proportion of national income. No government in the world has recognized that simple mathematics dictates that the costs of social services, which cannot be other than labour-intensive, have to rise as a proportion of GNP as a result of economic growth. Because of this blind spot it has only been public pressure that has forced politicians to maintain health service, educational and pensions standards and to introduce measures like the Common Agricultural Policy (CAP) to enable those in the agricultural sector to earn incomes comparable with those employed in sectors in which labour productivity can be increased more rapidly. Of course, as growth in one sector continues to outpace the rates in the others, the cost of maintaining health services or agricultural incomes steadily rises and powerful lobbies have sprung up seeking to pull the entire CAP and welfare structures down.

THE CONCENTRATION OF INDUSTRIAL POWER

Besides making the provision of social services relatively more expensive, destroying jobs – first overseas and then at home – and then forcing the rest of the economy to share in the cost of supporting those it has consigned to the dole, the growth process has something else to answer for: the generation of monopoly power. Running alongside the changes in the distribution of income and wealth which took place in both the inter-war and postwar periods was a steady increase in the size and market share of the leading companies in most industrial and commercial sectors. This was a continuation of the trend towards concentration we detected during the 1873-92 Great Depression and, as then, more companies merged at times when their market was expanding either slowly or not at all, because at such times mergers were the fastest way that sales growth and hence profits could be achieved.

S. J. Prais's 1981 study, *The Evolution of Giant Firms in Great Britain, 1909-70* shows that mergers absorbed 26 per cent of all British investment expenditure during the twenties and thirties. No figures exist for the forties because of the war. For most of the fifties, until the home market became saturated, merger activity was low and took only 7 per cent of investment funds but, between 1959 and 1972 when domestic growth was more difficult, the proportion never dropped below 20 per cent. Since then, with Britain's accession to the EC, firms have tended to merge internationally and the number of firms disappearing at home has fallen to between a third and a half of its 1960s level.

Not surprisingly, these mergers cut the number of small firms and increased the market share of the large ones. There was a steady fall in the number of firms with ten employees or fewer from 1930 to 1960 and then a slight rise, possibly as the service sector - which favours smaller firms - began to become more important. The share of overall trade held by the hundred largest companies steadily increased, as a table from Prais shows:

Increase in market share by hundred largest firms, 1909–68

Year:	1909	1924	1935	1949	1953	1958	1963	1968
% market share:	16	22	24	22	27	32	37	41

If firms that are growing slowly tend to amalgamate, we would expect to find the greatest concentrations of corporate power in sectors in which the market is mature and in fact there is considerable evidence that this is the case. Consider the computer industry: in its early years, thousands of small firms became involved around the world and highly successful businesses began in garages. Now that the market has almost settled down, however, some twenty companies dominate the industry and are continually arranging marriages between themselves. In mid-1991, against a background of production cutbacks, even the most powerful company, IBM, felt it desirable to enter an alliance with Apple.

Perhaps the best example of a mature market might be the grocery trade, where the real value of food sold per head of population has scarcely increased since the early fifties. Here concentration has become intense. In 1950, the Sainsbury chain, which was founded in 1869, already had 244 branches, mostly in the London area, although it had taken over some in the midlands in the thirties. These outlets were relatively small and the company estimates that it had around 1 per cent of the British grocery trade. In 1989, by contrast, the firm sold 15.8% of all groceries supplied through shops in Britain. This growth was not achieved by increasing the number of its branches by any great extent – the total in 1989 was 292 – but their average size was now 4.5 times greater, with new branches on average over 7.5 times greater. Sainsbury shops were also more widely distributed – the most northerly branch by this time was in Tyne and Wear.

I find the fact that almost a sixth of Britain's food should be supplied through just 292 shops very worrying. In 1950 this volume of business would have been handled by almost 37,000 outlets, including bakers, greengrocers, off-licences and fishmongers, most of them family-owned, according to the information service at *The Grocer* magazine. Around 130,000 full-time and 24,000 part-time staff would have been employed to handle the trade, compared with 38,089 full-time and 61,912 part-time people at Sainsbury's in 1990. The number of food shops of all types in Britain fell from 221,662 in 1950 to 46,300 in 1988.

In 1950 a typical Sainsbury store carried 550 lines. By 1989 this had reached 11,700, and the very diversity of products handled destroyed opportunities for other traders. The firm had built up this range gradually: indeed it was not until the First World War that it started selling groceries at all in order to compensate for the shortages of provisions. Fresh fruit and vegetables were sold from 1955, household goods from 1961, beers, wines and spirits from 1962 and delicatessen products from 1971. The first in-store bakery was opened in 1973, petrol stations and freezer centres in 1974 and fresh fish counters in 1982.

By the early eighties, Sainsbury's realized that it was going to get progressively more difficult to expand its British food sales. Most of the independent grocers had been driven from the field, and chains like its own – including Asda, Marks and Spencer, Tesco and the Co-op – controlled all but 14 per cent of the trade, making it extremely hard to win more. Accordingly it looked for a new line of business altogether, and in 1981 diversified into the do-it-yourself market with the Homebase chain, which by 1990 had grown to over sixty shops. It also bought up a 66-shop

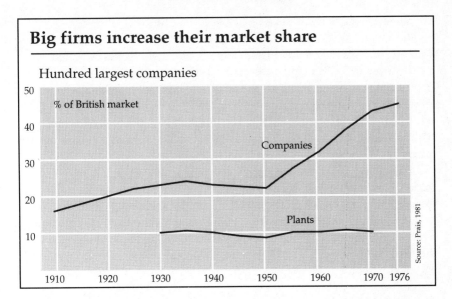

Big firms increase their market share

Hundred largest companies

% of British market

Companies

Plants

Source: Prais, 1981

1910 1920 1930 1940 1950 1960 1970 1976

Figure 6.3 Although the hundred largest British companies increased their share of the home market, individual plants still supplied about a tenth of the trade. This indicates that technological change did not require firms to get larger.

American supermarket chain in 1987.

The firm's current strategy can be seen as something of a mopping-up operation. It introduced over a thousand new products in 1990, destroying every niche market it could identify: the new lines included 'authentic' French patisserie, 'restaurant-style' pizzas, Italian, German and Russian breads and American-style dairy ice creams. Some of the new products represented a return to the standards of the fifties – twenty-five types of organic fruit and vegetable appeared 'all grown using environmentally-sound practices and avoiding synthetic fertilizers and sprays'. Traditional beef came back too, hung on the bone 'for long enough to let the flavour and tenderness develop fully'.

There is no evidence that the concentration of economic power in the grocery trade and elsewhere has brought significant benefits to anyone other than the shareholders. In 1969, only in a few industries – aircraft, mainframe computers, steel, electric motors, cars and turbogenerators – was the technology such that the most efficient plant required more than half of the British market to function properly, according to figures quoted by M. A. Utton in *The Political Economy of Big Business* (1982) and even in these activities, the cost penalties for being half the size of the optimum were 10 per cent or less of total costs except for aircraft and electric motors. Most other activities required a small fraction of the British market to be technologically efficient. A brewery, for example, required only 3 per cent yet in 1968 the five biggest firms in the business had 64 per cent of the total trade.

The graph on the previous page shows that, although the share of the domestic market taken by Britain's hundred largest companies increased rapidly after 1950, individual factories continued to produce around 10 per cent of home demand. Each company simply had more of them, owning an average of seventy-two plants each in 1972 compared with 27 in 1958 according to Prais, who notes that his study was unable to ascribe any substantial role to the technical need for greater plant sizes as a reason for the increases in firm size.

Indeed, big firms are frequently less efficient than small ones. Many studies have shown that small companies are more inventive in proportion to their turnover, switch from product to product more quickly in line with demand and use plant and machinery more intensively. They also get higher returns from the capital they employ. When John Dunning trawled through the 1965 balance sheets of 293 American companies operating in Britain for his 1969 pamphlet, *The Role of American Investment in the British Economy*, he produced the following figures:

Profitability by company size

Turnover	Number of firms	% Profitability
Over £25 million	11	13.3
£10-£25 million	14	13.5
£5-£10 million	22	21.0
£2.5-£5 million	46	26.2
£1-£2.5 million	77	22.2
£0.5-£1 million	60	21.1
£0.25-£0.5 million	40	27.2
Under £250,000	23	58.3

Where big firms score is in their access to cheaper capital and their ability to build brand names and to mount massive marketing campaigns. Neither of these advantages seems to benefit the consumer; in fact, the reverse may be true. If large firms use their greater financial strength or marketing might to eliminate their smaller competitors, as they evidently do, their customers are likely to suffer. Only if quality, convenience, price and service are the basis of competition rather than the size of the advertising budget is there a chance that the consumer will win.

In food retailing, not only has the British consumer lost the convenience of the corner store but the relationship between the nominally competing chains has become rather too cosy, according to Michael Campbell, director-general of RGDATA, the association of independent grocers in Ireland, who keeps a close eye on the British grocery trade. 'Net margins in the UK

are between 5 and 7 per cent compared with 2 to 3 per cent here,' he says.
'This is because all the British companies are structured in the same way and
are consequently under the same pressure from their shareholders to increase
the return on the capital they have invested.'

Both British and Irish grocery chains put enormous pressure on their
suppliers for lower prices and longer credit terms and, since only large, well-
capitalized companies are strong enough to resist, small food manufacturers
have been driven to the wall. In Ireland, where two chains, Dunne's Stores
and Quinnsworth, each control 23 per cent of the food market – the highest
concentration in any European country – firms used to be asked to pay
'hello money' to get their goods accepted into a store. When this was made
illegal, one chain started demanding between £3,000 and £10,000 to carry
out market research on the product instead. 'There are many ways of skin-
ning a cat,' commented a representative of the food manufacturers' association. 'The balance of power has shifted,' says Michael Campbell. 'A sales rep
can be dealing with a chain which takes a quarter of his company's output
by purchasing something which makes up only 0.1 per cent of the stores'
product range. The salesman needs the chain but they don't need him.'

ROOM FOR EXPANSION – OVERSEAS

Although the hundred largest firms in Britain increased their share of net
manufacturing output by 86 per cent between 1949 and 1968, it became
increasingly difficult for them to grow by takeover as there were progressively fewer firms left for them to buy up, especially without reference to the
Monopolies Commission. As a result the rate at which the big firms
increased their market share fell steadily – from 22.7 per cent between 1949
and 1953, to 18.5 per cent between 1953 and 1958, 15.6 per cent between
1958 and 1963 and only 10.8 per cent between 1963 and 1968. To escape
from this increasingly restrictive situation, they put considerable pressure on
Edward Heath, then Lord Privy Seal, to submit Britain's application to join
the EEC, and, since big firms contribute substantial amounts to
Conservative Party funds, in 1961 he did what they asked. Big business and
the banks then provided the bulk of the funding for the European
Movement, an organization which provided speakers and ran a major pro-
EEC propaganda campaign.

The justification offered for the inevitable loss of control over the country's affairs that joining the EEC would entail was twofold: that access to a
bigger market would enable British manufacturers to expand to benefit from
economies of scale, while for the consumer the increased competition would
lead to more choice at lower prices. In other words, both arguments said

that there would be an increase in GNP from which producers and public would benefit. However, economists estimated at the time that the gains from any increased efficiencies which might arise from larger scale production were, at most, 1 per cent of GNP. Harry Johnson, a professor of economics at Chicago University, stressed that this figure was a maximum:

It is extremely difficult to believe that British industry offers substantial potential savings in cost which cannot be exploited in a densely populated market of 51m. people with a GNP of £18bn. especially when account is taken of the much larger markets abroad in which British industry, in spite of restrictions of various kinds, has been able to sell its products.[3]

Britain's eventual membership of the EEC was therefore more about facilitating the growth of industrial giants than about the growth of the economy as a whole. Viewed from this perspective, the creation of the frontier-free EC of 1992 can be seen as a Sainsbury-style mopping-up operation involving the removal of niche markets occupied by the remaining small and medium-sized firms. Wisse Decker, the chairman of Philips, even helped to draft the Commission's 1985 white paper that laid out the plans for the abolition of frontier controls and the harmonization of product standards. Other industrialists, such as Jacques Solvay, head of Belgium's biggest chemicals company, and Giovanni Agnelli of FIAT were among those who lobbied hard for the single market.

Since only trivial gains to efficiency will arise because manufacturers no longer have to make products to different national standards and since most economies of scale are already fully exploited, the gain from the single market suggested by the European Commission – between 4.25 per cent and 7 per cent of the EC's annual output – looks grossly inflated. Ominously and dishonestly, the 1988 report on the effects of the single market prepared for the Commission by research teams under Paolo Cecchini says that it is impossible to predict where the gains will accrue. If the historical record counts for anything, the biggest companies and places within the 'golden triangle' made up by the Benelux countries, western Germany and northern France will gain at everyone else's expense.

Besides working for a greater freedom to grow within Europe, large companies have been attempting to use their governments to bring down barriers against them across the globe. Just as the industrial leader of the time – Great Britain – championed the cause of free trade in the nineteenth century because its manufacturers stood to gain, the present industrial, agricultural and service-sector leader, the United States, has been doing the same since the Second World War. The vehicle it chose was the General Agreement on Tariffs and Trade, an organization set up in 1947 to work towards international free trade. Countries belonging to GATT are committed to reducing tariffs and eliminating quotas and to abolishing preferential trade arrangements with particular states.

There have been several rounds of GATT talks since 1947, each leading to a relaxation of trading restrictions, each inspired by the United States. The latest was the Uruguay round, in which the main American goal was to eliminate non-tariff barriers to its exports, although it also sought to cut EC agricultural price supports, to let international banks operate freely, and to ensure that copyright fees were paid. Most non-tariff barriers – like the restrictions placed by some countries on the import of timber from the tropical rain-forest or the EC's ban on American beef from cattle injected with extra hormones – had been introduced for very good reasons but since they potentially conflicted with American corporations' interests, the United States wanted them swept away. Although the talks started in 1986, there was almost no public debate on the implications of the planned changes until about nine months before the agreement was due to be signed in December 1990. Not that public opinion would have counted for much anyway. The United States made little attempt to sell the tired old 'Free trade is good for everybody' line it had used in previous rounds; instead, it relied on threats to push through the agreement, which it assembled as a package, to be accepted or rejected as a whole. If any country was considering rejection, the United States made it clear that a trade war would break out with serious implications for that country's exports. It was 'a Rambo-like attempt to bludgeon the rest of the world into submission' commented *The Guardian* on the day the talks broke up without agreement, to be resumed the following year. As this book went to press in early 1992, it was by no means clear what the outcome would be.

The United States knew what it was doing when it dropped the 'benefits of free trade' argument. Even economists are beginning to lose faith in it, although it is one of the foundations of the discipline. According to the man *The Economist* calls the leading academic authority on the new approach to trade theory, Paul Krugman[4] of the Massachusetts Institute of Technology, 'the case for free trade is currently more in doubt than at any time since the 1817 publication of Ricardo's *Principles of Political Economy*' which introduced the idea of comparative advantage, on which the main argument for the benefits of international free trade rests.

The 'comparative advantage' argument is that if every country produces only those goods it makes best, and then trades them for everything else it needs, everyone everywhere will have more of everything, because the resources involved have been used most efficiently, *provided that there is perfect competition*. This latter requirement, however, makes the argument totally inapplicable in the real world, although Krugman and his colleagues are trying hard but vainly to adapt it to cope with markets dominated by a few large transnational firms. The argument is also valueless because it is based on the assumption that maximizing the output of goods is a country's only goal whereas in real life people and nations have many additional goals and try to come to the best possible compromise between them.

For example, work for most people is not just a means of earning money but the main way in which they develop and fulfil themselves as human beings and contribute to the community. Those who work producing useful goods and services are perceived – and perceive themselves – as pulling their weight in society, doing their bit. Even where the work itself is inherently boring, the fact that the person is being paid to do it means that he or she is valued. However, because the work people do is a major part of what they are or become, it is not enough for a country to offer reasonably paid jobs to its citizens – it is equally important that it offer fulfilling ones. And because everybody is different, a wide range of different occupations, each with its own level of responsibility, intellectual ability and manual skill, is needed if everybody is to find a suitable, fulfilling niche.

International trade, however, leads to international specialization – in other words, to a reduced range of jobs in each trading country. In Britain, whole categories of valuable jobs have been lost since the Second World War and most towns have a much more limited range of occupations than they had a century ago, especially for those who did poorly at school. This change is as bad economically as it is socially. If the economists' simplifying assumption that one worker's labour is the same as that of another is reject- ed for the nonsense it is, and if we treat each person as a unique collection of knowledge, interests and skills, then it is obvious that people can only be occupied optimally if we have a wide range of types of employment from which they can choose.

The lines along which free trade will force Ireland to specialize are already clear: the country will pay for its imports with earnings from tourism, forestry, and grass-fed beef and milk production. There will be no manufacturing, apart from the processing of wood, milk and meat for export, and the service sector will cater primarily for the export and tourist trades. These activities might provide the maximum return to land and capi- tal, but they will not use human resources well – anyone who cannot find suitable employment will have to emigrate – and, as a consequence, social life will lose its diversity. Apart from its human drawbacks, this type of spe- cialization is extremely risky. If disease strikes the country's monoculture Sitka spruce plantations, if an airline dispute damages the tourist trade, or if health worries hit beef consumption, Ireland will be plunged into an eco- nomic crisis, just as it was in the summer of 1990 when the combined effects of mad-cow disease and sanctions against Iraq brought the biggest beef-exporting company to its knees. In the natural world, a diversity of species tends to produce and maintain stability. It is the same in national economies. The more activities a country pursues the better, even if there is a financial cost, an 'insurance premium', attached to doing so.

In any case, the cost of such insurance is likely to be small. Apart from natural-resource-based products, which comprise a small fraction of the output of industrial countries (agriculture contributes less than 2 per cent to British GNP), almost everything produced in one country can be produced just as well in another using the same technology and raw materials. In other words, the gains from trade are largely a myth fostered by those companies and countries in strong trading positions that stand to gain from bigger markets.

International free trade inescapably leads to a levelling down. It means that salaries and wages will tend to converge at Third World levels, and social security provisions in industrial countries will have to be cut, since these are an overhead which economies cannot bear if they are to compete successfully with countries without them. Only the owners of the surviving transnational companies and of natural resources will escape the general impoverishment. Already the islands of prosperity are growing steadily smaller in an otherwise sick, dilapidated and hungry world. The quest for corporate growth has much to answer for.

7

Growth and the National Health

Growth for the sake of growth is the ideology of the cancer cell. – Edward Abbey

Although procreation had been taking place for some time previously, Philip Larkin suggests in one of his poems that sex did not begin until 1963. Much the same can be said about economic growth. What brought the concept to Britain's attention was a speech by the Chancellor of the Exchequer at the Conservative Party conference in 1954 which won headlines in the London *Evening Standard* that afternoon and, next day, in the newspaper which the Soviet Union then regarded as the authentic voice of British Conservatism, *The Yorkshire Post*. In his speech the Chancellor, R. A. Butler, said that if growth was to average 3 per cent a year in future, the standard of living would double by 1980, twenty-five years away. Butler subsequently made several speeches on the same theme, particularly during the 1955 election campaign, in which his party increased its majority. 'It's not pie in the sky but a sober picture,' he told his audiences, according to speaking notes kept in the Butler Papers at Trinity College, Cambridge. 'Moreover, we don't have to wait until 1980. Progress will come year by year if we concentrate on production and investment. The government will help with great new schemes. We will build roads and railways, develop atomic power and help with the re-equipment and modernization of the whole of industry.'

The reason it fell to Butler to set the target that has since dominated British life was that, although academics had been assembling their own GNP estimates since before the First World War, the first officially compiled UK national income figure is for 1938. This was published in 1941, when people had more pressing matters on their minds; consequently 1954 was the first year in which even a short run of official GNP figures was available that was not badly skewed by the war and its after-effects. British awareness of growth was ahead of that in the United States: the first presidential election campaign in which growth became an issue was the contest between Kennedy and Nixon in 1960.

Butler's twenty-five years are more than up. Growth failed to reach 3 per cent between 1955 and 1980: instead it was about 2.3 per cent, a high figure

Britain could double standard of living in 25 years—MR. BUTLER

'Our policy should be to invest in success'

From Yorkshire Post reporters

There was no reason why, in the next 25 years, the standard of living in Britain should not be doubled, Mr. R. A. Butler, Chancellor of the Exchequer, told the Conservative party conference which resumed at Blackpool yesterday.

"My motto is that our policy should be to invest in success," he said. "The meaning of that is that, as far as I am concerned, you are not going to get all the benefits rolled out at once. You are certainly not going to get lavish promises as with the Socialists.

"We have to draw back a bit, put our money into more investments in home industry, agriculture and the Commonwealth so that we can fortify ourselves and so that we shall not slip back into the morass from which we have just extricated ourselves.

"This does not mean that 'there won't be benefits for you. I think we may be just as successful at the next election if we show the public we are not out for a mass bribery campaign.

Without making any promises, the Government would do their best to keep the cost of living stable, always bearing in mind that, with a free economy, they could not count with the absolute certainty that they could under controls.

"We are suffering now by the greater plenty and the success of our policy," Mr. Butler went on.

GOVERNMENT SPENDING

He rejected the proposal for an outside Committee or inquiry into Government spending.

"I want to see no more May Committees or May reports. I propose to do the job myself with my colleagues. I propose to go on pruning expenditure with a view to reducing taxation, but there are limits to what I can achieve, if we are, at the same time, to have the boons of full employment and social welfare."

Dealing with external policy in trade, he said that a conference with Commonwealth representatives was to take place on GATT (General Agreement on Tariffs and Trade).

"Some of you, I understand, want to regut GATT. We should not do that. We should regut GATT. That is precisely what we are preparing to do."

While in Washington he found an "absolute acceptance of the policies of this Government and an understanding of the conditions which must be fulfilled before we could free the pound sterling. There was abroad considerable understanding and comfort about the progress we have so far made."

We were in an infinitely stronger capital position than we had been for years. The non-sterling capital position of the sterling area had improved by over £200 millions in the first part of the year.

Answering critics of the United States Mr. Butler paid tribute to the United States Administration and policy which, he said, had meant that the sterling area had not suffered from a nine per cent. fall in United States production.

Their wise foresight had meant that the working families of this country had profited.

'HELP THOSE IN NEED'

"We must also help those in need—the pensioners and others of fixed income. We must try to help especially o.a-age pensioners and the ex-servicemen and their wives."

Turning to external policy in trade affairs, he said: "If we are going forward as you request, with a truly Conservative policy, freeing markets, freeing the economy, and moving to liberty and the desirable goal of free payments and trade, then you must follow up externally the policy you pursue internally.

"You cannot open the Liverpool Cotton Exchange and trade in cotton and other commodities if you do not move into freedom in external payments.

"We shall not move until the conditions that I described in America are fulfilled, namely, that other people must do something for us if they expect us to do something for them.

"As I said in America, we expect some improvement in their trade practices ... in any quarter of the lowering our barriers any further or indulging in any further non-discrimination."

"What we want to achieve is overseas policy, as at home, is an approach which combines liberty with order.

"We want time, and we are going to have time, to carry through our job to the end and so to produce a policy that will preserve Commonwealth unity, and one line on which we can do it is on the line of freeing trade and payments. It is vital to carry Canada with us."

JAPANESE COMPETITION

Progress at the Commonwealth conference would be made in four ways—

"First, we propose to proceed with the examination of individual preferences, especially to meet the point of view of Australia. Second, we propose to review the value of the preferences today compared with the value on the date they were put on.

"Thirdly, we propose to fight for adjustments to meet the special needs of the Colonies. Fourth, in the interests of Lancashire, and not only of Lancashire but of England as a whole, we propose to secure that the unfair practices hitherto noticed in Japanese competition shall be dealt with in a fair and proper manner."

Mr. Butler said the Government would give constant attention to expenditure on education so that money could be diverted towards raising the status of the teaching profession and see that "every individual aggrieved by the exercise of Executive powers may seek redress from an independent Tribunal."

The subject of economic policy was introduced by the Keighley Conservative and Unionist Association, which submitted this resolution: "That this conference, while congratulating the Chancellor of the Exchequer on the success of his policies, exemplified by our stronger trading position, rising reserves, greater freedom and higher standard of living, urges him to carry these policies further, bearing in mind the desirability of moving towards a freer system of trade and payments and the need to reduce the still heavy burden of taxation."

The resolution was carried unanimously.

Mr. Marcus Worsley, of Keighley, moving the motion, said that the present scale and system of taxation was an intolerable burden on the people.

We must have more personal incentive if industry and the nation was to prosper. Just as serious, but less publicised, was the disruption which high taxation made in the ordinary processes of industry. He thought the first priority in lightening taxation should be given to the needs of productive industry.

Some of the Conservative conference delegates as they left their hotel yesterday. They are (left to right): Sir David Eccles, Mr. R. A. Butler, Lady Eccles, Mr. Duncan Sandys and Mr. David Gammans. (A Yorkshire Post picture.)

BUTLER: STANDARD OF LIVING CAN BE DOUBLED

We must try to help fixed income groups

Evening Standard Reporter: Blackpool, Friday

Mr. Butler, the Chancellor of the Exchequer, was loudly cheered at the Tory Party conference here today when he declared that he could see no reason why, in the next quarter of a century, Britain should not double her standard of living.

Britain, he said, must develop her vast family Commonwealth resources. And he added: "It is not a play on words to say our policy is to augment our Commonwealth."

Mr. Butler said he did not propose to reveal any major future proposals. They would come, in good time, "like the cat from the bag."

He was prepared, however, to give a few preliminary mews or whiskers.

Not all at once

The country would not be getting future benefits all at once. We had got to "draw back a bit" and invest money in home industry and agriculture and the Commonwealth.

"We must so fortify our Island and Commonwealth so that we shall never slip back into those crevasses and

● Back Page, Col. Three

Figure 7.1 How two newspapers reported the most significant shift in national economic strategy for generations.

nevertheless by historical standards if one remembers that from 1857 to
1913 the average British rate was 1.6 per cent. But missing the 3 per cent
target made only four years' difference, and Britain doubled its national
income by 1984. However, as population also went up during those years it
was 1988 before GNP per head had doubled in real terms. In theory at
least, all citizens were twice as rich as their parents had been at the same
age.

But how did it work out in practice? Did this growth fulfil Butler's expectations? We will never know – his papers give no indication that he thought
much about what the richer world he was trying to build would be like –
any more than growth's subsequent advocates have done. What can be said
is that the period between 1954 and 1988 was exceptional in many respects.
No major wars or recessions damaged Britain, and those crises that did take
place such as the 1973 and 1979 oil price rises and the Suez and Falklands
campaigns, were less serious than anyone had the right to expect. So, if we
find that growth has not delivered everything we were encouraged to believe
it would, something must have been wrong with (a) the promises that were
made to us, (b) the nature of the process itself, or (c) the economic system
that brought it about. We cannot blame the historical circumstances.

But if Butler did not spell out what growth would accomplish, an
economist did. In *The Theory of Economic Growth*, a classic book that
appeared in the same year as Butler's conference speech and was also, in its
way, a token of the coming of age of the new concept, Sir Arthur Lewis
wrote: 'The advantage of economic growth is not that wealth increases happiness, but that it increases the range of human choice.' He elaborated:

It is very hard to correlate wealth and happiness. Happiness results from the way
one looks at life, taking it as it comes, dwelling on the pleasant rather than the
unpleasant and living without fear of what the future may bring. Wealth would
increase happiness if it increased resources more than it increased wants, but it does
not necessarily do this and there is no evidence that the rich are happier than the
poor or that individuals grow happier as their incomes increase. Wealth decreases
happiness if, in the acquisition of wealth one ceases to take life as it comes and worries more about resources and the future. There is, indeed, some evidence that this is
the case; in so far as economic growth results from alertness in seeking out and seiz-
ing economic opportunities, it is only to be expected that it should be associated
with less happiness than we find in societies where people are not so much concerned with growth. There is evidence of much greater mental disturbance in the
United States of America than there is in other countries and, even when allowance
is made for differences in statistical reporting, it is at least plausible that the higher
suicide rate is causally connected with the drive for success in an already rich community. We certainly cannot say that an increase in wealth makes people happier.
We cannot say either that an increase in wealth makes people less happy, and even if
we could say this it would not be a decisive argument against economic growth,

since happiness is not the only good thing in life. We do not know what the purpose of life is, but if it were happiness, then evolution could just as well have stopped a long time ago, since there is no reason to believe that men are happier than pigs, or than fishes. What distinguishes men from pigs is that men have greater control over their environment; not that they are more happy. And on this test, economic growth is greatly to be desired. The case for economic growth is that it gives man greater control over his environment and thereby increases his freedom.

The idea that, although growth is not guaranteed to make people any happier and indeed might cause more suicides and mental distress, it has to be undertaken if we are to fulfil life's purpose, has never been stressed by advocates of the process, as most people would reject the argument out of hand. However, Lewis's other concept – that growth leads to increased choice – is still common currency. The spirit of the United Nations Development Programme's *Human Development Report 1990* is entirely his: 'Human development is a process of enlarging people's choices ... Growth in national production (GDP) is absolutely necessary to meet all essential human objectives.' Only two ideas in this report would not, perhaps, have been stressed by Lewis. One is its admission that 'the link between economic growth and human progress is not automatic.' The other is its identification of free markets with development: 'Human freedom is vital for human development. People must be free to exercise their choices in properly functioning markets ...' the UNDP says.

Unfortunately, the growth process destroys choices as well as creating them. As we have seen, growth depends on the introduction of new technologies and all successful new technologies tend to eliminate or restrict their predecessors. Thus a new transport technology, the car, increased the options of those who could afford to use it until vehicle numbers rose to such a point that they began to take options away by making it unpleasant to walk, unsafe to use a bicycle, impossible to take the train because the station had been closed and slower and less convenient to go by bus. Eventually the car began to destroy choices for its own users as roads became congested and there was nowhere left to park.

There is therefore no theoretical basis for saying that growth will permanently increase choice. The only period in which it will do so is during the transition phase when both new and old techniques exist side by side and even then the only beneficiaries are likely to be the better-off who can afford to adopt the new technique. Once everyone gains access, as with the holidays in the Algarve, the choice is no longer worth having, or, as with the car, effectively non-existent. What generally happens is that influential, well-off people promote new technologies because of the increased choices and freedoms – and possibly financial gains – they will bring *them*. By the time it comes to the ordinary person's turn to share in the benefits, these have largely if not entirely vanished and the promoters have moved on to the next set of promising techniques.

Most people probably support economic growth because they have been convinced it will bring them a higher quality of life. They are not interested in a more rapid rate of consumption for itself: it is a means rather than an end, the end being that they and their children can live more healthily, comfortably, securely and fulfillingly than they do at present. Indeed it is doubtful whether they are very worried about having a wider range of choices, except perhaps as far as it affects their ability to fulfil themselves. Certainly the fact that a hundred makes of nearly identical cars are on the market rather than fifty is neither here nor there: it might even create worry and confusion. So, did the growth between 1955 and 1988 improve the general quality of life?

There is no space here for an exhaustive discussion of what happened to the twelve factors we identified in chapter 1 as important components of the quality of life. A proper examination of, say, how the education system changed during the third of a century we are concerned with would need at least a book to itself. Moreover, even if we had space for such in-depth examinations, we would still be unable to say whether the overall quality of life had improved unless all our statistics moved in the same direction, because we could not set off gains in one area against losses in another without a common measuring rod. Do better teeth outweigh fewer butterflies?

There is a way around both problems, however. As we have seen, the best indicator of how satisfied people are with their lives is whether or not they are happy with their state of health and that people's feelings about their health bear a close relationship to their objective state of health as determined by a doctor. This enables us to venture that if people actually get healthier they will feel themselves to be healthier and will be more satisfied with their lives. Thus if the health of the British people improved during the 1955-88 period, it seems fair to suggest that their total welfare went up.

Many studies have shown that people tend to fall sick when they pass through an emotionally disturbing time. For example, although it has been known for some time that angry or bitter people and those who have been through a traumatic experience such as the death of a spouse are more likely to develop breast or lung cancer, a recent study at the East London Polytechnic has shown that a family row can cause a cold four days later. The researchers, Philip Evans and Nick Edgerton,[1] think this is because smaller quantities of a disease-fighting protein, immunoglobulin A, are produced when someone is upset, allowing the cold virus to invade the body. Researchers at the University of Miami have also shown that teaching people techniques for handling stress can improve their immune defences.

Changes in health, then, seem to be an ideal quality-of-life measuring rod. Moreover, as all the factors involved in determining the quality of our lives – the beauty of the natural environment, for example, or the strength of our personal relationships – have a bearing on the way we feel, it is one that turns out to be rather versatile.

WHAT HAPPENED TO HEALTH?

The public's perception is that Britain is steadily getting healthier. The public is wrong: the incidence of illness increased substantially between 1955 and 1988, and the deterioration accelerated as our study period wore on. The misconception that health is improving is due to the fact that most infectious diseases, like TB and whooping cough, have become much less common, and because life expectancy at all ages has improved. Infant mortality, for example, fell from 25.8 per thousand births in 1955 to 9.0 per thousand in 1988 and the number of stillbirths was down from 7.9 per thousand in 1955 to 4.9 per thousand in 1988. A boy born in 1955 could expect to live for 66.2 years whereas in 1988 the estimate was 72.2. Similarly, in 1955, 33.1 women and 54.4 men out of every thousand of those aged sixty-five to seventy-four died within the year while in 1988, the figure had dropped to 23.2 and 41.2, respectively.

However, these improvements disguised what was really going on, for two reasons. One is that they were produced by a system which had gained in medical knowledge and skill, gains entirely unrelated to economic growth. Even better life expectancy figures were achieved in Barbados and Dominica, with half and a quarter of Britain's GDP respectively. The second is that the health of an average seventy-year-old is the combined product of living conditions since before he or she was born, not just those in the past one or two decades. If a nation becomes less healthy it may take years, perhaps decades, for this to show up in the mortality statistics, if it ever does: illnesses are not necessarily fatal. As a result, the first indication that a nation's health is deteriorating may be that the level of chronic illness goes up.

Such a rise in fact took place in Britain between 1955 and 1988. According to the government's General Household Survey for 1988, 33 per cent of the population had a long-standing illness that year, up from 21 per cent in 1972 and, whereas only 8 per cent of those interviewed in 1971 had reported being acutely ill during the preceding two weeks, in 1988 14 per cent did. Similarly, the average number of days for which the state paid out sickness and invalidity benefits to each insured worker rose from 8.8 in 1962 to 12.2 in 1988. Again, 226 million prescriptions – 4.7 per head – were issued in 1961, when they were free and newspapers complained that spongers were using them to obtain items as cheap and trivial as bottles of aspirin; in 1988, the number was 427.7 million – 7.5 per person – despite the deterrent of a £2.60 charge. In addition, hospital admissions almost doubled and would have been higher still had the Health Service been able to cope. Despite the assistance of the DHSS, I was unable to trace any research into the causes of this increase, particularly the proportion due to the greater number of elderly people. No-one I spoke to, however, suggested that an ageing population was the main factor. 'There has been a big increase in minor disorders,' the director of the Office of Health Economics, George Teeling Smith, told me. 'The incidence of serious illnesses like cardiovascular disease has declined but ill-defined complaints like aches and pains have become much more common. There is a widespread malaise.'

Many studies[2] have demonstrated a link between income and health but the higher incomes some people get as a result of the growth process do not necessarily make them healthier. In *Health and Lifestyles* (1990), Mildred Blaxter reports that when she surveyed households containing a total of 7,000 people, she found that £250 a week before tax was the ideal income in 1984-5 because people living in households with incomes below *or above* this sum had more illnesses, more difficulty sleeping, and were more worried and depressed.

Relative income levels in fact are much more important than absolute ones in determining health. In a 1985 study,[3] Elsie Pamuk looked at changes in the mortality rates of men in 143 occupations that could be consistently identified for the span from 1921 to 1971. She found that mortality rates for occupations in social class V (such as labourers), tended to improve more rapidly than those for social class I (doctors, accountants, lawyers) in the period up to 1951, when war, economic depression and government policies pushed relative incomes in favour of the less well-off.

After 1951, however, relative incomes moved against people in class V occupations although their absolute incomes continued to rise until the end of the seventies. This can be seen in the graph opposite, which shows that the pre-tax proportion of national income going to the bottom half of the population was almost stable from 1949 until 1976 and then fell sharply. The proportion of income going to the wealthiest 10 per cent, on the other hand, declined in favour of middle-income earners until the mid-seventies and then, after 1978, swiftly recovered all its losses – largely at the expense of the poor. In other words, even during the fifties and sixties the poorest half of the population suffered a relative decline in economic status, first in comparison with the middle 40 per cent – the group that set the standards they were encouraged to aspire to – and then, after 1978, in relation to the very rich as well. Moreover, changes in the tax system aggravated these

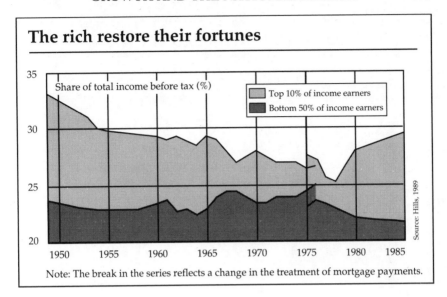

The rich restore their fortunes

Note: The break in the series reflects a change in the treatment of mortgage payments.

Figure 7.2 The proportion of national income going to the wealthiest 10 per cent of wage earners fell until the mid-1970s in favour of the middle 40 per cent. It then increased sharply, largely at the expense of the poor.

trends, with the result that incomes for the poorest one-fifth of Britons fell not only relatively but absolutely between 1979 and 1985, dropping by 2 per cent according to a 1989 Child Poverty Action Group report, *Changing Tax*.

Pamuk's study showed that when the various classes' incomes ceased to converge, the difference between mortality rates ceased to converge as well. This was largely because the absolute death rate of class I people continued to fall while the Class V death rate behaved erratically, even worsening from time to time. Later work[4] has shown that the mortality gap between the classes continued to widen until 1981 at least; when the 1991 census results have been analysed, they are likely to show that the gap has widened further still.

Pamuk also found that wives' mortality rates moved in parallel with those of their husbands. Another study, published by the Department of Health and Social Security[5] in 1984, showed that children were affected too: the difference in height between eight-year-old children from the five social classes was at a minimum in 1950, neatly confirming the income trend Dudley Seers spotted as early as 1951, as we saw in chapter 4. The link between relative incomes and relative health provides a remarkably sensitive social indicator.

Richard Wilkinson of the Trafford Centre for Medical Research at the University of Sussex has studied this link since the mid-seventies. 'The relationship between income distribution and health is quite robust,' he told the

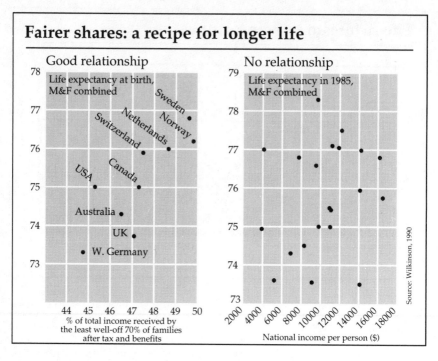

Fairer shares: a recipe for longer life

Figure 7.3 People in countries with higher national incomes do not necessarily live any longer. However, citizens of the more egalitarian countries do.

British Sociological Association conference in 1991.[6] 'It has now been demonstrated four times using different measures of income distribution from different countries at different dates ... About two-thirds of the variation in life expectancy between these countries is related by differences in their income distribution.' Wilkinson produced the above graphs to show that there was no link at all between GNP per capita and life expectancy in twenty-one OECD countries and that the proportion of national income going to the poorest 70 per cent of families explained most of the international variations. Even the proportion of national income devoted to health care had a negligible explanatory effect:

Since the early 1970s, Japan has gone from the middle of the field in terms of life expectancy and income distribution to the top in both. Japan now has the highest recorded life expectancy and the most egalitarian income distribution in the world. On the other side of the coin, while Britain's income distribution worsened dramatically during the eighties to produce the largest inequalities for over a century, its relative position in terms of life expectancy has also worsened. Each year since 1985 mortality rates among both men and women between the ages of 16 and 45 have actually risen – a trend which is not attributable to deaths from AIDS.

Getting sicker year by year

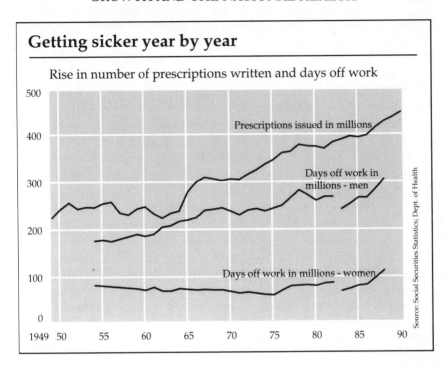

Rise in number of prescriptions written and days off work

Prescriptions issued in millions

Days off work in millions - men

Days off work in millions - women

Source: Social Securities Statistics; Dept. of Health

Figure 7.4 People take more days off work sick than they did in the 1950s. These figures are for workers claiming sickness or invalidity benefit: the break is due to an increase in the eligibility period from three to four days.

Wilkinson is certain that differences in absolute poverty do not account for the differences in death rates among rich countries. 'We are not dealing with the effects of residual poverty in the developed world – there are too few people in absolute poverty in each of the developed countries for their death rates to be the decisive influence [on the overall statistics],' he told the BSA conference. Some people in rich countries were unable to eat properly even though they had incomes which were theoretically adequate to cover the cost of essentials because they were forced to buy 'inessentials' like rounds of drinks if they were to participate in ordinary activities in their communities. Others had to live in damp housing. However, neither of these circumstances could account for most of the increase in the gap between death rates. Far more important, he suggested, was that 'relative poverty is a demeaning and devaluing experience and a sense of relative deprivation will reduce people's sense of self-worth and self esteem,' which then affected their health. 'What people feel about their housing, their financial and social circumstances and what that does to their morale is likely to be more important [to their health] than their objective conditions,' he said, suggesting that health statistics could be used as an indicator of the subjective aspects of the quality of life, just as we are doing here.

However, if we accept that the decline in people's health does indeed show that the quality of life worsened, we still have to demonstrate that economic growth, or the quest for it, was responsible for the deterioration, rather than the continuous struggle that takes place between social groups in all societies to improve their income share. In fact I can find no evidence that the quest for growth had much to do with the change in the distribution of income for thirty years after 1949: the adverse health trend began before growth became the prime national goal and the redistribution which took place was largely as a result of middle income people gaining at the expense of the very rich. On the other hand, the widespread feeling that growth was making things better for everyone meant that no attempt was made to increase the share of national income going to the poor. This was a sin of omission and can, perhaps, be excused. Mrs Thatcher, however, was guilty of a sin of commission because it was her belief that growth would accelerate if the better-off kept more of their earnings. The continuing decline in health after 1979 – as shown by the days lost off work through illness and the rise in the number of prescriptions issued – can therefore be attributed to her pro-growth policies. We can also state confidently that, if politicians really want to improve the lot of the poor, it is much better to redistribute income towards them instead of encouraging growth and hoping that some of the extra consumption it generates will eventually trickle down.

THE INCREASE IN CHRONIC COMPLAINTS

While changes in the distribution of income can explain much of the general increase in sickness between 1955 and 1988, they cannot account for most of the detail. Why, for example, did the incidence of asthma increase so sharply, becoming the most common chronic disease in the developed world? Almost 30 per cent of British children now suffer from it at some time during their childhood and by 1990, hospital admissions for children up to the age of fourteen were ten times higher than they had been thirty years previously. According to a 1990 report by the Office of Health Economics, an estimated two million people in Britain are asthma sufferers and the number of people consulting their doctors about it increased from 380,000 in 1955 to 875,000 in 1981/2. The number of deaths, however, stayed constant at around 2,000 a year.

The National Asthma Campaign blames the increase on changes in the way houses are furnished. Fitted carpets and more upholstery provide ideal breeding grounds for the dust mite, it says, pointing out that 85 per cent of asthmatics are allergic to a protein in the mites' excreta. This widely believed explanation is unlikely to be true, however. According to a Medical Research Council environmental epidemiologist, Keith Godfrey of Southampton University, there is no scientific evidence that exposure to dust mite faeces has increased over the last thirty years. 'The mite was only fully characterized in the 1960s and there are no longitudinal studies assessing any changes in the population levels over many years,' he told me. 'Although upholstery increases the house dust mite population, central heating reduces it by virtue of lowering the humidity.'

Moreover, asthmatic children in whose homes dust control measures have been carried out fare no better than those in untreated houses as Donald Lane and Anthony Storr point out in their 1981 book *Asthma, the Facts*:

Why have the results of dust control been so unimpressive? Partly because control has to be almost inhumanly rigorous to reduce the mite load to negligible proportions and partly because, even when skin testing and bronchial provocation suggest house dust mite allergy to be important, there are in fact many other trigger factors. The loss of one trigger might not make a detectable difference to the overall pattern and frequency of asthmatic episodes in the child.

Asthma is an allergy and the incidence of all allergies has increased over the period we are considering. Allergies are due to damage to the body's immune defence system; this causes it to act inappropriately when exposed to substances like mite excreta or grass pollen, which trigger allergic reactions but are not their fundamental cause. The increase in asthma is therefore linked with the increase in other diseases also associated with immune-system damage, notably AIDS and myalgic encephalomyelitis (ME), the chronic fatigue syndrome. As we will see, there are many things that could be causing this damage such as food additives, pesticides and atmospheric pollutants, to say nothing of magnetic fields and electromagnetic radiation.

DEBASED DIET

Not only have there been significant increases in certain types of illness since 1955 but the pattern of illness that people are presenting has changed. Walter Yellowlees, a family doctor, has watched the steady decline in the health of his patients in a valley in the Scottish Highlands near Perth since the early fifties. In a classic paper[7] read to the Royal College of General Practitioners in 1977, he said that some health problems were getting worse, although Britain had more doctors per head than ever before:

In 1918, coronary thrombosis was virtually unknown; so was diverticular disease of the colon. Both are now among the commonest diseases seen in practice today. The decay of our arteries as seen in coronary thrombosis is matched by the continuing incompetence of our veins: about 10 per cent of the population has varicose veins and many sufferers are greatly incapacitated by their complications. Duodenal ulcer, which at the beginning of the century was very rare, remains a common, crippling abdominal disease. The arthropathies and rheumatic complaints continue to cause disability on a vast scale.

Since the closing decades of the last century there has been a real increase in gall-bladder disease, appendicitis and diabetes. Recent evidence from Glasgow appears to show a considerable increase in diabetes in children. In Scotland, so terrible is the state of the nation's teeth that 44 per cent of adults aged 16 and over have no teeth at all.

The worst of all our afflictions is cancer. Since 1930 there has been a 62 per cent increase in Scotland's crude mortality rate for cancer which, when standardized, gives an increase of 15 per cent.

I believe it is true to say that in those countries which have achieved unparalleled advance in technological skill in medicine and in what is called standard of living we are witnessing the decay of man – the decay of his teeth, his arteries, his bowels and his joints on a colossal and unprecedented scale.

Most of the complaints Yellowlees mentions are the so-called 'diseases of affluence'. He attributes their increase to the 'continuing use of unnatural food', especially refined sugar and white flour. High intakes of animal and dairy fats, on the other hand, he thinks blameless, citing a 1966 study showing that the first record of angina was in the eighteenth century but that coronaries were unknown until the twentieth century. 'The Victorian and Edwardian servant-keeping classes, one-third of the population of England and Wales, ate as much or more animal fat than is being eaten today. And they were lazy,' Yellowlees said. 'The main feature of the modern Highlander's diet is the absence of fresh vegetables and salads and of whole-grain cereals and the massive intake of refined carbohydrates. Porridge no longer adorns the breakfast table and the Scottish high tea of scones, cakes, biscuits and tinned jam is a festival of sugar and starch.'

John Yudkin, now emeritus professor of nutrition and dietetics at London University, has been urging people to cut down their sugar consumption for at least thirty years. His 1986 book *Pure, White and Deadly* suggests that sugar may be a cause of childhood obesity, earlier sexual maturity, cancer, dental caries, short and long sight, dermatitis, gout, coronary disease, diabetes and various digestive conditions, although, as he notes, 'the evidence … is not equally convincing for all of them.'

Until recently, official bodies refused to be convinced that sugar was harmful, largely, as Yudkin shows, because of the pressures put on them by sugar manufacturers. The dam broke in 1990, however, when the World Health Organization published a report, *Diet, Nutrition and the Prevention of Chronic Disease*, which suggested that less than a tenth of dietary calories should come from sugar, compared with the 15 to 20 per cent level found in many countries at present. Naturally this made the British government's position untenable and in 1991 the Department of Health's Committee on Medical Aspects of Food Policy backed the WHO figure. Yet commercial considerations still prevented firm governmental action to get sugar consumption down. 'We must not be dictatorial or prescriptive,' the Food Minister, David Maclean, was quoted as saying. Accordingly, although the total amount of food advertising was £605 million and 40 per cent of the commercials on children's television were for high-sugar or high-fat foods, the minister allocated just £1 million to the Health Education Authority for a nutrition and dental health education campaign.

During our study period, sugar consumption rose from 50 kg per person a year in 1955 to 54 kg in 1970, double what it had been a century previously, as people bought more fizzy drinks, confectionery, cakes and other processed foods. Since then it has remained on a plateau with a fall in sucrose consumption being balanced by the use of glucose and high fructose syrup in processed foods. At present, seventy per cent of British sugar consumption is concealed in manufactured foods, showing just how intimately our level of intake is tied to economic growth. After water, sugar is one of a food manufacturer's cheapest ingredients, and the pressures to add more are strong. It can always be argued that people like their food sweet and manufacturers are only responding to market demand; however, since the preference for sweet foods is an acquired one, I suspect that the commercial pressure to add sugar to products gradually created its own demand.

With other food additives we are on surer ground. It was certainly not consumer demand that led to an estimated tenfold increase in the use of flavours, colours, preservatives, emulsifiers, anti-oxidants and other food additives in Britain between 1955 and 1985. The needs of food manufacturers dictated the change and the systematic food adulteration they permitted. As the London Food Commission puts it in its 1988 book *Food Adulteration,*

There are economic pressures on a manufacturer to debase food. If one manufacturer uses phosphates to add extra water to bacon and drops the price by a few pence, there is increasing pressure on the others to follow suit. When all the manufacturers in the same price range have watered their bacon, the cycle of dilution is repeated as soon as a manufacturer decides to shave a few more pence.

The commission says that about 3,800 additives are used to perform about a hundred functions. At the end of the Second World War, there were fewer than a thousand processed food products, but by 1988 the total had risen to 10,000, and 75 per cent of an average person's diet was made up of processed food. The result was that each Briton ingested about 3.6 kg of additives a year, or 10 g a day. Only about a tenth of the additives were subject to government control – there were 3,500 flavours alone which had not been systematically tested and approved, although work on this had started. But even approved additives could not be said to be safe. Erik Millstone, a lecturer in science policy at Sussex University, tells me that 85 of the 299 permitted additives listed in his book *Additives: a Guide for Everyone* (1988) are of doubtful safety, with 60 being suspected of causing allergic reactions in a significant minority of people and the remaining 25 possibly toxic to the population as a whole. In April 1991, when the Minister for Agriculture, John Gummer, assured Sir James Goldsmith, the former owner of a major food manufacturing firm, that all additives used in British food were safe, because they had been tested, the response was blunt: 'Don't give me that. I started out in the pharmaceuticals business. I know how chemicals are tested. I know experts can't know about long-term effects when a chemical is new.'

Even those additives which have been tested have only been checked in isolation. The London Food Commission points out:

A single meal may contain a cocktail of twelve to sixty additives. The combinations of additives may react with each other and with foods to produce new chemical substances ... In a rare test on mixtures of additives and low fibre food it was found that the rats developed 'unthrifty' fur, alopecia and extensive diarrhoea and there was a marked retardation in weight increase. This synergistic effect was not found when the animals received only one of the additives.

While food manufacturers were increasing the number and quantity of additives in their products in response to competitive pressures, farmers were under identical pressures to use more fertilizers and pesticides to increase yields and labour productivity. In fact almost the whole switch from organic to inorganic food production took place during the period under review. World fertilizer use grew from 14 million tonnes in 1950 to 143 million tonnes in 1989. The use of pesticides grew even more rapidly because it started from a smaller base, and by 1988, 1,000 million gallons of herbicides, insecticides and fungicides were being sprayed in Britain annually. Both developments caused a deterioration in food quality, since pesticides leave potentially harmful residues, and fertilizers cause a loss of flavour and nutritional value. On the other hand, the physical appearance of fruits and vegetables was improved.

Nitrogenous fertilizers can raise the amount of nitrate in the final crop to four or five times the level found in the compost-grown equivalent, while at the same time cutting vitamin C and dry matter levels. This change is potentially serious, since nitrates can be turned into powerfully carcinogenic nitrosamines by bacteria found in the mouth, while vitamin C has been shown to protect against cancers. Whether nitrosamines are in fact being made in the mouth is unclear, although oesophageal cancer has increased in step with increased nitrate exposure over the past thirty years, and Austria, Germany, the Netherlands and Switzerland limit the levels of nitrate allowed in several vegetable crops as a precautionary measure. Nitrate levels have also risen substantially in British drinking water as a result of fertilizer use. The only problem which this has been proved to produce so far has been the 'blue-baby syndrome', in which bottle-fed infants are poisoned when their stomach bacteria convert nitrates to nitrites and these are absorbed by their blood. Fortunately, no cases have been notified since 1972.

Although a 1985 study[8] by the Ministry of Agriculture, Fisheries and Food showed that 43 per cent of 1,649 samples of home-grown and imported fruit and vegetables contained pesticide residues, the London Food Commission thinks the proportion would have been higher had more sensitive tests been used. It says that 3,009 pesticides were approved for use in Britain that year and that, of their 426 basic ingredients, 164 have been implicated in causing cancer, reproductive effects ranging from impotence to birth defects, genetic mutations or irritant reactions. In the United States the position is as bad, if not worse: 30 per cent of the total weight of insecticides applied, 60 per cent of herbicides and 90 per cent of fungicides could cause tumours, according to the National Research Council. As a result, the riskiest American farm products to eat, in order of declining potential toxicity, are tomatoes, beef, potatoes, oranges, lettuce, apples, peaches, pork, wheat, soyabeans, beans, carrots, chicken, maize, and grapes.

Food additives and pesticide residues have both been suspected of causing health problems ranging from cancers and genetic damage to rashes and asthma. However, proving that they do so is almost impossible since few groups have not been exposed to both at some time. Even the link between food colourings and some cases of hyperactivity in children has not been conclusively proved despite the wealth of anecdotal evidence. In 1989 Ronald Finn, a consultant physician at the Royal Liverpool Hospital, told a meeting of the McCarrison Society, which studies the links between food and health, that he had treated a child whose academic record had been so poor that it had been decided to send him to a special school. However, after the removal of artificial colours from his diet, the boy had become top of his class in mathematics. Dr Finn suggested[9] that as food additives cause some children to become violent, they might cause adult violence as well. 'Lead poisoning from water pipes and wine storage has been suggested as a cause of the insanity which affected many of the Roman emperors, leading eventually to anarchy and the collapse of the Empire,' he said. 'If environmental toxins are reaching dangerous levels, their effects will first show themselves on our most sensitive cells, which are in our brains.'

Another factor that makes the health effects of the increased use of food additives and pesticides since 1955 so hard to determine is that the air over Britain has become considerably more contaminated. This was despite a successful effort to cut levels of sulphur dioxide, the gas that killed 4,000 people in the infamous London smog of December 1952, when it became sulphuric acid in the fog's water droplets and caused asthmatic attacks. The reductions were achieved by phasing out high-sulphur fuels and by building taller chimneys on power stations so that their fumes were blown away from urban areas. As a result, average levels of atmospheric sulphur dioxide were halved between 1970 and 1988. However, because of the rapid increase in the number of motor vehicles, efforts to bring down levels of two other 'traditional' pollutants – the nitrogen oxides – failed. The best that could be achieved was to hold them to their 1970 level.

The years after 1955 saw a rapid increase in the release of 'toxic trace pollutants' by transport and industry. The effects of these are much less well understood than the traditional gaseous pollutants. They fall into four major categories: heavy metals, such as beryllium, cadmium and mercury; volatile organic compounds (VOCs) such as formaldehyde and vinyl chloride; radioactive particles and gases; and fibres such as asbestos. Of these, VOCs present the biggest danger because they are released in large and growing quantities by the increasing volume of traffic, by the production and use of natural gas, the refining of oil and the processing and use of organic chemicals. They include ethylene oxide, formaldehyde, phenol, phosgene, benzene, carbon tetrachloride, chlorofluorocarbons (CFCs) and polychlorinated biphenyls (PCBs). As the OECD report *The State of the Environment* (1991) says, 'many ... are highly reactive and have considerable environmental health implications ... All are produced mainly by human activities and they are almost all known or suspected carcinogens. Several, also, are possible mutagens or teratogens' (i.e. substances which increase the incidence of congenital malformations).

Apart from having a direct effect, the VOCs react in sunlight with oxygen and the nitrogen oxides to form low-level ozone. 'High levels of ozone increase susceptibility to infections and respiratory disease and irritate the eyes, nose, throat and respiratory system' according to a 1990 Department of the Environment report,[10] which quotes figures showing that the total amount of VOCs emitted in Britain rose from 1.78 million tonnes in 1978 to 1.85 million tonnes in 1988. Fifty-seven per cent of the emissions came from chemical processes and solvents and 30 per cent from road transport. The OECD report estimates that the United States discharges 3.3 million tonnes of VOCs into the air each year and that the amount is likely to continue to grow because 'the chemical industry is expected to grow faster than any other industry and that growth is likely to increase the range and quantity of toxic substances released into the environment.' The report goes on:

It is much more difficult to estimate the exposure of a population to toxic trace pollutants than to the traditional air pollutants because the former are not routinely monitored in most countries; it is even more difficult to estimate the health risk. To date, negative health effects have been observed only at occupational levels which are higher than those normally found in the ambient or indoor air. For most of these pollutants, data regarding their effects on humans are not available but are deduced from animal studies. In addition, it may not be sufficient to know the health risk associated with one of these toxic pollutants since they can be additive, cumulative and, possibly, synergistic.

Although a few of the toxic trace pollutants present an ambient air problem in the outdoors, many of them constitute a greater risk to people indoors (at home, in vehicles, in the office and other working places) where concentrations are much higher ... Most people spend 90 per cent of their time indoors. A US study of comparative risk placed such indoor air pollution among the top environmental problems facing the nation.

This report connects toxic trace pollutants with the 'sick building syndrome' which causes people to complain of eye, nose and throat irritations, fatigue, headaches, nausea, irritability and forgetfulness. 'Although these irritations are unpleasant, they may still be considered to be relatively minor. On the other hand, many of the toxic trace pollutants are known to cause chronic, irreversible effects that may ultimately lead to premature death,' the OECD concludes.

In 1975 the Registrar-General published an analysis of the incidence of over one hundred different types of cancer in England and Wales in 1968-70, distinguishing between patients living in urban and rural areas. The figures showed that there was a large and increasing excess of cancers (particularly male lung cancers) in urban areas. 'We have an average total of 13,000 people dying of cancer in England and Wales every year who would not have died if they had all lived in a rural environment,' commented John Fremlin, former professor of applied radioactivity at Birmingham University, in his book *Power Production: What Are the Risks?* (1985).

Unfortunately, no similar records of the urban/rural ratio are available subsequent to 1970 but total cancer death rates in 1984 were over 28 per cent greater than in 1969 and show no sign of effects of the reduction of open fires which was already under way in the 1950s. It must be remembered that cancers take decades to develop: most of those observed must be due to factors acting soon after the war and it will be a long time before we can disentangle the falling effects of coal and the increasing effects of vehicles.

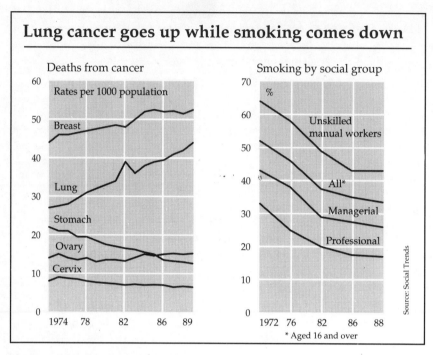

Figure 7.5 Although all social classes reduced the number of cigarettes they smoked, the incidence of lung cancer continued to rise. Other forms of air pollution were the likely cause.

As the graph above shows, deaths from lung cancer have risen by over 50 per cent since 1974 even though the number of smokers has declined steadily. We can only conclude that new forms of pollution as a result of the growth process are more than making up for coal fires and cigarettes.

MAGNETIC AND ELECTRICAL POLLUTION

Although little may be known about the cumulative and combined effects of the air and food pollutants to which the British were increasingly exposed during the 1955-88 period, the ignorance about 'electro-pollution' is even more profound. Government scientists at least accept that additives, pesticides and toxic trace pollutants can cause health problems; with electro-pollution, officialdom remains unconvinced and scientists working in the field tend to get labelled as cranks because the mechanisms by which electromagnetic radiation and electrical and magnetic fields can affect the human body are poorly understood. However, the situation is changing rapidly and in mid-1990, after a two-year study, the US Environmental Protection Agency suggested that the electromagnetic fields near power lines were causally linked with lymphoma, leukaemia and brain cancer in children, and called for further research.

Evidence that electro-pollution can affect the human body has in fact been available for over four decades. In 1950 the US Public Health Service found that workers frequently exposed to alternating current – power station operators, linesmen, electricians, welders, and telephone engineers – had significantly higher cancer rates than the population as a whole. In 1968 the Russians reported much the same thing, and in 1975 a Romanian team published the results of a study of technicians whose exposure to microwaves averaged eight years. These showed that nearly three-quarters of the men had less than the usual amount of sperm and that what sperm they did have was weak. They also showed a loss of sex drive, and 70 per cent had the loss-of-energy symptoms associated with myalgic encephalomyelitis.

But the main credit for bringing the matter to public attention must go to an American epidemiologist, Nancy Wertheimer, who was checking the birth addresses of Denver children suffering from leukaemia looking for a common environmental cause in 1974 when she noticed that most of the houses she was visiting were close to electricity distribution transformers. She sought the help of a physicist friend, Ed Leeper, and after extensive investigations they published a joint paper in the *American Journal of Epidemiology* in 1979. Its first paragraph reads:

Electrical power came into use many years before environmental impact studies were common and today our domestic power lines are taken for granted and generally assumed to be harmless. However, this assumption has never been adequately tested. Low-level harmful effects could be missed yet they might be important for the population as a whole since electric lines are so ubiquitous. In 1976-1977 we did a field study in the Denver area which suggested that, in fact, the homes of children who developed cancer were found unduly often near electric lines carrying high current.

The EPA statement eleven years later essentially confirms that they were right. Anything else would have been surprising as low-level electromagnetic fields have been shown to inhibit cell division in moulds, seeds, chicks, rats and human embryo tissue and it is widely believed that computer monitors or 'VDUs', which create fields of this type, have caused miscarriages, deformities, and premature and low-weight births. Ursula Huws' guide, *VDU Hazards* (1988), quotes a Japanese study of 4,500 female VDU operators which showed that of the 250 who had become pregnant while in the job, 91 had had abnormal pregnancies, including eight miscarriages, eight premature births, and five stillbirths. Two-thirds of the women who spent more than six hours a day at the screen reported pregnancy problems, while only one-quarter of those who spent less than one hour did.

It is not just magnetic fields due to cathode ray tubes, power lines and transformers that present health hazards: transmissions on the whole of the radio-frequency spectrum can do so too up to the microwaves used for line-of-sight communications and for cooking. Microwaves may even induce severe depression. Roger Coghill points out in his book *Electropollution* (1990) that of twenty-three British microwave scientists who have died while working on defence-related projects since 1982, three died of brain tumours and the rest in circumstances suggesting suicide.

Electricity consumption in Britain increased almost four times between 1955 and 1988 as a result of the growth process. However, the risks to health increased considerably more because the voltage carried by many overhead lines was raised to increase their capacity. In addition, many people acquired dangerous appliances, like all-night electric blankets, which the EPA has called 'probable human carcinogens', and bedside radios which could scarcely be more hazardous as their transformers create magnetic fields within a foot or two of a sleeper's head. There has also been a huge rise in the volume of radar, radio, television and microwave signals since 1955. It is impossible to quantify this increase but some indication of its size can be gained by remembering that there were only two television channels and three national radio stations in 1955; car phones, local radio stations and additional television channels have all developed since then. One novelty, the cordless telephone, which could represent a particularly serious threat because the handset is held right beside the head during use, has been classified as a 'possible human carcinogen' by the EPA.

The health effects of radio signals and electromagnetic fields are thought to be cumulative, and we can expect them to become increasingly apparent over the next ten or twenty years. A consensus seems to be growing that they lower the body's ability to resist disease by damaging the immune system, and Coghill suggests they are linked with some cases of AIDS. The immune defences of the large number of people suffering from myalgic encephalomyelitis may also have been damaged by electro-pollution exposure.

INCREASING NOISE

A rather less insidious cause of ill health as a result of economic growth is noise, particularly that from transport. Because the OECD is dedicated to achieving 'the highest sustainable economic growth and employment and a rising standard of living in Member countries' the information it gives on noise pollution in *The State of the Environment* (1991) is of especial interest:

Over the period 1970 to 1990, the state of the noise environment and the level of exposure to noise stabilized, at best, in the case of blackspots but got worse in the grey areas as far as transport noise is concerned. The major cause of increased noise levels in OECD countries ... has been the large growth in transport ... However, the trend of exposure to noise, as measured by the level of noise at the facade of the dwelling, has varied since the 1970s. During that decade, the situation at every level of exposure worsened, mainly because of the increase in traffic and urban development ... Subsequently, from the early to the mid-1980s, there was relatively little overall change as improvements in noise blackspots were offset by increases in grey areas ... Governments never really got to grips with the problem.

The report estimates that every second person in OECD countries is exposed to 'uncomfortable and unsatisfactory' levels of noise. This has had serious effects on their health:

For a long time it was thought that the body could adjust fairly well to noise, i.e. 'get used to' it, but recent observations have shown that this is not the case. For example, Europe-wide research has shown that even after several years of exposure to noise, cardiac response remains high.

Hearing damage is only one of the harmful effects of noise; continuous noise can induce non-auditory physiological and pathogenic effects (such as a rise in blood pressure or an increase in the risk of cardiovascular disorders). Noise thus comes under the vast category of contributory stress factors in disorders of the cardiovascular and digestive systems. It has been observed that the number of medical prescriptions, psychiatric and psychotherapy sessions, and the level of consumption of tranquillizers and sleeping pills are higher in noisy urban districts than quiet rural ones.

Sleep serves to repair the consequences of physical and mental fatigue and thus helps to maintain the metabolism in good working order and to keep people fit. Research has shown that exposure to noise during sleep both changes the duration of sleep and diminishes its quality by altering the phases (from deep to light sleep) – something the sleeper does not perceive.

THE LONG-TERM CONSEQUENCES

What all these examples demonstrate is that, just as humankind is threatening the health of the planet by the scale and nature of its activities, it is also threatening its own. We have adulterated our diet, polluted our soil, water and air, and exposed ourselves to noise, to unknown quantities of biologically active chemicals, to electromagnetic radiation and to magnetic and electrical fields. No-one can say what the consequences will be, except that they are bound to be bad. The increase in cancers and allergies is evidence of that.

Something even more fundamental may be going wrong, however. Ronald

Finn was incorrect when he said that our most sensitive cells are in our brains. They are in our ovaries and testicles and, since a woman has her life's stock of eggs from the time she is born, she has to be particularly careful not to let radiation and chemicals damage them although each one is naturally very well protected until a few weeks before it passes into the womb. But despite this protection and no matter how careful she is, some damage will be done and her fertility will decline rapidly after the age of thirty. Moreover, a thirty-five-year-old woman is twice as likely to have a genetically faulty baby as one of twenty-five.

A normal man, on the other hand, makes a thousand sperm cells every second and it is thus in human semen that the first evidence of any genetic damage we are doing ourselves is likely to turn up. Additives, pesticide residues, many organic chemicals, electromagnetic fields and radio waves all have a harmful effect on human sperm. At the February 1991 meeting[11] of the American Association for the Advancement of Science in Washington, Gladys Friedler of the Boston School of Medicine said: 'Paternal exposure to drugs, alcohol, radiation and workplace toxins has been reported to produce a wide spectrum of problems, including stillbirths, spontaneous abortion, growth retardation before and after birth, childhood leukaemia, brain tumours and behavioural changes.' In her experiments, she added, the learning power of the offspring of male rats dosed with morphine some time before mating had been impaired.

Another speaker, Leonard Nelson of the Medical College of Ohio, pointed out that a man's testicles were extremely sensitive and that sperm could be easily damaged by substances including tobacco, industrial chemicals such as flame retardants and plasticizers, pesticides, and common analgesics and antihistamines. According to World Health Organization figures, he said, about half of a normal man's sperm was damaged. Yet when I inquired, Patrick Rowe, a medical officer in the WHO's human reproduction division, told me that as far as he knew, no studies had been carried out to establish whether there had been a long-term decline in the quality of sperm. A literature search and contacts with other specialists in the field also failed to trace a single paper on trends in either male or female genetic health,[12] although several reports on seasonal variations in semen quality turned up. Dr Nelson told me that he had called attention in his talk to the absence of studies of environmental contaminants on the male reproductive function. The work that had been done had focused on the woman whereas both partners were quite clearly at risk, he said.

When this book was at final proof stage, *The Independent on Sunday* reported that a research team in Copenhagen had studied data from almost 15,000 healthy men in industrial countries and found that the average sperm count had fallen by half between 1940 and 1990. Further details were not available because the findings had not yet been published in an academic journal. However, a researcher told the newspaper that he thought a build-up of toxins in the environment was to blame.

'You'd be alarmed at what I see here,' a doctor at the Well Man clinic in Dublin told me. 'Damaged sperm, sperm with no tails, a real mess. The motility is often less than 10 per cent. Something must be going wrong.' It seems almost certain that we are damaging our ability to reproduce ourselves, and the quality and health of future generations, and very little research is being done on the subject. Could the fact that reproduction rates have fallen below replacement levels in every member-country of the Council of Europe except Ireland, Cyprus and Turkey be due in part to the way we have exposed ourselves to radiation and chemicals in pursuit of economic growth?

8

How Growth Damaged Family and Community Life

When accumulation is rushing forward at a headlong pace ... under the wild kicks of technical progress ... society reels along blindly in everything that ultimately matters to the quality of its members' lives.

The ultimate fruits of civilization are slow growths that need a stable environment and the economic motive running loose in circumstances that permit or compel violent economic change must wreck this environment ... Name a society whose economic advance delights its statisticians and you name one in which the good qualities of an earlier life are decaying and in which no new civilization has emerged. – D. M. Bensusan-Butt, *On Economic Growth* (1960)

Strictly, we have done enough. We have seen that since healthy people are happy people, the fact that the level of health declined in Britain between 1955 and 1988 because of attempts to accelerate the growth rate means the British people almost certainly became less happy about their lives, just as Arthur Lewis warned they might. We have also seen that long-term health and, probably, genetic integrity and reproductive success were being progressively undermined by pollution produced by the technologies required to make growth occur. We would be quite within our rights if we stopped our inquiry at this stage, concluded that Britain's doubling of national income had had disastrous consequences and began to investigate how growth could be stopped.

Packing up now, however, could be a mistake. The growthmen are unlikely to accept that they are beaten. They might, for example, argue that there is no such thing as a free lunch and that the benefits of growth could not have been expected to be costless. But what are the benefits? The ones that most people name are the greater numbers of young people undergoing further education, the shorter working hours, longer holidays with pay, better housing and of course the vastly greater stock of consumer durables like videos, washing machines, fridges and cars. We therefore need to look at these to see to what extent they really were benefits and, if so, the products of economic growth. We must also review the other quality-of-life factors we identified in chapter 1 to see whether changes in those areas strengthen or weaken the case against growth. Let us start with the factor that people interviewed in the SSRC survey thought was most important – the strength of family and community life.

In the beginning, the inhabitants of Britain lived as members of tribes or clans, on which they relied for security and support. Later, in areas conquered by the Normans, they received assistance in times of hardship from the church or their local lord, who was bound by the code of *noblesse oblige*. Later still, when the growth of commerce and the rise of the town caused the feudal system to break down, the extended family provided support, until it too was displaced by the nuclear family, in which husband and wife brought up their children alone and relied on the state rather than relatives for help in life's crises. In the years after 1955, however, even the nuclear family went into decline, with increasing numbers of people living alone – the proportion rose from 17 per cent in 1971 to 26 per cent in 1988 – and with 14 per cent of children being raised by just one parent. Six times as many marriages broke up in 1988 as in 1955, and 25 per cent of all children were born out of wedlock, compared with 5 per cent thirty-three years before.

But are these radical changes in social patterns of relevance to us? Did growth cause them? And if it did, do they really represent a deterioration? Could it not just be that people had more freedom than ever before – as the growthmen had promised they would – and were thus able to get out (or stay out) of relationships that had become insufferable?

Economic factors – especially the increasing monetarization of life – played a role in bringing about the breakdown of the nuclear family, as the historical sequence suggests. David Barker of Relate (which was known as the Marriage Guidance Council until the number of cohabiting couples made that title out of date) thinks that social, financial and legislative factors were all involved. 'It's not unreasonable to say that the financial ability of women to survive after divorce caused a lot of the change,' he told me. 'An increasing number of divorces are at the instigation of women. The men are often surprised: they thought they were doing nicely, but the women say enough is enough. They think that life will be better after divorce, but it often does not work out like that.'

Duncan Dormor, the information officer of another organization obliged to change its name – from the Marriage Research Centre to One Plus One Marriage and Partnership Research – thinks that increased employment opportunities for women played a part in the growth in numbers of divorces. Other factors were a decline in religious belief and a change in people's values. 'Research has shown individualism and materialistic attitudes to be associated with divorce,' he says.

The national obsession with raising GNP caused the main value change. A society was created in which wealth creators – those actively involved in the productive process – felt superior to other mortals. Paid work became much more important than anything done in the home, even something as literally vital as raising the next generation. As a result, the woman's traditional roles as mother and homemaker were seriously undervalued and increasing numbers of women felt that they had to realize themselves in other ways.

Other growth-related changes encouraged this value-shift. It was extraordinarily boring, especially for someone who had previously held a high-powered job, to be stuck on a housing estate all day with toddlers, scarcely seeing another adult. In earlier generations, a middle-class mother had servants to supervise and a nanny with whom she could leave her children when she wished to get on with other aspects of her life. The working-class mother had friends and neighbours dropping by, and usually lived close to the rest of her family; she also lived near the shops, which provided another point of social contact. Today nannies and family support systems have largely disappeared, and isolation is heightened because people move house more often, usually in connection with the husband's job; the average stay at one address is now seven years. A survey[1] by the Henley Centre for Forecasting found that a majority of people, and especially those under thirty-five, had very little in common with their neighbours and had limited contact with them.

Consumer durables have also helped to make women more isolated. For the middle class the arrival of a washing machine meant that the washerwoman or the laundryman no longer had to call; for the working class, it saved visits to the launderette. The fridge meant that shopping for perishables could be done less frequently, cutting down chances for people to meet. Television removed the need to go out to be entertained. Even the telephone reduced face-to-face contact. But the consequences of the car were most serious of all: not only did its widespread use destroy the corner shop and allow houses to be built long distances from community meeting places but by using it, people cut themselves off from the contacts they would have made had they walked, cycled or stood queuing for a bus. Moreover, as a study[2] in San Francisco has shown, contacts with people across the street fall sharply as the volume of traffic grows. People living in quiet streets with 2,000 vehicles a day passing averaged three friends and just over six acquaintances. In busy streets, however, those with 16,000 vehicles a day, they averaged 0.9 friends and 3.2 acquaintances.

Because views about what comprises depression and people's readiness to acknowledge that they have it may have changed substantially over the years, there is no evidence that the increasing isolation of women at home with young children has led to an increase in the illness, although this may well have been the case. Nevertheless, twice as many women as men seek medical help for depression, and married women with children are particularly vulnerable. 'High rates of many mental illnesses for women are particularly accounted for by married women: single women have lower rates although for those divorced, separated and widowed, rates are often high,' writes Eugene Paykel, professor of psychiatry at Cambridge University in a 1991 paper on depression in women.[3] 'For men, the ratio is reversed: those who are single have higher rates than those who are married. For men, marriage appears to be protective, for women, detrimental.'

Paykel cites studies showing that married women aged between twenty and forty – those in their child-raising years – are particularly liable to neurotic as opposed to psychotic depression. He reviews alternative explanations for the greater incidence of depression among women, such as hormonal changes and a greater readiness to visit the doctor, and concludes that these can only account for a small part of the excess and that social factors are much more important. 'The housewife role is associated with low social status. Social discrimination makes it difficult to achieve mastery by direct action and assertion, inequities lead to legal and economic helplessness, dependency on others, chronically low self-esteem, and low aspirations. Learned helplessness is induced, starting from childhood socialisation, self-images and expectations.'

In view of their isolation and low status as housewives, it is no wonder many women are so eager to get back to work after having a baby. However, this can actually cause depression if there is bad social support, as Paykel points out. Moreover, although being at work again can relieve isolation it does not always fulfil a woman's need for the deep relationships that previous generations of women were able to generate with their children, relatives and personal (as opposed to place-of-work) friends. A vague sense that something is missing in their lives can creep over women and cause some to embark on affairs. Moreover, since the fact that they are working brings them into regular conflict with their husbands over whose job takes precedence and who is principally responsible for the children – battles they usually lose – it is all too easy to think the grass is greener elsewhere.

Unfortunately, the argument that marriage deteriorated because of conditions engendered by the emphasis on growth cannot be proved; the statistics to support it do not exist. Marriages have always broken down: the fact that divorce increased does not necessarily show that any more were doing so, although we may suspect that this was the case. What we can say with certainty is that economic, moral and legislative changes made divorce a more popular solution to an age-old problem than it had been in the past. We can also say that divorce was very damaging for the couples involved. A 1991 report by One Plus One based on the results of more than eighty research studies showed that divorced people were far more likely to die prematurely than married people. 'Marital breakdown generates a great deal of continuous stress over a long period which has an impact on both bodily function and on mental or psychological function,' the report said. As a result, the body's immune system was compromised and the incidence of cancer rose significantly. Divorced people of both sexes were four times more likely to commit suicide than those remaining married and divorced men were twice as likely to die from heart disease and 2.4 times as likely to die from strokes. Health problems experienced by both sexes included headaches, anxiety, muscular tension, hypertension, chest pain, coughs, asthma, indigestion, diarrhoea, dry skin and tiredness. In short, the One Plus One data go a long way to confirm an American finding[4] that an unsatisfying marriage is better than no relationship at all.

Divorce has also had long-lasting and extremely damaging consequences for the children affected by it. The National Survey of Health and Development, which has followed the fortunes of 5,362 babies born in the same week in March 1946, assessed children from broken homes in their early twenties and found[5] that half were under-achievers, educationally disadvantaged and in poor jobs, a much higher proportion than was the case for children whose parents' marriages were intact. The children of divorced parents also drank and smoked more. They lacked self-confidence, put themselves down, and were often still very angry. Delinquency was much higher, particularly among those whose parents had split up before the children were five. When they were aged thirty-six, the pattern persisted: the men were in low-paid jobs or unemployed, and many of the women (but not the men) were drinking a lot and suffering from significant psychiatric symptoms.

Similar repercussions for children have been reported in a study of sixty middle-class families that began in California in 1971. This project, however, unlike the British one, also followed the progress of the parents involved. The most surprising aspect of the study, the first fifteen years of which are described by Judith Wallerstein and Sandra Blakeslee in their book *Second Chances* (1989), is how few problems divorce seemed to solve. It did not end the conflict between the parents, who continued to fight over the phone and when dropping off or picking up children. Nor did it give many parents a happier future: after ten years, half the children had seen a father or mother get divorced again. At this stage, too, 50 per cent of children still had a parent who was angry, 25 per cent had suffered a severe drop in their standard of living and 60 per cent felt rejected by at least one of their parents. Nor had the fact of the divorce eased the children's memories of the behaviour which preceded it. 'Children who witnessed violence between parents often found these early images dominating their own relationships ten or fifteen years

later. Therefore, while divorce can rescue a parent from an intolerable situation, it can fail to rescue the children,' the authors write.

The damage to the boys tended to show itself in disruptive behaviour at
school but both boys and girls suffered nightmares, bed-wetting, nail-biting,
and speech problems, some of which persisted. The most serious effect on
the girls, however, was that they felt abandoned physically and emotionally
during adolescence and lacked a model for their own relationships. This led
them to enter multiple relationships with men and to make impulsive marriages.

Besides divorce, British children have also suffered from the rise in illegitimacy and the increase in cohabitation. Of the 25 per cent of children
born outside marriage in 1988, over a third had their births registered in
their mother's name alone. The rest had their father's name placed on their
birth certificates too, indicating, in the view of some commentators, that
their parents were in a fairly steady relationship. Yet that these relationships
fell far short of marriage is clear from an analysis of Office of Population
Censuses and Surveys data by Ronald Gordon, reported in the *British
Medical Journal* in January 1990. Out of every thousand legitimate children,
3.4 died in the first four weeks after birth; the corresponding figure for
babies born to cohabiting couples was 5.2 and to single mothers, 7.2. As a
result, the number of babies dying in their first four weeks is higher in
Britain than in some other European countries. In Britain in 1986, for
example, the overall figure was 5.3 per thousand; in Ireland, where cohabitation and illegitimacy are less common, it was 4.8.

The human cost of promoting wealth creation above social goals has
therefore proved extraordinarily high. If British divorce rates stay at their
present level, one-third of all marriages will break up and between a fifth
and a sixth of children will be the subject of bitter battles between their
divorcing parents before they reach sixteen. Alternatively, fewer couples
might marry – 22 per cent of men aged 30-34 were unmarried in 1987 as
against 15 per cent in 1980 – and the illegitimacy rate could reach the 50
per cent figure it is in Sweden.

But if the pursuit of growth has damaged family life, how has community
life fared? Has it blossomed as a result of increased personal mobility and
additional leisure time? The answer is no. In almost every field – in women's
groups such as the Townswomen's Guild and the Women's Institute, in the
churches, amateur dramatic societies, local sports and gardening clubs, and
youth organizations like the scouts and guides – the level of participation
has fallen. Even the local pub has suffered, with more people preferring to
drink at home. There has been a major cultural shift away from seeking
recreation with one's neighbours and towards finding it with one's friends or,
more often, at home with the television.[6]

DETERIORATION IN THE WORLD OF WORK

In 1958 an economics professor at the London School of Economics, A. W. Phillips, published a paper[7] that was to have a profoundly damaging effect on millions of lives, although all he did was use historical data to confirm a relationship which non-economists had hitherto regarded as entirely self-evident. By plotting the annual rate at which wages in Britain rose against the percentage of people unemployed for each year from 1867 to 1913, he produced what became known as the Phillips Curve. He then checked his curve against data for more recent years and found that their points lay grat-ifyingly close. But this was not surprising: basically, all his curve showed was that in years in which the economy boomed, unemployment was generally lower and wages went up more rapidly than when the economy was less buoyant. Nothing really to write home about.

Phillips, however, thought there was. 'The statistical evidence ... seems in general to support the hypothesis ... that the rate of change of money wage rates can be explained by the level of unemployment and the rate of change of unemployment,' he wrote in the concluding paragraphs of his paper. On the basis of the historical data, he added, unemployment would have to run at just under 2 per cent to achieve a zero rate of inflation, given that productivity went up by 2 per cent a year. 'These conclusions are of course tentative,' he went on. 'There is a need for much more detailed research into the relations between unemployment, wage rates, prices and productivity.'

Phillips's idea – that the level of unemployment might explain the level of inflation, and that if this were true, running the economy so that unemploy-ment stayed somewhat above the typical mid-fifties rate of just over 1.5 per cent might stop price rises altogether – proved enormously attractive to the politicians who immediately forgot the author's caveats, just as they had with Pigou. They were excited because Phillips's work made it entirely defensible for them to let unemployment figures rise, as, the higher the figures were, the more downward pressure they could say they were placing on the inflation rate. Lower inflation, of course, meant more competitive exports, and hence better prospects for growth, quite apart from preserving the wealth of those with monetary assets. In essence, what everyone except the radical Left came to accept was that it was unfortunately necessary for an increased number of people to be out of work in order that the rest of the community might benefit through higher incomes. Any moral scruples could be assuaged by supporting higher rates of unemployment benefit.

From this point on the level of unemployment began to rise and rise. In the mid-eighties, as we have already noted, the number of people needing work almost reached 4 million (although the official figures were 'massaged'

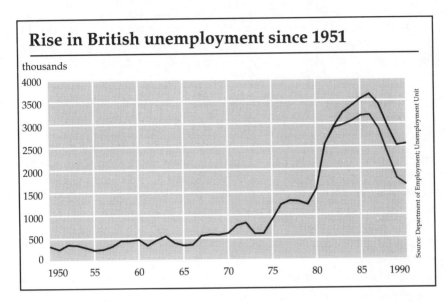

Figure 8.1 Unemployment rose to ten times its mid-fifties level because controlling inflation was more important than human welfare. The official figures were 'massaged' down: the top line shows the position using consistent counting methods.

down as the graph shows by changing the basis on which they were compiled. This was because, at 15 per cent of the work force, they were far above anything that Phillips had suggested might be necessary to stop prices going up). Predictably, Phillips's hypothesis was not rejected when unemployment reached this level: it is supported to this day by the vast majority of professional economists and by the Chancellor of the Exchequer, Norman Lamont. Instead the unemployed were blamed for failing to make the theory work because many of them stopped looking for jobs once they had been on the dole for a year or so and were thus no longer effective in keeping wages down. As a result, dole offices were instructed to make sure long-term claimants were still actively seeking employment before paying out their benefit.

In 1955, with only 232,000 people registered as out-of-work in Britain, economists believed that unemployment was at an irreducible minimum – after all, there would always be some people in the process of moving from one job to another who signed on for a few weeks until they got themselves fixed up. Anyone who did not fall into this category, it seemed safe to say, was unemployable, not seriously seeking work or being unrealistic in their aspirations. In other words, true long-term unemployment did not exist.

Nobody could make that claim in 1988 when fourteen times as many people were without work (the unmassaged February figure was 3,273,400) and the climate was such that those becoming redundant either found another job quite quickly or remained unemployed for the rest of their working lives. According to the Unemployment Unit, 948,200 people, 41 per cent of the jobless total, had been out of work for over a year.

Few people realize just how serious the effects of this massive increase were for the unemployed themselves. The most comprehensive recent assessment was carried out by Christopher T. Whelan and two colleagues at the Economic and Social Research Institute in Ireland. There are very few similar British studies, and those that exist have either used much smaller samples or, because of the difficulties inherent in measuring the mental strain caused by being out of work, have refrained from trying to do so. 'The relationships between unemployment, poverty, financial strain and psychological distress have been the subject of surprisingly little empirical research,' the Dublin team comment in an aside which speaks volumes about social scientists' attitudes.

The ESRI study, *Unemployment, Poverty and Psychological Distress* (1991), was part of a major survey of the extent of poverty and the uptake of welfare services in Ireland. Interviewers asked 6,095 adults a number of questions, to which they could answer 'yes,' 'no,' 'more than usual,' or 'less than usual.' The questionnaire had been developed by D. P. Goldberg in 1972 and used all over the world, so the researchers had some idea of what to expect. The questions were:

1. Have you been feeling unhappy and depressed?
2. Have you felt capable of making decisions about things?
3. Have you felt that you could not overcome your difficulties?
4. Have you been feeling happy, all things considered?
5. Have you been thinking of yourself as a worthless person?
6. Have you felt able to enjoy your day-to-day activities?
7. Have you lost much sleep over worry?
8. Have you felt that you are playing a useful part in things?
9. Have you felt constantly under strain?
10. Have you been able to concentrate on what you are doing?
11. Have you been losing confidence in yourself?
12. Have you been able to face up to your problems?

The questions are so arranged that a 'healthy' person will give negative and positive answers alternately. If anyone gives more than two 'wrong' answers they are likely to be judged to have a clinically significant psychiatric disturbance if interviewed by a clinical psychiatrist. In the Irish survey,

17.1 per cent of the sample had scores of three or more, which was similar to results obtained from an earlier large-scale Australian study. 65.2 per cent of the Irish sample gave no unhealthy answers at all.

The scores were analysed by social class, with the unemployed assigned to their former occupation. The results showed that people in group I – higher professional and managerial (a category which, as we saw in the last chapter, had the lowest mortality rate in Pamuk's studies in England) – had the lowest incidence of psychiatric symptoms, one-third of the level of those in group V, the unskilled manual workers and their spouses. The full results were:

Higher professional and managerial	8.1%
Lower professional and managerial	10.8%
Other non-manual	13.4%
Skilled and semi-skilled manual	19.3%
Unskilled manual	23.2%

When analysed by sex, the scores showed that on average women had a slightly higher rate of distress than men: 19.0 per cent had three 'wrong' answers or more, compared with 15.1 per cent. However, when these figures were further broken down according to marital status, the main reason for the difference appeared, with divorced and separated women having twice the disturbance rate of the same category of men, whose rate was in turn 50 per cent higher than those of their fellows whose marriages were intact. Widows were also under considerably more stress than widowers; and although deprivation as a result of poverty accounted for some of the pressures on them and on divorced and separated women, a significant difference remained when this was allowed for. Single men were the least disturbed group, but most of them were young and probably possessed a youthful optimism.

Psychological stress by marital status

	Married	Separated/ Divorced	Widowed	Single
% Women	17.2	44.3	29.6	14.9
% Men	15.7	22.5	15.5	13.1

When the women's scores were analysed according to whether they were in paid employment or engaged in 'home duties', the team concluded:

Women at work have higher distress scores than men at work. It is not clear whether this arises from differences in their work situations or expectations relating to work and non-work roles. Overall, women in home duties have particularly high distress scores. These are to some extent accounted for by the fact that a number of women are separated/divorced or widowed while others have husbands who are out of work. However, even when we allowed for such factors, women in home duties continue to display lower levels of mental health than men or women at work. The results are consistent with arguments which stress the negative aspects of housework such as its unending and repetitive character, and the manner in which it can prevent women from pursuing avenues to self-development.

Of course, as Whelan comments later on, since many paid jobs for women are also unending and repetitive, the high distress scores of those doing home duties could equally be due to their isolation there.

But regardless of sex, the most remarkable difference in distress scores was between those of the employed and the unemployed (retired people were found to have results similar to those in work). For example, 34 per cent of the unemployed said they were unhappy or depressed, compared with 9.5 per cent of those in jobs. Similarly, almost a quarter of the unemployed said they felt permanently under strain, and a fifth or more felt they could not overcome their difficulties, were not playing a useful part in life, had been losing confidence in themselves, or had had problems sleeping. Many had more than one of these problems – the average number of 'unhealthy' answers for an unemployed man was 2.57 compared with 0.47 for a man in work or on a government employment scheme.

Psychological stress by employment status

	Men		Women	
	Married	Single	Married	Single
% Employed	6.5	4.5	9.4	7.2
% Unemployed	40.4	29.8	24.7	30.9

The stress rate in unemployed married men, most of whom would have had children to support, is particularly striking. But were their problems due to unemployment, perhaps because of the social stigma attached? (The lack of stigma attached to retirement could be the reason that retired people do almost as well as those in jobs.) Or could it be that the relative, if not absolute, poverty unemployment always brings was really responsible for their stress, and that higher dole payments would therefore make those without work as mentally fit as their neighbours in jobs?

Whelan investigated this by comparing how many necessities the unemployed had to do without in comparison with those in work. He selected eight necessities from a list that a 1983 MORI opinion poll in connection with the television series *Breadline Britain* found that everyone should have. These included having a waterproof coat and two pairs of strong shoes, the ability to pay the rent, electricity and gas bills on time, not having to do without heating on a cold day, and the home-manager having had a substantial meal each day for the past fortnight. 22.9 per cent of the employed turned out to be deprived on this measure compared with 52.9 per cent of the unemployed. As one might expect, the degree of deprivation got worse the longer unemployment persisted. 69.1 per cent of those out of work for more than four years lacked one or more necessities compared with 44.4 per cent of those unemployed for less than a year.

Then he compared the psychological distress scores for employed and unemployed people with the same level of primary deprivation. Of manual workers and their spouses who were both unemployed and deprived, 44 per cent could have been judged to be significantly psychologically disturbed, because they gave three or more 'unhealthy' answers. When such people were in work, however, only 23.6 per cent could have been so categorized. Very few manual workers who were not deprived were disturbed when they were in employment – only 8.5 per cent – but 31.1 per cent of unemployed labourers were mentally ill.

Among non-manual workers and their spouses the pattern was similar. 19.1 per cent of those in work and deprived were mentally ill compared with 47.1 per cent of those deprived and unemployed. On the other hand, when they were not suffering from primary deprivation, 7.9 per cent of those in work and 24.7 per cent of those without it suffered from severe mental stress.

The verdict is clear: deprivation is bad, but unemployment is worse. For both manual and non-manual workers the level of psychological stress produced by unemployment among the non-deprived is higher than that produced by deprivation among the deprived. If the deprivation and unemployment occur together, as is common, the number of stress symptoms becomes extreme: five times as many deprived and unemployed people were above the mentally-sick level as were non-deprived workers or the retired. In fact, after correcting for differences in deprivation between the five social classes, Whelan concluded that the different rates at which they experienced unemployment were sufficient to explain all the differences in the incidence of severe psychological symptoms.

But does unemployment-induced psychological stress translate itself into the higher rates of physical illness and death many studies have detected among the unemployed? Whelan's team found that those with three or more 'unhealthy' answers to their questionnaire made on average twice as many visits to their doctors as those with lower scores. And, since visits to the doctor in Ireland are regarded as a waste of time unless one comes away with at least a cough-bottle, they also had twice as many prescriptions written for them. (Amazingly, the average number of prescriptions issued to these psy-

chologically stressed Irish people, 5.6 a year, was less than the 1988 average
for the overall British population, 7.5.) Beyond this, however, Whelan felt
unable to go because social scientists have not yet entirely proved that being
unemployed makes you physically ill: it could just be that the higher rate of
physical illness among the unemployed was due to the fact that employers
tend to dismiss people who are frequently off sick.[8] Nevertheless, in view of
Evans's and Edgerton's evidence we noted earlier that low morale can make
people ill by damaging their immune response, it seems highly likely that
making someone unemployed damages their health and lowers their life
expectancy, since it inevitably dents their morale in a society with a strong
work ethic.

Whelan's study also shows that the psychological stress induced by unemployment disappears quickly once people get back to work. I have paid considerable attention to his results because they show clearly that it is morally
unacceptable for governments to adopt policies that involve an increase in
unemployment however important such policies might be for increased
competitiveness, the control of inflation, or the promotion of growth. Even
if social welfare benefits were increased so that unemployment did not
involve deprivation, policies that caused long-term joblessness would still be
unacceptable because of the psychological stress, illness and premature death
they would entail.

As earlier chapters have argued, two factors – growth itself, through the
introduction of labour-saving technology, and attempts to create an economic climate that would speed growth along – were responsible for the rise
in British unemployment after 1955. In view of this, and given the distress
Whelan has demonstrated that unemployment causes, it is impossible for
anyone to claim that the rush for growth led to net welfare gains, no matter
how big the benefits it is found to have brought in other areas. If attempts at
growth lead to long-term unemployment, they have to be abandoned, whatever the benefits of that growth might be claimed to be. The trade-off
Phillips proposed is ethically impermissible.

Just as Phillips confirmed something non-economists always knew, so too
does Whelan: that work for most people is far more than simply a way of
earning money, and that its loss therefore cannot be made up by cash alone.
Work structures a person's time, gives social contact with other people, provides a source of ideas and experiences and permits the exercise and development of personal skills. But perhaps its most important non-monetary
role is the way in which it not only defines and develops the person's identity
and self-perception but also affects the way in which others see him or her:
an employed person is generally valued in society and paid work is seen as a
morally correct activity. An American psychologist, J. Jahoda, has even
argued[9] that work is the strongest tie a person has to reality and that there is

no need for it to be pleasurable to be beneficial.

Unfortunately, the growth process has undermined at least one of these benefits: the scope that work provides for the development of abilities and skills. As a Marxist writer (and time-served coppersmith) Harry Braverman trenchantly put it in *Labour and Monopoly Capital* (1974), new materials, techniques and machines have been used in an effort 'to dissolve the labour process as a process conducted by the worker and reconstitute it as a process conducted by management.' To this end, he says, individual workers have been regarded as if they were pieces of machinery, and 'progress is seen as a matter of indefinitely increasing the number of tasks that can be carried out by machine. The final triumph is achieved when all the human components have been exchanged for electrical or mechanical ones.'

Braverman's claim may seem rather strong, but there is no doubt that people have tried to find the simplest way of doing things throughout history, and specialization has happened whenever the market has been big enough to warrant it. Xenophon wrote in the fourth century BC: 'In small towns, the same man makes couches, doors, ploughs, tables and often he even builds houses ... In large cities, one man makes shoes for men, another for women, there are even places where one man earns a living just by mending shoes, another by cutting them out.' The only difference made by the Industrial Revolution was that it enabled jobs to be divided up so that they could be mechanized as well, not just so that less-skilled, and therefore cheaper, workers could be employed to do them.

As a result of mechanization and specialization, work has become less satisfying because the average worker now undertakes a more limited range of tasks and has much less responsibility for the product. These changes have also enabled the level of craft education to be cut: instead of long apprenticeships designed to transmit all the skills required for a particular craft, most people now go on brief training courses which only enable them to perform specific tasks. Far from being broadened by the experience, they are narrowed instead.

In his book decrying these changes, *Architect or Bee?: the Human Price of Technology* (1987), an engineer, Mike Cooley, argues that the de-skilling of producers has required the de-skilling of consumers too. 'The elimination of high-level skills in carpentry and cabinet-making is possible because large sections of the public do not appreciate the difference between a tacky chipboard product and one handmade with real wood and fitted joints, or between a plastic container and (say) an inlaid needlebox.' He denies that a concern for quality is élitist, pointing out that quite ordinary working-class or rural families used to pass furniture down from one generation to the next which, although simple, embodied fine craftsmanship and materials. What proportion of the products sold by furniture retailers like MFI will become heirlooms in the years ahead? Not only has work been devalued by the growth process but the products of work have too.

If the effects of growth were bad for adults in the home and at work, they were scarcely better for their children, who, apart from the effects of marriage break-up, lost an important element of their childhood: their freedom to play. The two pictures opposite clearly identify one of the causes: the increased number of vehicles that monopolized the streets. In the fifties it was still safe to let children go out into the street by themselves. They could walk home from school unaccompanied, and get into all sorts of adventures on the way, or use their bicycles to ride round to their friends to ask them to come out to play. The girls would skip in the street or play hopscotch on the pavement; the boys played football, piling their jumpers on the ground to mark out the goals, or cops and robbers, hiding behind walls and hedges so as to be able to jump out and surprise their friends. While daughters generally stayed fairly close to home, often because they had a younger brother or sister to look after, parents did not worry if they had not seen their sons all day: although they were written a generation earlier, Richmal Crompton's 'William' books paint a true enough picture of an early-fifties schoolboy's world, or so at least it seemed at the time to someone who was one.

In 1969, 90 per cent of seven-year-olds in Britain were allowed to cross the road outside their homes by themselves. By 1990, just 22 per cent were allowed to do so, according to *One False Move*, a major Policy Studies Institute report on the effect of traffic on children's lives. Even as late as 1971, over 70 per cent of seven-year-olds went to school unaccompanied by an older person; by 1990 just 7 per cent did. In fact accompanying them had become a major adult activity, taking up 900 million hours a year of their escorts' time. But this was not all. Around a third of primary school pupils were taken to school by car, compared with 9 per cent in 1971. The extra road congestion this caused cost other people time, and it is estimated that, all told, seeing children to school and back took the nation 1,356 million hours in 1990 and cost between £10,000 million and £20,000 million, depending on the value placed on people's time and on the consequences of congestion.

This huge cost was probably the least serious aspect of the growth of traffic as far as the children themselves were concerned. Their lives became much more restricted in every way. By the age of ten 79 per cent of children were allowed to go to leisure places alone in 1971: in 1990 only 43 per cent were. In 1971, 79 per cent of ten-year-olds were allowed to use buses by

Figure 8.2 Children's street games in the early 1950s ... and a similar street today.

themselves, but only 32 per cent in 1990. In 1971 two-thirds of the primary school-goers who owned bicycles were allowed to use them on the road, by 1990, although more of the age-group had bicycles (up from 67 to 90 per cent), only a quarter could do so.*

The fact that more children had to be accompanied meant that they did fewer things. The PSI report's researchers went into their sample schools on Monday mornings and asked children to tell them all the things they had done over the weekend. In 1971 they found that the average child had done 3.4 things by himself and 2.4 accompanied by a parent. In 1990 he had done only 1.8 things by himself – half as many as nineteen years earlier – and 1.7 things with his parents. In total, his number of activities had fallen by 40 per cent. Many parents were unhappy about this: 89 per cent of them said they were 'quite worried' or 'very worried' about their child's safety on the road and almost 80 per cent said they had had 'more' or 'far more' opportunities to go out on their own when they were children.

'The lack of a safe environment enabling opportunities for informal play and socializing outside the home has almost certainly led to an increase in indoor leisure activity,' the report's authors say. 'Children's lives are increasingly monitored around the clock, at home, at school and out of school hours.' They think that this matters, because growing up is essentially a process of becoming progressively independent. Moreover, a child's cultural identity is created by his interactions with the various surroundings in which his life is spent, but the scope of these interactions is being limited. 'The need for independence, in the sense of the capacity to satisfy one's material and spiritual needs by oneself, is common to all children and ... the loss of a private life and the diminishing of psychological identity have emerged as fundamental problems,' they conclude.

Something else that diminished children's opportunities for development between 1955 and 1988 was the increasingly early age at which they started school. In the mid-fifties very few went to school before they were five, and even as late as 1965 only 15 per cent of three and four-year-olds did so, according to the Department of Education and Science.[10] By 1988, 48 per cent of the age-group did, with half of them – mainly the four-year-olds – attending full time. One in every twenty two-year-olds was even going to school.

---

*Many modern parents are worried that their children could be abducted or sexually abused and give this as an additional reason for not letting them out alone. Although the statistics show that this type of crime has not become more frequent since 1955, unattended children could be at increased risk today because so many other children are being escorted everywhere.

Three factors produced this change: the lack of anywhere else safe for the children to go, the desire of mothers to get back to work out of boredom or financial necessity, and the wish of parents to see their children 'get on' in a world in which their eventual educational attainments would determine much of their future. (The situation has deteriorated sharply since 1988 with the introduction of official examinations for seven-year-olds: parents feel that children who arrive at infant school able to read and write will have a head start and the British Association for Early Childhood Education has been getting enquiries about paid coaching for three and four-year-olds.)

Some experts have become extremely worried by the world-wide trend to an earlier start to formal education. David Elkin of Tufts University in Massachusetts wrote in the autumn 1990 issue of the journal of the Irish Pre-School Playgroups Association:

Glenn Doman, best-selling author and founder of Doman's Better Baby Institute, has persuaded hundreds of thousands of parents that early instruction can make children more successful and this, they are convinced, lays the foundation for success in adulthood. [His methods do] work, in a limited sense. [They produce] 'precocious' children who seem wise and able beyond their years, who boost parental ego and entertain guests. Unfortunately, all reliable evidence shows that these gains are short-lived and that the long-term risks to the children are profound.

Superkids are victims of mis-education ... They are confronted with stress that their young psyches and bodies cannot handle. The Domanites ignore the point that the primary factor in learning is the child's internal clock, not the parents' ambition. With rare exceptions, children are not ready to learn symbolic rules, the basis of reading and mathematics, before the age of six or seven ... When parents disrupt a child's natural development, it can backfire. Premature learners often have more learning problems (and fall behind their peers) later in school ... Rather than being equipped to compete in our rapidly-changing world, they are saddled with a crushing handicap.

Among the repercussions of too-early schooling, Elkin says, are classic stress symptoms like headaches, stomach aches and depressions. Children can also become abnormally aggressive because of feelings of inferiority. 'When young children are asked to master skills before they are ready, they develop a heightened fear of failure and a sense of helplessness. As pre-schoolers, they are often problems in their day-care centres and nursery schools. When they reach adolescence, they are prone to drop out of school and engage in delinquency,' he writes.

Although some of the best kindergartens concentrate on play and successfully resist parental pressure to teach the three Rs, their 'play' is carefully controlled and structured and takes place in a limited area, or with the children sitting down. It is very different from the energetic, imaginative and highly physical play that children undertake if left alone. Nor are after-school hours any better: children are collected, taken home, and dumped in front of the television while a meal is prepared, or, if the weather is suitable, allowed out into the back garden to exercise, just as if they were a cat or dog. The scope for running about with other children, climbing trees, walking along the tops of walls and generally having adventures has become very limited indeed.

In short, the increase in traffic during our study period circumscribed the development of most children, and there is strong evidence that this in turn led to at least part of what seems to have been a remarkable rise in the incidence of dyslexia, the learning disorder that prevents its victims from seeing words as a whole, thus making it hard for them to read and write: perhaps sufferers' most common symptoms are that they write letters backwards and are unable to spell. I used the phrase 'what seems to have been' deliberately because, as with depression, no figures exist to prove that there was an increase and if so, to indicate its extent. 'Dyslexia is a vague and nebulous condition' was the reason a spokeswoman for the British Dyslexia Association gave for the lack of data.

The conventional explanation for dyslexia is that it is congenital. Its apparent increase is put down to the fact that teachers and parents only became aware it existed relatively recently: previously, a child's inability to spell was ascribed to stupidity. The fact that middle-class children seem to suffer disproportionately is said to be because their parents are better informed and sufficiently motivated to bring the problem to someone's attention.

An alternative explanation for some cases of dyslexia is gaining ground, however, particularly among educationalists influenced by Rudolf Steiner and Maria Montessori and among occupational therapists familiar with the work of Jean Ayres. It is that if children do not get enough stimuli from their senses, their brains will not become adequately organized and they will have learning difficulties. Getting an adequate sensory input from the eyes, ears and nose rarely presents problems. However, neglected children can be starved of touch (there were some embarrassing moments in 1991 when customs officers asked Irish occupational therapists on their way to work as volunteers in Romanian orphanages what they intended to do with the vibrators in their luggage), and a lack of opportunity for types of play involving movements of the whole body can mean that children do not develop proper processing systems for information about the relative positions of its various parts.

Traditional children's activities such as catching balls, riding rocking-horses, skipping, swinging and hopscotch all involved the child's brain in handling information about relative movement. Playground soccer did so too, and, like some of the others, involved a factor occupational therapists consider particularly important: 'crossing the midline' – using the limbs on one side of the body to do something on the other side (for example, catching a ball on one's left side with one's right hand). But these games are almost extinct, and in those places where they do survive it is generally 'common' children who play them. Middle-class children have picked up the idea from their success-oriented parents that many traditional games are childish and silly and that life has to be taken rather more seriously if they are going to get on. In any case, they might dirty their clothes.

It is easy to see why a child who has not engaged in enough physical play might show symptoms of the 'clumsy child syndrome' such as finding it difficult to stand on one leg with the eyes shut, confusing left and right and being unable to catch. Another sign is nystagmus, involuntary rapid eye movements when trying to focus on something. In 1990 Rod Nicolson and Angela Fawcett of Sheffield University showed[11] that these symptoms are linked with learning difficulties. Many activities, like driving a car, depend on carrying out basic operations without consciously thinking about them. It is this type of automatic activity that dyslexic children are unable to do: they have to think consciously how to perform every step.

In one test Nicolson and Fawcett asked dyslexic and ordinary twelve-year-olds to stand on a wooden beam raised slightly above the floor. All the children were able to do this equally well; however, when they were asked to count, 16 of the 23 dyslexics tested were unable to maintain their balance, and only one was not affected at all, whereas all the normal children had no problems doing the dual task. Moreover, the degree of difficulty the dyslexic children experienced was correlated with their reading age deficit.

The idea that 'clumsy child' symptoms might be linked with spelling and reading problems was first advanced by Jean Ayres, an American occupational therapist in her 1977 book *Sensory Integration and Learning Disorders*. In a more recent book, *Sensory Integration and the Child* (1979), she describes the treatment given to Bob, a boy of almost nine who, after four years at school, could read no better than the average five-year-old. Bob was also behind in spelling and maths, although intelligence tests showed that he was as bright as most other children. Ayres found that when wooden shapes were placed in his hand unseen, he had difficulty telling a square from a triangle by touch alone; he also had considerable difficulty understanding what was said to him, especially if there were other noises at the same time. He disliked being touched and was hyperactive and easily distracted.

The boy's treatment consisted of allowing him to swing for hours on end on a swing made from a single elastic rope – an activity he himself chose. 'If I had not learned to trust children's inner drive and direction, I would not have let him spend so much time doing the same thing over and over.

Sometimes I did feel that maybe I should be arranging a more varied kind of programme but I allowed his inner drive to take over,' Ayres writes.

After four or five months of doing this for two-and-a-half hours a week, Bob switched activities himself and began to climb 'anything and everything', jumping down from wherever he had reached. Later he would swing from a rope hanging from the ceiling and kick a cardboard barrel around the room, making a good deal of noise. Yet after a year, during which he had only had six months of actual treatment, his reading had advanced by three years, his spelling by eighteen months and his arithmetic by about a year. Nor was he unique: many case histories in the sensory integration literature show that children's learning ability can benefit from being allowed to use many different types of play equipment for a few hours spread over several months. If such limited periods of whole-body activity are so remarkably effective, the type of society which the single-minded pursuit of economic growth has created must have left some modern children's play lives extremely circumscribed.

THE CAUSES OF CRIME

If children's lives were restricted by the growth of traffic, those of their parents were limited by the growth of crime. In 1988, 1,680 inhabitants of Islington, an inner-London borough, were asked a wide range of questions about their attitudes to crime by researchers from the Centre for Criminology at Middlesex Polytechnic,[12] repeating a survey carried out three years earlier. The results were astonishing. 81 per cent said they were more afraid to go out alone at night than they had been at the time of the first survey. 49 per cent of the women and 23 per cent of the men said they sometimes felt unsafe from criminals in their homes, up from 37 per cent and 18 per cent three years before. 68 per cent of the women under twenty-five said they took some sort of precaution if they went out at night, such as avoiding certain streets for fear of crime or carrying a weapon. 43 per cent of all women said they were too frightened to use public transport after dark.

These fears were justifiable. During the previous year, 6.6 per cent of the sample had been burgled, 21 per cent had had their vehicles damaged and 17.9 per cent had experienced the effects of some sort of vandalism. The researchers not unreasonably concluded that the level of crime had had a very detrimental impact on the quality of their sample's lives. 'In this sense crime is now a green issue,' their report says.

In terms of offences recorded per head of population, the level of crime in Britain increased eightfold between 1955 and 1988. Although all types of crime went up, the various forms of theft remained the most significant and constituted about 90 per cent of the total at the end of the period, clearly suggesting that most crime has an economic motive and is not aberrant or irrational behaviour, as so often thought. In his contribution to *The Economics of Crime* (1980), David Gordon mentions that in 1965 researchers for the US Presidential Crime Commission got an amazing 91 per cent of the adults they interviewed to admit that at some stage in their lives they had committed acts for which they might have gone to jail, a statistic that indicates that crime is the norm. As the American economist Gary Becker says,[13] 'a person commits an offense if the expected utility to him exceeds the utility he could get by using his time and other resources at other activities. Some persons become "criminals" therefore, not because their basic motivation differs from that of other persons but because their benefits and costs differ.'

The most recent and conclusive analysis of British crime demonstrates its economic basis by showing that in years when economic growth is rapid, crime increases less than in slower-growth years. By drawing graphs of two time series side by side so that that it was possible to see how their movements compared, Simon Field of the Home Office showed[14] that the annual change in property crime and the economic growth rate move very closely in step, as can be seen in the graph overleaf. (Note that the line for growth has been inverted so that the two lines make their turns in the same direction.) One can sense Field's excitement at his discovery:

The relationship is so strong that the last two decades of British economic history are, in effect, written into the history of recorded crime during the same period, with each peak and trough of the economy being accurately mirrored by a trough and a peak in the growth of crime undertaken for gain ... There [were] falls in property crime in 1972-73, 1978-79, 1983 and 1988. Each of these troughs in property crime growth [was] broadly coincident with peaks in consumption growth. The boom in consumption growth during 1987-88, such that consumption growth during 1988 reached a post-war record, appears to explain a large part, if not necessarily all of the decline in recorded property crime during [the same period].

Having found this relationship, Field rushed off to see if it applied at other times and in other places. Sure enough, it did. It explained most of the variations in crime in England and Wales between 1900 and 1949, in the United States from 1970 to 1986, in France from 1973 to 1986 and in Japan after 1972. Curiously, though, it did not apply in Sweden and the relationship took a different form in Germany. For those countries in which it did apply, no alternative variable, such as current or previous levels of unemployment, worked nearly so well.

The relationship exists, Field suggests, because since it is easier to make money legitimately in times of high growth there is less need to turn to crime. But this explanation only covers the year-to-year differences in the

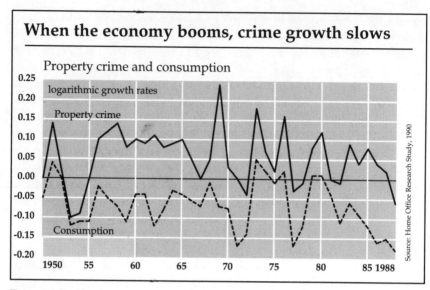

Figure 8.3 Rapid economic growth slows down the rate of growth of crime because there are more legitimate opportunities for young men during a boom. However, the growth process has destroyed many exciting jobs for this group. Note that when growth increases, the line representing it on the graph falls as the scale has been reversed.

rate of increase in property crime, not its steady upward trend, which displays, in his words, 'consistent long-run growth', with surges frequently following years in which the rate of increase has been low. What can account for this? Perhaps more goods were stolen simply because there was more to steal as the growth process moved along. However, Field finds statistical evidence that when the number of young men grows – and young men are the most frequent offenders – there is a disproportionate increase in crime. This, he suggests, is because the opportunities for social advancement cannot suddenly expand to meet the extra demand and there is a consequent search for opportunities outside the law.

But there must be more to it than this. There were 3.36 million young men between fifteen and twenty-four in 1955 and the number rose to just over 4.1 million in 1966. It then stayed roughly the same for ten years before rising to 4.73 million in 1986 and then falling to 4.46 million in 1989. If crime was simply related to the number of young men it would not have increased between 1966 and 1976 and would now be starting to fall. Neither of these happened: a headline in *The Guardian* in June 1991 read 'Car theft tops list as crime leaps 18%'. What Field's statistical analysis picked up were short-term variations in the crime rate as a result of changes in the availability of lawful opportunities whenever the growth rate altered. He failed to account for the long-term rise in crime brought about by the steady erosion of opportunities because of growth. Free trade and new technology have reduced the number and range of exciting jobs open to poorly educated young men. In 1955 the merchant navy offered adventure to 172,000 men, but by 1989 its employment had dropped to 36,000. The armed forces had also cut their recruiting. In 1955, 217,400 young men joined up, including those on national service. By 1989, the figure was only 36,412 and much higher educational standards were demanded.

What economic growth and changes in military technology created between 1955 and 1988 was a sub-class of young men who sought in crime the excitement, status and money they could no longer get legitimately. Indeed, since society measured success by a person's rate of consumption and stock of possessions, they had no other option. Property crime figures are in fact sensitive indicators of the pressures placed on young men when suitable alternative avenues for advancement are denied. The doubling of the suicide rate among them between 1960 and 1990 also indicates that these pressures increased.

DRINK AND VIOLENCE

Field was also able to explain much of the annual variation in crimes of violence, which increased by an average annual rate of 9 per cent between 1950 and 1987, by changes in the amount of beer people drank. He plotted a time series for the annual growth in beer consumption alongside the annual growth of violent crime, and found, as he had with growth and property crime, that both series generally changed direction simultaneously, suggesting that when people drank more beer they became more violent. The consumption of other forms of alcohol did not show this statistical link. When he then put data for unemployment into his model he found that domestic violence went up a year after an unemployment rise, suggesting that long-term unemployment eventually provoked marital disputes.

Field thus had two mechanisms linking violence with growth, one of which tended to counteract the other. When people's incomes rose, he found, they went out more often to pubs and clubs and drank more beer, which led to an increase in violence. On the other hand, when the growth rate was inadequate to generate enough new jobs to replace those being destroyed by the steady introduction of labour-saving technologies, people became unemployed, and the stress they experienced after months of idleness led to increased domestic strife.

The verdict is clear. Property crime increased because society allowed growth to destroy exciting and profitable opportunities for young men, while at the same time urging them to display their status in the form of material possessions. Violent crime increased because when the economy grew, more people went out and got drunk. On the other hand, in periods when the economy contracted and people became unemployed, the pressures that that imposed led to violent marital disputes. Growth loses on every score.

But growth and alcohol combined to create another harmful effect. British drink prices halved in relation to people's earnings between 1958 and 1984 and, since the amount drunk is very price-sensitive, consumption per adult almost doubled. This brought a host of problems apart from violent crime: prosecutions for drunken driving soared, and deaths from cirrhosis of the liver almost doubled. Estimates of the fatal consequences of alcohol consumption prepared by the Centre for Health Economics at York University show[15] that 161,500 years of people's lives were lost in England and Wales in 1986 because of illness, road accidents, fires, drownings, murders and suicides in which alcohol was the prime cause. Unfortunately, there are no comparable estimates for the mid-fifties nor has anyone found an indicator to enable us to track changes in the total level of misery that alcohol creates. The presumption has to be, however, that there was a large increase.

Can we blame growth for these consequences? One of its effects, of course, is to reduce the price of goods made using its new technologies so that, other things being equal, people tend to buy more. But what if this increased consumption does harm, as it does with alcohol? Are members of the public to blame for not limiting their purchases voluntarily? Or is it the government, for not forcing them to do so? Or is it the growth process, for bringing about the changes that cause the problem to occur? With alcohol, growth has to get an acquittal between 1955 and 1988 since there was no need for the reduced price of drink to have been allowed to stand: the government could have increased its tax take and held consumption down. In future, however, this freedom will be lost as taxes are harmonized within the EC. If alcohol consumption increases still further because of even lower prices, the blame for the consequences will have to be placed at growth's door, particularly as the EC was primarily established to facilitate economic expansion.

However, the quantity of alcohol drunk is decided by things other than its relative price. If growth caused people to become dissatisfied with their lives, or stressed as a result of unemployment, or ill because of pollution, and they sought refuge in drink, then the process is responsible for the unhappy results.

THE RETREAT OF CIVIL LIBERTIES

It is ironic that, as one of the arguments in favour of growth is that it increases 'freedom', its pursuit has led to a loss of civil liberties. The outcome was inevitable, however. Since growth involves concentrating manufacturing activity and other forms of economic power, essential services become more exposed to terrorist, criminal and union action and governments are compelled to take draconian steps to protect them from disruption. In addition, technological developments such as the computer and the telephone have given governments the power to keep a closer eye on their citizens, and it would be unrealistic to expect this ability not to be used. Computers, for example, were used to trace people attempting to evade the poll tax in Britain. They checked through the names and addresses on housing, social services and education department records right across the country, an operation that would have been impossible by hand. It may have been legitimate to use computers this way – the government's attitude was that as the law required every adult to pay the community charge it was entirely fair to check up on those using state services – but it established a precedent, and next time the motives for using a computer to hunt someone down may be rather more malign. As it was, the Data Protection Registrar was sufficiently worried to warn the government of the inherent conflict between an effective collection system and individual privacy.

In telecommunications, privacy has already disappeared, because an equipment manufacturer, Plessey, has installed an automatic call-tracing system in its System X telephone exchanges that allows calls to be intercepted or recorded without any physical connection being made to the line. According to *The Observer*,[16] British Telecom employed twice as many tapping engineers in 1988 as in 1980 and 30,000 lines were tapped in the later year at a cost of £10 million. *The Guardian* and ITV's 'World in Action' disclosed[17] in 1991 that trade unionists, disarmament campaigners and even the Vatican had had their calls intercepted. One government listening post, at Palmer Street, London, is linked by cable to BT's international telex exchange and intercepts thousands of messages every day, while another, at Bude in Cornwall, checks private civilian telephone calls transmitted by satellites over the Atlantic and Indian Oceans. At both locations, computers are programmed to spot combinations of key words and names. Supposedly, these intelligence activities are governed by the Interception of Communications Act 1985, but there is no enforcement mechanism, and the brief section of the Act dealing with safeguards covers only calls intercepted legally under warrants issued by the Secretary of State. People who find that their calls are being tapped without warrants cannot take legal proceedings against those responsible without the consent of the Director of Public Prosecutions, who is scarcely likely to give it if the intelligence services are involved. Their only consolation is that illegally gathered information could never be used in court.

There is no doubt that a huge amount of illegal yet official tapping is going on, particularly as an administrative officer on the Joint Intelligence Committee, Robin Robison, resigned in early 1991 in protest at the extent of the abuses. Significantly, the 1985 Act allowed phones to be tapped not just to catch terrorists and criminals but, for the first time, to 'safeguard the economic well-being of the United Kingdom'. Robison told 'World in Action' that British intelligence had engaged in industrial espionage, not only against foreign companies but on British firms including Rolls-Royce, Marconi, and oil and mining companies. 'Anything that was seen to be an integral part of the British economy was looked at quite carefully,' he said.

Police powers were also increased significantly in response to the rise in crime and the heightened exposure to terrorist threats. The Police and Criminal Evidence Act 1984 gave the police the power to stop and search people on the street, to set up road blocks, to detain suspects without charge for up to ninety-two hours and to take fingerprints (and, in Northern Ireland, mouth swabs) by force. The increased road-block powers were used almost immediately to prevent striking miners from moving about the country, in direct contravention of Article 13 of the Universal Declaration of Human Rights. Road blocks were also used against strikers at Wapping in 1987. The Police and Criminal Evidence Act also reduced the freedom of the press by giving the police powers to seize unpublished journalistic material.

Under the notorious Prevention of Terrorism Act 1984, people can be detained for up to seven days without charge and without anyone having to be told of their detention for the first two days. In 1988 the European Court of Human Rights in Strasbourg ruled that the Act contravened the European Convention on Human Rights, to which the British government is a party. The same Act also established a form of internal exile, as under it UK citizens can be banned from entering Northern Ireland or Great Britain. Exclusion orders are imposed without trial, affected persons are not told of the evidence against them, and there is no right of appeal.

A Briton's traditional right to freedom of peaceful assembly and association was taken away by the Public Order Act 1986, which introduced controls over open-air meetings and pickets. It gave the police wide discretionary powers, particularly over the right to demonstrate, and introduced some new, and widely drawn, public order offences. In 1988 another hallowed right, that to trial by jury, was taken away for three offences – taking a car without the owner's consent, driving while disqualified, and common assault – and the list would have been longer had Parliament not objected. Where the right to a jury trial was preserved, the Act abolished the defendant's right to challenge members of the jury without cause. The prosecution's right of challenge was restricted but maintained.

In his 1989 book, *Decade of Decline: Civil Liberties in the Thatcher Years*, Peter Thornton, a barrister, made this assessment of the extent to which freedom has been lost in Britain:

Civil liberties have not just been eroded: they have been deliberately attacked and undermined. The scale of the assault is breath-taking ... First, the state has increased its own power at the expense of individual freedom. It has developed, for example, state censorship by banning radio and television programmes, by interfering with the right of the press to publish. It has effectively extended the laws of secrecy to deny the public's right to be informed. It has increased government control over the individual in the collection and use of personal information.

Secondly, the Government has taken away basic rights in order to stifle legitimate protest. It has diminished freedom of association and freedom of expression. Workers have been sacked for belonging to a trade union. The police have been given wide discretionary powers to ban and restrict demonstrations.

Thirdly, the Government has strengthened the powers of the servants of the state, with a corresponding reduction in the level of accountability of these servants to democratic control. The police have been given unacceptably wide powers of arrest and detention without adequate safeguards for suspects. The police are now controlled and armed by central government and autonomous chief constables. The Special Branch's responsibility is largely undefined. The security services are accountable to no one.

Fourthly, the Government has created a climate of intolerance, with institutionalized prejudice and discrimination. The immigration laws are racially discriminaory. Individual acts of racism are on the increase. Homosexuality has been attacked by Clause 28.* Travellers have been treated as outcasts.

All this has been done with the growing confidence of a long period in office ... The future is bleak.

Thornton's gloomy prognosis has proved valid. Shortly after his booklet went to press, Parliament passed the Official Secrets Act 1989 which makes it a criminal offence, unique in British law, to disclose anything about the past or present activities of the security or intelligence services, even if those activities were illegal.

GROWTH AND THE ENVIRONMENT

We need not delay here. Other chapters of this book describe the ways in which growth has damaged the world's environment by causing pollution,

---

*Clause 28 has become Section 28 of the Local Government Act 1988. Its intention is to prevent teachers openly recruiting children to homosexuality but it has so broad a sweep that it may interfere with local authorities' attempts to curb discrimination against gays and lesbians. The Arts Council has even been advised that almost any artistic or literary activity with an element of homosexuality may now be in breach of the law.

the threat of climatic change, the thinning of the ozone layer and the destruction of topsoil, forests and other resources.

Even if one ignores the world scene and looks at Britain in isolation, the story is the same. In almost every aspect the environment is worse than in 1955. In the countryside, for example, almost all permanent pasture has been ploughed or fertilized since the Second World War, with the result that its rich population of wild flowers has been seriously reduced. The labour-saving switch from hay to silage-making also reduced plant diversity, because, as silage is cut earlier, the annual flowers normally found in a hayfield are denied the chance to spread seed for the next generation. Three-quarters of the country's heathland has been 'developed', 100,000 miles of hedges have been pulled up, and between a third and a half of all ancient woodlands have been felled.

The result? For humans, the countryside has lost much of its appeal. Many more species of plants, birds and mammals can now be seen in a London park than on a walk over a typical farm. For wildlife, there has been a sharp loss of habitat, with many species confined to a handful of sites. Thirty species of birds, three butterflies, six moths and several mammals, such as the otter, dormouse, and pine marten, are perilously close to extinction.

Lapwings, grey partridges, snipe, thrushes, owls, gulls, swallows, green woodpeckers and skylarks are among the species under threat, and the only type of wild birds to be increasing their numbers noticeably in Britain are feral Canada geese and members of the crow family.

According to Robert Fuller of the British Trust for Ornithology, speaking at the British Association for the Advancement of Science in 1989, new farming methods are reducing the abundance of food for birds and other animals.

Shifting the season for sowing many cereals from spring to autumn involved the loss of stubble, which provided autumn and winter food for seed-eating birds. This change also means that many cereal crops are much taller and thicker in the spring than they once were, which makes the land unsuitable for ground-nesting birds, and the increased use of inorganic fertilizers has reduced the number of worms.

Another damaging trend has been to put cattle in stockyards during the winter instead of allowing them to remain in the fields. Food dumps in the winter, which used to be left for the cattle, were important food sources for many seed-eating birds. Now they are no longer there.

Many wild birds used to make their nests in wet, badly drained fields but now that these fields are increasingly ploughed, another important bird habitat is lost. When such fields are ploughed, the bordering strips of rough grass are lost. Rats and mice used to live in these strips and they are vital to the diet of owls. Increasingly, the owls have less to eat.[18]

Fuller's conclusions are those of a scientist. For the real flavour of what it means to see a place one loves destroyed we might turn to Robin Page, who grew up in the forties and fifties on his parents' farm in a Cambridgeshire village and described its decline in his 1975 book:[19]

The parish of meadows and trees has been transformed and disfigured by new developments and modern agricultural techniques that have, in places, completely destroyed its former beauty and peace. Each year more hedges are grubbed out, trees are felled and, at weekends, the high-pitched whine of chainsaws belonging to part-time woodmen competes with the steady hum of the internal combustion engine as week-end motorists drive at a leisurely pace along the roads. The large hedge dividing Tinkers Field in two was uprooted as birds were beginning to incubate and, looking eastwards from the brook, the land has become a treeless tract of gently undulating desolation.

Nearly all the fields now come under the plough, the few remaining hedges are trimmed mechanically each year, and Father's cows are the last to graze on old-established grass. South of the brook, the once lush meadows are cultivated, the last remnants of the rabbit warren have disappeared and all that remains of a once fine row of elms is a pile of unburnt tree stumps in the corner ...

With the increased use of sprays, even where grass fields remain there is an unusual silence, for on hot summer days the chafing trill of grasshoppers has grown steadily rarer and the roadside verges, trim and neat, are usually silent. Bees often vanish as quickly as they appear after acres of flowering field beans have been dampened by a fine drizzle of spray, and wild flowers wither and die. In the autumn, wandering along the hedgerows looking for mushrooms is still a pleasure, but on returning home the basket is nearly always empty, and the only things certain to be found on the land are the machines that dominate it; large self-propelled combines, and the powerful tractors on the larger farms that can pull, with ease, six furrows through the soil.

The aftermath of the harvest has taken on a different aspect and there is a new feeling in the air. With the decline of livestock, little straw is needed and after the combines leave, the fields are fired and the stubble burnt. At dusk, the crackle of hungry flame grows and a fierce glow lights the night sky, while on still, warm days the sun is shrouded by a pall of mist and smoke which its rays only weakly filter through. Where care is not taken, hedges and trees are lapped by flame, fanned out of control by dry winds, and the scorched branches never again burst into new life. The fields wait charred and black for the ploughman, relieved only by the spotless white undersides of the lapwings as they take to the air in sudden and erratic flight.

The only really positive environmental change to take place during our period was that many rivers were cleaned up between 1958 and 1980. By 1985, however, 2.5 per cent of them had deteriorated again, largely as a result of pollution from farms,[20] and a more recent survey by the National Rivers Authority[21] has produced evidence of a further decline. In fact, wherever one looks, locally, nationally or globally, economic growth has had extremely grave environmental consequences.

Sir Arthur Tansley, the ecologist who coined the term ecosystem, was once asked what exactly he understood by conservation. He replied: 'It usually means keeping things much the same as they were when the speaker was young.' When I first heard this remark I thought he was suggesting that environmental concern was motivated by a false nostalgia. However, after reviewing the evidence in this chapter of the extent to which the quality of life has declined, I am sure he was not. The widespread feeling that things were better in the past is not false and should not be dismissed as a natural yearning for the energy and optimism of youth. But if our instincts are correct and things were better, why are we so reluctant to admit that our system has caused us to go so badly wrong?

9

What Has All the Growth Done?

'After bathrooms they want central heating and poodles,' Mrs Arkwright thundered on. 'We all know what central heating does to you. Dries up yer natural juices dun't it?' – Jeanette Winterson, *Oranges Are Not the Only Fruit* (1985)

So far, the weight of evidence about the impact of growth in Britain between 1955 and 1988 has been depressingly negative. Surely the process must have brought some benefits, especially as it has been advocated so enthusiastically by so many for so long? To achieve a balanced appraisal, we must make a determined attempt to identify any good things it has brought about.

SUPPOSED BENEFIT 1: THE EXTRA GOODS AND SERVICES PRODUCED AND
CONSUMED

As the population of Britain was well fed, clothed and cared for in 1955, any gain in the quality of their lives produced by the increased availability of consumer goods and services is likely to have been small. Indeed, if their level of wants was increased by the growth process, as Nordhaus and Tobin and Sir Arthur Lewis warned it might, there could even have been a deterioration, especially if there was an increase in the number of 'regrettable necessities' they were forced to buy to ensure that the changes taking place all around them did not damage the way they lived. We have already seen that the incomes of the bottom half of the population fell in relation to the middle class. This could have left them less satisfied with their stock of possessions, even though it was far greater than that of their parents. Moreover, this effect could have been heightened because advertising expenditure went up by more than five times in real terms between 1950 and 1986, and was deliberately deployed to make people dissatisfied and yearn to consume more. Similarly, the middle class may have been exposed to even more pressure to keep up with their peers in a segment of society that, having adopted the growth target, placed material accumulation above almost everything else.

So, was there a net welfare gain as a result of the increased consumption? We cannot tell as there is no way of measuring welfare directly. However, two indicators – the level of savings and the level of consumer debt – might give us a clue. If people save, it could be argued, it means they are relatively happy with what they have and want to make provision for their future. Conversely, if they borrow to buy a better house or a new car, the obvious implication is that they are dissatisfied with their present ones and are prepared to sacrifice part of their future income to replace them.

On this line of argument, there is no doubt that the level of satisfaction in Britain in 1988 was very low: net consumer borrowing as a proportion of disposable income reached almost 17 per cent while savings dropped to 1.3 per cent in the third quarter, the lowest since quarterly records were first kept in 1955. However, since it could also be argued, as the Treasury did at the time, that 'if people find that they are wealthier than they expected to be, they are likely to feel less need to save and more likely to take on more borrowing, so that the buoyant equity and housing markets have probably contributed to the fall in the savings ratio,' then the boom in borrowing was because people felt secure, happy and expansive and were buying more possessions for the significant extra satisfaction they would bring.

In the present state of economics, no-one can say whether the 'more secure' or 'more dissatisfied' explanation best covers the increase in debt. I suspect both might apply, but to different groups of people, since only a section of the population got wealthier. Some people certainly got into debt out of necessity. In May 1987, while the housing and stock markets were soaring upwards, the National Consumer Council stated that debt had become the most common problem being reported to it. One-third of all clothes, shoes, furniture, cars and household goods were being bought on credit, and the proportion of accounts in arrears had grown from 5 to 7 per cent since 1974. 'The figures tell a story of human misery, as families struggle with mounting bills, demands, summonses and court orders, and experience the fear of disconnection, eviction and the loss of household possessions ... For families on low incomes, difficulties in paying bills are the rule, not the exception,' the council said.

If there was an increase in misery, with families at the bottom getting deeper into debt buying consumer goods out of need or to keep up with the class above them, then, as Pigou said, even if the quality of life of the majority improved by leaps and bounds, we cannot say that there was a gain in the national quality of life as we cannot set off one group's gains against another's losses. Moreover, just because most households had a car, television, video, vacuum cleaner, washing machine, fridge, freezer and microwave in 1988 does not automatically mean that there was a gain in the quality of life over 1955 when they had not. We do not want consumer durables for themselves but for the services they give. No-one gets a television set because they want a cathode ray tube in a plastic case: they want entertainment. Similarly with the fridge and the freezer: we do not buy them because they look nice but to keep food fresh so that we have to go to the shops less often.

People in the early fifties did not have to manage without the services that today's consumer durables provide but obtained them in other ways. They did not need refrigeration as they had marble slabs and porous pot containers in their pantries to keep foods cool. In any case shops were nearer home, so they could purchase perishables more frequently, and if they could not shop themselves, an errand boy would call. The well-off sent their washing to the laundry or had it done by a charwoman; the less prosperous did it themselves with a washboard and tub. Today most laundries have ceased business, chars have become extinct, and washboards are no longer made. In those days entertainment came from the radio, friends, the pub, and the cinema, although television was developing rapidly, particularly after the launch of ITV in 1955. Now only city-centre cinemas are left, and friends in most cases live further away so a car is needed to go out for the evening. In short, because life-styles have changed and many services have been discontinued, people have had to purchase consumer durables to enable them to cope. As a result, we cannot rely on economic principles to tell us whether the acquisition of these goods made anyone better off.

However, to say that consumer durables are regrettable necessities that replace discontinued services is to sell them short. A washing machine, a car or a microwave might, for example, save time. But time-saving is not an end in itself: the only point in saving time is to be able to spend it in another way. Consequently, if the widespread introduction of household appliances has given people more time, this will show up in the hours they spend at work or at leisure and we will be able to assess its benefits when we examine those areas. Alternatively, life in a house equipped with consumer durables might save its occupants trouble. For example, it could enable them to enjoy a wider variety of foods or entertainment than was available to them previously. They might not have to plan quite so carefully, remembering to put the laundry out or what to order from the butcher. Nor need they struggle out to be amused at the end of a hard day: diversion is there, on tap.

But even if increases in leisure and convenience can be established, that will still not enable us to say that growth was beneficial. The amount of energy, labour or raw materials needed to provide every household with appliances like washing machines, televisions and refrigerators – everything, in fact, but its car – is really very small. In 1955 Britain produced 1,725,000 radio sets, 417,000 radiograms, 1,771,000 televisions, 1,238,000 vacuum cleaners, 918,000 electric washing machines, 2,963,000 irons, 333,000 electric blankets, 328,000 toasters and £16,644,000 worth of domestic fridges. In other words, the country had the resources to produce the stock of consumer durables it has today, provided the goods were made to be reasonably long-lasting. If the increase in the stock of consumer goods was beneficial – a matter that is open to doubt – growth cannot take the credit because the mid-fifties economy had the resources to accumulate that stock anyway.

SUPPOSED BENEFIT 2: INCREASED PERSONAL MOBILITY THANKS TO THE CAR

Whatever about televisions and washing machines, there is no doubt that the productive resources of the mid-1950s were inadequate to build, maintain and fuel and to provide roads for Britain's 1988 fleet of 18,432,000 cars and 647,000 freight vehicles, both totals more than five times their 1955 level. But while growth made the increase in traffic possible, it also made it necessary: the graph opposite shows just how closely the distances people travel and the amount of freight moved are linked to the level of GNP. Growth and the need for transport go hand in hand. So the question we really need to ask is, 'Were there any beneficial aspects of the increase in travel and transport other than the fact that they made possible the process of economic growth itself?' If we establish that there were, we have to ask whether the gains outweigh the losses that traffic growth imposed.

The motor car serves two functions. That it is a status symbol is demonstrated by the fact that most people wealthy enough to buy a new car sell it long before it ceases to give comfortable and reliable service because it would not do to be seen in anything shown by its numberplate to be more than two years old. Although the possession of a new car can give its owner a great deal of satisfaction for two or three months, I am going to ignore this contribution to human welfare, for three reasons. One is that the new owner's pride of possession has to be set against the envy his purchase generates in other people. The second is that during its life, the new vehicle will cause the succession of people who own it considerable pain: the anguish after the first scratch, the worry as reliability begins to decline, the feeling of slumming as it rattles and coughs its way through its last year's journey to the crusher. And the third reason? Simply that if people did not have cars to show their status they would undoubtedly find other ways.

The other function of the car is the provision of transport, and in this it is like other consumer durables, because moving about in one is generally not an end in itself. A car's job is to get people from place to place so that they can do other things and, consequently, we can judge its value by looking at how many more things people were able to do in 1988 than their predecessors found possible in 1955. Increased activities to do with work we

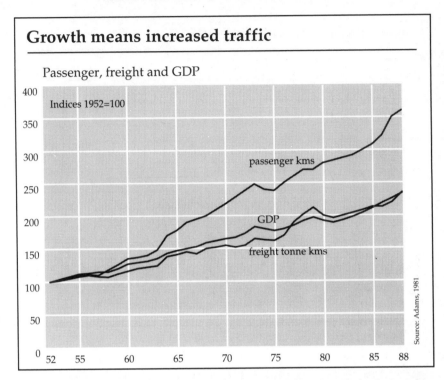

Growth means increased traffic

Passenger, freight and GDP

Indices 1952=100

passenger kms

GDP

freight tonne kms

Source: Adams, 1981

Figure 9.1 The volume of goods moved about Britain increased in step with the rise in national income. However, the distance that people travelled grew even more rapidly.

ignore, since those were part of the growth process: we are looking for welfare gains rather than economic ones. However, if it made the actual getting to work more comfortable and convenient, that would count as a plus. Consequently, the only improvements that concern us are in people's leisure lives, which we will look at later, and in the level of comfort and convenience with which they were able to travel about outside working hours.

Cars obviously made some aspects of travel pleasanter during our period – for example, their owners no longer had to wait at bus-stops in the rain. However, it also made some things less pleasant: traffic congestion meant that buses moved more slowly and all road users spent more time stuck in jams. By the late eighties, the average speed at which people could move in many cities was below that in the days of the horse, and 54 per cent of all journeys in central London were being undertaken on foot. Indeed, things were so bad that in May 1990 the Lord Mayor of London announced that the City's prosperity was threatened by its crowded streets.

The increased traffic and, in particular, the larger freight vehicles (the maximum size allowed by law in 1955 was 24 tonnes; in 1988 it was 38 tonnes) made it too dangerous for people to use the fastest method of travel

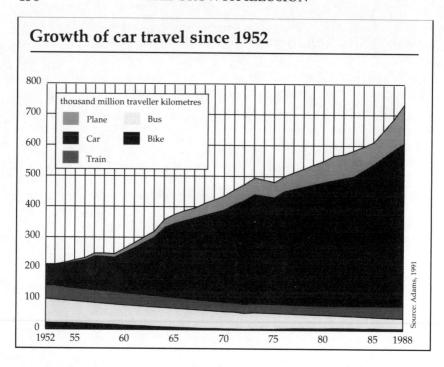

Growth of car travel since 1952

thousand million traveller kilometres

Plane   Bus
Car   Bike
Train

Source: Adams, 1991

Figure 9.2 Although the British travelled much further each year during the eighties than they had during the fifties, they made fewer separate journeys. As the length of journeys increased, they walked or cycled less.

over short distances in a city: the bicycle. Between 1952 and 1988, a period in which car travel increased tenfold, bicycle use dropped by 80 per cent and bus travel halved despite the fact that the average Briton was travelling three-and-a-half times further in the course of the year. This extra travel was not because everyone was making more trips – in fact they were making fewer[1] – but because journeys got longer as the level of local facilities declined. Thus, while the car seemed to be a convenient way of travel, its widespread use created more inconvenience through increased congestion and by reducing the level of services in people's own neighbourhoods. It also removed other, possibly more convenient, travel options, like the bike. As a result, although I cannot prove this, I am convinced that the increase in car numbers produced a welfare loss in transport comfort and convenience alone. However, once one adds in the harm done to other facets of the quality of life, there can be little doubt that the growth in vehicle numbers cut the level of national welfare significantly.

This reduction (if one accepts that it took place) was produced at great cost. In fact a great part of the additional resources generated by the growth process was devoted to moving goods and people ceaselessly back and forward, and in producing the roads, parking and packaging that this activity required. In 1957 the average family spent only 7.9 per cent of its income on motoring and fares; by 1987, according to the Family Income Survey, the figure had soared to 15 per cent, almost all of which was spent on buying, running and maintaining a car. In other words, since incomes roughly doubled, family spending on transport almost quadrupled. Government spending on roads tripled in the same period, rising from £1,401 million in 1955 to £3,915 million in 1988 (both sums in 1988 prices).

SUPPOSED BENEFIT 3: THE IMPROVEMENT IN THE HOUSING STOCK

Perhaps the most obvious improvement in Britain since 1955 has been in its housing stock. Not only was the actual number of housing units in 1988 62 per cent higher than in the earlier year, but their average level of comfort had gone up appreciably too. But, as with the stock of consumer goods, neither the increase in the number of houses nor their internal improvement can be attributed to the growth process. Britain had the resources in 1955 to increase its stock of houses without the need for growth at all. Indeed it was building 317,700 houses a year, a rate that has been exceeded in only eight years since; and had this level of investment in construction continued, either the housing stock would have been much bigger than it is today or the standard of each house would have been much better. Growth in fact made the standard of housing worse, by causing certain areas to decay as a result of pollution and traffic and by encouraging the diversion of resources, especially in the public sector, from house construction to 'productive' projects that it was hoped would generate a national income gain. 203,000 council houses were built in 1955 and only just over 30,000 in 1988. If anyone thinks that this collapse of public authority house building was linked with the growth in homelessness (117,500 families were officially listed as homeless in 1988 according to figures given in Parliament, not counting several thousand people living in cardboard boxes on the streets) they might not be too far from the truth.

Instead of providing proof that growth brings benefits, developments in the housing sector are probably the clearest evidence that it does not. The population of Britain would have been better served if governments had continued taking direct action to improve housing conditions – the reason for the high level of council house building in the early fifties – rather than taking an indirect approach and concentrating on growth in the hope that some of its supposed benefits would manage to trickle down.

On the anniversary of Shakespeare's birth in April 1991, Prince Charles made a carefully researched speech in which he expressed deep personal alarm over the low educational standards being reached in British schools. His views met with widespread support, particularly as that same day the official schools' inspectorate published the results of a survey of seven hundred classes which showed that many primary school pupils were not being taught English satisfactorily. Some months previously the inspectorate had published the results of a maths teaching survey that had revealed similarly inadequate results.

There is evidence that British schools have been growing steadily less successful in teaching basic English and arithmetic for at least a quarter of a century. In 1964, as part of an international research project, English and Welsh 14-year-olds were asked to find the average of 1.50, 2.40 and 3.75. Half of them got the right answer. In 1981, when a similar group were asked the same question, only a third were successful. Other tests, this time by the government's Assessment of Performance Unit, show that performance in maths continued to worsen until at least 1987. In 1982, 61 per cent of eleven-year-olds could divide 256 by 8; in 1987, only 50 per cent could do so.

Although some education experts blame changes in teaching methods in the seventies, recent evidence suggests that a growing lack of parental interest is the real culprit. In a twelve-year survey of forty-nine schools in Buckinghamshire, an educational psychologist, Mike Lake, found[2] that the reading ability of seven to eight-year-olds began to deteriorate after 1985, and that this was accompanied by a reduction in general knowledge – the range of facts that pupils acquire primarily at home. Lake argues that general knowledge is the best single measure of children's ability to learn, their linguistic development, and the time their parents take to discuss things with them. Children who come to school with an interest in learning about the world because of parental attitudes are more likely to take to reading and to most other things than those brought up in an atmosphere of apathy and distrust, he says.

The average decline in reading ability Lake observed was small – about 3 per cent – but it was much worse in areas with a high proportion of disadvantaged families. The deterioration was linked to the length of time spent watching television: Lake mentions that the Assessment of Performance Unit has shown that primary schoolchildren who watch over six hours of television a day obtain significantly lower reading scores than those who watch between two and five hours. 'It certainly looks as though any deterioration in reading is more connected with worsening background factors than with faulty teaching,' he concludes, expressing concern that a decline in performance should be seen in Buckinghamshire, one of the more stable and privileged areas of the country. 'What would one expect to find in a generally far less privileged one?' he asks.

Another cause of the worsening educational performance is the steady erosion of teachers' status, as reflected by the decline in their salaries in comparison with other professions. In 1974, after the implementation of the Houghton Report recommendation that teachers' pay be increased substantially to restore their parity with other jobs, the average teacher got 36 per cent more than the average non-manual worker. By 1988, however, teachers were only earning 8 per cent more and their situation has slipped further since. As a result, it became impossible to attract and keep enough high-calibre people in the profession and the government was forced to mount recruiting drives overseas. According to *Only a Teacher*, a report published by the Royal Society, the British Association and the Association for Science Education in 1991, shortages were particularly acute in science subjects and thousands of teachers without specialist qualifications were having to be used. A quarter of science teachers did not believe they had the experience to teach the subject properly, the report said.

A third cause of the decline is the improper goal the educational system has had set for it by society – and which, to its shame, it has accepted. The public debate that followed Prince Charles's speech illustrated this well. It concentrated almost entirely on how damaging a poorly educated labour force could be for Britain's competitive position. Even the Prince had mentioned this – 'What worries me so much is how we are going to survive in the Europe of 1992 and beyond with such manifest handicaps' – although most of his speech was a robust attack on the attitude that prompted such fears: that the schools' primary function is to supply the economy with suitably grounded young workers rather than to build well-rounded young people. He said he felt 'an overwhelming sadness' that Britain should have allowed such a short-sighted approach to prevail. 'I don't want my children, or anybody else's, to be deprived of Shakespeare or of the other life-enhancing elements which I have suggested should be part of the schooling entitlement of all the children of this country.'

The term 'life-enhancing' is crucial. The purpose of education is to widen the interests of the child and to equip him or her to cope with all aspects of the post-school world, not just the world of work. Getting children through exams – an aspect of an age obsessed, as Prince Charles said, 'with the tangible, with discernible results and with that which is measurable' – should not be a school's main goal. Exams exist to allow employers and others to slot individuals into categories in an increasingly impersonal world. Instead schools should see their role as developing the child's range of interests and enthusiasms. If a young person leaves school with just one overwhelming passion, whatever it may be for, his teachers have succeeded supremely well, regardless of what his exam results may show. In fact, a student with a passion for something will be highly self-motivated and gain better results in exams than someone who does not care. The two tasks of the educational system – to arouse enthusiasms and to impart knowledge – are far from incompatible; it is just that Britain, in its search for growth, has been putting the wrong one first. In any case, how can badly paid, socially disregarded teachers arouse enthusiasms when many have none themselves?

A market research study in 1990[3] found that a lack of passion and enthusiasm was the main characteristic of a sample of 2,000 young people aged between eight and eighteen. Most youngsters, it said, were intellectually and politically passive. Almost the only evidence of dissatisfaction with the status quo was that far more of them intended to vote Labour or Green than Conservative. Their interest in environmental matters was simply a way of rebelling in a safe, arm's-length way: 'There is more interest in the future of the Amazonian rainforests than in the plight of the urban homeless, but even concern for the environment goes little further than ... buying an ozone-friendly aerosol,' the report said. Conformity and escapism went hand in hand. 'While young people are encouraged at every turn to amuse themselves, their interest in the real world around them is diminished.' Few of the sample read books but there was a vast appetite for comics and magazines. Their favourite newspaper was *The Sun*.

Admittedly, the average child spent a few months longer at school in 1988 than in 1955 but, in view of the market research findings, it is hard to believe this did pupils much good as people, or even as future recruits to the work force. Indeed, keeping children who want to be off in the world at school could well be inimical to their future intellectual development, putting them off many of the subjects they are forced to learn for the rest of their lives.

Schools have so much power to damage their pupils that it is by no means clear that a longer education is necessarily a good thing. Not only do schools often make less-academic children feel failures, a self-fulfilling prophesy which dogs its victims for life, but they deliberately establish a set of bad attitudes which is also likely to be permanent. In *The Six-Lesson Schoolteacher*, a widely reprinted article[4] which first appeared in the May 1991 issue of the American publication *The Sun*, John Taylor Gatto, who won the New York State Teacher of the Year Award in 1989, 1990 and 1991, writes that the first lesson he teaches his pupils is: 'Stay in the class where you belong.' In other words, 'Know your place'. The remaining five lessons are:

- Stop whatever you are doing, however interesting, when the lesson ends.
- Surrender to a predestined chain of command.
- Wait for the teacher to tell you what to do and what to study.
- Accept outsiders' judgments of your personal worth.
- Realize that you are under constant surveillance and have no private time.

'This is training for permanent underclasses, people who are to be deprived forever of finding the centre of their own special genius,' he writes. 'It is training shaken loose of even its own special logic – to regulate the poor ... "School" is an essential support system for a vision of social engineering that condemns most people to be subordinate classes in a pyramid that narrows to a control point as it ascends ... With lessons like the ones I teach day after day, is it any wonder we have the national crisis we face today? Young people indifferent to the adult world and to the future; indifferent to almost everything except the diversion of toys and violence ... School is like starting life with a twelve-year jail sentence in which bad habits are the only curriculum truly learned.'

Gatto argues that it takes only about fifty contact hours to transmit basic literacy and arithmetic skills well enough for children to teach themselves from that point on, and there is no doubt that schools designed to help children to develop and follow their own interests would be very different places. However, even if we accept the doubtful premise that the extra* months at school were, on balance, beneficial to those children who enjoyed the experience and did no serious damage to those who did not, was economic growth necessary to generate the resources to enable the nation to provide them? The answer is clearly 'no' since schools are labour-intensive and require relatively few of the goods produced by the growth process. As a result, it is only in relation to higher education that it might be possible to argue that things improved after 1955 as a result of growth. Certainly, the number of full-time students in universities and colleges of further education approximately doubled between our two years, reaching 255,733 by 1988.

However, in an economy that is becoming rapidly more knowledge-intensive as a result of depending on a constant stream of innovations to generate the profits it needs to survive, the level to which the work force has to be trained must rise continuously. Indeed one of Britain's constant fears since the Second World War has been that it has not been training its work force as well as its rivals, particularly those on the Continent. There is not necessarily any intrinsic virtue in carrying out more of this form of training:

*The Department of Education could not supply figures for 1955 but the increase in the average age of leaving school between 1965 and 1989 was only three months, from 15.77 years old to 16.04.

it is simply another activity, like transport, that is necessary to make a modern economy run. The fact that more and more of it is needed is one of the costs of the growth process. Only if the extra training enriches the lives of those who undergo it as well as the economy can it be counted a gain. Personally, I feel that it is enriching to a limited extent, although I have no evidence for saying so, and it is quite impossible to measure the size of any gain.

Although most university and college courses involve elements of both education, which is wide in scope and opens many doors, and training, which is highly job-specific and opens only one, academics seem to agree there has been a pronounced increase in the training content since 1955. If this is so, present-day students may get less intellectual benefit from their studies than their predecessors did. We do not know. But even if we accept that the increased number of people going to college and university in 1988 represented some sort of unquantifiable improvement, was growth necessary to bring it about? The answer, again, is 'no'. In 1955 every fit young man of 18 was required to undertake two years' service in the armed forces. A total of 460,000 men were so occupied that year, far more than the number of full-time students of both sexes in 1988. Naturally, national service tied up a lot of resources – training personnel, equipment, buildings, food, clothing and transport – which, if society had wished, could have been used in other ways. In particular it would have been possible to give the same number of young people an academic education instead of military training and had this been done, 300,000 more students would be at university or college today. On this basis, therefore, despite the doubling of national income, Britain devoted fewer resources to further education and training in 1988 than in 1955. In other words, if there were improvements in education during our study period, economic growth was not necessary to bring them about. However, the evidence we have discussed seems to show that, on balance, things deteriorated and for much of this decline, the drive for growth was at least partly responsible.

SUPPOSED BENEFIT 5: THE INCREASE IN LEISURE

This is the crunch. So far, we have failed to identify any aspect of British life that improved in quality as a result of growth and that could not have been so improved had the expansion not occurred. Instead, in area after area, life seems to have become substantially worse. Unless we find that there was a remarkable increase in leisure – and evidence that additional leisure was what people really wanted out of life – we will be forced to conclude that the growth rush has failed almost totally and in a way that threatens us all.

Increase in paid holiday entitlements

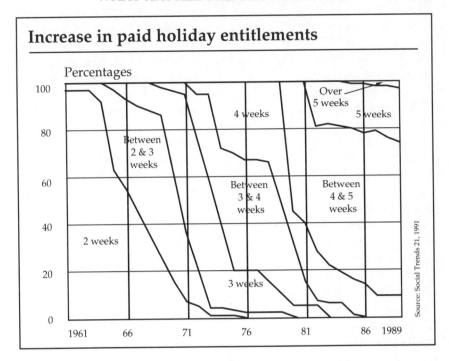

Figure 9.3 The number of weeks' paid holiday to which the average worker was entitled grew from two to five. However, competitive pressures meant that not everyone felt able to take them.

In one aspect of leisure, however, the gain is clear: people are getting longer holidays. In 1955 most employees were allowed a two-week paid break each year while in 1988 they typically got between four and five, as the chart shows. Taking public holidays into account – six days in 1955 and eight in 1988 – the average number of days of paid holiday rose from sixteen to thirty.

However, this gain seems to have been achieved by working longer for the rest of the year. The longest-running series of studies of how the British people spend their time has been carried out by the BBC as part of its audience research. The first survey was in October 1939, and similar ones were carried out in 1947, 1948, 1950, 1952, 1961, 1974/5, 1983/4, and 1988/9. Unfortunately, although the earlier BBC results provide a fascinating insight into life at the time they were done (for example, in 1939, 31 per cent of workers lived close enough to their jobs to go home for lunch) they are not usually directly comparable with the two most recent ones. In spite of this, Jonathan Gershuny of Nuffield College, Oxford, has been able to combine the BBC results for 1961, 1974 and 1975 with those from two surveys by the Economic and Social Research Council in 1983/4 and 1987 to reveal trends covering most of our period.[5] His figures show that in 1961, the average man devoted 45 hours 9 minutes to paid work, including travelling time. By 1987 this had fallen to 40 hours 15 minutes, which is, on the face of it, a significant reduction. However, if we correct both figures to allow for the rise in the level of male unemployment between the two years from 2 to 12 per cent, we find that the average employed man spent 46 hours 4 minutes each week in 1961 either working or travelling to or from his job, and that this had fallen to just 45 hours 45 minutes in 1987.

Further corrections are also required to cover the additional fourteen days' holiday people took in 1987 and the fact that many men were retiring earlier. For example, in 1961, 25 per cent of all men aged 65 and over were still in employment but by 1985, only 8.2 per cent were working. Many younger men were stopping work prematurely too, so that by 1985 only 53 per cent of men aged between sixty and sixty-four were economically active and 82 per cent of those in their late fifties. Ten years earlier, however, 84 per cent of those aged sixty to sixty-four had been at work and 94 per cent of those in their late fifties. In most cases these early retirements were not voluntary. Many were the result of company reorganizations that gave people little choice but to accept a golden handshake and go. Others were as a result of the increased stress associated with modern business life: in a 1977 study of 3,500 retired people for the Office of Population Censuses, Stanley Parker found that three-quarters of those taking early retirement had done so because of ill health or disability, while some of the remainder had done so because they felt they could no longer stand the strain. Unfortunately, Parker's work was done before early retirement became as common as it is today and it seems unlikely that his results would still hold.

When we allow for extra holidays and early retirement, we find that the average man must have spent about 49.5 hours a week in connection with paid work in 1987, compared with 47.9 hours in 1961. The figure of ten hours per working day seems about right: certainly, everyone who travels into London to work is away from home for at least that length of time. Moreover, the figure corresponds closely to one given in the 1991 edition of the official publication *Social Trends*, which states that men spent 48.9 hours on employment and employment-related travel in 1989.

In short, the time saved by increasing labour productivity has not meant a shorter working week. Instead, it has pushed some men out of work altogether, into unemployment or involuntary early retirement, and given many of them too much free time, while those still in work have to spend slightly longer over it than they did in 1961. For this group, any negotiated reductions in the working week have been swallowed up by increased travel times – how many workers come home for lunch now? – and by work that has become more pressured because of the heightened competition. Many salaried employees (and the proportion of these has greatly increased since the late 1950s) feel they have to put in a lot of extra unpaid hours if they are not to be made redundant. According to the Equal Opportunities Commission, British male managers work, on average, 52 hours a week, a figure which takes no account of travelling time, while another study shows that executives' working hours went up by 20 per cent during the 1980s in OECD countries. A third survey, this time of 1,300 businessmen, showed that 40 per cent were taking two weeks' holiday a year or less.

Because Gershuny's averages have to cope with a 600 per cent rise in male unemployment, they can only give tantalizing hints of exactly how employed men's time-use outside work changed between 1961 and 1987. They show, for example, that the average man spent half an hour less sleeping and eating in 1987 than in the earlier year. As unemployed or retired men typically spend ninety-six minutes more in bed or at the table than men in work, the reduction by those in employment must have been even greater, suggesting that workers were living under increased pressure. Similarly, employed men spent less time watching television or listening to the radio in 1987 than in the earlier year, although Gershuny's overall average time went up by four minutes a day to 160 minutes: this is because the surveys found that non-employed men watch eighty-six minutes' more television each day than those in full-time work, and in view of the large rise in unemployment, those working must have watched less.

How the average man spent his day

	Paid work	Unpaid work	Sleep and eat	Outside leisure	Radio, television	Home leisure	Total
1961	6h 27m	1h 34m	10h 47m	1h 24m	2h 36m	1h 12m	24h
1987	5h 45m	2h 7m	10h 15m	1h 50m	2h 40m	1h 23m	24h

Variations from the mean:

Full-time worker	1h 13m	−21m	−22m	−10m	−12m	−9m	0
Unemployed	−5h 41m	1h 41m	1h 14m	41m	1h 14m	50m	0

Women, on the other hand, do seem to have more leisure as a result of the changes since 1961. The question is: which women? Gershuny's figures show that the average woman did about thirty-nine minutes' less work around the house in 1987 than in the earlier year, a change he attributes largely to the extra thirty-three minutes of daily housework being done by the average man and not to the increased stock of domestic appliances. However, since most of this extra housework was done by unemployed men, the majority of women may not have benefited very much. Moreover, since the proportion of women registered as unemployed rose from just over 1 per cent to 8 per cent between our two years and this category of woman spent much more time watching television and on other leisure activities, it is hard to say if the typical housewife, who possibly had a part-time job, had any more discretionary time than her counterpart a generation earlier. What is certain is that the average woman, like her man, felt it necessary to reduce her sleeping and eating time, not something one would expect her to do if we had genuinely attained a more leisurely age.

How the average woman spent her day

	Paid work	Unpaid work	Sleep and eat	Outside leisure	Radio, television	Home leisure	Total
1961	2h 47m	5h 16m	11h 6m	1h 13m	2h 10m	1h 28m	24h
1987	2h 41m	4h 37m	10h 47m	1h 49m	2h 17m	1h 49m	24h

Variations from the mean:

Full-time worker	3h 38m	−1h 54m	−32m	−13m	−23m	−33m	0
Unemployed	−2h 31m	1h 19m	20m	11m	19m	22m	0

In summary then, we can say that although employed men got 112 more hours' paid holiday in 1987 they worked harder and spent longer on activities connected with their jobs to earn them. With women, only those who were unemployed or had an unemployed husband probably had more 'free time' but they were more stressed in other ways. In short, the increases in labour productivity did not bring anyone in work appreciably more leisure: instead, the potential gains were squandered by making three or four million people unemployed and giving many others unwanted early retirement.

But why did economic growth not give people the option of working less and using the time saved on other things, as economic theory predicts it should? The answer is clear: people do not *want* more time to spend at home with their families or out at the pub with their friends. One can have too much of a good thing, particularly if the alternative is to be earning at overtime rates. The more one earns, the more costly it is to take time off. What people did want – and got – were more blocks of days in which they could do something completely different, like going off on holiday or repapering the bedroom. Half an hour off the working day is neither here nor there – which is why people were prepared to use it for commuting – but a completely clear day or two makes a huge difference to the way one feels and behaves.

Leisure is a supplement to work, a dessert rather than the main part of the meal. Few people relish the thought of having nothing but sport and socializing to fill their time for the rest of their days: most want some form of purposeful activity as well, which is why many retired people work for a voluntary organization or join an evening class. In her study *Leisure and Unemployment* (1989) Sue Glyptis suggests that we cannot properly experience leisure without the contrast of paid work, because in a society imbued with the work ethic, leisure has to be earned psychologically.

In the light of Gershuny's work it is not surprising how few leisure activities people undertook in the mid-1980s. The 1983 General Household Survey, for example, shows that only one in four of all men and one in ten of women had taken part in an outdoor sport or activity in the previous four weeks, if walking was excluded. The higher a person's social class, the more likely he or she was to have taken part: including walking, 53 per cent of Group I had been active outside compared with only 20 per cent from Group V. The same applied to indoor sports, such as snooker or swimming, the two the most popular: while on average one-third of men and just less than one-fifth of women had participated in an indoor activity, more than twice as many professionals had done so than had people from the unskilled manual class.

Taking the population as a whole, only 8 per cent had been to a spectator sport such as a football match, 7 per cent to the cinema, 11 per cent dancing and 9 per cent to bingo. On the other hand 98 per cent had watched television, 87 per cent had listened to the radio, 56 per cent had read a book, 44 per cent had gardened, 40 per cent had gone out for a meal and 54 per cent to have a drink, and 92 per cent had either visited or entertained friends and relatives.

Watching television was therefore the most popular leisure activity in Britain in the eighties, taking up an average of 3 hours 46 minutes a day in 1989, according to BBC figures which do not seem to square with Gershuny's ESRC data; the comparable BBC figure for 1955 was just 1 hour 48 minutes, so the increase in viewing has been quite considerable. What effect did this increase have? We do not know, since so many other things were changing at the same time. However, some research results from Canada can give us a fair idea.

In 1973 Tannis Williams, a psychologist at the University of British Columbia, learnt that a town of 2,500 people which had been unable to receive television was to be provided with a signal in a year's time. She immediately began to study the town, which she called 'Notel', using standard psychological tests, and arranged for the same tests to be carried out in two similar towns in the same area, Multitel and Unitel, which had been receiving television for years. Guy Lyon Playfair describes what she found in his book *The Evil Eye: the Unacceptable Face of Television* (1990):

One of her findings was completely unexpected: Notel adults were a good deal brighter than those of the two other towns. They were much better at creative problem-solving tests, and even those individuals who were unable to solve the tasks they were given would try for much longer than Multitel or Unitel people before giving up. As for the children of Notel, they came out at the top of the three-town league when they were given the Alternative Uses Task, a standard test in which subjects are asked how many things they can do with something, like a sheet of newspaper. This is a more revealing test than it sounds because it points to what psychologists call ideational fluency, or the ability to form ideas and mental images, and is considered to be a good indicator of overall creativity and the ability to think properly. The Notel youngsters did not come out top in all tests, however. In one they came last – that which tested them for aggression. It soon became clear to Dr Williams that both the young and old of Notel were making much better use of their brains than their counterparts in the other two towns.

A year after television arrived things were quite different. There was 'a dramatic drop' in community participation, with fewer people going to public dances, parties, meetings, concerts, parades and bingo than before they had television in their homes. Moreover, when the young people were re-tested for verbal and physical aggression they now scored above the two control towns. Reading skills had also suffered, particularly among those who found it difficult anyway, and Williams suspected that individual personality had been lost and that people had become mentally more passive.

In sum, then, we can say that there has been no overall increase in leisure as a result of economic growth and that those groups that do have more – the old and the unemployed – are the least well equipped to use it fully. Moreover, the effect of the main shift in leisure activity during our study period – the increase in television viewing – has probably been to make people more isolated, mentally passive and aggressive while at the same time less creative and less skilled in reading and thinking.

THE WRONG LIGHTHOUSE

Even on the most generous interpretation, it is hard to believe that these changes are the sort of benefits people imagined growth would bring them when they looked into the future from their vantage point in the mid-1950s. Why have the benefits of economic growth proved so meagre? The fact is that those who were driving the process along were being guided by the wrong lighthouse, just as Roefie Hueting suggested. Their guiding light was profit, not the welfare of the community. It is scarcely surprising that we have failed to arrive at a destination we never attempted to reach. The 'invisible hand' that was meant to ensure that personal profit and public welfare were one and the same has let us down.

As a consequence, the increased resources produced by the growth process have been largely wasted. They have been employed to keep the system running, not to bring anyone – even the wealthy – much joy. They have been used to provide pallets and corrugated cardboard, non-returnable bottles and ring-pull drinks cans. They have built airports, supertankers and heavy goods lorries, motorways, flyovers, and car parks with many floors. They have enabled the British banking, insurance, stock-broking, tax-collecting and accountancy sector to expand from 493,000 to 2,475,000 employees during our thirty-three years. They have financed the recruitment of over three million people to the 'reserve army of the unemployed'. Is it surprising that so little was left for more positive achievements when all these had taken their share?

There is, however, a more fundamental reason why growth has been such a disappointment. It is that a high proportion of the resources we supposed it had created *were never really there*: they just appeared to be because suppliers had put their prices up. Think back to Erewhon, whose combined agricultural and industrial sector was able to increase its output per employee by adopting new technologies but whose service sector was not, because teaching and nursing cannot be done by machines. In such an economy, industrial workers ensure that their wages rise in step with their own increases in productivity and with rises in the cost of living as well. Service-sector workers, many of whom are represented by the same unions, naturally seek to retain wage relativities. However, because their productivity has not increased, the price of their services has to go up if these increases are to be given.

This means two things. One is that the growth process is inescapably inflationary; the other is that the national income figure will be distorted by the service-sector wage rises because, although incomes in it have increased, the sector's output has not. When statisticians add up everyone's earnings to calculate national income, they will overvalue service sector output. They will try to correct for this by deflating their GNP total according to the rise in the cost of living index but, as the price of service sector output will have risen by more than that of the industrial sector because it has a higher labour content, some error will remain. Moreover, the bigger the service sector becomes in relation to the industrial sector, the more serious the error grows. In fact, in industrial countries whose service sector is steadily increasing in comparison with the actual production of goods, growth figures are becoming more and more unreliable. Essentially, industrial productivity increases are yielding rapidly diminishing returns while at the same time making the relationship between wages and raw materials costs increasingly distorted. The incentive to shed labour and use more energy and materials is strengthening at an accelerating rate.

Quite simply, the 'additional resources' gained from growth were increasingly a sham, and most of those that were not false were wasted. A large proportion of the increase in incomes measured by the GNP statistics went to people who were charging more for doing the same thing, or to parasites – like the two million extra people recruited to the financial services sector – whose existence is possible only because our system measures money and not real resources or real benefits. A doubling of national income could never have made 'each man twice as rich as his father was at the same age' as was expected in the 1950s because of the inevitable path the growth process takes when propelled by people who measure their success solely in terms of monetary profit.

At the end of chapter 3 I asked whether people living around 1700 would have preferred to live in the society and economy of the 1900s and decided that perhaps they would, but for non-materialistic reasons. I do not have to ask the same question about the late twentieth century: an experiment has actually been carried out. A group of 274 people living almost exactly as their ancestors had done in the 1820s was brought to Britain and invited to stay.

The experiment began in October 1961 when the volcano that dominates Tristan da Cunha, the remote island some 1,900 miles west of the Cape of Good Hope, began to erupt. A huge river of lava approached the narrow coastal strip on which the inhabitants had built their houses, and total evacuation seemed the only safe course. The refugees were welcomed to Britain, housed in a former army camp in Hampshire, and helped to find work.

To outsiders, Tristan is a most unattractive place. The climate is harsh, the soil poor and the landscape bleak. Official visitors have always recommended evacuation. As Michel Bosquet wrote[6] in *Le Nouvel Observateur* in 1965:

When it was evacuated in 1961, the community was still living as it had in 1827. The staple food was the potato, hand-cultivated in the meagre soil of the coastal strip. The island's 700-odd sheep provided the 280 inhabitants with a little meat and a little milk, and above all with hides and wool for clothing. When the sea permitted, the men fished for crayfish; what they caught, sold dirt cheap to the ocean-going trawlers of a deepsea fishing company, enabled the islanders to buy a few industrial products: paraffin and acetylene lamps, rubber boots, fishing equipment, a little sugar and tea during periods of 'prosperity'. To a foreigner, these conditions of life indicated a level of destitution, of starvation almost, which would be intolerable to a civilized man.

After two years of life in modern Britain, the refugees learnt that the danger was over. Should they go back? Their sheep, which had been left on the island, were all dead, the stock of seed potatoes was almost totally destroyed; and the potato fields themselves had been overrun by pests. Their houses had either been burned or wrecked by passing sailors. Lava covered the beach, and there was no trace of the crayfish plant. A vote was taken and, apart from six young women who had married Englishmen, the decision was unanimous: they would go home. Why? 'If life were as free in England as it is in Tristan,' one of the islanders said after his return, 'I wouldn't mind living [there]. But I'm not used to working for a boss. Here I work when I feel like it.'

So some things are more important than the level of production and consumption, than economic growth. As Bosquet concluded: 'For anyone who still believes in the absolute value of progress, the lesson of Tristan da Cunha is a terrible one.'

10
Growth Must Have a Stop

A society which is dependent on world trade for rising prosperity, high employment levels and the elimination of poverty must seek these objectives through increased productivity and constant innovation. We need higher productivity because our competitors already have both a higher and a faster growing output per man. We need innovation because we must constantly adapt our response to a ceaselessly changing world. – Margaret Thatcher (1977)

Two remarkable publications appeared within a month of each other in early 1972. One, *The Limits to Growth*, set out quite clearly that if things went on as they were there would be a sudden and uncontrollable decline in world population and industrial capacity within the next hundred years. More hopefully, it also said that if changes were made soon enough, a global equilibrium could be reached under which everyone's basic needs could be met. The other, a special edition of the magazine *The Ecologist* called *A Blueprint for Survival* (which in fact appeared first), set out in detail the steps to be taken to reach this equilibrium. It called for economic growth to be brought to a halt by taxes on the use of raw materials, an energy tax, and an amortization tax, which would discourage the production of short-life goods.

Both publications sold well and attracted worldwide attention. 'Those were heady times. The *Blueprint* authors and the *Limits* team were lionized. They could do no wrong. Those who sought to refute them could not be heard,' Michael Allaby, one of those who helped compile *Blueprint* wrote afterwards. *Blueprint* eventually appeared in book form in twenty different languages and sold 500,000 copies after being endorsed by over two hundred leading scientists, including two Nobel laureates and several Fellows of the Royal Society, making the front page in several London daily papers, and getting discussed in the House of Commons and the British Cabinet. Around the world, *Limits* received similar treatment. It appeared in thirty languages, and two million copies were printed.

About three months later the United Nations held a conference entitled 'Only One Earth' in Stockholm for which Barbara Ward and René Dubos prepared a background report with the same title, which also sold well. The conference drew up a Declaration on the Human Environment, consisting of a preamble and twenty-six principles, some of which read as if they were written by the *Blueprint* or the *Limits* teams. The Declaration is now part of the UN Constitution, alongside the Declaration on Human Rights, but almost no-one knows it exists. The conference also set up the UN Environmental Programme (UNEP) to try to co-ordinate international efforts to measure changes in the atmosphere and the seas.

And that was it. A few months later all the fuss had died away. The UNEP was starved of funds and it was almost seventeen years before there was another international conference on the environment that attracted a comparable level of public attention – the March 1989 'Save the Ozone Layer' meeting in London called by Margaret Thatcher in conjunction with the UNEP. (The UNEP's two earlier conferences on the same topic – at Vienna in 1985 and Montreal in 1987 – were much more significant events because they led to the first restrictions on the production of chlorofluoro-carbons (CFCs) under the Montreal Protocol – 'the UNEP's single most important achievement since it came into being,' Jonathan Porritt, then of British Friends of the Earth, said later. However, neither excited public interest nor the commitment of a national leader to anything like the same extent.)

So what happened? Why did seventeen years slip away, with almost everyone happy to ignore the *Limits* team's warning that if the achievement of ecological and economic stability was delayed, the chance of humanity fulfilling its basic material needs in the foreseeable future would be sharply reduced?

One reason for the wasted years was that the *Limits* prophecies were not believed, mainly because the idea that we can all become better off is very attractive and people are reluctant to give it up. But a more fundamental reason was that the prophets did not really believe their predictions them-selves, or, put another way, if they believed them intellectually they doubted them emotionally. Four years after *Blueprint*, Michael Allaby wrote in *Inventing Tomorrow* that 'what emerges is a picture of a world that is far too robust to be easily destroyed by man,' and this view was widely held. John Maddox, then editor of *Nature*, a leading British scientific magazine, said in his 1972 book *The Doomsday Syndrome* that the scale of human activities was too small to threaten the plankton in the seas or to enhance the natural greenhouse effect. 'The threat of calamity by the greenhouse effect is at once uncertain and remote,' he wrote.

Maddox's book was widely seen as a successful rebuttal of the *Limits* case, although it was nothing of the sort. Its main theme was that human ingenuity was making things better and better. 'Famine is receding, minerals are more plentiful than ever ... Air pollution has been decreasing for the past decade in British and U.S. cities ... The pace of population growth has begun to decline ... The world is not in nearly as bad a state as the conservationists and the ecologists say that it is ... The technology of survival has been more successful than could have been imagined in any previous century' are some of the phrases he used in it.

Maddox's opposition to the 'doomsday' warnings, which he felt were exaggerated or premature, stemmed from his belief that they could undermine the human spirit. 'The environmentalist movement tends towards passivity and true conservatism. Widespread acceptance of what the doomsday men are asking for could so undermine the pattern of economic life as to create social stagnation. It gives offence to suggest to relatively poor sections of the community that the time has come for the search for material prosperity to cease.'

The idea that something would turn up, that humankind's inventiveness would get it out of any future difficulties, was enormously popular. Julian Simon, an economics professor at the University of Maryland, wrote a book about human ingenuity in 1980, calling it *The Ultimate Resource*. The book, which dismisses *The Limits to Growth* as 'outrageously bad', 'a public relations hype' and 'not worth detailed discussion or criticism', presents a graph that purports to show how the bigger the population a country has, the more scientific research it undertakes if one allows for differences in national income. 'This fits in with the idea that more people imply faster increases in technology and economic growth,' the caption reads. Simon went on to make something of a speciality of casting doubt on the validity of warnings about the future. In 1984 he edited *The Resourceful Earth* in collaboration with a futurologist, Herman Kahn, which, according to the jacket, 'is both a devastating indictment of all doomsday books and also the most scientific inquiry into the future ever organized'. It is neither.

Many authors trotted out the anonymous and possibly apocryphal nineteenth-century prediction that if the volume of traffic in New York continued to grow at the existing rate it would not be long before the streets were buried beneath six feet of horse manure. Predictions in 1865 by the economist W. S. Jevons that the consumption of coal in Britain would rise in a geometric progression and that reserves would be exhausted, with disastrous results for the national economy, were also exhumed to discredit the current prognostications. And Malthus – who had inspired Jevons's thoughts on coal – was himself dismissed because his forecasts about the relative rates of increase of population and of agricultural land had not been fulfilled – yet. It was of no use for one of the rare anti-growth economists, E. J. Mishan, to write in 1976: 'If growthmen can spin telling analogies, so can the growth sceptics. A man who falls from a hundred-storey building will survive the first ninety-nine storeys unscathed. Were he as sanguine as some of our technocrats, his confidence would grow with the number of storeys he passed on his downward flight and would be at a maximum just before his free-fall abruptly halted.'

In spite of Allaby's remark that those who sought to refute the *Limits* and *Blueprint* teams could not be heard, the public very quickly picked up the comforting idea that the ideas in both books had been proved fallacious. I can remember academic economists dismissing the idea that running out of fossil fuels or minerals could halt growth, a concept they said had been put forward in *Limits*. 'It doesn't work like that,' they would say. 'You don't just run out of something and come to an abrupt halt. What happens is that as something becomes gradually scarcer, the price rises and this encourages substitutes to be found.' This is true enough in itself. However, *Limits* had never suggested that a lack of energy or mineral resources would prove to be the problem. In one of the runs of the computer model on which all its predictions were based, the amount of available resources was assumed to be unlimited. The results were the same: pollution increased, leading to an increase in the human death rate which cut food production and increased the death rate still more. And if pollution was successfully cut by 75 per cent so that the death rate did not rise so rapidly, then population continued to grow until all the world's arable land was used up, whereupon it started to fall anyway. But arguing that a lack of natural resources would not constrain growth certainly paid off for Robert Solow, who did just that in the *American Economic Review* in 1974 and elsewhere. In 1987 he won the Nobel Prize for Economics.

Academic misinformation about what the *Limits* team were saying influenced relatively few people. Far more damage was done by stories in the media that the *Limits* computer model had been found to be faulty. These arose because the Science Policy Research Unit at the University of Sussex decided to do one of the standard tests performed on all predictive computer models: to run it backwards and see how well its results fitted in with what actually happened in the past. The SPRU (which in fact used an outdated version of the *Limits* model for their test) thought the results unimpressive and said so publicly[1] although other people doing their own tests thought their results were fairly good. What nobody said was that even if the model was adjusted to give a better historical fit and then run forward again, it still predicted disaster, although a few years later on. By the time this was known, no-one was interested any more. From a journalistic point of view, the story was dead.

The fact is – and this should have surprised nobody since it is simple common sense that you cannot have indefinite growth in a finite world – that the *Limits* predictions were right in their fundamentals, if not in their details. In simple terms, what the team said was that if things carried on growing as they were, industrial output and food production would decline sharply around the year 2010, because of a lack of resources. This would cause population to decline precipitately a generation or so later. Even if double the *Limits* level of resources was available, either as a result of prospecting efforts or of our inventiveness, pollution from an ever-growing industrial sector would rise so much that it would cut food production and increase the death rate a few years after 2010 anyway. And if we found a way to deal with pollution by cutting it by 75 per cent, and managed to invent our way out of all resource constraints, humankind would then run out of land, and the population would peak in about 2070 because of declining food supplies.

There was no way out of this problem. Even if we were able to double the productivity of land to avoid a population decline, pollution would become the problem again a few years later since industrial output is assumed to be constantly rising and the effect of the additional waste that industry creates would be to ensure that population still peaked before 2100.

The reason pollution always seemed to get us in the end is that, however much emissions from a particular process are cut, there will always be some. Consequently, if industrial growth takes place year after year, the level of emissions will eventually grow enough again to outweigh the gains from cutting pollution back. And it will do so surprisingly quickly. Suppose an industry cuts pollution by half. If it is growing at an average rate of 6 per cent a year, it will be back up to its old pollution level in twelve years. If it grows at 3 per cent, the problem will be as bad as it is today in twenty-four years. So, although the *Limits* team did not pretend to be able to say in exactly what year pollution would cause population to fall, they could be absolutely sure it would, give or take a few years, *so long as industrial output continued to grow.*

Where the team fell down of course was in not knowing exactly how pollution would act. After quoting a 1970 paper by G. Evelyn Hutchinson in the *Scientific American* saying that 'many people ... are concluding on the basis of mounting and reasonably objective evidence that the length of life of the biosphere as an inhabitable region for organisms is to be measured in decades rather than hundreds of millions of years' as a result of human activities, they pointed out that scientific efforts to measure the effect of these activities were only very recent. 'We are certainly not able at this time to come to any final conclusion about the earth's capacity to absorb pollution.'

What they could and did say was that pollution seemed to be increasing exponentially, generally at a faster rate than the increase in population. 'We have almost no knowledge about where the upper limits of these pollution growth curves might be. The presence of natural delays in ecological processes increases the probability of underestimating the control measures necessary and therefore of inadvertently reaching those upper limits' – a statement that appears, with hindsight, to be a clear warning of our situation at present in relation to the greenhouse effect and the damaged ozone layer.

To this day, every *Limits to Growth* critic has played the pollution problem down. In 1973 the Science Policy Research Unit argued that the effects of pollution were local, not global, and that it was invalid for the *Limits* people to lump pollutants together and assume that they behave in a composite way. By doing so, they had diverted attention from 'urgent and still soluble problems ... into speculation upon an imaginary race against time between "Life" and "Global Asphyxiation"'. In 1981 Julian Simon limited his discussion of the greenhouse effect in *The Ultimate Resource* to the sentence: 'Also in dispute is the amount of oil and other fossil fuels that man can safely burn without creating excessive atmospheric levels of carbon dioxide.' He then went on to claim that if life expectancy was taken as the best index of the seriousness of pollution, things were getting better. CFCs and acid rain he completely ignored, although sulphur dioxide emissions, he claimed, were being reduced.

Three years later, in the introduction to *The Resourceful Earth* (1984), Simon was prepared to give a little ground on the dangers of carbon dioxide, probably because he felt that in doing so he was not admitting that growth would one day have to stop:

The CO_2 question is subject to major controversy and uncertainty – about the extent of the build-up, about its causes and especially about its effects. It would not seem prudent to undertake expensive policy alterations at this time because of this lack of knowledge ... [but] if it is considered desirable to reduce the amount of CO_2 released into the atmosphere by human activity ... only two possibilities are feasible: reduce total energy consumption or increase energy production from nuclear power plants. Reduction in total world energy consumption ... is clearly unacceptable to most nations because of the negative effects on economic growth, nutrition and health, and consumer satisfaction. This implies an inverse trade-off relationship between CO_2 and non-fossil (especially nuclear) power.

Since the main constraints on the expansion of nuclear power production were merely 'various political interests, public misinformation and cost-raising counter-productive systems of safety regulation,' Simon wrote, economic growth could continue indefinitely since 'nuclear energy is available at costs as low or much lower than from coal ... in unlimited quantities beyond any conceivable meaningful human horizon ... costing fewer lives per unit of energy produced than does coal or oil.'

Simon did bring himself to mention acid rain this time, but said it would be cured by the switch to nuclear power. CFCs, on the other hand, continued to escape his attention, although one of his contributors did say that there would be no appreciable change in climate as a result of the CFC-induced depletion of the ozone layer and that any increase in skin cancer the loss of ozone caused was outside the scope of his chapter.

How things have changed! Simon's brand of relentless techno-optimism lost much of its public support after Bhopal and Chernobyl although some influential planners and politicians remain on his side. These apart, however, it is hard to find an informed person who does not accept that global pollution, in one form or another, has become a threat to life on the planet, exactly as *Limits* predicted it would.

To acknowledge that the three atmospheric pollution crises facing us – acid rain, global warming, and the loss of the ozone layer – are threats is one thing; to do something about them is quite another. The simplest one to treat, the loss of ozone, is also much the most urgent. Just how well, or badly, we deal with it will give a fair indication whether we will be able to cope sufficiently well with the other two to avoid catastrophe. So how well have we handled the ozone depletion so far? The answer is not encouraging.

CFCs were invented in 1930 by Thomas Midgley, who also gave us leaded petrol, and he was showered with honours for his pains. They were developed as a safer replacement for ammonia in refrigerators and proved ideal: they are non-poisonous, non-inflammable, and very stable. Almost inevitably, other uses came to be found for such apparently benign chemicals: as aerosol propellants, solvents and blowing agents for plastic foam. A related family of chemicals, the halons (in which the chlorine is replaced by bromine) was widely adopted in fire extinguishers. Production soared.

The first indication that both types of chemical might be building up in the atmosphere came through chance and one man's curiosity. The chance was that a remarkable independent scientist, the man who later developed the Gaia hypothesis, James Lovelock, bought a holiday cottage overlooking Bantry Bay in the south-west of Ireland in 1968. In his Schumacher Lecture in 1988, Lovelock told what happened next.[2]

Most of the time the air was so clear that islands fifty miles away could be seen from the mountain top, but occasionally, the air was so hazy that nothing more than a mile away could be seen. The haze looked and smelt to me just like the photochemical smog of Los Angeles but how could it have reached this remote rural region? Next summer, to the disgust of my family, I took a homemade gas chromatograph on holiday. I had the idea that it should be possible to decide if the haze was a natural phenomenon or was man-made by measuring the level of CFCs in it. CFCs are unique among chemicals in the atmosphere in being unequivocally of industrial origin: all other chemicals have natural as well as man-made sources. My idea was that if the haze was pollution it would come from an urban industrial area and in it there would be more of these CFCs than in clean Atlantic air.

On the first few days of our holiday it was sparkling clear and I was surprised when I measured the air to find a strong signal for one of the CFC gases at about 50 parts per trillion. A few days later, the wind shifted and an easterly drift of air blew from Europe. With it came the haze and the pleasant confirmation of my idea about the origin of the smog, for in the hazy air there was three times as much CFC as in the clear air. So the haze was man-made. Later investigations showed it to be photochemical smog, rich in ozone, and to have come from the South of France and Italy, having drifted in the wind nearly 1,000 miles, carrying the exhaust fumes of millions of cars of European holidaymakers.

Lovelock's investigation might have ended at this point but he began thinking about the 50 parts per trillion of CFCs in the pure Atlantic air: had they come from the United States or were CFCs building up in the atmosphere because there was no mechanism for their removal? The only way to find out was to travel by ship to Antarctica and back, measuring CFC levels along the way. And this he did, hitching a ride on the research vessel *Shackleton*. His wife paid the costs out of the family's housekeeping, because his applications for research grants were turned down. His gas chromatograph, which he had invented and built himself, showed that not only were CFCs ubiquitous but that other gases – methyl iodide, carbon tetrachloride, dimethyl sulphide and carbon disulphide – were building up too.

But there was no hint from Lovelock's work that the CFC build-up was doing any harm. The first suggestion came from two American scientists, F. S. Rowland and M. J. Molina, in a paper in *Nature* in 1974. However, their suggestion that the chlorine in CFCs might be catalysing the destruction of atmospheric ozone met with a sceptical reception from Lovelock. In a book review in the *New Scientist* in 1988 he wrote:

I didn't doubt the scientific validity of their hypothesis – that CFCs would accumulate and become an ever-increasing source of atmospheric chlorine, and that this chlorine would probably react with and deplete ozone. What I did doubt was that the 50 parts per trillion of F11 and the 80 parts per trillion of F12 were a significant threat in the mid-1970s. F11 and F12 are the most widely used CFCs. I also had a feeling that the potent greenhouse properties of these compounds might be a more serious danger, if and when they increased to the levels now present. CFCs seemed, to me, to be things to keep a watch on and curtail if and when they became a menace. Hardly something to lose sleep over or legislate against in the 1970s.

Nevertheless, the Rowland-Molina hypothesis generated widespread concern in the United States. 'The public wrote more letters to their congressional representatives about CFCs and ozone depletion than they had on any other issue since the Vietnam War,' says Carolyn Hartman of the Public Interest Research Group in her study of the tactics American CFC producers used to obstruct efforts to control their output, *Du Pont Fiddles While the World Burns* (1989). The result of the letters was that in December 1978 the United States banned the non-essential use of CFC in aerosols with Canada and Sweden introducing similar legislation the following year.

As one might expect, these bans were achieved in face of bitter opposition from the CFC producers whose first move was to deny that their products were doing any harm. 'There is no experimental evidence supporting the chlorine-ozone theory. To the contrary, a study by London and Kelly indicates that the concentration of stratospheric ozone has actually increased during the past decade,' Raymond McCarthy, the technical director of Du Pont – the biggest CFC producer – told a House of Representatives subcommittee in December 1974, before going on to argue that research should be carried out to see if the hypothesized reactions were taking place before any controls were introduced.

Apart from the aerosol ban, the efforts by American CFC producers to prevent their government restricting their activities were completely successful, and other uses of CFCs were allowed to continue. Britain did not even ban CFCs in aerosols because ICI, the main British supplier, convinced politicians that it was too dangerous to use butane as an alternative propellant because of the risk of an explosion or fire. Eventually, when atmospheric monitoring by NASA failed to show any changes in ozone concentrations, public pressure for restrictions died away and both Du Pont and ICI felt it safe in the early 1980s to call off or scale down their search for CFC substitutes.

But the UNEP never lost interest in the Rowland-Molina hypothesis. It was discussed by its Governing Council in 1976, and an international conference of experts was called the following year. This in turn parcelled out investigation work among other UN organizations, the results of which were sufficiently worrying for twenty countries to sign the Vienna Convention for the Protection of the Ozone Layer in April 1985. This is the foundation for all the international agreements to phase out CFCs that have been reached since; had the UNEP not been working away quietly during those years, the world reaction time to the crisis would have been longer.

A month after the Convention had been signed, events began to move more swiftly. This was as a result of another paper in *Nature*, this time by an atmospheric chemist working for the British Antarctic Survey, Joe Farman, who announced that ozone concentrations above Antarctica had begun to fall sharply after 1978. One of the reasons for the delay in letting the world know about the fall was that, as ozone levels fluctuate widely from year to year and there can be a 30 per cent change from day to day, it was 1982 before anyone spotted a possible downward trend. By this time the drop had become so pronounced that Farman and his colleagues thought their measuring instrument must be faulty, especially as NASA had not reported anything from its satellite surveys. A newer instrument was sent out from England, and by October 1984 the team was convinced that something significant was happening. However, a further six months passed before the paper they wrote appeared in print. It turned out that NASA had failed to spot the downward trend because it had programmed the computer processing its ozone data to ignore 'anomalous' figures – any reading 30 per cent or more above or below its expected level.

The reaction of the American CFC producers was to suggest that the loss of ozone Farman had reported did not matter. 'Although the observed reductions in the ozone over the Antarctic area are real, the ozone levels return to near normal soon after the October springtime begins and no plausible mechanism has been proposed to explain this phenomenon,' a spokesman for the Alliance for Responsible CFC Policy – a grouping of CFC manufacturers and users – said in 1986. Even as late as March 1988 Du Pont was arguing that 'the scientific evidence does not point to the need for dramatic CFC emission reductions. There is no available measure of the contribution of CFCs to any observed ozone change. In fact recent observations show a decrease in the amount of ultraviolet radiation from the sun reaching the United States.' The second largest American CFC producer, Allied Signal, showed what it thought of the findings in a more direct way – it expanded its production in 1986, and began convincing computer firms to switch to CFC-113 for cleaning electronic components. In March 1988 too, American firms sold equipment to India for a factory to build refrigerators cooled with CFCs.

But in May 1989, exactly four years after Farman's paper appeared, eighty-one governments met under the auspices of the UNEP in Helsinki and agreed to phase out CFC production by 2000 – a remarkable step by historical standards, and an accord achieved in a very short time. Most non-participating countries fell into line at a further conference in London in June 1990 at which it was agreed that Third World countries including India and China should be given financial assistance to acquire the necessary replacement technology.

By any standard other than a historical one, however, the response time was simply not fast enough. 'We were very slow about tackling the crisis and we should be phasing out CFCs much faster,' Joe Farman told an RTE interviewer after the London meeting. Many commentators agreed. 'By the time CFCs are phased out in ten years, there will have been a 30 per cent increase in total global production of the major ozone-depleting substances, CFC-11 and CFC-12,' Greenpeace's Director of Science, Jeremy Leggett, wrote in *New Scientist* a week later. 'Production of these substances is set to increase from the 18 million tonnes produced between 1930 and 1990 to 24 million tonnes by the end of the next decade.'

In April 1991 the Environmental Protection Agency released NASA figures showing that twice as much ozone had been destroyed in the previous ten years as had been thought, and that a much wider area was affected for a longer period. Over North America, Europe and northern Asia, the layer had thinned by 4 to 5 per cent, and at British latitudes the winter loss was 8 per cent and extended into early spring. In the Southern Hemisphere the loss was 2 per cent higher and persisted for longer still. Yet even these data were not enough to halt CFC production at once. Du Pont planned to stop production in the year 2000 in line with the Montreal agreement, ICI by 1997 as agreed by the EC, until early 1992, when it was discovered that dust in the upper atmosphere from the eruption of Mount Pinatubo in the Philippines the previous year was providing such good conditions for CFCs to wreak their havoc that a quarter of the ozone over North America and Europe was likely to be destroyed before the layer began to repair itself in the spring. President Bush immediately ordered that US production was to stop in 1995; the next day, ICI followed suit.

The delay in phasing out the use of CFCs and the continued use of other ozone-depleting chemicals means that the average level of atmospheric ozone will drop by a further 3 per cent by the end of the century. What might this mean? Public discussion on the effects of the CFC build-up has concentrated on the increased incidence of human skin cancer because of the higher levels of ultraviolet radiation penetrating the reduced ozone layer: every 1 per cent loss of ozone causes a 2 per cent increase in UV radiation and a 3 per cent increase in the incidence of non-melanoma skin cancers. On the basis of the 1991 NASA data the EPA now estimates that there will be twelve million additional cases of skin cancer in the United States alone over the next fifty years and that these will result in 200,000 deaths.

Strangely, the effects of higher UV levels on land plants and plankton have largely been ignored, although these could be much more serious. UV radiation is widely used in industry to sterilize water and in March 1988 Donat Haber of Marburg University told a meeting of the American Society of Photobiology that his work had shown that a 5 per cent increase in UV levels – less than the rise already recorded in the Southern Hemisphere – would halve the life-span of some types of micro-organism, including those found in plankton. 'Our data say that marine phytoplankton is already under very drastic ultraviolet stress,' he said.

Three weeks later Sayed El-Sayed of Texas A&M University reported a 10 per cent rise in the level of UV radiation was enough to kill plant plankton because it slowed down photosynthesis. 'The plankton is eaten by krill, a shrimp on which whales, squid and numerous other animals depend. If anything happens to the krill, the whole ecosystem collapses. We can say goodbye to the whales, the seals, the penguins and so on.' He did not observe that we can also say goodbye to humanity, but others – notably the American astronomer Carl Sagan – have since. UV radiation reaching the surface of the seas around Antarctica has doubled at certain times of the year and there are increases of at least 20 per cent as far north as Tasmania and New Zealand. Early research into the effects of this rise on the plankton is not reasssuring, although in 1990 Don Lubin of the University of Chicago found that stratus clouds, typical of the Antarctic sky, often absorb half the UV radiation, and that organic material in the sea itself can weaken certain wavelengths. Some types of phytoplankton are more sensitive to the radiation than others. When Barbara Prézelin[3] from the University of California measured UV levels in the water near icebergs in the Bellingshausen Sea during the southern spring of 1991, she found that the most common type of plankton, an alga, *Phaeocysis*, suffered far more than diatoms, which contain silica. Overall, the production of plankton dropped by between 6 and 12 per cent and the loss was proportional to UV exposure. The highest levels of UV radiation were occurring at just the wrong time of year – when the plankton made most growth.

All animal life and most plants apart from blue-green algae have evolved under the protection of the ozone layer and are damaged by high levels of UV radiation, because it splits up the molecules in their cells. This is the cause of the skin cancers in humans and slower growth, poorer pollination and, above a certain level, death in plants. Marine plant plankton and land plants put the oxygen into the earth's atmosphere, and they continually top up its level by taking in carbon dioxide and stripping out the carbon they need for their own growth. If the growth rates of both types of plant were seroiusly damaged by high levels of UV radiation, not only would food supplies plunge but the greenhouse effect would accelerate as untreated carbon dioxide built up and prevented excess heat being radiated off into space.

If things ever reached this stage, events would spiral out of control. The accelerated greenhouse warming would destroy much of the remaining land plants and encourage vast fires, which would not only produce even more carbon dioxide and thus speed up the warming but also increase the rate of damage to the ozone layer. Paul Crutzen, an atmospheric chemist at the Max Planck Institute in Mainz, Germany, fears this could happen because large quantities of methyl chloride are released when vegetation burns and this, like the CFCs, breaks down and releases chlorine in the upper atmosphere, destroying the ozone there.

And yet the public is largely unaware that the world could be teetering on the brink of an unstoppable death plunge, a final environmental catastrophe. There is a very real chance that the quantity of CFCs already released is enough to destroy most life forms on earth – several million tonnes of them are already swirling around in the atmosphere, gradually floating up towards the ozone layer, a journey that can take 120 years. The 6 million tonnes that will be manufactured or released because of the ten-year phase-out period will obviously increase this danger, and many environmental groups have been calling for an immediate halt to production. These organizations also want to see the recovery of CFCs from the insulation and cooling coils of refrigerators as these are scrapped: in 1990 an estimated 1,500 tonnes of CFCs escaped into the atmosphere in Britain from old fridges alone.

In view of the seriousness of the crisis, why was the ending of production put off for so long? Apologists for the agreements point out that the important thing was to get as many countries as possible to participate and that this meant the phase-out had to be much longer than many countries thought desirable. They add that it is open to any country to phase out production before the year 2000 and that several countries have announced that they are going to do so. Also, since any country that continues making CFCs when many of its competitors have stopped can expect to be subjected to considerable moral, commercial and diplomatic pressure, the actual phase-out might take place ahead of target.

On the other hand, there is an economic incentive to continue CFC production for as long as possible. Carolyn Hartman quotes from a 1988 study by Douglas Cogan of the Investor Responsibility Research Centre that estimates that the price of CFCs could rise so much as production is phased out that the remaining manufacturers would make $5,700 million in extra profits over the ten-year period. Certainly the main opposition in London and Helsinki to an early cut-off date came from Britain, the United States and Japan – all major producers. In 1987 Britain only dropped its resistance to proposals for a reduction in the production of CFCs throughout the EC after the then junior Minister for the Environment, William Waldegrave, had been given permission to do so by his opposite number at the Department of Trade and Industry, Giles Shaw. Survival did not come into it. Previously, Shaw's department had refused to allow Environment to agree to anything beyond a pledge that Britain would not increase its production.

Britain's main concern was that ICI should have its highly priced and environmentally damaging substitute in production before the company's CFC plants were closed down. (The substitute, HFC-134a, is a greenhouse gas, only slightly less warming than CFC-12. It also attacks the ozone layer, but because it contains less chlorine it is thought to do less damage especially as most of it is said to break down before it reaches the upper atmosphere. 'It should never have been suggested,' Farman says; but its advantage as far as ICI is concerned is that it will earn it more money: it costs £30 per kilogram compared with £5 per kilogram for CFC-12.) Britain also insisted that ICI's exports to countries which had not signed the agreements be allowed to continue for fear that other countries' manufacturers would take over these markets. (ICI has made full use of this freedom, increasing its sales to India from 39 tonnes in 1987 to 315 tonnes in 1990 and trebling its

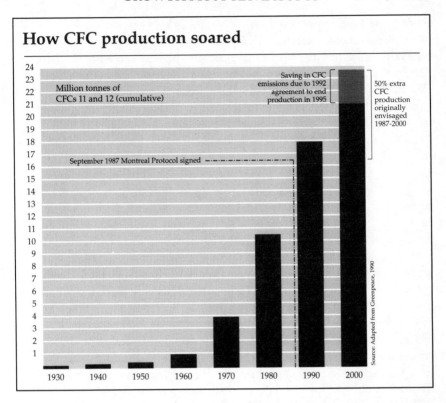

How CFC production soared

Figure 10.1 The world had made 14 million tonnes of CFCs when the hole in the ozone layer was discovered. So reluctant were governments to cease production that an extra 7 million tonnes would have been made by the year 2000, the date it was originally planned to stop, had alarming results not come in from a high-altitude flight over the Arctic in 1992. Production will now stop in 1995.

sales to Pakistan.) No consideration was ever given to requiring British refrigerator manufacturers (the main CFC market) to use propane or water instead of CFCs in their cooling coils or to accept non-CFC foam for fridge insulation. Not only would both have been feasible but the fridges would have been 10 per cent more energy-efficient. The idea of closing factories if products could not be made without CFCs was never mentioned at all.

Although Du Pont was encouraging its customers to write to their congressmen opposing CFC restrictions as recently as June 1989, the real problem in stopping production was not the commercial interests of the countries involved, important though these were: the true culprit was the growth process itself, because it can lead – as it did in this case – to huge increases in production before anyone realizes that things are going wrong and tries to correct them. Even if governments had been prepared to ban CFCs immediately the scientific evidence was in, their response might have been too slow to save the world. There was five times as much CFC in the atmosphere on the day the Helsinki agreement was signed in 1989 as there was in 1971 when Lovelock first noticed the problem.

There are at least three lessons to be learnt from the world's CFC performance. One is that governments are likely to put their national economic interests before those of the planet and to delay making changes until their producers are ready to exploit the new opportunities that implementing a ban will create. The next is that chemicals that seem harmless and have been used for years can prove damaging and even take scientists like Lovelock by surprise. And the third is that serious – and possibly irreparable – damage can be done before we notice anything is wrong, because of the speed with which manufacturers take up new technologies (and the chemicals they entail) in order to stay competitive. 'It's very worrying – industry can grow so fast these days,' Farman told RTE. 'How many times can we stop them?'

Of course, CFCs are not the only synthetic chemicals that have been released into the environment with serious consequences. DDT was the first to come to public notice, exposed by Rachel Carson's 1962 book *Silent Spring* which told of the effects pesticides and herbicides were having throughout the world, of mass kills of birds and fishes and of DDT entering the food chain where it was concentrated at the top: in human body fat and mother's milk. Although the book generated a tremendous outcry and encouraged the production of a generation of safer pesticides, the effects of DDT have proved less damaging than we had any right to expect. There is no evidence that its presence in human fat is harmful – one can apparently eat a pancake laced with DDT and merely vomit – and the only serious consequence detected so far is the thinning that its breakdown product, DDD, produces in birds' eggshells, which nearly led to the extinction of many birds of prey.

The long-term effects of a family of 209 chemicals discovered a few years before the CFCs look much more threatening. These are polychlorinated biphenyls (PCBs), and some scientists think they will destroy the oceans as a source of human food unless governments act promptly. As with DDT and CFCs, commercial production began long before anyone had second thoughts about them. Deliveries began in 1929, and it was only in 1966 that it was realized that they were entering the food chain when scientists working on DDT residues in the fatty tissues of animals found that their results were being thrown out by the PCBs in the tissues too. Follow-up studies have shown that the children of mothers who ate mildly PCB-contaminated fish from the Great Lakes in Canada have suffered significant learning and behavioural defects as a result of taking in the poison both in breast milk and while in the womb. PCBs have also been implicated in cancers, birth defects, infertility and liver damage and are said to reduce the body's immune defences and to lead to hypertension and strokes. Production was stopped in the early 1970s when the dangers became known – previously some of them had been thought safe enough to use in insecticides to 'increase their effectiveness and persistence' and, terrifyingly, in kiss-proof lipstick.

A professor at the University of Western Ontario who has studied PCBs since 1968, Joseph Cummins, estimates that about thirty per cent of the 1.2 million tonnes of PCBs manufactured before production ceased has already escaped from the transformers and hydraulic equipment in which it was used and been carried, in water and through the air, right around the world. Like DDT, PCBs become concentrated at the top of the food chain. 'Levels of PCBs in the adipose tissue of polar bears increased fourfold between 1969 and 1984. If current PCB inputs continue, the bears will exceed the 50 ppm [parts per million] limit designating them as toxic waste about the year 2005,' he wrote in *The Ecologist* in 1988. 'I can foresee an end to the effective use of the ocean fishery within a decade and yet nothing whatsoever is being done internationally to check the release of PCBs into the environment,' Cummins told *Green* magazine in 1989. 'If the fifteen per cent of world PCBs at present in use, storage or simply dumped in developing countries were released to the general environment, the extinction of marine mammals would be inevitable.' He added that he would like to see an international agreement under which the countries that manufactured the chemicals in the first place bought back their lethal products.

The CFC and PCB disasters – the full consequences of which are still unknown – have not made us significantly more cautious or stopped us releasing more and more synthetic chemicals into the environment. Since these chemicals play a key part in generating growth, few people are prepared to give them up. In *The Closing Circle*, another landmark book to come out in Britain in 1972 (a vintage year!), Barry Commoner argued that the reason for the increased pollution in the United States was not primarily that the population had grown or was living better. 'Total production has increased by 126 per cent since 1946 while most pollution levels have risen by at least several times that rate,' he wrote; 'what has drastically changed is the technology of production.' The growth that had taken place 'has had a surprisingly small effect on the degree to which individual needs for basic economic goods have been met,' because the average American was eating, drinking and wearing about as much as before. What had changed was the way these needs were satisfied. His food was now grown with the help of larger quantities of pesticides and fertilizers; his clothes contained more synthetic fibres and were washed with synthetic detergents instead of soap; his beer came in cans rather than returnable bottles; his house was built with concrete and aluminium rather than wood; and his car was heavier, more powerful and more polluting.

As we have seen, the growth imperative forces producers to adopt new technologies if they wish to enter or stay in business. Besides the increased use of fossil fuel, many of the technologies introduced this century have involved the use of synthetics, and as a result the Western world's chemical manufacturers more than quadrupled their output in the twenty-seven years up to 1989. They produced 600 million tonnes of approximately 20,000 different compounds in 1990, and, according to the Chemical Industries Association in London, output is doubling roughly every eighteen years. Nobody knows how many new compounds go into commercial production each year, but some idea can be gained from the fact that the *OPD Chemical Buyers' Directory* listed 816 more substances in 1990 than in 1989. Few if any of these new chemicals would have been assessed for their environmental impact before being placed on the market. In Britain, even chemicals for which there is a legal regulatory procedure, such as pesticides, are not properly checked but are approved for use on the basis of inadequate data because of a shortage of staff in government laboratories, according to a report in a 1990 issue of *Food Matters Worldwide*. Indeed, chemicals that have been on the market for many years are unlikely to have been checked thoroughly, and even if they have been, we still cannot be confident they are safe, so complex are the systems in the natural world.

Unfortunately, as if we had not got problems enough, we are about to create another set. In thousands of laboratories all over the world new life forms are being created by genetic engineering. Most of these new creatures, like most chemicals, would probably prove harmless if they were released or escaped into the outside world, as they probably lack the ability to survive there. However, it is almost inevitable that there will be exceptions and that some of these will do tremendous harm.

To a lay person, the amount of genetic investigation and manipulation going on is amazing. 'For a university biology department it's as basic as having a microscope in the lab,' says David McConnell, a biology professor at Trinity College, Dublin, one of several centres in Ireland where this work is carried on. 'It is an extremely powerful way of analysing all biological systems and if you are not using the technique, your competitors certainly are. And science these days is very competitive.' Fifty-five people are involved in genetic research at Trinity alone. Some have followed the evolution of different AIDS viruses by looking at the genetic codes they contain; others are developing potato varieties that are resistant to all major viruses, tracking hereditary blindness or helping the Thais to develop a new range of medical drugs. Even ornithologists are using genetic engineering techniques. 'Suppose you are studying the breeding behaviour of finches. If you take a small sample from each chick in a nest you can tell how many parents they had and consequently whether the mother bird had more than one mate. This is much more reliable than observation,' McConnell says.

Most of this work involves no risk at all. Dangers are only likely to arise when new life forms are created and released. Environmental activists in the United States became concerned in 1982 when two Californian scientists deleted a gene from the bacterium *Pseudomonas syringae*, which prevented the organism from acting any longer as a nucleus around which frost crystals could form. A company, Advanced Genetic Sciences, took over their work and developed a product containing the altered bacteria, Frostban, which it hoped to sell to strawberry growers to spray on their crops to prevent frost damage.

The Environmental Protection Agency discounted protests and gave consent for two field trials in 1987. However, worries persist that the formation of ice crystals in rain clouds will be affected if the altered form survives in the environment and displaces the natural strain. This could change the world's climate; it might mean that less snow falls, cutting the amount of solar energy the earth reflects and causing the polar ice-caps to retreat.

Fergal O'Gara, professor of food microbiology at University College, Cork, pooh-poohs this fear, saying that there are a great many other types of ice-nucleation bacteria available instead. He is working on another type of *Pseudomonas*, trying to develop a natural fungicide to replace potentially harmful chemical sprays. His form of the bacterium is found naturally in the soil, where it manages to co-exist with its fungal neighbours by grabbing the iron salts the fungi feed on and making them unavailable. The natural form stops locking iron away when it has created enough living room for itself. However, it might be possible to make it protect farm crops from fungi as well if it could be induced to go on mopping up iron indefinitely – in other words, if its genetic switch-off mechanism was removed. O'Gara's team has already done this: they analysed the DNA of the bacterium, found the gene that controlled the switch and cut it out. The altered form began greenhouse trials in 1985, and after these proved satisfactory, tests were started in an open field in 1990. Eventually the research could lead to *Pseudomonas* being routinely included in the dressing applied to seeds before they go out to the farms.

But most environmentalists think that no genetically altered bacteria should ever leave the laboratory. In O'Gara's case, they fear his creation could run amok, knocking out fungi that are essential for recycling of plant nutrients in a healthy soil. They also fear that the altered gene could transfer to other types of bacteria with unknown results. 'We have no formula for assessing the risks at all,' says Tom Whitty of Earthwatch, the Irish arm of Friends of the Earth. 'We want a moratorium on releases until one can be worked out. Nobody anticipated the damage that rhododendrons would do when they introduced them to Ireland,' he said, referring to the way the plant has spread through native oakwoods, choking out everything else and preventing the oaks from regenerating. O'Gara, however, insists that the most his new microbe will do is alter the soil's fungal balance.

O'Gara has also been trying to increase the amount of atmospheric nitrogen fixed by two legumes – soya and alfalfa – and has permission from the Irish Recombinant DNA Committee to move genetically altered *Rhizobium* bacteria out of the greenhouse and into the outside world. This step seems non-controversial because the only way that the bacteria have been changed is to make them take up more nutrients from the plants on whose roots they grow, so that they have more energy to fix nitrogen faster. However, previous studies have shown that the changed genetic material could spread to other species of *Rhizobium* and that it is capable of transferring to human gut bacteria under laboratory conditions.

While his applications for both releases were awaiting approval, O'Gara told me that very little risk was involved in letting *Pseudomonas* and *Rhizobium* loose in the environment, because no potentially harmful effects had been detected during the greenhouse trials. Also, as he had not put any genetic material from other species into his strains, the results he had achieved could have been obtained, eventually, by conventional breeding methods. Nevertheless, if the Recombinant DNA Committee thought it advisable, he said, he would introduce a change into the bacteria so that they self-destructed at a certain stage in their life cycle and were unable to spread. However, the committee had no legal power to force him to do this, as Ireland had no genetic-engineering legislation. In the event, the committee made no such condition. 'We have to keep the area fenced and burn all the crops at the end of the season,' one of O'Gara's colleagues told me after the open-field trials had begun.

As recently as 1989, Denmark was the only EC state to have laws to control genetic engineering. However, the European Commission has since developed directives covering contained use and release into the environment which had to be incorporated into member-states' legislation by the end of 1991. Such is the strength of the growth imperative that while the directives were being prepared, PR companies lobbied the Commission hard, both directly and through magazine articles, stressing that EC controls on genetic engineering should not be too stringent lest multinationals shift their research to the United States. A great deal of money was at stake, they said, particularly as the American market for genetically engineered products was expected to reach $10,000 million before 1999. However, a civil servant who followed their activities closely feels that their efforts to loosen the proposed restrictions were largely ineffective. 'The firms left their lobbying quite late, and no significant changes were made,' she says.

The dangers we face from the tremendous efforts being put into genetic engineering around the world are impossible to assess. However, if studies that could accidentally reduce the fertility of the soil by limiting the growth of soil fungi or alter the functioning of the human gut are going on in a small department in a small university college in a small country with very limited funds to put into research, it is impossible not to be thoroughly scared about what might be going on in the thousands of bigger and better-funded laboratories elsewhere. And we should never forget that whatever risks we are running are considerably heightened by the extraordinary pressure on firms to get their products onto the market before their rivals.

Western capitalist society is the only society in the history of the world to put a premium on rapid change, to reward those who do things in new ways and to penalize those who do not. Just as living creatures have evolved over time to fill particular environmental niches, so have human societies. Most of the genetic mutations that occur in a particular species of plant or animal make it less fitted for survival within its specialized environment and the individuals that carry the new, altered genes eventually die out. Similarly with a traditional human grouping such as a clan or a tribe: over the centuries it has worked out a near-optimal way of living within its environment and is reluctant to change this because, almost invariably, different means worse.

James Scott gives an example of just how sensible this refusal to change can be in his book *Weapons of the Weak*. Scott looked at thirty years' rice harvest figures for an area of south-east Asia and showed that, although the indigenous varieties of rice gave smaller yields than the seed companies' strains, their crops were more reliable. Had the people depended on the imported varieties, he said, they would have starved, because of the extreme fluctuations. The native strains saw them through every year.

It seems that capitalist man, however, can never say no. In 1950, only seven years after DDT's first large-scale use, George Decker, an adviser on insect control to the US Department of Agriculture, told a meeting of the American Association of Economic Entomologists that 'when pesticides are properly used, they are a very valuable tool, but, like the atomic bomb, if unwisely or wrongly used they may lead us to our doom. It seems to me that we are in the position of a drunk in a high-powered car approaching a stop-and-go light. We had better sober up and look and listen for danger signs before we proceed much further.'

We have not done so. We have introduced and are introducing changes at too rapid a rate, long before their effects can be assessed, because the firms and the farmers that adopt new technologies early on make the highest profits, and those that adopt them more slowly or cautiously are driven to the wall. Decker's car is still being driven much too fast, and although we've seriously damaged it as we ploughed into obstacles we refused to believe were there, most of its passengers are shouting for it to go faster still.

If we release new organisms, if we increase our output of chemicals or if we introduce new substances – all of which we are doing every year – it is equivalent to increasing our speed. We need to throttle back; but, for as long as the growth imperative compels firms to move ever faster and to adopt untried techniques, it will be impossible to do so, and we will be in continual and increasing danger. As Rachel Carson tried to impress on us when she used some words of Albert Schweitzer's for the opening of *Silent Spring*, 'Man has lost the capacity to foresee and forestall. He will end by destroying the earth.'

11

Growth in the Greenhouse

The most striking thing about modern industry is that it requires so much and accomplishes so little. Modern industry seems to be inefficient to a degree that surpasses one's ordinary powers of imagination. Its inefficiency therefore remains unnoticed. – E. F. Schumacher, *Small Is Beautiful* (1973)

While the elimination of CFCs is the most urgent problem facing the human race, halting the increase in concentrations of greenhouse gases in the atmosphere to stop global warming is the most intractable. The main problem is not that five different types of gas have to be dealt with but that all five are the products of economic expansion and their elimination or reduction will end the growth process, at least as it is now understood.

The surprising and frightening thing about atmospheric pollution is how recently and rapidly the damage has been done. As late as 1960 we had added only 20 per cent to the pre-industrial level of greenhouse gases. Thirty years later we are 40 per cent above that level and we will be 100 per cent above it by around 2030 if present policies continue. Until recently, it was thought that the seventeenfold increase in the output of CFCs between 1950 and 1980 was adding substantially to the greenhouse effect, but it is now known that it has destroyed so much high-level ozone, another greenhouse gas, that it has produced no net warming. However, methane, whose concentration in the atmosphere doubled between 1960 and 1990, is certainly guilty, now contributing 16 per cent to the human-made greenhouse effect. It is the result of increases in the world cattle population, the expansion of the area under lowland rice, and releases from rubbish dumps, coal mines, and the oil and gas industry. Another culprit is nitrous oxide, a by-product of nitrogenous fertilizer use, of the burning of fossil and biomass fuels and of the conversion of land to agriculture. It provides 8 per cent, about the same amount as low-level ozone – the joint creation of vehicle exhausts and sunlight. But the biggest contributor of all, at over 66 per cent, is carbon dioxide from fossil fuel consumption, deforestation, and new types of land use.

These figures show clearly that priority must now be given to reducing fossil fuel use, since this would cut not only carbon dioxide emissions but also those of methane, low-level ozone and nitrous oxide. Unfortunately, the cuts required are so deep that most governments regard them as outside the realm of practical politics. An authoritative estimate of how severe they would need to be has come from the 170 scientists from forty countries who make up the Intergovernmental Panel on Climate Change (IPCC). In May 1990 this group published a report that concluded that a 60 per cent cut was necessary to stabilize concentrations at current levels. 'The longer emissions continue to increase at present day rates, the greater reductions would have to be for concentrations to stabilize at a given level,' they warned.

If no cuts were made, the global mean temperature would go up by 3° C before 2100, they said, the most significant rise in the 10,800 years since the last Ice Age ended; indeed the change would be so rapid that nature would be unable to adapt. Isolated remnant vegetation, currently protected in nature reserves, would die out, and some species of animals, already stressed by loss of habitat, would become extinct too. Northern forests would be particularly badly affected, because many trees cannot cope with even small increases in temperature or reductions in rainfall. Deserts would expand, particularly in the lands bordering the Sahara.

The sea level would rise by 0.65 m over the same period, uprooting vast numbers of people – ten million live within 1 m of the high tide level on the river deltas of Bangladesh, Egypt and Vietnam alone. Entire countries such as the Maldives, Tuvalu and Kiribati would be threatened with submergence, and other countries would have to spend huge sums on building up their sea defences. Drinking water would become short as lakes and rivers dried up – the Great Lakes would fall by 2.4 m and New York could well have only 60 per cent of the water it needs by 2050. Violent winds and rain would probably increase and diseases such as malaria could return to continental Europe.

But perhaps most worrying of all is the risk that the earth could leave its present stable climatic regime and rapidly move to another, very different one, either much hotter or much colder – and there would be nothing we could do to stop it. Such sudden flips have apparently happened before. Larry Ephron, a leading proponent of the 'differential greenhouse effect' hypothesis until his death in 1990, claimed[1] that analysis of pollen deposits showed that the final shift at the beginning of the last Ice Age from a warm inter-glacial climate to tundra conditions in which it was too cold for fruit and nut trees to grow took less than twenty years. His view was that a greenhouse-induced warming in the tropics would lead to an increase in cloud cover around the poles and a spread of snow and ice there. 'The tropics, paradoxically, are hotter in an ice age,' he said, arguing that the earth's periodic 90,000-year cold spells were its natural way of reducing carbon dioxide levels and restoring soil fertility, both by the rock-grinding action of

Who is planning what for their greenhouse gases		
Country	% contribution to world CO_2 emissions	Policy Plans
USA	22.0	Against emission controls but committed to stabilizing total contribution to global warming at 1990 level by 2000, in part by phasing out CFCs.
USSR	18.4	Not in favour of emission controls at present.
Japan	4.4	Will stabilize per capita CO_2 emissions at 1990 level by 2000 if other countries do so too.
Germany	3.2	Aims to cut CO_2 emissions by 25% below 1987 level by 2005, with biggest falls in the east.
Britain	2.8	Will cut 1990 contribution to global warming by 20% by 2005 if other countries do so too.
Canada	2.0	Aims to stabilize all greenhouse gases at 1988 level by 2000 'as a first step'.
France	1.9	Aims to stabilize CO_2 emissions at 1990 level by 2000. Considering 50% cuts by 2030.
Italy	1.8	Aims to stabilize CO_2 emissions at 1988 level by 2000. Parliament has requested 20% cut by 2005.
Australia	1.6	Will stabilize emissions of all greenhouse gases at 1988 levels by 2000 and cut them by 20% by 2005 if others do too.
Netherlands	0.65	Committed to stabilization of CO_2 emissions at 1989 level by 1995 and 3-5% reduction by 2000.
Belgium	0.5	Has accepted EC target of stabilization of CO_2 emissions at 1988 levels by 2000.
Denmark	0.3	Programme in place to cut CO_2 emissions by 20% below 1988 level by 2005.
Finland	0.26	Will stabilize CO_2 emissions at 1990 levels by 2000 'at least'.
Sweden	0.22	Will stabilize CO_2 emissions from parts of the economy not subject to international competition if other countries do as well.
Norway	0.22	Aims to stabilize CO_2 emissions at 1990 level by 2000.
Switzerland	0.2	Interim target of stabilization of CO_2 emissions at 1990 level by 2000. 20% cuts proposed.
Ireland	0.14	Has accepted EC target of stabilization of CO_2 emissions at 1988 levels by 2000.
New Zealand	0.1	Aims to cut CO_2 emissions 20% below 1990 level by 2000.

Source: Climate Action Network, November 1991

the glaciers and the distribution of desert dust by the higher winds generated by greater temperature differences between the equator and the poles.

In view of these possible harsh consequences, what would the IPCC's 60 per cent reduction mean? In 1988, the world's consumption of all fossil fuels was the equivalent of 54 billion barrels of crude oil, roughly ten for each person on the planet. A 60 per cent cut would bring the average down to four barrels, 140 imperial gallons, or half a tonne of oil a year each – a figure which, by historical standards, is very high. Half a tonne of oil contains 56 million kilocalories. This is roughly ten times the energy available to a peasant farmer relying on animal power, the sun, and the wind, or twice the average used per person in the early stages of industrialization.[2] In fact, it is around the level Portugal and Greece used in 1965, according to World Bank figures, and was very close to the average consumption for that year in Latin America and the Caribbean. Given the economies in fuel consumption we know are possible and the progress in developing renewable energy sources that has already been made, the target seems quite reasonable.

Except for one thing. Half a tonne is very much less than the industrialized countries are using now. If the United States had to reach the per capita target level, it would need to cut consumption by 93.5 per cent. The equivalent figures for some other countries are: Britain, 87 per cent, Ireland, 81 per cent and the Netherlands 90.5 per cent. India, on the other hand, would be able to *increase* its fossil fuel use two-and-a-half times. When one remembers that the average family car covering 11,000 miles a year burns at least two people's fossil fuel allowance to do so and that heating a typical British house requires almost four allowances, one can see that cuts of the size needed are going to hit so close to home that it is impossible to see politicians taking the initiative and making them: only tremendous public pressure or a desperate crisis will get them to act.

So far public pressure has been small, and we can still pretend there is no crisis. It was thus politically practical in mid-1990 for President Bush to call for further research before setting any carbon dioxide reduction targets for the United States although in taking this line he was ignoring the near-unanimity in the world scientific community that if greenhouse gas levels carry on growing, if a warming is not already happening one will certainly begin. He was also ignoring the precautionary principle, the philosophy that you do not do anything which *might* damage the planet irrevocably. The mere risk of causing climatic change by continuing the present rate of emissions is enough to warrant cutting back: it is not necessary to prove that damage is actually being done.

Bush's statement came shortly after he had met lobbyists from the American coal companies and read a report from the George C. Marshall Institute, a right-wing think-tank financed by several large corporations.

The institute's report suggested that the warming of 0.5 degrees Celsius that has taken place since 1880 could be due to a rise in the level of heat given out by the sun and that, as similar periods of high solar radiation have been followed by cooler periods in the past, the twenty-first century could be 1 degree colder than at present. 'I have little respect for the vociferous people who are insisting, without looking at this evidence, that the earth is getting steadily hotter,' said Robert Jastrow, one of the report's four authors – a group of scientists previously best known for a series of pamphlets on strategic defence. 'I suspect that they are motivated by an anti-growth, anti-business ideology,' he added, revealing perhaps more than he had intended about his own ideological position. Bush's chief of staff at the time, John Sununu, whose attitude on measures to deal with the threat of global warming is encapsulated in his phrase, 'we are not prepared to talk about changing the American way of life,' was later described by Stephen Schneider, a leading climate-modeller, as 'brandishing the [Marshall] report as if he were holding a crucifix to repel a vampire'. Although many experts called the document 'junk science', it provided the President with exactly what he wanted – an excuse to do nothing. Perhaps it is significant that the Marshall Institute is named after the general who, as chief of staff of the US Army in 1941, rejected Dutch intelligence that the Japanese fleet was sailing towards Pearl Harbor over a week before the raid. When American sources confirmed the Dutch report several days later, the general was out riding and unavailable for eight hours. Eventually he did send a warning, but classified the message 'deferred precedence', and it arrived after the attack had been carried out.

Mrs Thatcher performed little better than President Bush, despite her undoubted personal concern about the problem and her belief that the human race was conducting a 'massive experiment with the system of this planet itself'. All she offered was to return British carbon dioxide emissions to their 1990 level by 2005, although her statement was deliberately phrased to give the impression that she was doing rather more. 'Providing others are ready to take their full share,' she said in May 1990, 'Britain is prepared to set itself the very demanding target of a reduction of up to 30 per cent in presently projected levels of carbon dioxide emissions by the year 2005.' Only those in her audience who knew that Department of Energy figures predicted that British emissions would increase by 30 per cent by 2005 unless something was done could have understood that this meant stabilizing emissions, not cutting them.

It was not overwhelming political pressure which caused Mrs Thatcher to make her pledge so weak. True, Wilfred Beckerman, the Oxford don who wrote *In Defence of Economic Growth* in the early seventies, had written an article earlier that year in *The Sunday Correspondent* which seemed to suggest that if the world was warmer, life would be better for those living on the streets; but this was hardly a consideration likely to influence the Prime Minister.

Nor was she likely to have been influenced by a pamphlet called *Mounting Greenery* published in 1989 by the industry-funded Institute of Economic Affairs in which Robert Whelan, a leading disciple of the American growthmonger Julian Simon, had written:

Before we start dismantling the engine of industrialism which has given Western nations the highest standard of living the world has ever known, and which promises the same degree of progress for the less developed nations, we do at least have the right to ask: are you sure? It would be a mistake which could have grave consequences to allow ourselves to be swayed by the apocalyptic rhetoric of the Greens into allowing irrational, panic station policies to choke people's efforts to establish a higher standard of living for themselves.

These contributions had been far outweighed by hundreds of radio and television programmes and newspaper articles on the effects that warming could have and details of the cuts that would be required to stop it. Mrs Thatcher would have had wide support for almost any action she cared to take, even within Parliament: the all-party House of Commons Select Committee on Energy prepared a 60-page report that called for specific policies to achieve cuts of up to 50 per cent in carbon dioxide emissions and declared that 'our civilization is hanging by its fingernails from the cliff face'.

So why did Mrs Thatcher not act more positively? And why was inertia 'too positive a word to describe the American position', to use a British civil servant's phrase about President Bush's plans to combat global warming? The explanation is that, although deep cuts in fossil energy use and hence carbon dioxide emissions can undoubtedly be made over a period of years without reducing GNP seriously, this is a once-only effect and when these savings have been made, increased energy consumption is essential if economic growth is to continue. For both Bush and Thatcher, stopping or even slowing growth was unthinkable; some American analysts even totted up the billions of dollars of national income that would be lost if growth slowed by one or two percentage points and regarded this as the cost of the anti-emission programme. So large were the sums involved that they concluded that, in spite of the risks and costs involved in global warming, they had no option but to let it continue. Mrs Thatcher's offer to return carbon dioxide emissions to their 1990 level by a date by which she could be sure to be safely out of office really was the best she could do.

One of those who attempted to calculate the costs and benefits of combating global warming was an economist whose work on GNP we have already discussed, William Nordhaus of Yale University. In an essay[3] in *The Economist* in July 1990 that is certain to become a classic of its kind, Nordhaus declared that the Intergovernmental Panel on Climate Change 'should have known better' than to call for cuts of 60 per cent in carbon dioxide emissions because industrialized countries get few benefits from the natural world, at least in monetary terms.

The social and economic impacts of [climate] change are *terra incognita*. In any attempt to assess them, the main factor to recognize is that the climate has little economic impact upon advanced industrial societies. Humans thrive in a wide variety of climatic zones. Cities are increasingly becoming climate proofed by technological changes like air-conditioning and shopping malls.

On the whole, thanks to technological changes, people now tend to move toward warmer regions in North America and Europe. Climate warming will probably be a boon to Alaska, which is America's least productive state in terms of GNP per square mile. Studies of the impact of global warming on the United States and other developed regions find that the most vulnerable areas are those dependent on unmanaged eco-systems – on naturally occurring rainfall, run-off and temperatures, and the extremes of these variables. Agriculture, forestry and coastal activities fall into this category.

Most economic activity in industrialized countries, however, depends very little on the climate. Intensive care units of hospitals, underground mining, science laboratories, communications, heavy manufacturing and microelectronics are among the sectors likely to be unaffected by climatic change. In selecting whether to set up in, say, Warsaw or Hongkong, few businesses will consider temperature a weighty factor.

Greenhouse warming would have little effect on America's national output. About 3 per cent of American GNP originates in climate-sensitive sectors such as farming and forestry. Another 10 per cent comes from sectors only modestly sensitive – energy, water systems, property and construction. Far the largest share, 87 per cent, comes from sectors, including most services, that are negligibly affected by climate change.

Continuing in this optimistic vein, Nordhaus says that greenhouse warming will reduce yields in many crops but the associated fertilization effect of higher levels of carbon dioxide will probably offset the climatic harm over the next century. 'Snow skiing will be hurt but water skiing will benefit ... Construction in temperate climates will be favourably affected because the weather will be warm for more of the year ... In sum, the impacts of climatic change on developed countries are likely to be small, amounting to less than 1 per cent of national income over the next half-century. In contrast, small and poor countries with large agricultural sectors are likely to be particularly vulnerable.'

Although Nordhaus accepted that catastrophic climatic changes such as sea level rises of six metres or more in a few centuries or a shift in the Gulf Stream so that Europe froze could not be ruled out ('Geological history is filled with odd events'), he seemed unsure how to react. 'A vague premonition of some potential disaster is insufficient grounds to plunge the world into depression ... Move cautiously, gather information and use markets wherever possible' was the best advice he could give.

But by November 1990, the professor's work had progressed and in a paper called *To Slow or Not to Slow – the Economics of the Greenhouse Effect* which he circulated privately, he came to the conclusion that the United States should spend very little to check the emissions of greenhouse gases. This was because his estimate of the net economic damage a 3-degree warming would do to the American economy was only about 0.25 per cent of GNP in terms of the factors he was able to quantify and he thought that a percentage point or so more should cover the rest. 'My hunch is that the overall impact upon [US] human activity is unlikely to be larger than 2 per cent of total output ... Climate change is likely to produce a combination of gains and losses with no strong presumption of substantial net economic damage.' On the other hand, the annual cost of reducing greenhouse gas emissions rose rapidly the larger the cut that was made. While it cost an estimated $120 million to reduce emissions by 2 per cent, the figure for 20 per cent was $16,300 million and for 40 per cent, $108,000 million. As it obviously did not make sense to spend more on cutting emissions than the value of the benefits achieved, he suggested that the largest cut worth making might be of the order of one-third, while at the same time admitting that his analysis 'has a number of important oversimplifications', some of which were 'the issues of uncertainty' – such as the risk of a climatic flip.

The main problem with Nordhaus's work is not his simplifications or the fact that he suggests that the United States need not worry too much about the effect of global warming on its domestic economy; it is that his analysis is entirely concerned with the costs and benefits of reducing emissions below their present level and thus makes no allowance for the effects of economic growth. His position is therefore as sensible as that of someone trying to get down an escalator while ignoring the fact that it is going up.

Economic growth and increased energy use are inseparable, Nobel laureate Solow to the contrary. All human activity involves the use of energy, and most economic growth has come about either from the monetarization of activities which were previously done for nothing or through the progressive substitution of increasing amounts of fossil energy for that from human, animal and other renewable sources. This is because, apart from improved plant varieties, most of the technologies introduced by entrepreneurs responding to the growth imperative involve the use of fossil fuel, even those that use humans or animals as their motive power. Consider the bicycle, a device that greatly increases the speed at which a person can move from place to place for the same expenditure of energy as walking. It is essentially a solid lump of fossil energy: the power that was used to make it.

Not surprisingly, there is a close relationship between the level of energy used in a country and the level of activity measured by its GNP, as the following table shows:

Energy consumption and GNP, 1988

Kilograms of oil equivalent used per head		GNP per head	
Canada	9,683	Switzerland	27,500
Norway	9,516	Japan	21,020
United States	7,655	Norway	19,990
Sweden	6,617	United States	19,840
Finland	5,550	Sweden	19,300
Netherlands	5,235	Finland	18,590
Australia	5,157	West Germany	18,480
Belgium	4,781	Denmark	18,450
West Germany	4,421	Canada	16,960
New Zealand	4,339	France	16.090
Switzerland	4,193	Austria	15,470
Denmark	3,902	Netherlands	14,520
United Kingdom	3,756	Belgium	14,490
France	3,704	Italy	13,330
Austria	3,396	United Kingdom	12,810
Japan	3,306	Australia	12,340
Ireland	2,610	New Zealand	10,000
Italy	2,608	Ireland	7,750

Source: World Bank Development Report, 1990.

Obviously the relationship is not exact: there are discrepancies caused by the way a country's GNP is made up and its climate. Warmer countries seem to use less energy than colder ones with a similar GNP while Canada and Norway have disproportionately large energy consumptions because both are involved in energy-intensive metal extraction. Similarly, the Netherlands uses a great deal more energy than it would if it did not make so much fertilizer and plastics and refine so much oil. Switzerland's GNP on the other hand is very high in relation to its energy use, because its manufactured goods are knowledge- and skill-, rather than material-intensive and it has large financial services and tourism sectors. Japan's high-value, low-weight manufactured goods also give it a high earnings/energy ratio. Overall, though, the relationship holds: the higher the energy use, the higher the GNP.

The intensity of energy use varies from industrial sector to sector. Fortunately, however, those sectors which supply humankind's basic needs – food, clothing and shelter – have the lowest energy requirements, as the table overleaf shows:

Energy use by sector in Britain, 1984

	Value of output (£million)	Energy use (million therms)	Therms/£100 output
Transport	23,609	14,999	63.53
Iron and steel	7,276	2,935	40.34
Chemicals, syn. fibres	19,573	3,659	18.69
Glass, concrete etc.	7,743	1,440	18.60
Wood, water, rubber	10,335	1,506	14.57
Non-ferrous metals	3,741	502	13.42
Paper, print, publishing	15,326	820	5.35
Food, drink, tobacco	33,948	1,584	4.67
Cars, ships, aerospace	18,265	712	3.90
Textiles, clothing	11.488	441	3.84
Agriculture	14,375	550	3.83
Mechanical engineering	28,060	1,042	3.71
Electrical engineering	20,958	446	2.13
Construction	43,850	409	0.93

Source: Institute of Fiscal Studies Commentary no. 19, January 1990.

Most industrial countries have reduced the amount of energy they require per dollar of GNP over the past decade, as the graph opposite shows, and there have been claims that these reductions were due to increased energy efficiency. These claims are misleading, however. Most of the savings arose because the highly energy-intensive industrial sectors of these economies grew much more slowly than they had over the previous fifteen years with the bulk of the increase in GNP coming from the expansion of less energy-intensive industries and other low-energy activities such as services.

Other factors helped save energy too. Every mature industrial country moved its production 'up-market', trying to emulate Switzerland and Japan by producing high value, high quality goods while leaving bulk production to the developing world. As the graph shows, the energy used per unit of GNP in developing countries rose; this was largely because they were mining ore and smelting metals for export to the wealthier parts of the world. The share of part-processed goods in OECD imports grew significantly during this time, and certain types of unsophisticated shipbuilding moved from Japan to Korea. As a result of the rise in semi-manufactured imports, European steel production, a heavy energy user, declined from a peak of 141 million tonnes in 1979, the year the EC's energy use also peaked, to 110 million tonnes in 1983. Production also declined in the United States and Japan.

Not in my backyard

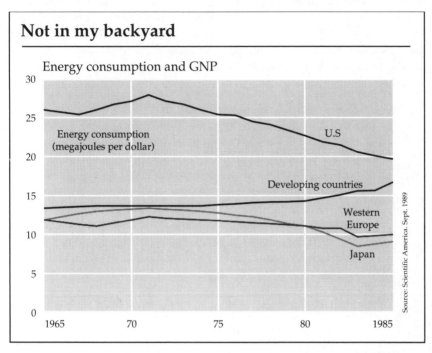

Figure 11.1 The industrialized countries seem to have cut the amount of energy they need for each dollar's worth of GNP. However, this is because they have increasingly come to rely on the Third World for imports like ships and steel, which embody a lot of energy. As a result, the Third World is using more energy per unit of national income.

Whenever industry expands rapidly, energy use expands rapidly too. In the sixties and seventies, this was true despite the effects of the 1973 oil price shock, as the next table shows. In the eighties, when industrial expansion was slow and other sectors of the economy provided the growth, the rate of increase in energy use was slower. However, only Germany managed the trick of continuing to grow industrially while consuming less fuel, and in its case, both the energy saving and growth were small. In both 1990 and 1991, Britain's GNP fell while its carbon dioxide emissions rose.

While there is undoubtedly scope for increased energy efficiency, the reductions in carbon dioxide emissions that this will produce will not be enough to enable 80-90 per cent cuts in current emission levels to be made while at the same time allowing growth to go on indefinitely. The most optimistic forecast of the potential for cutting carbon dioxide emissions in Britain was prepared by the Department of Energy for submission to the IPCC. It estimated that 60 per cent reductions were possible if the best current technologies were adopted and the pay-back period for conservation measures was not limited to the ridiculously short period of two years, as had been government policy. However, once these cuts had been made, further ones would become increasingly difficult to accomplish, and their yield would become progressively smaller. In any case, if growth continued at 3 per cent, the whole of the 60 per cent saving could be expected to be exhausted in around thirty years unless the make-up of GNP changed considerably.

Energy growth compared with industrial growth

	1965-80		1980-88	
	% Energy	% Industry	% Energy	% Industry
Japan	6.1	8.5	1.9	4.9
Netherlands	5.0	4.0	1.3	0.8
Canada	4.5	3.5	1.6	3.0
Ireland	3.9	*n.a.*	1.5	1.7
France	3.7	4.3	0.4	0.1
Italy	3.7	4.0	0.3	1.1
Germany	3.0	2.8	-0.2	0.4
Belgium	2.9	4.4	0.0	1.1
Sweden	2.5	2.3	2.4	2.9
US	2.3	1.7	0.9	2.9
UK	0.9	-0.5	0.8	1.9
OECD average	3.0	3.1	1.0	2.2

Most industrial countries have been considering the extent to which they can reduce their carbon dioxide emissions since the target of a 20 per cent cut by the year 2005 was proposed by an international conference in Toronto in 1986. The table on page 195 shows the reductions individual countries have set themselves.

The European Commission published[4] its thinking on the matter in September 1989 and the result of one of the three scenarios it presented seems encouraging because it appears that the EC can cut emissions by 16 per cent below its 1987 level by 2010 while still growing at 3.5 per cent from 1990 to 2000 and then by 3 per cent to 2010. However, when the figures are examined more closely it becomes apparent that this result has been obtained by sleight of hand: the growth of energy-intensive industry is halted after 1995 (presumably to be carried on elsewhere, as we have just seen) and the use of gas as a fuel is increased by 61 per cent. (Gas, of course, gives off less carbon dioxide per calorie than oil or coal because of its higher hydrogen content.) In addition, nuclear energy is assumed to displace 200 million tonnes of oil equivalent without releasing any carbon dioxide, a major error, since nuclear power requires the use of fossil fuels for the construction of generating plant, for the mining and concentration of uranium and for the disposal of

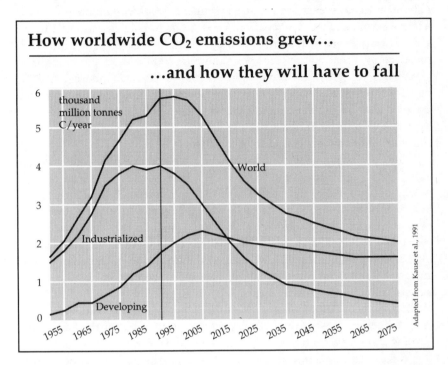

How worldwide CO_2 emissions grew...

...and how they will have to fall

Figure 11.2 Carbon dioxide emissions need to be cut by at least 60 per cent to halt global warming. This graph shows that the industrialized countries will have to cut their consumption to about a quarter of their 1950 level unless they can buy the right to burn more from more frugal countries.

its waste. One estimate, by John Gever, Robert Kaufmann, David Skole and Charles Vorosmarty in their book *Beyond Oil* (1987), is that a nuclear station gives out about four times as much power as the fossil energy used to build it and to provide its uranium. If the energy costs of decommissioning are deducted, the net yield might be zero: 'It now appears that the United States will be lucky if the nuclear industry eventu-ally produces as much energy as it has consumed,' the authors say. The   argument in the Commission's defence is that the carbon dioxide releases occasioned by uranium mining take place outside its area, those connected with building nuclear stations are already included under other headings, and those caused by decommissioning occur after the period under con-sideration.

The EC document also presents another, less optimistic scenario in which energy-intensive industries continue to grow until 2000, but then stop. In this version, energy savings do not arise to the same extent as in the first version, governments do not interfere with the free market, people spend their increased income on bigger cars and traffic congestion worsens.

(The first scenario envisaged that governments would simultaneously build new roads and shift passengers from private cars to public transport!) In the second scenario – which seems the more likely to come to pass – growth is projected to run at 3.5 per cent per annum to 2000 and 2.5 per cent thereafter, with carbon dioxide emissions rising 45 per cent above the 1987 figure. However, this might prove to be an underestimate as the projection assumes that 39 per cent more nuclear energy will be generated in 2010 than in 1987: if the public refuses to let this happen but allows growth to continue, emissions are bound to become worse.

Why, one asks oneself, did those who prepared the EC study stop the growth of energy-intensive industry? Was it because the results were too bad to contemplate if they did not? And if they were prepared to halt that, why not the growth of manufacturing as a whole? It would have saved them a lot of knock-on problems, like the 60 per cent growth in the volume of transport they predict. The answer is that halting the growth of the manufacturing sector would eventually have limited the expansion of the other sectors and caused the growth rate to tail off. This was unacceptable because, in the paper's words, 'zero growth means a permanently lower standard of living for large parts of our populations.' Yet this is not necessarily true. What zero growth does mean is a fixed overall level of consumption for the EC; it says nothing about how high that level will be nor how it will be distributed.

Similar intellectual dishonesty – or, more charitably, self-deception – permeates the whole document, right from the first paragraph written by the EC's Commissioner for Energy, Cardos e Cunha. In this he asks himself if sustainable energy growth is possible. The answer is obviously no: the infinite growth of anything is impossible in a finite world. Moreover, at current rates of consumption, human society uses in a year an amount of fossil fuel that it took nature roughly a million years to produce. Such a high rate of use is obviously unsustainable unless one has a very short time horizon: only a world system totally dependent on renewable energy supplies can be regarded as ultimately sustainable. But the Commissioner is not interested in the ultimate, just up to 2010. He adjusts his definition of sustainability accordingly: 'Essentially, the question is: "Can we continue to develop the world's energy supplies on a secure and economic basis sufficient to maintain economic growth whilst at the same time ensuring that the global environment is protected and, indeed, improved?"' he writes, knowing that his staff have assembled figures that enable them to say: 'Yes, so long as EC governments agree to regulate their markets in accordance with an energy policy we will devise.'

By using the phrase 'economic basis', however, the Commissioner has strayed further into the mire. Although he trained as a chemical engineer and ought to know better, he has evidently been misled by economists into thinking that the availability of energy is a question of price: that if one is prepared to pay enough then any amount is available. Not so. The factor determining how much energy can be supplied is energy: if it takes more energy to extract oil from a well than the energy that oil delivers, the well will never be economic, no matter how high the price. This is the reason the shale oil industry has not developed. In 1972 the American Petroleum Council forecast that when the price of a barrel of oil exceeded $6, shale oil extraction would be economic. Although this price has been exceeded by a factor of two or three for most of the period since, the shale oil has stayed in the ground. 'The faulty forecast simply arose through imagining that the costs of extracting shale were independent of current energy costs whereas the costs ... were essentially determined by the price of oil to those industries that manufactured the inputs and physical capital,' explains[5] Malcolm Slesser of the Resource Use Institute at Edinburgh University. 'Shale oil should not be priced against crude oil but through it,' he adds, speaking as a pioneer of energy accounting as opposed to accounting of the financial kind.

The energy cost of obtaining oil has risen substantially. In the 1940s, one hundred times as much energy was produced by an average oil well as had been expended in finding and developing it. By the 1970s, the ratio had fallen to twenty-three to one, according to John Gever and his colleagues in *Beyond Oil* and it is almost certainly even less now. 'By 2005 it will be pointless to continue exploring for oil and gas in the United States: after that more energy would be used to look for these fuels than the oil and gas we found would contain,' they write, claiming that the United States will have abandoned all its oil and gas fields by 2020 – not because they will be empty but because the energy required to extract the residue will be more than the energy gained. 'World oil and gas supplies will last perhaps three decades longer [that is, to 2050] or more if Third World economies fail to develop,' they conclude. They say that the net returns from coal have fallen considerably too: American strip-mined coal releases only $2^{1}/_{2}$ times the energy used to mine it if scrubbers are fitted to remove the sulphur dioxide it produces when burned.

The energy accounting approach enables us to see that the economists' response to the *Limits to Growth* projections I mentioned in the last chapter – 'You don't suddenly run out of something. When something becomes scarcer, the price rises and this encourages substitutes to be found' – was only partly correct. The only thing for which there is no substitute is energy, although there are alternative sources of it, and some of these might become more attractive when the net yield from others falls.

This problem with economics is of recent origin. When the value of currencies was directly or indirectly linked to gold, the world was essentially on an energy standard because the amount of gold mined in a year was determined by the cost of the energy it took to extract it. If energy was cheap and abundant, gold mining would prove profitable, and a lot of gold would find its way into the banks' reserves. This would enable them to increase their lending and their currency note issue, causing interest rates to fall and the economy to expand. If the increased activity drove up energy prices, the flow of gold would decline, slowing the growth of the economy too – a neat little balancing mechanism. But this link has been broken and now there is nothing to back a currency but confidence. An unreal situation and one which economists have failed to appreciate, with the result that their strategies, based as they are on the assumption that it is financial stocks and flows that matter rather than energy ones, are equally unreal.

Malcolm Slesser, who trained as a chemical engineer and who now specializes in energy systems analysis, and Bert de Vries, a physicist from the Centre for Energy and Environment Studies at the University of Groningen, decided that they would check the European Commission's energy and emission projections using resource accounting techniques. They took the Commission's basic scenario which is intermediate between the two we have just discussed – neither optimistic nor pessimistic – and ran their computer model, ECCO, for each year from 1984 to 2084 to check for stability. According to their March 1990 report,[6] they found that the EC's projected industrial growth rate of 1.5 per cent was not high enough to support a 2.5 per cent growth rate in personal consumption and a high growth rate in services because it generated insufficient output to maintain the EC's growing capital stock – houses, roads, factories, machinery, etc. As a result, the growth rate of the services sector started to fall after 2004 and its total output reached a peak at around 2030.

In other words, more energy was required to keep the EC growing steadily than the Commission had allowed, because the energy-intensive industrial sector had to expand faster than it had calculated. This, and the fact that the official scenario made no allowance for the additional energy required to implement fuel conservation measures, meant that the EC could not keep within the carbon dioxide levels projected by the Commission after 1990. 'We do not believe that such a scenario could persist until 2084,' the authors conclude, pointing out that if it did the EC's output of carbon dioxide would be 16,800 million tonnes per year, equal to 60 per cent of the world's current, excessive, output. So much for the Commissioner's sustainable energy growth.

Slesser and de Vries then looked at what would happen to carbon dioxide emissions if the growth of personal consumption was limited to a minimal rate, 0.5 per cent. They assumed that in each year after 1989, 10 per cent of capital spending would be devoted to energy conservation (the money the EC forgot); they stopped building all fossil-fuel power stations after 2000, doubled the rate of construction of nuclear plants, and made up any energy shortfall with wind and solar (photovoltaic) energy. By 2014, as far as they looked into the future, they found that renewable energy generating capacity (but not output, given the nature of these sources) would exceed that of either nuclear or fossil-fuelled plants. Carbon dioxide emissions would peak in 2004 and then slowly decline. Industrial output, as measured by the amount of energy embodied in its products, would begin to decline from 2010 but the population's rate of consumption of goods and services would continue to move up.

ECCO is by far the best available method of predicting energy trends. Consequently, we have to pay attention when it shows, as it did on this last run, that even with only 0.5 per cent consumption growth, carbon dioxide emissions would not fall sufficiently to meet the 20 per cent cuts proposed in Toronto or even Mrs Thatcher's pledge of stability at 1990 levels by 2005. The question is therefore no longer how much growth we are going to be able to have while preserving the environment, it is how many of our current activities we are going to be able to keep. The European Commission's projections showing that we can go on as we are are at best misleading, at worst dishonest. They delay the proper consideration of the situation and hence the date on which a truly sustainable development strategy is adopted. They should be ignored.

What the Slesser and de Vries analysis shows is that a high proportion of the energy we consume is taken up by the growth process itself. In monetary terms, most industrialized countries use around 18 per cent of everything they make to generate growth but, in energy terms, the proportion is much higher because the production of steel, aluminium and cement are very energy-intensive: Slesser estimates that 55 per cent of all energy is consumed by the investment process. As a result, if we can devise an economic system that does not need continual investment to keep itself from collapse, we can cut our energy consumption very considerably. After all, the amount of energy actually required to feed, clothe and house a human is not very high, as the table on page 202 showed. Our problem is that we have created a system that makes it so.

As the IPCC pointed out, if we fail to make the change now because we have deluded ourselves into thinking that things will be all right for a little longer, in the way the EC Commission has done, or pretend, like Professor Nordhaus, that the problem will not have too severe an impact in the industrial world, then our situation will get significantly worse. By climbing further up the energy consumption ladder we will have further to climb down – or fall. The longer we delay, the harder will be the adjustment we will have to make. Moreover, just as energy is getting more costly in energy terms, raw materials are as well, so that when a crisis eventually forces us to make a change, the real cost of doing so will be very much higher. Renewable energy systems – wind-turbines, wave-power stations, photovoltaic arrays, and so on – will all require inputs of cement, steel, copper and other energy-intensive materials for their construction, and the energy cost of these is steadily rising. Slesser quotes an estimate from P. A. Bailey's book *Mining Engineering* to the effect that, while 1 kg of copper took 3.5 kg of coal to produce in 1976, 10.1 kg will be required by 2000, because the average grade of copper ore can be expected to have fallen from 0.7 per cent to 0.2 per cent. In short, the sooner we change, the more favourable the outcome will be and the more comfortably will we be able to live on a sustainable basis.

So how do we bring about the necessary cuts in carbon dioxide emissions, given that capitalism depends on continuous economic growth for its survival and that we can either reduce greenhouse gas levels or continue to grow, but not both? There is no way that we can scrap the capitalist system and replace it with another one in the few years we have available. Capitalism is the only working economic system in the world today, and we have no option but to use it.

What we can do, however, is change its nature. As we noted in the Introduction, politicians have taken pride recently in leaving decisions to the market, with the result that market forces have shaped society rather than society shaping the market. This is the tail wagging the dog. We have forgotten that the people are the point of economic activity and behaved as if economic activity is the point of people.

All this must change. Society has to tell the capitalist system in which direction it wants to go. It has to give it signals in terms that it understands – prohibitions, taxes and incentives – so that it takes us very quickly and efficiently, as it can do, to our desired end. Naturally, we have to agree what that end is to be, something we have avoided doing of late, preferring to work for an increase in the undifferentiated bundle of goods and services that is GNP rather than towards the accomplishment of particular, and finite, objectives. Fortunately the decision has been largely made for us: we have to reduce greenhouse gas emissions by an amount that, within fifty years, will stop global temperatures rising beyond the increase of 1 to 2 degrees to which we are already committed. True, some people would accept a lesser target and limit temperature rises to 0.1 degrees a decade, a rate to which they think it may be within the power of natural systems to adapt. But for now that does not matter because both schools of thought agree on the path we must take for the first part of the way.

Another thing that we can agree on – in principle if not in practice – is that the cut in emissions must be achieved without making life worse for the world's poor and disadvantaged, if only because it was the rich who caused

Equality of
SACRIFICE?

THE MAN AT THE TOP—
"Equality of Sac-
rifice—that's the
big idea, friends!
Let's all
step down
one rung!"

THE
UNEMPLOYED
MAN

VOTE LABOUR

global warming in the first place. However, there is a problem here as a result of our having to use the capitalist market system to get us to where we want to go. Ted Trainer prints a wonderful definition in big capital letters in his book *Developed to Death* (1989). 'A market economy is an ingenious device for ensuring that when things become scarce only the rich can get them', a statement so blindingly true you wonder why you never realized it before. What it means in our case is that unless we are careful about the way we limit fossil fuel consumption, the rich will still use as much as they ever did before, leaving the poor to go without. Fortunately there is an answer to this, which, since it has frequently been used in capitalist countries in times of war, may be considered to be ideologically sound. It's called rationing.

The right to burn 500 kg of oil a year or its equivalent in other fossil fuels belongs to every human being, not just those who by hard work or good fortune have the money to pay to do so. However, if every country implements an initial 20 per cent cut in its consumption, as the Toronto conference urged, the situation will be equivalent to the 'equality of sacrifice' proposed by the wealthy gentleman in this thirties cartoon, and those on the lowest rungs of the ladder will be submerged. The only way to avoid this is to distribute fossil fuel ration cards to everyone on earth, giving us all the same basic entitlement; when we want to buy a litre of petrol or a tonne of coal we pay over a specific number of coupons to the merchant before we receive our supply.

If such a system were implemented, an unofficial market in energy coupons would quickly spring up. No attempt should be made to discourage this, because it would enable people who were prepared to organize their lives so that they could manage without using some of their coupons to be well paid for their efforts by others who were more profligate. In fact an international trade in coupons would build up as the energy-intensive nations paid the traditional ones for the right to burn more than their natural share. This trade would not only bind into the system those countries that might otherwise want to go their own way but it would also represent a substantial shift of resources from rich to poor, a reversing of the trend to financial concentration. And, as we saw in chapter 4, shifts in income from rich to poor have done more historically to improve people's well-being than overall rises in national consumption ever appear to have done.

It seems an awful lot of work to distribute a ration card to everybody on earth – and, as someone is bound to say, 'think of all those trees to provide the paper.' Unfortunately, there is no alternative, because if allocations were made on a national rather than an individual basis, many governments would distribute the fuel bureaucratically or to political supporters, or – to raise income for themselves – would sell the right to supplies on the open market using carbon taxes. These alternative methods of allocation have serious flaws. Distributing fuel in line with government decisions centralizes power, opens the door wide to corruption, and is liable to generate the mis-allocation of resources that eventually brought down the centrally planned economies of eastern Europe.

However, the worst drawback of the alternative methods is that none of them automatically does anything for the poor. This makes them unaccept-able, because whatever system is adopted, the price of goods with a fossil energy content will move up, and unless the less well-off are compensated, people who are already living on the margin will be tipped over the brink. The poor must be protected not least because, in their search for renewable energy sources, wealthier nations will start using land now under food crops to produce alcohol for their cars and rapeseed oil for their lorries. Food prices will rise as its supply drops and the poor will need additional resources if they are not to go hungry.

The principle of 'one person, one vote' is widely accepted as the best way of ensuring that a country has a government that takes its people's interests into account. Other systems might be less troublesome or more efficient but they rarely work out well in the end. The distribution of energy ration cards to everyone is equivalent to giving people the vote. Politicians are bound to think they could manage the distribution of energy just as well without rationing, just as they think they could run their countries as well, if not bet-ter, without regular elections. In both cases, though, it would be a mistake to let them try.

The beauty of a rationing scheme is that it kills a lot of birds with one stone. The World Resources Institute published[7] some heroic estimates in 1990 that suggested that 45 per cent of West Germany's annual contribu-tion to the greenhouse effect came from CFCs while methane from rice-growing and livestock made up 45 per cent of India's. Brazil and the Ivory Coast, the WRI thought, were just as bad as the United States as polluters, although their fossil fuel usage was very much lower, because of the carbon dioxide released when their forests were burned. A rationing system could easily be adapted to make allowances for this: an international commission could assess each country's non-fossil-fuel contribution to the greenhouse effect annually and adjust the number of coupons its citizens got accordingly, allocating extra coupons to countries that worked to slow down the warming by planting trees. Special allocations would also be possible to pay countries to preserve their tropical rain-forest for the good of us all.

It is easy to see why sixty-five or so of the world's governments would happily support an international rationing scheme: on average their 2,000 million people use less than the 500 kg annual allowance, and the right to sell coupons they do not need would in effect give them something for nothing. But why would the remaining more powerful countries (a group that includes China, whose 1,088 million people used 580 kg of fuel each in 1988) go along with something that essentially means they have to pay more for something they are probably finding rather expensive already? The answer is that there is no certainty that they will – in fact, the precedents are against it. Human society has a very bad record (except, strangely, in wartime) of making sacrifices today for the sake of a better tomorrow. It will take a tremendous effort by ordinary people working through pressure groups to defeat the forces defending the status quo, although one hopeful sign is that GATT suggested an energy rationing scheme with tradeable coupons in a report it published in early 1992 in preparation for the Earth Summit.

A consideration that should ease the task of getting governments to accept rationing is that its initial effects would be very mild. In the first year, enough coupons would be issued to cover all but, say, 3 per cent of the previous year's total world greenhouse emissions. These would be distributed to everyone in the world, but the price they would be worth on the unofficial market would be so low – as demand and supply would be so nearly in balance – that the whole exercise might not seem worth undertaking. However, this would be an illusion. Once investors believe that the world really is going to cut emissions they will plunge huge funds into designing, developing and producing the systems to enable it to do so. The growth imperative would at last start running in the planet's favour as any country that failed to adapt fast enough would find itself buying coupons from its thriftier neighbours, while those that cut back fastest would find that they had coupons to sell. Similarly, those firms that developed the best ways of saving energy would become the most profitable, licensing their systems or exporting their equipment all over the world.

Each year the number of coupons issued would fall, but by the time the really deep cuts in consumption came to be made, rather than the shavings off the flab, national economies would be much better prepared to make radical changes and there would be powerful industrial lobby groups to force everything through. And what about countries that refused to play ball, or fell by the wayside as the cuts got tough? Economic sanctions should do the trick; at the very least mavericks' exports should be subjected to tariffs based on their energy content to 'level the playing field' for their virtuous competitors.

There are already encouraging signs that the growth imperative is beginning to encourage countries to restrict energy use. The Germans, shocked at the damage done to their forests by pollutants from the burning of oil and coal, realize that their economy cannot continue to develop along the lines it has followed since the Second World War. If they restrict fossil energy use now, they reason, their industry will be forced to develop systems to cope, and these systems will then be able to be sold throughout the world when other countries are forced to economize too. A massive export market could open up; low energy technologies could be the source of a whole new round of German industrial expansion.

Accordingly, in conjunction with the Dutch and the Danes who think the same way, they have pushed the Environmental Directorate of the European Commission to propose the introduction of energy taxes throughout the EC. 'The EC target is to be world leader in carbon dioxide reduction,' an Environmental Directorate official, Leo de Nocker, told a conference on ecological taxes I attended in Germany in spring 1991. The Commission's plan is that a $3 a barrel tax on oil be imposed in all EC countries in 1993 rising by a dollar a year until the year 2000. This would bring the total tax-take up to $10 and add approximately 50 per cent to the pre-refinery price of oil. Taxes would also be imposed on other power sources on the basis of their energy yield and the carbon dioxide they release: nuclear power would bear the least tax and the cost of coal would double. However, these rates will not even stabilize the EC's carbon dioxide emissions: it is estimated that an $18 a barrel tax on oil and proportionate levies on other fuels would be required to do that. And although these rates represent a doubling of the price of oil and a quadrupling of that of coal, much higher taxes still would be required to provide a long-term answer to the greenhouse effect if that was the control method chosen.

Although I have argued throughout this chapter that continuing GNP growth is incompatible with a drastically cut, constant level of fossil fuel use, at least some sectors of the economy would grow for a period if we began reducing carbon dioxide emissions. We need them to do so because the total restructuring of the economy we are discussing requires a very different national capital stock, with fewer cars and more public vehicles, better insulated houses, and power stations based on renewable rather than irreplaceable energy.

Investment would probably continue for generations, but at a steadily declining rate, bringing us ever closer to our goal of a stable society in which there would be no net change in overall output levels from year to year. Of course some sectors would undoubtedly decline as a result of the economy's new course – and they would need to do so to release the energy and other resources required for the expanding sectors. In consequence, it is impossible to say whether the GNP figure would go up or down – not that it matters, anyway, because GNP, as we have seen, is a largely meaningless figure. What does matter is that in the short term we keep the level of investment high to avoid the slump that Geoffrey Lean feared would necessarily result from Green Party economic policies. However, with our knowledge of the relationship between interest rates, the level of investment, and inflation, there should be no fear of that.

As we approach our goal of the stable state, the rate of return from our investment will fall off while, as our capital stock grows, the level of resources we need to devote to maintaining it will steadily rise. Eventually the annual amount we invest will be vanishingly small while most of whatever we produce which we do not ourselves consume will go into maintenance. It may be that output growth will never actually stop because technological improvements will permit more and more to be made from the same inputs of land, labour and solar and fossil energy without placing the environment under threat. However, each improvement will tend to yield a smaller benefit than the last as we asymptotically approach an ultimate level. The important difference between this path and the one we are on is that stability, rather than growth, will be our aim.

The transition from a growing to a stable economy will be exciting if it is carried out in a planned way while we still have the energy resources to do so. It will be a period in which cultures and communities blossom rather than being trampled underfoot by a one-economy world. In *Energy and Equity* (1974), which was born out of the energy crisis of the early seventies, Ivan Illich maintains that the use of large quantities of energy degrades social relations as inevitably as it destroys the environment.

Only a ceiling on energy use can lead to social relations that are characterized by high levels of equity. The one option which is presently neglected is the only choice within the reach of all nations. It is also the only strategy by which a political process can be used to set limits on the power of even the most motorized bureaucrat. Participatory democracy postulates low energy technology. Only participatory democracy creates the conditions for rational technology.

What is overlooked is that energy and equity can grow concurrently only to a point. Below a threshold of per capita wattage, motors improve the conditions for social progress. Above this threshold, energy grows at the expense of equity. Further energy affluence then means decreased distribution of control over that energy.

Illich argues that once some people move faster than the speed of a person on a bicycle, a speed everyone can achieve and afford, there are no limits at all to the resources and energy the better-off will pour into faster and faster travel modes for themselves so that they can control ever larger parts of the world. Exactly the same argument can be made in relation to manufacturing industry. Unless there is a limit to the amount of energy an entrepreneur can employ, he will take over larger and larger shares of the market at the expense of less energy-intensive competitors.

The first casualty of a move to a lower energy world would be transport, the most energy-intensive sector of all. Higher transport costs would allow small producers to re-emerge to use local resources to supply local markets. This would, in turn, create greater local, regional and national autonomy, reversing the concentration of economic power that has taken place in the last century. What a flowering of cultures, communities and individuals there could be!

12

The Dutch Dilemma

At Christmas, the joyous anniversary of Jesus' birth, light breaks through in a world darkened by Man's egotism and lust for domination over his fellow man and Nature. We feel that darkness today in all its frightening gloom as the future of creation itself is now at stake. What we are now seeing is not the destruction of the earth at a blow but its demise in a silent drama ... The earth is slowly dying, and the inconceivable – the end of life itself – is actually becoming conceivable. – Queen Beatrix of the Netherlands in her 1988 Christmas message

It's ten o'clock on a warm May morning in 1990 and sunbathers are already basking topless on the sandy beach at Scheveningen, a resort popular with the residents of The Hague, a short tram-ride away. All along the promenade, people are unloading wind-shields, beach chairs and picnic baskets from the boots of smart cars.

Yet something seems wrong. The sea is a dark peaty brown, only becoming blue about 800 m from shore, and all along its edge is a 100 mm high curd of greeny-beige foam. On the beach a tractor drives between the sunbathers scooping up sand and sieving out the soft-drink cans with a device mounted on its back. It seems to miss most of the plastic rubbish, though: chip trays and forks crunch under your feet as you walk and plastic bags lie like stranded jellyfish along the water line. But neither the sea nor the tractor cleans the dry sand between the permanent sun loungers, and as I pick my way through them and the surrounding orange peel and dog dirt I wonder how the Dutch, a people I had hitherto regarded as fastidious, can stomach using the beach at all.

The sea is brown with silt dredged from the shipping channels into Rotterdam that is routinely dumped just south of the port and carried north by the current. The foamy fringe is caused by an algal bloom, which is in turn due to the enrichment of the sea by phosphates and nitrates from the land. According to official figures, 159,000 more tonnes of phosphate were applied to Dutch farmland as fertilizers or added to its waters as detergents or sewage in 1986 than were taken up by crops or otherwise lost to the system. Eventually this entire surplus will leach into the sea. The nitrate run-off from fertilizers, animal waste and sewage is even larger: roughly 400,000 tonnes a year, a quantity that took 2 million tonnes of oil to produce. The algae are the least worrying aspect of this extraordinary wastage: the real problem is that both phosphates and nitrates are working their way down into the groundwater that is pumped up for human use and by 2005 their concentrations are expected to make it unfit for drinking without expensive treatment. Scientists calculate that a 70-90 per cent reduction in phosphate and nitrate use ought to have been implemented in 1986 if treatment was to have been avoided, but so far nothing concrete has been done beyond placing a ceiling on the number of animals farmers can keep.

Even though the first warnings about water quality were given as long ago as 1970 and the government had worked out its policy by 1983, it is easy to understand why the 1986 deadline was not kept: the measures it required were so drastic. Many environmentalists think the five million cows and twelve million pigs the country keeps – more per square kilometre than anywhere else in the world – will have to be reduced by half. This is in spite of government plans to encourage farmers to set up plants to dry, pelletize and export 20 million tonnes of farm slurry a year by 2000, a fifth of the total, and to build other plants to denitrify and dephosphate sewage and industrial effluent. Certainly, arable farmers will have to learn to manage with severely limited fertilizer applications and research is urgently going on to develop animal feedstuffs with a low phosphorus and nitrogen content.

'I don't swim in the sea,' says Lucas Reijnders, professor of environmental science at Amsterdam University and part-time co-ordinator of the Nature and Environment Foundation, the leading Dutch environmental organiza-tion. 'Pollution in the Waddenzee [a portion of North Sea enclosed by the West Frisian Islands, and nursery area for 80 per cent of North Sea's plaice, half its sole and significant quantities of its shrimp, dab, herring, whiting and cod] got so bad last summer that it became anaerobic and killed fish.'

Reijnders adds that some harmful chemicals, including PCBs, are being absorbed by the mud on the seabed and are having a harmful effect on the flatfish that live on top of it. 'You see fish with all sorts of cancerous growths on them – 20 per cent of fish lying in mud close to the shore are affected,' he says. 'In experiments, seals fed with fish caught off the Dutch coast had much less resistance to disease than those fed with fish from elsewhere. Eighty per cent of our seals died in 1988 from disease, possibly partly because of this.'

Johan Vijfvinkel agrees. He is information officer of the North Sea Working Group, a partially state-funded organization that aims to protect and restore the marine environment and which organized the Third North Sea Conference in 1990. 'Half the fish catch is being thrown back into the sea off North Germany because of its diseased appearance,' he says.

'Overfertilization due to agriculture is the main problem and even though the 1987 conference in London on the North Sea agreed that the input of nutrients should be halved from its 1985 level by 1995, it is generally accepted that the Dutch and the Danes will not achieve that target. The North Sea is not even mentioned in the Ministry of Agriculture's plans.'

Vijfvinkel stresses that algal blooms would occur from time to time even if the North Sea were not being fertilized by man. However, enrichment makes them almost inevitable. 'Blooms impose an oxygen stress on fish and make them more likely to be affected by other forms of pollution,' he says.

Several fish processors and merchants have their factories and offices on the dockside at Scheveningen, less than two hundred metres from the beach. 'Are you suggesting our fish are not fit to eat?' one of them says angrily when I ask him about cancerous growths. 'I've never seen anything like that.' Peter van der Toom, secretary-manager of the Scheveningen fish auction hall, also denies seeing ulcerated fish, and blames overfishing rather than pollution for most of the decline in landings through the port. His figures show that 42,105 tonnes of fish were landed in 1965 and that by 1989 this had dropped to 16,797 tonnes, half from foreign boats.

Indeed the shocking thing about the harbour basins at Scheveningen for those who knew them in the past is how few boats they contain. In the mid-sixties they were generally full of boats in the 15 to 30 m range, but the smaller boats, particularly those built in wood, were increasingly unable to compete with the bigger ones and were being sold off. By the early eighties, it was the middle-sized boats' turn to become obsolete, and half of the inner harbour was packed with rusting hulks.

'The worst boats were scrapped. Slightly better ones were sold off to African countries like Mauretania and the best went to Britain and Ireland,' says van der Toom. Only two types of fishing boat are based in Scheveningen at present: steel shrimpers of between 15 and 20 m that fish so close inshore it seems you could wade out and touch them, and huge stern trawlers which go to sea at the start of each week and return on Thursdays and Fridays. It is apparent from everything he says that the efforts of fishermen over the years to catch more and more fish have not only cut overall catches and severely damaged fish stocks but have concentrated the exploitation of marine resources in very few hands and made fishing methods highly energy-intensive.

The Scheveningen auction figures show that roundfish catches – mainly cod, whiting and herring – collapsed in 1989. 'It's overfishing,' van der Toom says. 'The use of echo-sounders has made it too easy to catch them, particularly as they go about in shoals. Flat fish don't give an echo.' On the other hand, catches of a flatfish, the sole, have increased and the total allowable catch limit imposed by the EC has gone up by 70 per cent. 'A biological miracle,' says Johan Vijfvinkel.

Peter van der Toom is worried that the huge fishing effort being applied by the Scheveningen fleet might be making things even worse. 'The seabed is being ground up almost continuously, favouring short-life species. Some areas of the seabed are closed to fishermen, but they are only kept closed for a few months, not even a full year.' He is also concerned about enrichment. 'Herring have been reaching sexual maturity earlier than in the past, because of the extra algal food. They have spawned too early in the year, when the water has been cold and the fry have been lost.'

Not everybody accepts that the situation is dire – in fact, Rudolf Boddeke of the Netherlands Institute for Fishery Investigations in Ijmuiden even thinks that the enrichment has brought positive benefits. 'It's been a blessing. There has been a clear growth in catches of sole, plaice and cockles and mussels since the fifties as a result of the eutrophication [nutrient enrichment] of the coastal zone. I calculate the value of the fertilizers flowing in from the land to be 400 million guilders [£133 million] a year as far as the fishermen are concerned.'

Boddeke also says it is 'complete nonsense' to suggest that fish other than the flounder have been developing ulcers. 'No fish are being discarded as a result of their diseased appearance, and you never see ulcers on plaice or sole. The flounder has been getting wounds for decades as a result of the sharp salinity gradients created by sluice works, which put enormous stress on the fish. Their ulcers have nothing to do with PCBs, and it is irresponsible to suggest that Dutch fish have had any harmful effect on seals – the Dutch seal population doubled between 1980 and 1988 to about 1,100 animals, although canine distemper cut numbers back to 450 in 1989.'

On the other hand, Boddeke knows only too well the damage 'development' can do. In a paper[1] on the Waddenzee he delivered with two colleagues in May 1990 he writes, 'Fisheries [have] changed drastically since the 1930s. Fishing for the "Zuiderzee" herring came to an end shortly after the closing off of the Zuiderzee. The anchovy fishery ceased in the 1960s, that for flounder in 1983. Oysters became extinct in the 1960s due to the over-exploitation of the natural beds ... whelks were fished until 1970 ... Increased turbidity [cloudiness] may have impaired life conditions for adult dab and have also prevented the recovery of sublittoral eelgrass beds after their disappearance in the 1930s due to a "wasting disease" ... Stocks of several bird species breeding in the area suffered great losses in the early 1960s due to a pesticide accident [but] most of the breeding populations have recovered. PCBs caused a reproduction failure among harbour seals in the 1970s.'

One of the few things Boddeke can set against this catalogue of disasters is that mussel cultivation increased ten times between 1950 and 1961; but this added to the sea's turbidity, which has increased fifteenfold. Not that the mussels were entirely to blame – the dumping of silt south of Scheveningen and dredging in the Waddenzee itself were more important causes. Cockle catches also went up until 1984 when three bad winters cut stocks back, and brown shrimp catches have improved since restrictions were placed on catching undersized ones.

The Netherlands' environmental problems are less visible inland, although there are dead and dying trees almost everywhere in the country: around the houses immediately behind the beach at Scheveningen, for example, and in Amsterdam's biggest public open space, the Vondel Park. 'Sixty per cent of our trees are now showing signs of distress,' says Reijnders. 'The figure was only 20 to 30 per cent ten years ago.' He explains that this is due to the quantities of sulphur dioxide and the two nitrogen oxides being deposited from the air, and that, because soil acidity builds up year by year, the trees' condition is steadily getting worse. 'Four-fifths of our trees will have died by the middle of the next century if we continue as we are. We need to cut emissions by 85 per cent to save them,' he says. 'The worst thing for them now would be a dry, warm summer.'

Already, a third of the plants that grew in the Netherlands at the start of the century have become extinct, mostly within the past twenty or thirty years. 'Fertilizer enrichment has affected the wet areas, streams have been canalized and water tables have been lowered. As a result, the plants that used to depend on those systems have gone. In other places soil fertility has improved because the level of nitrates in the rain favours fast-growing grasses at the expense of other species. Even heather, which used to be common on poor, sandy soils, is getting rare and the areas in which it grew are going over to grass very quickly.'

Insects and other animals have disappeared along with the plants. Thirty per cent of butterfly species have gone and anyone returning to Britain or Ireland in the early summer will realize on their first day home that they didn't see even a cabbage white during their stay. But then with no waste land for food plants and an average rate of pesticide application four times higher than anywhere else in the world it's surprising that any butterflies are left at all. 'We've lost our last otter,' Reijnders says. 'They were badly affected by PCBs, but this one was run over by a car.' But it is not all gloom. 'Frogs have made a come-back as a result of an effort in the sixties to clean organic chemicals out of sewage,' he adds.

The Dutch people are well aware of the environmental problems their economic development path has created. It would be hard not to be, since the stench of animal slurry spoils still summer evenings in the country, a red-brown haze of photochemical smog creates Turneresque sunsets in the town and two-thirds of people are said to have to put up with unacceptable levels of noise. Half a million people (out of a population of 14.5 million) belong to one environmental organization or another and their concern was, rather belatedly, picked up by the government in 1988. 'It was only then that the environment became the central issue in Dutch politics and the government started taking it seriously,' Reijnders says. One sign of the change was the publication that year by the National Institute of Public Health and Environmental Protection of a full-scale environmental survey, *Concern for Tomorrow*. Queen Beatrix's Christmas speech that year also made a very strong impression. 'She spoke about the end of nature. It was almost apocalyptic,' Reijnders says.

In May 1989 the government came forward with *To Choose or to Lose*, a massive national environment plan supported by twenty-seven further documents and memoranda. This was the first comprehensive environmental plan to be prepared by any EC member-state, but even before it had come off the presses it had achieved a world first as well: it had brought the government down over the financing of its proposals, the first to fall on an environmental issue. The collapse came when the junior partners in the ruling coalition, the Liberals led by Joris Voorhoeve, objected to proposals to scrap tax allowances for people who travelled to work by car and for the raising of excise duties on petrol and diesel. The party was duly punished in the subsequent election, losing five of its twenty-seven seats.

The election campaign became something of an auction, each party trying to better the others' environmental promises. Ruud Lubbers, the leader of the senior partner in the defunct coalition, the Christian Democrats, promised to cut emissions of sulphur dioxide and nitrogen oxides to control acidification and even to step down carbon dioxide releases by 2 per cent a year. The Labour Party offered to spend £1,000 million more a year on the clean-up than Lubbers but lost three seats to the small Green Left grouping of parties, which called for the doubling of motoring costs and the closure of factories using mercury and cadmium as well as those making PVC and CFCs.

'The public will to change is considerable,' Reijnders says. 'They are ahead of the politicians. A survey among young people showed that their main worry was about the environment, followed by AIDS and then the prospects of getting a job. With older people, the environmental priority is even more pronounced.'

However by late 1991, thirty months after the election, there was still no sign that the coalition it had produced, this time between Labour and the Christian Democrats, had been able to take advantage of its large parliamentary majority and of the public mood. Indeed, Lubbers had backtracked on his carbon dioxide promise despite the fact that this was embodied in the National Environment Plan, and, rather than holding to the target of a 2 per cent reduction each year, was working towards a 2 per cent per annum reduction in the rate at which emissions grew – which in theory would merely mean that they didn't grow at all. Moreover, even though cars are a major source of carbon dioxide and most environmentalists accept that their use will have to be cut by at least half, the government was planning to expand the motorway network by 70 per cent and to build four extremely expensive tunnels under canals to remove traffic bottlenecks. The effect of these would be to encourage even greater vehicle flows.

'The programmes the government has in place will not meet even the carbon dioxide stabilization goal,' Reijnders says. 'There has been considerable wrangling in the Cabinet between the Ministry of Economic Affairs, which acts as a lobby for industry, the Ministry of Agriculture, which speaks for the farmers, and the Environment Minister, with the latter often losing out. If this government fails environmentally, there will be a large Green Party vote in the next elections.' (No true Green Party candidates were elected in the 1989 election: Green Left is a coalition of communist, anarcho-syndicalist, pacifist and evangelical Christian parties, whose common elements are social concern and a commitment to environmental protection.)

The main problem the Dutch government faces is that the whole thrust of the country's development for at least a generation has proved wrong and that it takes a tremendous amount of courage and conviction to admit this and set off in a new direction, particularly as no-one has worked out in detail what that direction should be. Recent economic growth in the Netherlands has been based largely on the expansion of the chemical industry, whose output grew 900 per cent between 1960 and 1985, and the intensification of animal production – output from the agricultural sector grew at 7.8 per cent a year between 1980 and 1985. 'Every 2-3 per cent of GNP growth has led to 5 per cent extra pollution because of the sectors which expanded,' Reijnders comments. 'There is no doubt that the expansion of most traditional growth sectors must stop.'

Few people have so far reached the conclusion that all growth should stop and that the country will have to adjust to a declining GNP. Someone who has been saying this since the mid-sixties is Roefie Hueting, head of the environmental statistics section of the Central Bureau of Statistics in The Hague, whose ideas we discussed in chapter 1. Hueting incurred considerable unpopularity in the seventies and early eighties, even among members of the Green movement. 'They were telling people you could preserve the environment and have growth as well, and didn't like my questioning that,' he says. 'I was despised in Holland. Bitter personal attacks were made on me by my colleagues. I *hate* people who say we have to grow to generate the resources to save the environment. 80 to 90 per cent of economists say that and, since they are not dumb, they must be liars.'

His anger has its roots in 1974, when he was invited to join a group of scientists opposed to the construction of three nuclear stations. 'I saw that it was pointless to be opposed to nuclear energy without developing an alternative to conventional sources of power as well, because these have equally harmful effects such as acid rain,' he says. 'Even if you managed to cut emissions from conventional sources by half, within twenty-three years the situation would be as bad again if the economy grew at 3 per cent.'

In 1973 the group split over Hueting's argument that continued economic growth was incompatible with environmental protection and the Hueting faction stalked off and set up the Centre for Energy Saving. 'Our idea was to compare the growth-first scenario with one in which saving the environment was given priority, but it was 1980 before we could get any funds,' he explains. Eventually they got 2 million guilders (around £700,000) from the Ministry of Economic Affairs to compare the likely effects on national income and unemployment in the year 2000 for the two development strategies. The growth model assumed that the Dutch economy would grow at 3 per cent a year and not introduce any additional environmental protection measures. 'Both scenarios achieved economic growth: 64 per cent in the growth version, compared with 27 per cent in the environmental one. However, I think that we got growth from the environmental model mainly because we reduced atmospheric emissions by 30 per cent and we now know that an 80 to 90 per cent drop is required.'

The two models created an almost identical number of jobs. The growth scenario, however, produced six times the air pollution, a drastic deterioration of the environment, and a continued loss of plant and animal species. And in spite of these costs, the available income per citizen was only 11 per cent greater than for the environmental model, because a high proportion of the increased national income had to go to pay the interest on the investment it had taken to bring it about.

Hueting thought that he had proved his case and wanted to present the results to an OECD conference. Since the Dutch government had paid for the work, he asked them to submit it (a private individual cannot do so directly) but was turned down. 'They said they would not do so because they did not agree with my findings. That's a position I can accept,' he says. But when he asked the umbrella group representing most Dutch environmental organizations to submit it instead, both the group's referees turned the paper down as an inadequate piece of work.

'If the paper had been submitted to the OECD in all probability it would have been forgotten. As it was, I was determined to prove the referees wrong and I got it published in no less than nine learned journals around the world – completely unchanged,' he says. He also presented the paper in person at The Other Economic Summit (TOES) in London in 1984.

'It's not that I'm against growth. I'm entirely in favour of people having three cars and five houses if they want them, provided they can do so without hurting the environment, but unfortunately they can't. There is nothing incompatible between creating employment and preserving the environment – in fact, saving the environment creates a lot of jobs. The problem is the conflict between production and the environment.'

In the late eighties, however, public and professional attitudes to Hueting's views softened as other people began to publish similar results based on their own development models. In March 1989 the government's Central Planning Bureau published a comparison of three potential development scenarios and their environmental consequences up to 2010 as part of the work on the National Environmental Plan. All produced an approximate doubling of GNP, but under one of them, the continuation of present policies, carbon dioxide emissions rose by 35 per cent and bad smells by 10 per cent, and the number of people affected by serious noise went up by half. On the other hand, sulphur dioxide releases were cut by 50 per cent, nitrogen oxides by 10 per cent and ammonia by 33 per cent, while discharges into the Rhine and the North Sea were halved.

The second scenario involved the maximum enforcement of current restrictions on emissions. This did nothing for carbon dioxide levels, left the number of people affected by noise unchanged at its 1985 figure, and halved the numbers affected by bad smells. Sulphur dioxide was cut by 75 per cent, nitrogen oxides by 60 per cent and ammonia by 70 per cent, with North Sea and Rhine discharges going down by 75 per cent. The problem was that this course involved spending twice as much money as the first strategy.

The third scenario was as harsh as the planners thought they could realistically be. It involved sweeping energy conservation in houses and businesses, the construction of combined heat-and-power plants, the maximum use of renewable energy sources and a greater use of natural gas instead of coal and oil. More goods would be carried by rail and water instead of road and there would be a big shift from private cars to public transport and bicycles. Agriculture would maintain its animal numbers but use less fertilizers and pesticides. Industry would switch to cleaner production methods. The result? A drop of between 20 and 30 per cent in the release of carbon dioxide and around 80 per cent in levels of sulphur dioxide, nitrogen oxides, and ammonia. Up to 15 per cent of those affected by noise and 60 per cent by smells would cease to be so and a 75 per cent reduction could be made in discharges into the North Sea and the Rhine. The cost? Potentially no more than the second scenario because of the saving made in energy and raw materials, but energy prices would have to be raised to their pre-1985 levels to ensure this. Best of all, if other countries, particularly fellow-members of the EC, had to follow suit, there would even be 4 per cent more growth over the twenty-year period than with the second scenario.

So what are the snags? From the point of view of the planners, only that the numbers affected by noise and smells were not cut further – they had set themselves a 70-90 per cent reduction target for both. All the other cuts were close to the levels they felt ought to be achieved. But for environmentalists, the promised carbon dioxide reduction left a lot to be desired. 'We need a 60 to 90 per cent cut just to stabilize the atmospheric carbon dioxide concentration,' says Lucas Reijnders. 'We can't be more accurate, because we still don't know enough about how the natural sinks for the gas behave. Even if we achieved that reduction now, we'll still get at least a degree Celsius warming.' (Other scientists put the warming to which the world is already committed at twice that figure.)

Reducing sulphur dioxide, nitrogen oxide and ammonia emission levels is comparatively simple because the three pollutants are amenable to technical fixes. Reducing carbon dioxide emissions requires a change in life-styles. The National Environment Plan itself concludes: 'The [Central Planning Bureau] study shows that, in theory at least, it is not impossible to combine a doubling of consumption and production with reduced emissions of 70 to 90 per cent – with the exception of emissions of CO_2 – provided that the traditional end-of-pipe cleaning techniques are supplemented by structural modifications in the processes of production and consumption.' So serious is the carbon dioxide problem in fact that yet another report, *Climate and Energy*, prepared for the Ministry of the Environment in 1989, concluded that the necessary measures to curb it would be too draconian and the country had better prepare to build taller dykes. As a result, it is scarcely surprising that the Dutch government has already abandoned its pre-election promises about the gas.

So far, because growth is so fundamental to the country's economic system, no Dutch political party with parliamentary representation has seriously suggested bringing the quest for ever-higher consumption rates to a halt. 'A senior Labour Party politician told me that he agreed with what I was saying but that if he adopted it he would lose his job,' Hueting comments. Even the Green Left coalition, which is so radical in other areas, was undecided in mid-1990. 'We are divided between those who want to put the environment first and those who want to do something about poverty,' a spokeswoman, Marijke Vos of the Centre for Environmental Studies in Leiden, told me. 'After all, we can't make the poor pay the cost of putting the environment right. We want a 15 per cent shift of national wealth from the rich to the poor.'

Hueting believes the economic growth the country has experienced in the past thirty years has brought very meagre benefits because, although higher levels of consumption have been generated, this was at the expense of some of the other factors that also contribute to total human welfare with the result that there has been little or no net gain. Two factors in particular, he argues, the natural world and the chances of survival for our children and grandchildren, have been sacrificed to achieve the higher national income levels.

Marius Hummelinck, co-author of the pioneering work on the economic value of the natural world, *Nature's Price*, thinks that the results of recent attempts at growth may even have been negative. 'We are overgrown, definitely,' he says. 'We risk the destruction of our culture if we are not careful.' And, for the visitor walking through the streets of old Amsterdam, it is hard not to agree. The essence of the Dutch architectural style is its sensitive use of simple materials and its human scale, but many new buildings recently have ignored all that. 'Our architecture is chronically sick,' read a May 1990 headline in the Amsterdam daily newspaper *De Volkskrant*, and Hummelinck says that Prince Charles's views on architecture find wide support in the Netherlands too. Steel and glass Pullman Hotels, C&A shops and Post & Telegraph offices dominate the central areas of most Dutch cities, celebrating the concentration of corporate economic power that growth has brought about, while the fine canalside houses that prosperous merchants occupied for over two centuries are hollow, decaying echoes of another way of life. Walking from Laura Ashley to W. H. Smith and on to the Body Shop, one feels that the whole essence of Dutchness is in danger of becoming a sham.

Nobody has asked the Dutch, the twelfth-richest nation in the world in per capita income and the fourth-highest in quality of life according to the UNDP's 1990 *Human Development Report*, whether growth should continue. The question seems irrelevant: there seems to be no option but to carry on. Nor does there seem to be much chance that future growth will be less harmful than that in the past; the present government is ideologically opposed to intervening in the free market, although Lubbers wrote a paper on selective growth and the possibility of steering the economy in 1976.

Another, more intractable difficulty is that when state intervention was tried in the past, the EC objected to 'restraints on trade'. 'The Dutch, the Germans and the Danes are generally held back environmentally by the EC,' says Lucas Reijnders. 'If we had had a free hand we would have legislated so that new cars had to be fitted with catalytic converters at the same time as the US made them compulsory in 1983.'

Later, when the Dutch government started giving tax relief on cars with catalytic converters so that they cost no more than dirtier vehicles, it was taken to the European Court although eventually the case was dropped. On another occasion the Dutch wanted to restrict the use of cadmium in the plastics industry because the toxic metal was building up at between 1 and 2 per cent a year in the soil and marine mud. Again the EC discouraged national action, since it would interfere with trade, and offered to make a regulation itself, eventually producing a toothless directive as a result of opposition by Britain and Italy. Similarly, when Germany wanted to ban pentachlorophenol, the directive the EC produced to do the job actually legalized existing uses. 'We're getting the worst of all worlds,' Reijnders comments. 'What we are able to do legally within the EC is far short of what is required to stop environmental deterioration in the Netherlands. Still, what we can do is to legislate in defiance of the EC in the knowledge that it takes at least two years for a case to come to court.'

Environmentally, the Netherlands is infinitely depressing. Although the Dutch people and their government know they have to act and have the will to do so, they clearly lack both the theoretical framework – the knowledge of how to build an economic system that does not multiply its problems by aiming blindly for growth – and the power to create such an economy within GATT and the EC even if they did.

For Hueting, the solution is so simple and the situation so urgent that he can scarcely contain his impatience. 'Growth is the heart of the environmental problem. The National Environment Plan will never succeed, because it is embedded in growth. People's whole idea of progress is tied up with that damned evil figure, GNP, which was never meant to be used that way by Jan Tinbergen and Richard Stone, the people who developed it. It's not written in the Bible that we have to have economic growth. It's obvious what we have to do, so why all the fuss about a figure in a book?

'Carbon dioxide emissions are linked with energy use which is in turn linked with GNP, so if we have to cut CO_2 by 80 per cent, we have to cut GNP by 75 per cent unless cheap ways are found to reduce the emissions. People think that a 75 per cent cut would take us back to the Middle Ages but that's not true – the proper period is around 1952.

'Saving the environment without checking production growth is only possible if a technology is invented that is sufficiently cleaner, takes sufficiently less space, uses sufficiently less energy and resources *and* is no more expensive than current techniques. This is hardly imaginable, especially across the whole range of human activities.'

13
The Mahatma's Message

Economists must redefine poverty as a shortage of biomass rather than a shortage of cash. Gross natural product is more relevant to the poor than gross national product. – Anil Agarwal, environmentalist

It is not just in the Netherlands that you can tell by looking out to sea that things have gone badly wrong. In India, if you stand on the cliff just south of the beach in Gokarna, a seemingly idyllic village, all temples and coconut palms, in northern Karnataka about 50 km down the road from Goa, you can watch the dug-out canoes returning from fishing almost every afternoon at the end of the year. The season begins in August, just as soon as the sea is calm enough after the late monsoon storms to allow the men to launch their canoes from the beach. Not only are catches best at that time of year but prices are highest too because there is no competition from the big mechanized boats, which are still confined to port by the waves breaking on the harbour bars.

But go up to one of the three or four men in the canoe – a hollowed-out mango log stabilized with an outrigger – that you watched come in through the breakers and which has now been dragged to the top of the beach. In the past, he will tell you, they used to continue to set their gill nets until the end of December, but this year, well before the season is over, his family is on the brink of starvation, and for all the fish he's caught today he might as well look for other work.

Until 1984 each canoe could be expected to catch 60 kg of fish a day for most of the five-month season, giving its crew a daily wage of £4 to £5.50 each, a good income in a state where a graduate secondary teacher gets between £2.50 and £5 per day. But since then catches have declined drastically and are now at a third of their former level. 'The fishermen are getting insufficient food even for their own families,' a social worker told me in December 1986. 'Any fish that is caught has to be sold to buy filling foods like rice, and the infants are showing clear signs of protein deficiency.'

The fall in catches is blamed on the introduction of mechanized boats. 'As soon as the mechanized boats start to fish, our catches drop,' a Gokarna canoe fisherman, Santha Ambige, told me. The previous year, when four

mechanized purse-seiners had put to sea before 1 September, the normal
start of the season for engined boats, they had been set on fire by traditional
fishermen and completely destroyed. Twenty-five people were injured in the
fighting. In Goa, clashes between fishermen were even worse and sixty people died.

The purse-seiners seek out shoals of mackerel and sardine and encircle
them with their nets, which have a mesh less than 10 mm square. Before
this method was introduced, both species were caught by the traditional
fishermen, who put out *rampani* nets, sometimes 5 km long, from the
beaches, and the whole community pulled from each end to help haul them
in. 'I remember a shoal of a million mackerel being caught in a rampani net,'
said Dr M. V. Pai of the Central Marine Fisheries Research Institute
(CMFRI). 'They were kept alive in it in the sea until trucks came to take
them to Bombay. That would have been 100 tonnes of fish and a huge sum
of money for the villagers.' He added that, until a few years previously, each
coastal village had had at least two rampani groups, but almost all had now
disbanded.

When the purse-seiners were introduced in 1976 there was an initial
increase in total catches but landings have now dropped below the original
level. In 1986 CMFRI stated officially that purse-seining had not increased
production and the activities of between 400 and 450 boats along the 300
km Karnataka coastline could damage the resource. In 1982 researchers at
the College of Fisheries in Mangalore warned that even 200 could prove too
many.

As in the Netherlands, mechanized fishing methods have damaged fish
stocks and allowed the wealthy to take over a resource that previously
benefited everyone in the coastal communities. 'Mechanized fishing boats
have to work from harbours, so the income they earn is concentrated in a
few places; the old methods spread it right along the coast,' Dr S. K. Salian
of the College of Fisheries in Managalore told me. 'Very few fishermen
were able to borrow the money to build purse-seiners and the politicians,
civil servants and businessmen who could do so got a gold mine. They have
ruined the industry and the economy of the villages.'

The purse-seiners are not the only problem. Even worse damage has
been done by trawlers which were introduced to Indian waters in the early
1950s by a Norwegian aid project in the neighbouring state of Kerala. The
new type of boat enabled a prawn and shrimp fishery to develop all along
the Kerala and Karnataka coasts. There are now so many trawlers in
Karnataka that the same areas are dragged daily and boats work along the
beaches right up to the point at which the waves begin to break.
Considerable damage is being done to spawning grounds. 'It's almost like
ploughing,' Salian says. None of the catch is eaten locally – it is too highly

priced. Instead, 90 per cent is exported to the United States and Japan.

Large quantities of small 'trash fish' are caught along with the prawns and shrimp and are dried on the sand and used as chicken feed or fertilizer. Many of them would have grown into larger fish to be caught by the canoes if trawls had not been used. As a result, apart from displacing the traditional fishermen, the mechanization of the fishing fleet in Karnataka has seriously depleted fish stocks, reduced the catch of fish for local consumption, caused starvation in the fishing villages, and entailed a greater expenditure of energy and capital on catching smaller but higher-value hauls.

So why was it allowed to happen, particularly as its results were clear in Kerala a decade before Karnataka was affected? The answer is simply that traditional fishermen are of low caste and less important to the politicians than the influential, moneyed class that invested in the new technology. Consequently, no-one was sufficiently concerned to ensure that a mechanism was put into place to ensure that the winners compensated the losers. Even the law that requires the mechanized boats to work more than five nautical miles off shore is totally ignored: there are no fisheries patrols, and fishing boats are not registered, so there is no way of identifying a vessel seen working illegally inshore.

In one way, however, the Indians are better off than the Dutch. They have a well-developed alternative to growth-dependent, wealth-concentrating capitalism: the concept of *sarvodaya* (the welfare of all) developed by Mahatma Gandhi. Unlike Western economics, which conceals its moral assumptions in an unconvincing attempt to be value-free, Gandhi's system is value-based and starts from the position that 'the end to be sought is human happiness combined with mental and moral growth.' Above all, it is concerned about the effect any measures might have on 'the last man' – the weakest and least in any community. Gandhi felt strongly that morality could not be divorced from economics, as he made clear in this passage from *Sarvodaya*, his paraphrase of Ruskin's *Unto This Last*:

Among the delusions which at different periods have affected mankind, perhaps the greatest – certainly the least creditable – is modern economics [since] it is based on the idea that an advantageous code of action may be determined irrespective of the influence of social affection. Of course, as in the case of other delusions, political economy has a plausible idea at the root of it. 'The social affections', says the economist, 'are accidental and disturbing elements in human nature but avarice and the desire for progress are constant elements. Let us eliminate the inconstants and, considering man merely as a money-making machine, examine by what laws of labour, purchase and sale the greatest amount of wealth can be accumulated. Those laws once determined, it will be for each individual afterwards to introduce as much of the disturbing affectionate element as he chooses.

This would be a logical method of analysis if the accidentals to be introduced afterwards were of the same nature as the powers first examined ... but they are not

... they alter the essence of the creature under examination the moment they are added. They operate not mathematically but chemically, introducing conditions which render all our previous knowledge unavailable.

Gandhi saw very clearly that the traditional Indian village, which was described by Sir Charles Metcalfe in 1830 as having within itself almost everything it wanted, was being destroyed by the competition its craftsmen faced from machine industry coupled with the free trade policies of the British-controlled Indian government and the export of raw materials. The result was large-scale unemployment and underemployment and massive poverty in the countryside, and the concentration of wealth in fewer and fewer hands in the towns. Moreover, Gandhi also realized that it would be impossible ever to find enough capital to absorb all the displaced rural labour in the industrial system – 'I wish to make it clear that India does not have enough money to employ everyone with modern technology,' he wrote in *Young India* in 1924 – and that, even if that capital could be found, the drain on the planet's resources to keep everyone employed would be unsustainable. Consequently, he rejected the introduction of any technologies that displaced labour where there was already a labour surplus. He was also a pioneer of the concept of appropriate technology, encouraging devices like the *charka*, the spinning wheel that became his symbol, which was cheap enough for everyone to buy and allowed them to use their free time profitably.

Much of Gandhi's time between 1934 and his death in 1948 was spent preparing a concrete programme for the regeneration of the village economy through the revitalization of its industries and the decentralization of production. Probably the last thing he wrote was a draft of a constitution for the Lok Sevak Sangh (Association of Servants of the People) whose members would go out into the villages to help them organize to become self-contained and self-supporting through agriculture and handicrafts, as they had been in the past. But even if he had not been assassinated the day after writing it, it is extremely unlikely that he could have persuaded the Indian National Congress to give up the power it had just won from the British, dissolve itself and join the Lok Sevak Sangh en bloc, as he was suggesting.

All governments, whether of newly independent countries or not, are very reluctant to dilute their powers by enabling communities to work without them. (In 1986 I attended a briefing in Pune organized for the Chief Secretaries of all the Indian states. It was about a Maharashtrian village, Ralegan Shindi, which has vastly increased its well-being through its own efforts. The 'Sir Humphreys', as the lecturer, Vijay Parulkar, had described them to me beforehand, were not impressed. 'If the village can do all that for itself, where does that leave us?' one of them asked in the discussion that followed.) Consequently, it was almost inevitable that Nehru would adopt a

Western-socialist model of development in India's first five-year plan which ran from 1951, although a nod was made in Gandhi's direction by its concentration on agriculture. However, in the Stalinist second plan, which ran from 1956, the emphasis was switched firmly to heavy industry, with the rural sector being deliberately milked of its savings to finance the steel mills and dams. Little had changed when the current ninth plan was introduced in 1990. In fact at the end of the eighties, the Indian government was spending more on civil aviation – a service used by perhaps 100,000 Indians – than on agriculture, a sector that provided the livelihood of 60 per cent of its people.

Nehru realized that the capitalist system could result 'in the concentration of wealth and of the means of production to the detriment of the common good,' in the words of the first plan, and he sought to overcome this tendency by putting industry under state control. This was done both directly through public ownership, and indirectly, through an increasingly complex system of bureaucratic regulation, which until recently required firms to seek official approval before raising their output by more than 5 per cent in a year or introducing a new product. But in spite of these handicaps, in conventional, GNP, terms the Indian economy did well compared with the pre-plan period, although growth was slow in comparison with other Asian countries including China. Between 1951 and 1959 Indian growth averaged 4 per cent compared with around 1 per cent a year previously. It then ran at around 3.5 per cent in the sixties and seventies and rose to 5 per cent in the early eighties. In total, between 1950 and 1986, a period in which British GNP went up 138 per cent, Indian GNP increased almost fourfold. Even though the population more than doubled, from 361 million to 781 million in the same period, net national product per head went up 72 per cent.

But these increases were not enough to prevent life for most ordinary people getting steadily worse and the country becoming sharply divided between the top 10 per cent of well-educated urban people, who enjoyed at least a quarter of the national income, and the poorest 10 per cent, who survived on around 3 per cent. 'The growth has not benefited the poor and the deprived,' Ramashray Roy of the Institute for Rural Development in Patna wrote in 1981. 'The hoped-for percolation has not materialized; benefits of growth have not gone downwards but only upwards and sideways. Inequality remains and has, in many respects, deepened.' But Roy was not saying anything new. As he pointed out himself, Nehru had said the same thing twenty years earlier when he wrote in a commentary on the third plan, 'Large numbers of people have not shared in [growth] and live without the primary necessities of life. On the other hand, you see a smaller group of really affluent people ... I think the new wealth is flowing in a particular direction and is not spreading out properly.'

Even the main achievement of the 1950-90 period, the 175 per cent increase in agricultural production as a result of the Green Revolution, was hollow. It was only the richer farmers who could afford the new types of seed and the fertilizer, pesticides and machinery to go with them, and many poorer farmers were displaced, exactly as happened in England during the Agricultural Revolution almost 200 years earlier. Moreover, the coarse grains consumed by the poorer people were less responsive to the new techniques, and their output fell. So did the production of pulses, on which most Indians rely for their protein intake: government figures show that the weight of pulses available per head almost halved between 1956 and 1987, dropping from 70.3 g per day to 36.2 g, a serious situation since dietitians recommend vegetarians (which most Indians are) to eat 80 g each day. And the surpluses of rice and wheat that seemed to appear after the record harvests in 1986 and 1989 were illusory, although the government had insufficient space in its famine-reserve warehouses to store all the grain the farmers wanted to sell. As Professor L. S. Venkataramanan of the Institute of Social and Economic Change in Bangalore commented to me, the excess only arose because the people who needed it could not afford to buy.

On top of all this, the richer farmers who successfully adopted the new techniques are caught in a nasty pincer movement. One jaw is that they have to apply ever larger amounts of fertilizer to maintain yields, pump water from increasingly deep wells and spray more and more pesticide as insects' resistance grows. The other jaw is that the prices of chemicals, tractors and of electricity for their irrigation pumps have risen remorselessly while the government has been trying to limit agricultural price rises, minimize wage pressures, moderate inflation and help the poor. As a result, many farmers have fallen into debt. Massive farmers' movements sprang up in the eighties to try to force the government to raise its buying prices and subsidize agricultural inputs, and the early part of 1988 saw hundreds of thousands of farmers blockading Meerut for twenty-five days before moving to Delhi and camping on the streets there.

Deep ploughing, irrigation and the increased use of fertilizers have had serious effects on the land. In an article in the Lokayan Bulletin in 1986, the environmentalist Vandana Shiva quoted a former British director of agriculture in the United Provinces as saying in his presidential address to the Indian Science Congress before independence, 'We need not concern ourselves with soil deterioration in these Provinces. The present standard of fertility can be maintained indefinitely ... In India, we have in existence a perfect balance between the nitrogen requirements of the crops we harvest and the processes which recuperate fertility.' Essentially, these processes involved lightly ploughing and harrowing a soil made friable by the fierce pre-monsoon heat. The first rains would then wash the surface soil into the deep cracks in the earth, exposing a new layer to serve as a seedbed. A mulch was also applied, which had the effect of recycling nutrients, building up levels of soil bacteria and increasing the amount of rain the soil was able to absorb.

'Soil loss on fields without mulch [has been] found to be 232.6 tonnes per hectare per year while that on mulched fields was 8.2 tonnes,' Shiva wrote, adding that 42 per cent of the rain ran off unmulched land but only 2 per cent if a mulch had been applied. The use of artificial fertilizers had meant that mulching had been largely abandoned, she claimed, while the use of heavy tractors in place of the plough oxen had caused soil compaction and further reduced the amount of rain the soil is able to absorb. As a result, the rate of soil erosion had greatly increased while less rain had been able to percolate through the soil and replenish the water table. Simultaneously, 10 million hectares of land had become waterlogged as a result of irrigation, and another 25 million hectares was affected by a growing salinity. 'In total ignorance of the essential ecological processes which sustain productivity, development strategies have been introduced which may well lead to the death of the soil,' she commented.

The other crisis in the Indian countryside is the destruction of its forests. The nation got a nasty shock in 1984 when satellite photographs showed that large areas shown on maps as 'state forest' had no trees at all and that 1.3 million hectares of woodland were disappearing each year, with the result that the area of the country under trees had dropped from 16.9 per cent to 14.1 per cent in just ten years. Several groups share the blame for this. What normally happens is that corrupt politicians connive with senior forest officers to sell off the best trees in an area to paper-mills or saw-mills, and once these are gone, the deforestation process is completed by firewood gatherers and by herdsmen with cattle and goats. In some cases, however, commercial enterprises are directly involved in the destruction. In Karnataka, for example, virgin forest was felled so that eucalyptus could be planted to provide a rayon factory with its cellulose supply, while the prosperous apple growers in the foothills of the Himalayas clear thousands of acres of forest each year because it takes the yearly growth of ten acres of forest to make the boxes to pack the annual output of one acre of fruit. Tobacco – a big business in India, which is the third largest producer of flue-cured leaf in the world and a major exporter – is another insidious destroyer. In the main producing state, Andhra Pradesh, roughly 5 per cent of the forests is felled each year to fuel the curing kilns.

Whether the loss of the forests has reduced rainfall is hotly debated, but it has certainly made droughts worse. When a hill is covered with trees, a lot of the water carried in the low clouds that sweep across it is stripped out when mist condenses on branches and leaves. Once the trees are felled, this water falls as rain instead, making rainstorms heavier than before and causing soil erosion and flash flooding, both of which are augmented by a faster run-off from bare hills. Forest loss has therefore meant that more rain escapes to the sea and that less gets time to soak into the soil and refill aquifers, that land is washed away and dams and canals silt up. The human consequences may be even worse, though. Thousands of tribal people depend on the forests for their livelihood as they gather honey, bamboo, tendu leaves, lac, resins, and fruits which they sell in the towns. Once the trees go, their way of life goes with them.

The hardships 'development' has caused in the countryside have driven millions of people to the towns – again repeating the English experience but on a vaster scale. 'Every year, an estimated 5 million people leave the parched lands and the flickering lamps in their villages and head for the distant glare of city lights in search of employment,' wrote the news magazine *India Today* in 1988. 'As a result: a fourfold jump in the country's urban population from 56 million in 1951 to over 230 million last year. The spiralling urban millions now account for a fourth of the country's people.' Not surprisingly, the cities are unable to cope. Already around a third of the population of Delhi, Bombay, Calcutta and Madras live in slums or on the pavement and half the population has no piped water. Transport, sewage and refuse disposal systems are breaking down. 'In Delhi, the sweeping flyovers and verdant parks contrast starkly with the ghetto-like conditions that exist on its periphery,' wrote *India Today*. 'In East Delhi's Nand Nagri and Seema Puri, man and animal live alike. Human excreta floats around in clogged open drains, rats and rag-pickers scurry around in reeking garbage piles, pigs roll in the slush, queues around public water taps stretch for a mile and, at night, people lie littered around in corners with torn tarpaulins as roofs and newspapers as blankets to beat the cold.' The director of the Indian Institute of Urban Affairs, O. P. Mathur, was quoted as saying: 'Big cities are beginning to reach their critical mass and meltdown has begun,' and it has been the deterioration and overcrowding in the cities that, more than anything else, has made the urban middle class realize that the system that looks after them so well in many ways will have to be changed.

But if rural policies have been a social and environmental disaster, the consequences of expanding India's industrial sector since 1956 have been equally bad, in spite of the emphasis given to it in national plans. It is not that Indian industry did not grow, although it grew more slowly than elsewhere in the non-communist world and slipped from the world's tenth biggest industrial power in 1955 to its twentieth in the mid-1980s. Between 1960 and 1985 production of coal increased threefold, of iron ore fourfold, of aluminium fifteenfold, and of nitrogenous fertilizer fortyfold, and overall the index of industrial production went up 336 per cent. The problem is that, as in eastern Europe where the same development strategy was tried, the industries chosen for expansion were especially environmentally damaging ones, which, because they were in state ownership, other arms of government failed to control.

The lack of a proper system of checks and balances meant that anyone whose land was required for, say, an opencast mine or a dam was displaced with minimal compensation and little attempt at resettlement; if they protested they were branded as anti-national. One of the worst examples of government companies running out of control is in Singrauli, an ancient tribal princely state between the Mirzapur district in Uttar Pradesh and the Sidhi district of Madhya Pradesh. Until thirty years ago Singrauli was almost untouched by modern industry and its people made their living by grazing animals, collecting forest produce, and a blend of fixed and shifting cultivation. In 1961 the opening of the Rihand dam to generate electricity undermined all that. Nearly 200,000 people lost their land as the dam's waters rose – their villages were flooded without notice as the easiest way of making sure they moved quickly away. No-one knows where 50,000 of them went, but the rest settled on the only land they could get, the valley sides.

The next step in the development programme was to build an aluminium smelter to use the power the dam was generating. This required the construction of a railway line to bring in the alumina. Other chemical factories, such as one making sodium hydroxide, also moved in. Then, in the late sixties, coal was found in the narrow valleys, and huge opencast mines were opened to extract it, and, rather than haul it away, three 'superthermal' power stations were built close by. Three more even larger ones are under construction today. As Suresh Sharma wrote in the *Lokayan Bulletin* in 1986:

Bare statistics hardly convey the anguish and trauma of the suffering. To begin with, the people accepted terrible hardship in the innocent belief that it was for the greater good of all. But uprooting of homes has become a permanent feature of life in Singrauli. People have been displaced from their homes as many as six times in twenty years. And this has happened as a part of what is supposed to be planned development. The near absence of the most elementary concern for human decency makes the hardship unbearably humiliating. People are driven out of their homes like cattle and dumped anywhere, even in pouring rain ...

With each passing year, the world around appears to the inhabitants of Singrauli less and less within their control and comprehension. Forests have disappeared as the reach of the Forest Department and contractors extended into the hinterland ... to satisfy the demand for timber in the large cities ... but the small cultivators and the landless, for whom the forest has been an unfailing refuge for food and fuel since time immemorial, have to bribe or steal wood even to cremate their dead [and] women and children have to spend more and more time foraging for fuel to cook the family evening meal.

Penetration of the modern market into the hinterland has undermined both the viability and legitimacy of local crafts and skills. The massive ecological disturbances entailed by large-scale mining and power generation have created serious problems of soil erosion and pollution. Benefits that flow from coal mining, power generation and timber felling ... have become the prerogative of the better-off sections of society and the large urban centres. Local inhabitants are expected to be content with paying the social and cultural costs entailed in development.

During a visit to Singrauli in 1988, its muddy hillsides, bare except for an occasional lopped tree, gave me the impression of a First World War battlefield. Slums and shanties surround the aluminium works, although further away there are smart housing colonies, complete with schools and hospitals. These are almost exclusively for the workers imported from the plains: very few of the tribals have been able to get jobs with the industries that have moved in. 'Outsiders are taking the jobs and the tribals' land,' a social activist, Prembhai, told me. 'This area is going to be the energy capital of India, but its people are not.'

There are many public projects like Singrauli in India and, without exception, they have involved the taking of resources away from the poor. This has convinced many Indians that it was not enough for Nehru to restrict private enterprise to avoid its harmful consequences. State enterprises with the same goal as capitalism – economic growth, the increase in output above all else – can be equally bad, or perhaps worse, as once the state is involved directly there is no-one to adjudicate between the exploiters and the oppressed. 'Economic growth is a new colonialism, draining resources away from those who need them most,' says Vandana Shiva, and looking around Singrauli, with its yawning gulf between the prosperous newcomers and the tribals they have displaced, you can see what she means.

FAILED POLICIES

There is broad agreement in India that the policies followed in the various national plans have failed. 'Forty years after independence, 80 per cent of the rural population has neither drinking water, schools, hospitals, jobs, nor, most ironically, any benefits from the energy which monstrous projects such as Singrauli produce,' said a letter to the editor of *The Statesman* of Calcutta in May 1990. During my visit there was a power cut every night. 'They give preference to factories over people,' Prembhai explained.

Many Indians think the growth-before-people policies have created two states within the same land area. One state, India, with a population of around 80 million, is so technically advanced that it ranks ahead of the Netherlands in industrial output, builds nuclear reactors, and probably has the atomic bomb. The other state, Bharat, the old name for the sub-continent, has a population of 720 million people living and working in conditions of extreme hardship largely as a result of the 'internal colonization' to which Shiva referred. Rajni Kothari put the phenomenon – an exact parallel of Disraeli's two nations at a similar stage in British development – like this in the magazine *Seminar* in January 1987:

Two Indias, one consisting of those with access to wealth and resources and the other of those denuded of it all thanks to the type of 'development' we have had.

Two Indias, one consisting of an upper caste crust immersed in social privilege and the other of the social peripheries that have been rendered impotent under the impact of a narrowing structure of opportunities and access to such things as education, social mobility and 'welfare'.

Two Indias, one consisting of those with growing resource endowments and expanding living spaces and the other of those whose minimal resource base – even its access to natural resources – is being continuously eroded under the impact of a deeply discriminating and destabilizing technology.

Two Indias, one consisting of growing hordes of VIPs and their urban entourages enjoying culture, even popular culture, while the other, the populace itself, is denied its own cultural and aesthetic resources thanks largely to the conversion of culture into commodities to be exhibited, museumized and exported by the government.

And, above all, two Indias, one consisting of those with access to state power and the privileges and perquisites it confers and the other of those pushed out of the democratic process and the institutions of the state.

There are three basic reactions to the two nations phenomenon. One is to call for even faster economic growth. 'Growth has been inadequate,' wrote Kirit S. Parikh in India's academic *Economic and Political Weekly* in March 1988. 'Poverty, hunger and illiteracy persist amidst abundant foodstocks: much of our industry remains internationally non-competitive and requires the import of technology [while] the public sector does not generate a sufficient surplus and remains inefficient.' He then went on to urge that the country adopt a 7 per cent annual growth target, twice the average level achieved between 1951 and 1985, although he made no estimates of how much good this would do to the poor. They should be given food for work, he suggested, 'till the time trickle-down reaches them.'

A more common reaction is to admit that the current system has failed to deliver and cannot be made to do so. 'The Indian economic system is poised for change because it can no longer manage in the old way the pressures and compulsion it has generated,' P. N. Dhar, one-time principal secretary to the Prime Minister, wrote in the *Indian Economic Review* in 1987. P. C. Joshi, a former member of the government's Planning Commission who worked on the first five-year plan and many of its successors, was even blunter. 'We were swept away by a tidal wave of development ideas from the West forty years ago,' he told a seminar at Delhi University in 1988. 'This eroded our autonomy but now, confidence in the West's ideas has gone and there is a total holiday from theory.' He went on to say that economists – like himself – had been everywhere when the plans were drawn up, and people from the other social disciplines were nowhere. As a result, key factors had been left out – women, water, forests, land – and there had been many development disasters. 'Existing received theory is a rationalization of the interests of government,' he said.

Another former Planning Commission member and economist, J. D. Sethi, wrote in *Seminar* in 1987 that 'development strategies have become inimical to development itself ... India has reached a point where survival has become uncertain.' He argued that the time had come for the adoption of a new paradigm, a combination of Marxism and Gandhianism. 'Classical marxism has been shattered both by experience and by its critiques provided by the neo-marxists. [It] can be saved only if it is structurally built into the alternative Gandhian paradigm: one representing the forces of production and the other the forces of moral checks and obligations.'

The fact that these men had controlled the state planning apparatus until shortly before they made their statements is remarkable and illustrates the extent of the intellectual ferment. Many ideas have been put forward to fill the theory gap, and there has probably been more consideration of alternative development strategies in India than anywhere else in the world. Western science and technology have been put in the dock along with Western economics. 'Descartian methods, the vehicle of progress in the seventeenth century, became a fetter on the progress of science later,' wrote Sailendranath Ghosh in *Seminar* in June 1987, echoing Gandhi's *Sarvodaya*. 'Separating facts from bias came to be understood as divorcing facts from values. This stripping of values later became the excuse for the destruction of reverence for life.'

Others have argued along similar lines, suggesting that science has replaced morality. 'Scientific rationality, the ideological basis for modern development, enables the elite to shrug off all costs as necessary and inevitable in order to secure a better future,' Harsh Sethi and Smitu Kothari wrote in the editorial in the *Lokayan Bulletin* of October 1985. 'A global and secular process of creating innumerable new victims demands from its proponents a world-view which arms them with legitimacy and an unshaken belief in their correctness. Science thus becomes the religion of the secular modern elite.' A postgraduate student at a Delhi University seminar on inadequacies in development theory called for a 'people's science' that was not alienated from the sources of life and from nature. The Union Carbide plant in Bhopal had been set up to provide the pesticides required by the Green Revolution, Madhulika Banerjee said, and the poison gas leak had been the inescapable result of Western science. She attacked the idea that technology was neutral and value-free and necessarily led to the right type of development. 'We can progress without Western technology,' she said.

The third response to the crisis of confidence over the country's development path has come from thousands of educated Indians who have decided not to wait until the theorists have sorted things out but to do something practical now. Few of them are specifically Gandhians – they come from all backgrounds: Marxist, Christian, Hindu, Muslim, Sikh – yet all have been deeply influenced by Gandhi and have taken on the role he proposed for the Lok Sevak Sangh, of going out and working with the people to help them improve their lot. A massive movement has grown up which has been little noted in the West. It is estimated that some 7,000 voluntary agencies – the Indian contraction is volags – have been set up by these idealists, the equivalent of one for every hundred villages in the country, although they operate in urban areas as well. In fact the effort has become so big, effective and well-financed (one estimate is that £100 million, around half of their annual income, comes from foreign charities like Oxfam) that the government has imposed stringent conditions on their activities for fear of losing control. A special agency, CAPART, channels state funds to the volags, which naturally gives it considerable power, and any organization that wishes to receive funds from overseas has to obtain permission from the Ministry of Home Affairs, which can withdraw its consent at any time.

But the main motive for the state's involvement with the volags is not control but the recognition that the voluntary organizations are better run and more highly motivated than its own civil service. In Koraput, a remote tribal area of Orissa, the government's medical personnel collected their vaccine requirements from the voluntary New Hope Rural Leprosy Trust until recently, because this was the only way they could be sure it had been kept cool since it left the factory: New Hope's vaccine is carried by special messenger in an ice-filled flask on its 24-hour journey to the hills, but nobody could be sure what had happened to the official supplies. Today, however, the government workers call no more: New Hope has been given responsibility, and state funding, to provide health care in 1,500 villages, almost all of which can be reached only on foot. 'We'd have taken over responsibility for all Koraput if they'd let us,' says Eliazar Rose, who set up the trust.

Like many volags, New Hope uses health care as an entry point into the communities it serves and then, as public confidence in its workers builds up, begins to suggest new answers to old problems. It has introduced the Oxfam pot chlorination system for wells in its area. 'The government workers would just dump bleach into a well, which made the water undrinkable,' Rose says. Now, a mixture of sand and bleach powder is put in a porous pot which is lowered into the well, and the bleach leaches slowly out.

But New Hope's main long-term goal is to reverse the environmental decline in the area so that the Bhonda tribals can have better lives. The main problem is deforestation caused by a paper-mill at Rayagada and by the inability of shifting cultivators to leave the steep hillsides fallow long enough for the forest to regrow before clearing it and planting again. Rose's answer is to get the people to grow more tree crops so that they need to plant fewer annuals, an approach that will also make them less liable to famine during droughts: Koraput is the district in which several hundred tribals died of starvation during 1987 and 1988 when successive monsoons failed. He has set up a thirty-acre demonstration farm and many thousands of trees have been planted by tribal women in the villages.

'We see women as the key to our work. If you teach women you can do anything. They carry the burden of the whole community; the men just get drunk and fall asleep,' Rose says. 'We did a survey of 1,500 children and found that 55 per cent of them were suffering from protein and vitamin A deficiencies so we are experimenting with the leaf-juice concentrate prepared according to the method developed by an organization called Find Your Feet in the UK.'

Some of the volags are almost independent countries. '"Prembhai wants to set up a parallel state" is written on my intelligence dossier,' says the secretary of the Banwasi Sewa Ashram in the Singrauli area proudly. As indeed he does: he has a rudimentary local currency scheme in operation and the ashram runs eight primary schools and a secondary school, fifty mobile libraries, a health service with a clinic, ten health posts and 150 village health workers, a demonstration farm, and innumerable productive enterprises, including a flour mill. Half a million people have been taught to read since the ashram was set up in 1954, 10,000 acres brought under irrigation, 1,200 small dams built, and 7,000 acres levelled and reclaimed.

Petty-minded officials frequently obstruct the volags, largely because they resent someone showing them up by doing 'their' work better than they do it themselves and also because the best volags are informing the people of their rights and teaching them how to demand them, a course that frequently causes trouble for civil servants. But in spite of the radicalizing effect the volags are having, some far-left intellectuals scorn them as 'the new delivery system of capitalism' or because of what they consider to be their urban, petty bourgeois ideology. 'They refuse to unite to overthrow the state and seize power on behalf of the oppressed,' one of them told me. More moderate commentators see them as a bridge between state and people and chuckle at the spectacle of groups protesting against the system while being part-funded by the state.

Most Indians accept that there are tremendous physical and human resources lying wasted in the villages and that unless rural development becomes a mass movement there is no salvation for their country. Most too would probably agree that the volags' work can at best be only part of the creation of such a movement and that a radical change in political attitudes and the national development strategy is also required.

Towards Green Villages: a Strategy for Environmentally Sound and Participatory Development might contain the blueprint the country needs. This 1989 book by Anil Agarwal and Sunita Narain of the Centre for Science and the Environment in Delhi calls for economic and political power to be returned to villages, exactly as Mahatma Gandhi wished. 'Before the advent of the modern state, grazing lands, forest lands and water bodies were mostly common property and village communities played an important role in their use and management,' the authors write.

The British were the first to nationalize these resources and bring them under the management of government bureaucracies. In other words, the British initiated the policy of converting *common property resources* into *government property resources.*

This expropriation has alienated the people from their commons and has started a free-for-all. Today even tribals, who have lived in harmony with forests for centuries, are so alienated that they feel little in felling a green tree to sell off for a pittance. Repeatedly we have been asked by tribal groups, what is the point in saving the forests, because if they don't take them first, the forest contractors would take them away. The desperate economic conditions of the poor, made worse by the ecological destruction, has often left them with no other option but to survive by cutting trees. Unless people's alienation from their commons can be arrested and reversed, there cannot be any regeneration of common lands.

ONE COMMUNITY'S RESPONSE

'People will care for their environment only if they have the legal right to manage it and to its products,' Agarwal says, and the book gives case histories of villages which have been able to take responsibility for their surroundings. One example is Ralegan Shindi, the village on which the Chief Secretaries were briefed. It lies about 60 km east of Pune in a low rainfall area and the overall impression is of rocks and bare, brown earth, relieved by the occasional mango tree. However, once the road dips into the valley where the village stands there is a remarkable change: although the earth is still dry and dusty, there is greenness everywhere as a result of the thousands of trees the people have planted. Only the surrounding hills are still naked. 'Come back in a few years and see them then,' Raut Thakaram, headmaster of the secondary school, told me in 1987. His large two-storey school has hostel accommodation for ninety-six children from surrounding villages and stands close to a small, one-room library. Both buildings were constructed by the villagers themselves with financial assistance from the state.

The progress that Ralegan Shindi has made is largely due to one man, Anna Hazare, who returned there in 1975 after fifteen years' service in the army. The community he found was in social and economic decline; few of its 315 families were able to grow enough to support themselves, and over forty of them were engaged in illegal distilling to help out. Not all the product was sold: 'They drank like anything and behaved like beasts,' Thakaram says. Hazare, a bachelor, went to live in the temple and spent all 20,000 rupees of his resettlement money on rebuilding it. Gradually other villagers began to help with the work too. He still lives there in a small room filled with files, and all the village's decisions are made at mass meetings in the square outside.

His first move was against the distillers. After an incident in which drunks from another village beat up a local man, he forcibly closed down the stills with the help of some young supporters. But the families involved in the drink trade had to live, so he arranged for some of their sons to join the army so that they could send money home. He also arranged for other people from the village to get work on government labour schemes.

The next step was to sink a well to water 45 acres of the village's common land. Everybody gave their labour free, but a bank loan was necessary to finance the pump. This was repaid in two years, as crop yields increased tenfold. Other common wells have since been built, and many families have also been able to sink ones on their own land. The water table has remained high, however, because thirty-five small dams have been built in gullies to prevent water running away uselessly during the monsoon.

Confidence began to grow and a spate of developments followed. Each household was persuaded to dig an underground soakaway for its waste water to prevent mosquitoes breeding in it, and eight tubewells were sunk so that people did not have to drink water from the open wells. The effect was to cut the incidence of illness by half. Communal latrines, which are kept spotlessly clean, were built near the village square to feed a gobar (methane digester) plant supplying gas to cook meals; by 1987 there were another twenty-seven gas plants and more blocks of latrines were going up.

A ten-room school was built without any state support, and as the ministry refused to pay the teachers' wages, the villagers found qualified volunteers prepared to work for just their board and lodging. At the end of the first school year, however, the ministry still refused to recognize the school and prevented the children sitting their exams. It took a mass hunger-strike by 250 villagers in the district capital to break the deadlock.

The schoolchildren started a tree nursery and sold trees to the government forest department, using the proceeds to level a playing field. They also planted out a fruit orchard, and each year they distribute all the crop free. Over a million trees had been planted by the villagers by the time I was there and almost all of the 2,200 acres of land in the village were irrigated, some of the water coming by canal from a dam 60 km away. So successful had the village been in fact that there was no longer enough labour to carry out projects, and schemes were either being delayed or employed workers brought in from other villages.

But Anna Hazare's achievement should not be seen purely in material terms. His thinking has been greatly influenced by the Hindu philosopher Vivekananda since he bought a book about him on a railway station in 1964. He was particularly attracted by the swami's teaching that the noblest thing a man can do is to work for the good of others; and when he was the only uninjured survivor of an air attack on his truck during the war with Pakistan in 1965, he was convinced that God had saved him for some purpose. 'Getting a better house or being able to buy a motorbike is not development,' he says. 'What is important is one's relationship with one's neighbour'. In line with this philosophy, those farmers in the village whose land happened to be best placed to take advantage of irrigation water voluntarily give a proportion of each harvest to help those less able to benefit. Similarly, the entire village has set up a scheme to help people who lost their land under the waters of the dam that supplies their irrigation canal.

Ralegan Shindi has made a point of never accepting outside financial help except from the government – 'That is the money of the people anyway,' Hazare says. He is convinced that existing state schemes are adequate to allow other villages to work similar transformations, so long as they know how to go about using them, and he has helped many other communities start on the road to change. A large party of farmers was going round the village the day I was there. But finding the money is not enough. 'To change our nation we have to change our villages and to change our villages we have to change ourselves.'

And change is happening. There has been a massive shift in urban middle-class attitudes to environmental issues in India during the past ten years, although this has not yet been passed on to those in government, a time-lag common to many countries. 'Care for the environment was seen as a diversion, a Western ploy to stop us developing, until around 1984 and Bhopal,' says Sujit Patwardhan, who helped set up the Parisar environmental group in Pune in 1981. 'Now, however, the scepticism is gone. It was the ordinary people who were quickest to make the connection between, say, deforestation and the need to drill deeper wells. The most educated were most difficult to convince: for them, atomic meant modern. I've been depressed in my dealings with the government, but not with the people. The politicians are waiting to see which way the wind blows.'

Baba Amte, India's grand old social activist who was called 'Brave Defender' by the Mahatma himself, is trying to raise that wind. He set up

Green Front in June 1989 in collaboration with eighty prominent environmentalists, in the hope that it would become a massive pressure group that would force the political parties to take notice of 'the innumerable millions who suffer from the degradation of the environment and the destruction which so-called development projects wreak.' Green Front's first protest, three months after its foundation, gained media attention all over the world. It got thousands of ordinary people, many of them tribals, to gather in Harsud, a small town in Madhya Pradesh, to protest against the building of the Narmada Sagar dam. 'There will be fifty feet of water where we are standing today,' one of the local organizers told the crowd, many of whom had been notified officially that they would be made homeless by the project. Two politicians turned up for the protest, one of them Maneka Gandhi, who became India's environment minister two months later when V. P. Singh's government came to power. Both, however, were kept off the platform and left in a huff.

Since then, the Narmada Valley project – which involves the building of 30 major, 135 medium and 3,000 minor dams over the next thirty-five years – has become the battleground on which those Indians who reject the Western development model have chosen to show their strength. They have picked their ground well, because the project's human and environmental cost will be colossal. If things go as planned, by the time the whole scheme is finished 1.5 million people will have lost their homes and 3,500 square kilometres of India's few remaining forests and 2,500 square kilometres of its best land will have been submerged.

These non-monetary costs are so high that, as the magazine *Business India* wrote in 1989, 'the mega-project has come to symbolize all that is wrong with the prevailing model of development: ecological destructiveness; callous unconcern for the displaced tribal people and the rural poor; fascination with gigantic, enormously costly and ill-conceived schemes which benefit relatively few and are unable to alleviate widespread poverty.'

Four large dams have already been built, with disturbing consequences. Yields of all crops have fallen in the irrigated areas and so much land has been lost because the clay soil has become waterlogged that 700 wells have had to be sunk to try to pump excess water away. Many of the people displaced have become landless labourers or are living in city slums.

Amte's group analysed[1] the results of the 1,500 big dams built in India so far and showed that they have benefited only a small number of rich farmers and the urban élite while making the country more drought-prone because they permit inappropriate crops to be grown. Millions of people have been displaced and impoverished by them. 'The nation's rivers cannot be strangulated to meet the needs of the exploiting class within society,' Amte added in a personal note. 'No river-valley project in India has ever raised enough revenue to meet even annual expenses. The [Narmada] project is simply not viable financially.'

Amte's view was confirmed by a Pune economics professor, Vijay Paranjpye, in evidence he gave to a US House of Representatives sub-committee in October 1989. 'Cumulative losses from big dams in India between 1973 and 1982 were $1,500 million and the principal beneficiaries were the big landlords who still use irrigation water at highly subsidized rates,' he said. India had not got the funds to complete 141 dams it had already started within the next five years, let alone the Narmada ones, he told the committee.

Equally serious arguments have been made against the dams in the past, to no avail. R. L. Gupta, one of the chief designers of the whole Narmada scheme, told me before his death in 1988 that the river had 20 per cent less water in it than he had thought, and that consequently the Narmada Sagar dam would never fill. Moreover, although 1,000 MW of generating capacity was to be installed, only 78 MW would be generated when the other dams in the scheme were finished. Gupta was also worried that building so many dams in the valley could trigger earthquakes, as happened elsewhere in India. He wrote to the then Prime Minister, Rajiv Gandhi, pleading for construction to stop, and suggesting cheaper and less ecologically damaging ways of meeting Gujarat's water needs. He never received a reply.

Amte too believes that alternatives exist and that small dams will irrigate many sites for between 10 per cent and 25 per cent of the cost of the large ones. 'We need to work out an optimal mix of dry farming technology, watershed development, small dams, lift schemes for irrigation and drinking water and improve the efficiency of the major projects which are already complete,' he wrote in a pamphlet he published in early 1990. However, the World Bank, which plans to part-finance the project, has no time for this approach. Pointing out that almost 5 million people live in the rural areas to be watered by another of the big Narmada dams, Sardar Sarovar, which was at the time part-built, the bank's president, Barber Conable, replied to a critic by saying that 'modest alternatives would be inadequate to meet [their] needs'. Conable was wilfully ignoring the fact that the projected financial benefits from the dams only arise because the value of the land and the forest to be flooded has been grossly underestimated and because no adequate provision has been made for the cost of resettling the hundreds of thousands of displaced people, even if land can be found for them. Similarly, the value of the power generated and the rise in agricultural output as a result of irrigation is hugely overstated.

Why have the figures been fudged? Why are the politicians so keen to go ahead? One of India's leading environmental journalists, Claude Alvares, explained in *The Illustrated Weekly of India* shortly after the Hardwar protest:

'At a routine 15 per cent commission rate on the 150,000,000,000 rupee Sardar Sarovar project, politicians ... [stand] to make 22,500,000,000 rupees over a period of years.'

And why is the World Bank equally committed to the project? A clue is given by the fact that Japan is making $20 million available through the bank to help finance the Sardar Sarovar's turbines, which, one suspects, it hopes to supply. Small-scale, labour-intensive projects of the type envisaged by Amte don't generate much export business for the industrial countries that provide the World Bank's funds.

Although he doesn't believe he will win, Amte has decided to devote the rest of his life to fighting the scheme. In March 1990, aged seventy-five, he left Anandwan, the leprosy colony which he set up in 1951, to live in a hut built for him by local people on the banks of the Narmada river. He vowed not to leave the area until the project was cancelled or until he died, either from old age or by drowning as the dam's waters rose. Late in 1991, despite several arrests and at least one police beating, he was still there.

Environmentalists, economists and social activists from all over the world wrote to the World Bank asking it not to lend more money to the scheme, but it ignored their requests and instead announced a further loan in July 1990. This did not upset the project's Indian opponents too much, as they want the decision to scrap it to be made at home rather than abroad, since only that would mean that their country had really changed direction. In early 1992 the Bank was still funding the project but had a team of investigators in India reassessing the situation.

'The struggle for a new India is taking shape in the Narmada Valley,' Amte wrote to friends on the day he left Anandwan for what he and they believed was the last time. 'The conflict is a consequence of our rulers' complete insensitivity to the genuine needs of our people and of their lack of understanding of the pattern of development that India must follow. I am leaving ... to be part of the attempt to bring this life-rending conflict to an end.'

14
De Valera's Dream

That Ireland which we dreamed of would be the home of a people who valued material wealth only as the basis of right living, of a people who were satisfied with frugal comfort and devoted their leisure to things of the spirit – a land whose countryside would be bright with cosy homesteads, whose fields and villages would be joyous with the sounds of industry, with the romping of sturdy children, the contests of athletic youths and the laughter of happy maidens, whose firesides would be forums for the wisdom of serene old age. It would, in a word, be the home of a people living the life that God desires that man should live. – Éamon de Valera, Irish Taoiseach, in a radio broadcast on St Patrick's Day, 1943[1]

My wife and I have a favourite place for looking out to sea. Clew Bay is on the west coast of Ireland, just behind the weather forecaster's right shoulder on British television, and our house stands on a natural level close to the top of a low hill a few hundred metres from its southern shore. Each spring we drag a wooden bench from its winter store to where the heather of the hillside gives way to the grass of our plateau so we can sit and look out over what Thackeray thought 'the most beautiful view I ever saw in the world'.

About five kilometres to our left is Croagh Patrick, the mountain on which St Patrick meditated and fasted for forty days and nights in AD 441, wrestling with demons and 'extracting rash promises from God' on behalf of the people of Ireland. On the last Sunday of July thousands of those people arrive to climb his mountain, as pilgrims have done for at least 900 years.

Over to our right is Westport Quay, once a busy port with huge stone-built warehouses, now just a convenient place for sport-fishing boats to tie up. Then come the woods around Westport House, our local stately home, still owned by the Brownes, the family that built its first house on the site over 300 years ago. And at the edge of the picture comes the valley in which the Brownes built the town of Westport, but most of the houses are so cosily tucked away that we can see nothing of them except for a blue peat-smoke haze on a still winter day.

Most of our hillside is covered with trees, but in the fields below us the regular corrugations left by the raised beds in which people used to grow

DENSITY OF POPULATION, 1841

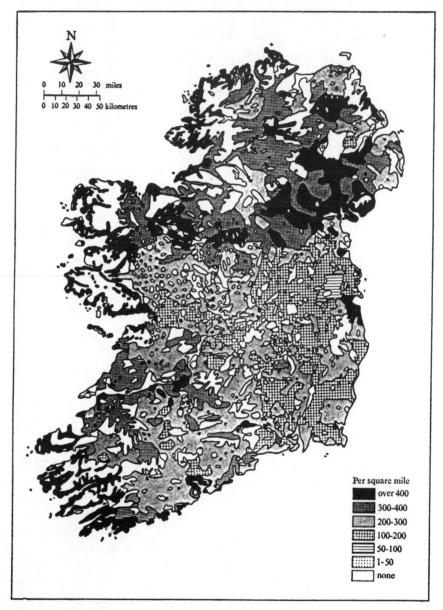

Figure 14.1 In 1841, before the Potato Famine, the west coast of Ireland was the most densely populated. From *The Irish Economy since 1922* by James Meenan (1970).

DENSITY OF POPULATION, 1961

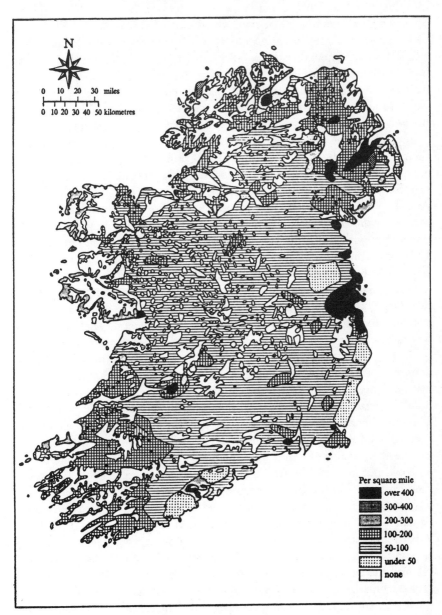

By 1961, the main areas of dense population were on the east coast.

potatoes can be clearly seen, especially when the setting sun etches the land into deeper relief. Only if one knows how densely the west of Ireland was once populated can one understand why the remains of these so-called 'lazy' beds can be seen stretching up almost every hillside from Kerry to Donegal. Yet, although I knew that the population of Ireland had been cut almost by half by the potato famine and by the emigration that followed, I had not realized the extent of the population loss hereabouts nor the degree to which Ireland's settlement pattern had shifted from west to east until I came across the two maps on the preceding pages while researching this chapter.

A grasp of the facts about emigration and population loss makes many things about Ireland understandable. The 1780s and 1790s were a period of great prosperity because the American War of Independence made it necessary for the British to send a large part of their Irish garrison to North America. To take the place of the missing troops a volunteer militia was formed by the landed aristocracy who feared that the French, who had allied themselves with the Americans and on whom Britain had declared war in 1778, would take the chance to invade. The membership of this force, the Irish Volunteers, came largely from the Protestant professional and commercial classes; and, as the British had severely curtailed trading opportunities during the previous 150 years, the recruits saw the formation of the Volunteers as an opportunity to put things right. Among their grievances was the fact that it had been made illegal to export Irish wool to prevent it competing with the British clip. Even the weaving of woollen cloth for domestic sale had been discouraged, forcing the Irish to buy from Britain instead. This was to maintain the country's subservience: 'For how can they then depart from us without nakedness?' the former Lord Deputy, Sir Thomas Wentworth, had asked in the 1630s; and the same policies had been pursued since. Only the linen industry had been allowed to develop – I can see the remains of a mill from my house – because British manufacturers could not meet the demand themselves. However, stiff import duties had been imposed and the Irish were forbidden to sell to any other country but England. Even the export of cattle had been banned until 1759, when Britain found it needed increased supplies during the Seven Years' War. What's more, those goods Britain deigned to import from Ireland could not be paid for in English gold or silver coin: the import of those was made illegal, and the currency here consisted of a motley collection of foreign coins, bankers' bills and notes and silver and copper tokens issued locally.

Not unnaturally, Irish manufacturing failed to develop in these circumstances and landowners, with no market for additional agricultural production to provide an incentive to develop their estates, frequently neglected them and moved to England to live on their rents. This created a set of problems which has dogged Ireland ever since, and is worth considering in detail.

Ireland is littered with the ruins of castles and churches built during the Middle Ages like the abbey at Murrisk at the foot of Croagh Patrick, just out of sight from my seat. This was built by Tadhg O'Malley, leader of the O'Malley clan, for the Augustinians in 1457, and when news of his plans broke, craftsmen arrived and stayed in the community until the job was done. Local quarries provided the stone and local woods the timber, and there was plenty of work for local people who wanted to take it on. Tadhg's pious project spread his personal prosperity through the area, recycling resources to the people who had generated them in the first place. This was the way things worked in those days. Whenever a technique was developed that enabled fewer people to satisfy the community's needs, there was never any question of the surplus labour being left unemployed: those benefiting from the changes had little else to do with their wealth but use it to maintain soldiers or pay for civil, ecclesiastical or defence construction within their own localities. Even if part of someone's prosperity was used to import wines or clothing – and the Middle Ages saw a flourishing trade between the west coast of Ireland and Portugal and Spain – it was largely a case of exchanging the products of Irish labour for those of labour abroad, since commerce was only partially monetarized.

Three centuries later, however, financial systems had become more sophisticated and resources produced in one part of the world could be consumed elsewhere with little or nothing coming back in return. Instead of being spent where they had been generated, Irish estate incomes were used by absentee landlords to support builders and craftspeople in England, and the only way the Irish people could benefit from the wealth they had generated was to emigrate. The mechanism that previously had automatically returned rents or tributes to tenants or clansmen had been destroyed. Consequently, as Irish industry was unable to expand as a result of English laws, and with what we would now call the service sector developing in England rather than at home, any rise in agricultural productivity made emigration or a rise in underemployment inevitable. (Unemployment was fatal, as, with no means of support, the displaced labourer and his family frequently died on the roadside.)

The Volunteers were determined to break out of this vicious system of exploitation. Like many Indians 150 years later, they pledged themselves to wear only home-produced clothes. They also threatened civil war unless the restrictions and taxes on Irish exports were lifted, and in 1779 the Lord Lieutenant gave way. The following year the ban on the import of English coins was lifted, and the Bank of Ireland was chartered in 1783. For almost twenty-five years Ireland enjoyed a period of prosperity that, in relative terms, has never been equalled. Many of the landlords returned to the country, and it was during this period that most of the terraces and squares of Georgian Dublin were developed, including two of its finest buildings, the Custom House and the Four Courts. Because the leakage of resources overseas had been stemmed, craftsmen and manufacturers set up everywhere, and people were able to find non-agricultural work in their own country. The period of Grattan's Parliament was a golden age.

But the British did not like it. They were constantly worried that a near-independent Ireland would provide a sympathetic staging-post for the French; and after a thousand troops under General Humbert landed at Killala, about fifty kilometres from Westport, in 1798 and gathered considerable local support before being defeated fifteen days later, the London government felt it had to act. In 1799 the British put a Bill of Union between England and Ireland before the Irish Parliament but it was narrowly voted down. The following year they tried again, having spent £1.5 million on buying out or bribing many borough-owners and place-men in the Irish House of Commons and creating more than twenty additional peers to see their measure safely through the Irish House of Lords. Peter Browne of Westport House, who was already Baron Monteagle, Viscount Westport and the second Earl of Altamont, was made Marquess of Sligo and an Irish representative peer in the British House of Lords in return for his vote. One local historian[2] claims he also received £15,000 in cash, which was spent on developing the town's tree-lined Mall, its most attractive feature.

Dublin ceased to be a brilliant social capital almost immediately after the Union: the wealthy and witty moved to London again, taking their property incomes with them and decimating the service trades. Irish industry was allowed some protection until the 1820s and consequently lasted a little longer. When protection ended, however, its decline was rapid as these figures quoted by Karl Marx in a report[3] to the Communist Association of German Workers in London in 1867 show:

DUBLIN

Master woollen manufacturers	91 (1800)	12 (1840)
Hands employed	4,918 (1800)	602 (1840)
Master woolcombers	30 (1800)	5 (1834)
Hands employed	230 (1800)	66 (1834)
Carpet manufacturers	13 (1800)	1 (1841)
Hands employed	720 (1800)	0 (1841)
Silkloom weavers at work	2,500 (1800)	250 (1840)

KILKENNY

Blanket manufacturers	56 (1800)	42 (1822)
Hands employed	3,000 (1800)	925 (1822)

BALBRIGGAN

Calico looms at work	2,500 (1799)	226 (1841)

WICKLOW

Handlooms at work	1,000 (1800)	0 (1841)

CORK

Braid weavers	1,000 (1800)	40 (1834)
Worsted weavers	2,000 (1800)	90 (1834)
Hosiers	300 (1800)	28 (1834)
Woolcombers	700 (1800)	110 (1834)
Cottonweavers	2,000 (1800)	220 (1834)

In the same report Marx quoted from an 1847 speech by Thomas Francis Meagher, one of the founders of the Irish Confederation, a pro-independence movement:

The cotton manufacture of Dublin, which employed 14,000 operatives, has been destroyed; the 3,400 silk looms have been destroyed; the serge manufacture, which employed 1,491 operatives has been destroyed; the flannel manufacture of Rathdrum, the blanket manufacture of Kilkenny, the camlet trade of Bandon, the worsted manufactures of Waterford, the ratteen and frieze manufactures of Carrick-on-Suir have been destroyed. That fortunate business which the Union Act has not struck down – that favoured, and privileged and patronised business – is the Irish coffin trade.

In Westport the linen trade was badly hit. Although flax had been grown and spun in south Mayo for some time, the first Earl of Altamont, John Browne, had encouraged weavers to come into the area by building houses specially for them in Westport, which he began to lay out in the 1750s. He lent them capital to buy yarn, provided their looms and bought up any finished cloth they were unable to sell. As a result, according to Arthur Young, who visited Westport in 1776, production had risen from £200 worth in 1772 to £10,000 in 1776, but the weavers were still only using about a tenth of all the yarn spun in the neighbourhood.

The trade brought the new town so much prosperity that the Bank of Ireland chose it as the site for its seventh branch, ahead of much larger places like Limerick and Galway. There was no need for emigration, and the population of the area increased. At its height, 30,000 people were involved in the linen business in the area. 'No trade gives such universal employment,' wrote Henry Inglis[4] in 1834, pointing out that sixty people were needed to prepare a web of linen and that growing and spinning the flax provided local farmers with all their extras above a bare living. But by the

Figure 14.2 Westport in the 1890s, with Croagh Patrick beyond. The workhouse is on the hill and dominates the town.

time Inglis visited the town the boom in employment had passed, not, in this case, as a result of the loss of protection but because the mechanized spinning and weaving techniques meant that far less labour was needed. 'The decline of the linen trade has produced a great want of employment and the condition of the agriculturalists throughout these districts has very much deteriorated,' he commented.

The combined effect of the Act of Union and industrialization was to destroy any options the people had except to rent a patch of land on which to grow potatoes, or to emigrate. Many took the latter course. Births exceeded deaths by 858,710 between 1831 and 1841, according to figures Marx gives in his report. Over half of this increase left: 450,873 people, or over 45,000 a year. So great was the flow that the British tried to slow it down by building workhouses throughout the country under the 1838 Irish Poor Law Act, although they were adamant that the cost of these should fall to Irish ratepayers and not to the United Kingdom as a whole. Westport's workhouse was completed in 1842, at a cost of £9,800. It could take 1,610 paupers, with a further 810 in an annexe, at a time when the population of the town was 4,500. However, it did not open for three years, although the government took legal action to try to force it to do so, because it proved impossible to collect sufficient rates within the area to pay its bills. In 1844 a warship and two revenue cutters were sent to the bay carrying special collectors backed by a contingent of troops to try to seize property to pay for its construction. They were so unsuccessful that it was estimated at the time it had cost the state a pound for every shilling the collectors had been able to gather.

Money as well as people flowed from Ireland to England after the Act of Union. Apart from the rent paid to absentee landlords, which Marx says amounted to £7 million in 1834 alone, there was also a considerable investment flow.

Middlemen accumulated fortunes that they *would* not invest in the improvement of the land, and *could* not, under the system which prostrated manufactures, invest in machinery etc. All their accumulations were sent therefore to England for investment. An official document published by the British Government shows that the transfers of British securities from England to Ireland, i.e., the investment of the Irish capital in England, in the 13 years following the adoption of free trade in 1821, amounted to as many millions of pounds sterling [as had been sent in rents]. And thus was Ireland forced to contribute cheap labour and cheap capital to building up 'the great works of Britain.'

The agricultural and social consequences of having no outlet other than emigration for the country's surplus labour were appalling. After visiting Ireland immediately before the Famine, Frederick Engels wrote in 1844 in *The Condition of the Working Class in England*:

If England illustrates the results of the system of farming on a large scale and Wales on a small one, Ireland exhibits the consequences of over-dividing the soil. The great mass of the population of Ireland consists of small tenants who occupy a sorry hut without partitions, and a potato patch just large enough to supply them most scantily with potatoes through the winter. In consequence of the great competition which prevails among these small tenants, the rent has reached an unheard-of height, double and treble and quadruple that paid in England. For every agricultural labourer seeks to become a tenant-farmer, and though the division of land has gone so far, there still remain numbers of labourers in competition for plots. Although in Great Britain 32,000,000 acres of land are cultivated, and in Ireland but 14,000,000; although Great Britain produces agricultural products to the value of £150,000,000 and Ireland of but £36,000,000, there are in Ireland 75,000 agricultural proletarians *more* than in the neighbouring island. How great the competition for land in Ireland must be is evident from this extraordinary disproportion, especially when one reflects that the labourers in Great Britain are living in the utmost distress.

The consequence of this competition is that it is impossible for the tenants to live much better than the labourers by reason of the high rents paid. The Irish people is thus held in crushing poverty from which it cannot free itself under our present social conditions. These people live in the most wretched clay huts, scarcely good enough for cattle-pens, have scant food all winter long or, as the report above quoted [Report of the Poor Law Commission on Ireland of 1837] expresses it, they have potatoes half enough thirty weeks in the year and all the rest of the year nothing. When the time comes in the spring at which this provision reaches its end, or can no longer be used because of its sprouting, wife and children go forth to beg and tramp the country with their kettle in their hands. Meanwhile, the husband, after planting potatoes for the next year, goes in search of work either in Ireland or England and returns at the potato harvest to his family. This is the condition in which nine-tenths of the Irish country folks live. They are as poor as church mice, wear the most wretched rags, and stand on the lowest plane of intelligence possible in a half-civilised country. According to the report quoted, there are, in a population of 8 millions, 585,000 heads of families in a state of total destitution; and, according to other authorities cited by Sheriff Alison [Archibald Alison, *The Principles of Population and their Connection with Human Happiness*, 1840] there are in Ireland 2,300,000 persons who could not live without public or private assistance – or 27% of the whole population paupers.

The total dependence of so many people on a single crop was bound to lead to disaster. There was no question about whether the Irish potato crop would fail – it had already done so in whole or in part at least twenty times since 1728, causing hardship and distress each time – and several official reports had given explicit warnings of the risks the country was running. It was simply a case of by how much and when. In the autumn of 1845 the failure was partial; in 1846 it was complete. In 1847 there was an abundant harvest, but in 1848 the crop failed completely again, and so weakened were the people by what had gone before that the death toll was higher than ever, particularly as the British, who had provided £7 million for relief up to mid-

1847, had changed their policy, transferring all financial responsibility for dealing with the Famine to Dublin and resolutely refusing to provide any more aid.

Thomas Carlyle visited Westport at the end of July 1849 when the Famine was at its worst because that year's potato crop was still not in. He could not leave the place quickly enough:[5]

Human swinery has here reached its *acme*, happily: 30,000 paupers in this union [workhouse area], population supposed to be about 60,000. Workhouse proper (I suppose) cannot hold above 3 or 4000 of them, subsidiary workhouses and outdoor relief the others. Abomination of desolation: what *can* you make of it! outdoor quasi-*work*: 3 or 400 big hulks of fellows tumbling about with shares, picks and barrows, 'levelling' the end of their workhouse hill; at first glance you would think them all working; look nearer, in each shovel there is some ounce or two of mould and it is all make-believe; 5 or 600 boys and lads, pretending to break stones. Can it be a *charity* to keep men alive on these terms? In the face of all the twaddle of the earth, shoot a man rather than train him (with heavy expense to his neighbours) to be a deceptive human *swine*. Fifty-four wretched mothers sat rocking young offspring in one room: *vogue la galère* ...

Westport Union has £1100 a week from the Government (proportion rate-in-aid), Castlebar has £800, some other has £1300 etc, etc, it is so they live from week to week. Poor rates, collectible, as good as *none* (£28.14.0 say the books); a peasant will keep his cow for years against all manner of cess-collection: spy-children, tidings run as by electric wires, that a cess-collector is out, and all cows are huddled under lock and key, *un*attainable for years. No rents; little or no *stock* left, little cultivation, docks, thistles; landlord sits in his mansion for reasons, except on *Sunday*; we hear of them 'living on the rabbits of their own park.' Society is at an *end* here, with the land uncultivated and every second soul a pauper. – 'Society' *here* would have to eat itself, and end by cannibalism in a week, if it were not held up by the rest of our empire still standing afoot!

Carlyle mentions that all Lord Sligo had to live on was the rent from his opera box in London. This is confirmed by the tenth marquess[6] whose family, unlike those of many Irish landlords, can be proud of their record at this time. The third marquess, George Browne, his local income gone, literally sold the family silver – his father's racing trophies and two Gainsborough paintings – before running himself into debt to pay the poor rate on his own land and that of his smaller tenants. Had he not done so, the workhouse would have had even less adequate funds. Moreover, he went considerably further than his legal obligations and twice paid for the workhouse to be kept open for two or three-week spells when its funds ran out rather than have the paupers sent away. With his cousin George Moore of Moore Hall (father of the novelist) he imported 1,000 tons of American flour, which was sold off at half price in 1846. Browne lost £3,012 on his share of the venture. He closed down Westport House to save money and lived in a smaller house in the centre of the town for most of the Famine.

The Bingham family in Castlebar, eighteen kilometres inland from Westport, adopted quite a different policy. Lord Lucan, the head of the family, regarded his tenants as vermin, and took advantage of their inability to pay rent to clear them from his lands, turning many of them out of their houses in winter, thus sending them to an almost certain death. Two hundred families were cleared in the Ballinrobe area to make way for a 2,000-acre cattle farm he let to a Scot called Simpson. Carlyle saw this farm from the coach on his way to Westport, and approved:

Lord Lucan's close by Castlebar and on the other side of it too: has *cleared* his ground (cruel monster! cry all people); but is draining, building, harrowing and leasing; has decided to make this ugly land *avail* after clearing it. Candour must admit that *here* is a second most weighty consideration in his favour, in reference to those 'evictions.' First-rate new farmstead of his, Scotch tenant (I think), for peasants that will work there is employment here; Lord Lucan *is* moving, at least, if all others lie motionless rotting.

No-one who has looked at this terrible period has suggested that the British reaction to the Famine, particularly after 1847 – when the Exchequer in London passed financial responsibility for its relief to Dublin – was deliberately designed to clear the land. However, the fact that local landlords were expected to pay most of the cost of famine relief after 1847 gave them a compelling motive to do so, particularly as the land was more valuable commercially after the tenants had gone, as it could be turned over to cattle, exactly as done by Lord Lucan. No one has suggested that the Encumbered Estates Act of 1849, under which indebted estates could be sold up compulsorily on the petition of a creditor, was designed to clear the land either. Again, though, it did just that, falling especially harshly on the better landlords who felt some responsibility to their tenants and had borrowed during the Famine to pay their share of poor relief. The new owners on the other hand had no links with their tenants, whom they were legally entitled to clear at will. Marx quotes from a Co. Galway account of 1852:

The tenantry are turned out of the cottages by scores at a time ... Land agents direct the operation. The work is done by a large force of police and soldiery. Under the protection of the latter, the 'crowbar brigade' advances to the devoted township, takes possession of the houses ... The sun which rose on a village sets on a desert.

Marx estimated that starvation, disease and exposure killed over a million people during the Famine itself, and quoted Colonial Land Emigration Office figures to show that 1,200,436 people emigrated during its course or its immediate aftermath up to 30 June 1852. But the haemorrhage did not stop then, and more than another million had left by the time the census was taken in 1861. In all, the population of the whole island fell from 8.2

million in 1841 to 5.8 million twenty years later.

Some people certainly welcomed the changes the Famine and the clearances brought about. *The Economist* commented at the time that 'the departure of the redundant part of the population of Ireland and the Highlands of Scotland is an indispensable preliminary to every kind of improvement … the revenue of Ireland has not suffered in any degree from the famine of 1846-47, or from the net emigration which has since taken place. On the contrary, her net revenue amounted in 1851 to £4,281,999, being about £184,000 greater than in 1843.' Marx thought the clearances were 'a silent revolution which must be submitted to, and which takes no more notice of the human existences it breaks down than an earthquake regards the houses it subverts. The classes and races, too weak to master the new conditions of life, must give way.' He regarded as 'hypochondriacal philanthropy' Sismondi's view that the technological causes of the displacement – the changed methods in agriculture and industry – should have been prohibited.

As any economist would predict, the decline in population increased wages, just as in Britain after the Black Death, and led to a fall in the labour intensity with which the land was worked. The acreage of arable land decreased and the yield per acre of those arable crops that were grown went down, while the area of land under livestock went up. Between 1855 and 1866 '1,032,694 Irishmen [were] displaced by about one million cattle, sheep and pigs,' Marx commented in a speech he prepared but did not deliver in 1867. The trend away from tillage was encouraged by price changes on the British market: beef prices doubled between 1850 and 1911 while wheat prices, undermined by imports from the United States and Australia, fell.

As a result, a high proportion of each generation had to emigrate and 5.8 million people left Ireland between 1841 and 1925. The combined effect of higher beef prices and a declining population, which by the 1926 census was almost half what it had been seventy years previously, was to improve living conditions for those who remained. Before the Famine, the per capita national income of Ireland is thought to have been about £9.80 (£370 in 1987 terms), about 40 per cent of the level in Great Britain and one of the lowest in Europe – only Romania, Greece, Yugoslavia and Bulgaria seem to have been comparable.[7] By the outbreak of the First World War, however, Ireland had caught up and was number ten or twelve out of twenty-three European countries, although its income per head was still only around 60 per cent of the level in Britain. This rise in the economic pecking order, however, was not due to economic growth, merely to better agricultural export prices and the smaller population.

When representatives of twenty-six of the thirty-two counties undid the Act of Union in December 1921 by signing the Anglo-Irish Treaty, some certainly hoped for a new period of prosperity akin to that of the 1780s and 1790s. One signatory, Arthur Griffith, had published an influential pamphlet, *The Resurrection of Hungary: a Parallel for Ireland*, in 1904 in which he had described the effects of Hungarian independence in glowing terms. Hungary had turned itself, he said, from a land that was worse off than Ireland into a powerful state which was the granary of Europe and in the first rank intellectually. A self-governing Ireland could do the same. 'Hungary's progress, not only in agriculture but in mining and manufacturing industry since the restoration of her national constitution might be, with small exaggeration, called marvellous,' he wrote, adding that coal production had risen from 200,000 to 7 million tons and iron output from an 'infinitesimal' amount to 500,000 tons.

But for the first ten years of its life the new Irish state made few efforts to re-establish the conditions that had led to the flowering 120 years previously, and disappointed those who had shared Griffith's vision. In particular, for fear that Britain, which took over 90 per cent of Irish exports, would impose duties or quotas, the Free State took only tentative steps towards erecting a protective tariff wall behind which its industry could develop. Equally importantly, it failed to restrict the flow of Irish savings into British investments, a flow that was largely the result of Irish banks lending on the London market those funds for which they could not find a borrower at the externally determined interest rates which ruled at home. In 1926, private Free State investments held overseas totalled £195 million, a huge sum, seven times total government expenditure for that year, whereas foreign holdings in Ireland were worth only £73 million. The effect of this haemorrhage was to create jobs overseas rather than at home.

It is unrealistic to feel that the new government should have done more than it did. The men who formed Grattan's Parliament in 1782 had the confidence that came from being born into the ruling class: they felt they knew what they were about, and that removing trade restrictions was it. Those elected to the Dáil in 1923 were, by contrast, predominantly lower middle-class farmers or property owners with no personal knowledge of how government worked. Their target was to demonstrate, first to themselves and then to the British, that they were capable of running a country, especially one that had just disgraced itself by fighting a civil war. Their lack of confidence in turn made them ultra-cautious and heavily reliant on the British-trained civil servants they found waiting for them with advice on what should be done. They badly needed this advice because achieving Irish independence had been the only goal that most of them had ever had. Now that had been won, what next? Even Griffith, who might have known, was not there to tell them: he had died of apoplexy the previous year.

Since just over half the Irish population depended for its livelihood on the land and most of its deputies had rural backgrounds, it is not surprising that the Cumann na nGaedheal government under W. T. Cosgrave decided to make agricultural prosperity the foundation of the new Ireland. Certainly there was little industry for the government to turn to as an alternative basis of development: only 56,400 people, 4.3 per cent of the work force, were employed in manufacturing in 1926, compared with 670,000 on the land, and one brewing company, Guinness, made up 30 per cent of national manufacturing output in value-added terms.

Unfortunately, however, agricultural development boiled down to being more of the same: increasing the export of beef cattle to Britain, the strategy that had been followed since the Famine. What had probably decided this course was that cattle production had proved very profitable during the First World War and prices in 1920 had reached almost three times their 1913 level. So, although they had slipped a long way back by 1922 when Cosgrave took office, cattle culture still seemed a good bet, and everything was done to try to ensure its success. Farmers were exempted from income tax, had their liability to rates (property tax) reduced, and, so far as was possible, their labourers' wages were held down. As things turned out, however, all the government could do was enable producers to hold their own against continuing price falls. Livestock numbers, which had reached 4.42 million in 1921 just after meat prices peaked, dropped back to 3.95 million in 1926 and then recovered slightly to 4.14 million in 1929, not a lot more than the total Marx gives for 1860 in *Capital*, 3.61 million, although his figure was for the whole island.

But even had meat prices moved more favourably, an expanded national herd could not have maintained rural populations unless Sismondi's advice to prevent changes in technology had been followed too. Beef production is a low-labour enterprise and as farm sizes gradually increased, less labour was needed to manage the herds. In addition, although the Famine had so shocked the Irish psyche that the average ages at which people married were the highest in Europe – 34.9 for men and 29.1 for women (5.8 and 2.5 years, respectively, above those in England and Wales) – births still exceeded deaths by 17,000 a year and the potential labour force was increasing, although the economy was not generating extra jobs for it. Emigration therefore continued throughout the early years of the new state at much the same proportionate rate as in previous generations, although the flow reversed towards the end of its first decade as a result of the depression overseas.

It must not be thought that the Cosgrave government was completely supine or its policies entirely barren. As its self-confidence increased it began, very cautiously, to introduce protection measures to encourage particular industries, taking care to lower as many tariffs as it raised so as not to increase the input costs to agriculture nor to provoke retaliation by the British. By the end of its term of office in 1932 at least a hundred firms around the country owed their existence to this course. Perhaps most important of all, it began work on the hydro-electric power station on the Shannon in August 1925 and set up the Electricity Supply Board in 1927 to distribute the output across the country. It invested over £10 million to do so, equivalent to £350 million today, and was roundly criticized for its extravagance.

But Éamon de Valera, a former member of Arthur Griffith's Sinn Féin (a party whose belief in self-sufficiency is hinted at by the English translation of its name, 'Ourselves') thought that much more should be done and made it clear that he was prepared to risk British countermeasures and a fall in living standards if his chance came. 'If the servant was displeased with the kicks of his master and wanted to have his freedom, he had to make up his mind whether or not he was going to have that freedom and give up the luxuries of a certain kind which were available by being in the mansion,' he wrote in a statement of economic policy prepared in 1928 for the party he had just founded, Fianna Fáil. He also accepted that halting emigration would mean that the country's resources would have to be spread out over more people. 'We should try to get for our own people the necessities of life and try to maintain our population,' he wrote in the same document, advising the nation to 'forget as far as we can what are the standards prevalent in countries outside this.' The previous year he had told the *Manchester Guardian*:

I think it is quite possible that a less costly standard of living is desirable and that it would prove, in fact, a higher standard of living. I am not satisfied that the standard of living and the mode of life in Western Europe is a right or proper one. The industrialised countries have got themselves into a rut and Ireland is asked to hurry along after them.

De Valera's chance came in March 1932, when his party secured a majority in the Dáil and formed a government. Within two months he had imposed import duties of between 15 and 75 per cent on a wide range of goods, and within five he had deliberately provoked an economic war with Britain by refusing to pay the interest and principal due on loans the British had raised to enable Irish farmers to buy out their farms from their landlords – a payment that a previous Irish government had twice signed undertakings to make. Britain hit back by imposing duties on its imports from

Ireland, ostensibly to make good its loss. These duties hit beef, Ireland's main export, especially hard – at one stage in the six-year struggle they amounted to two-thirds of the value of some animals – and there is no doubt that the financial cost of the war was greater by far than Ireland's financial gains, even though the sum involved was around £5 million a year, about a fifth of Irish tax revenue. The Irish government did not even escape paying the annuities as it was forced to provide exporters with bounties to prevent producers from being financially destroyed, and, indirectly, these amounted to the same thing.

But from a political point of view the economic war was a resounding success because it rallied the people behind the government and motivated them to do within months things that, without its stimulus, they would have done much later, if at all. Westport, for example, had just two manufacturing businesses in 1932: these were Pollexfen's, a flour mill at the quay, and Livingstone's on the main street, which bottled stout and mixed its own soft drinks, the remnant of a 150-employee brewery on the same site over a century before. However, lack of an industrial tradition did not deter two women, Margaret Gallagher and Katherine Reece, from attending a course on Achill Island run by a government development agency to learn to knit with 'hand-flat' machines. In 1932 they took over a disused ballroom in the centre of the town and, trading under the delightful name of Connaught Cosiwear, began to produce women's 'twin sets', helped considerably by the electricity from the Shannon scheme that had reached the town just two years before.

'It was partly out of patriotism, partly because they wanted something to do,' says Mrs Gallagher's son, Roger. 'My mother was twenty years younger than my father – that was often the way marriages were then – and had just been left some money by a relative. Mrs Reece who was Welsh also had her own funds.' The business quickly moved into making up women's underwear from a knitted cotton fabric imported from England, relying on the fact that imported underwear was subject to duty but the fabric was not. When duty was imposed on the fabric too, the basis of the business seemed threatened, and the women travelled to Dublin to see the minister responsible, Seán Lemass, who explained that he had introduced the duty because he wanted the fabric to be made in Ireland in future. So the pair went to England, bought four of the special knitting machines, and learnt how to use them, and by the mid-thirties Cosiwear was running two shifts, each with a hundred employees.

The next factory in the town opened in 1934. It was Irish Sewing Cotton, which had the sole right to produce sewing thread in the Free State. The firm was a fifty-fifty joint venture between two of the town's business families, the O'Malleys and the Hugheses, and one of the smaller British thread producers, which had been told that it would be given an exclusive licence if it located its plant in Westport, Ballina or Sligo and took Irish partners. 'It's difficult now to realize how important thread was then,' says Jeff O'Malley, the son of one of the founding directors. 'We became involved because we were selling the company's thread to the grocery shops we supplied from our wholesale grocery business. Every housewife in those days was always making and mending.' Before the outbreak of the Second World War, the company employed 120 to 130 men.

The town's third new factory grew out of the success of the second. A group of the town's businessmen began to discuss what other ventures might be viable, and several ideas, including setting four men to make nails, were researched before Charles Hughes, a director of Irish Sewing Cotton, persuaded them that a boot factory would be best. Hughes was already wholesaling boots, so his opinion carried some weight. All the main trading families in the town bought shares in the £12,500 equity, and the factory opened in 1936 and soon employed between eighty and ninety people.

Other towns and cities reacted to de Valera's artificial crisis in the same way, and the number of people employed in the production of so-called transportable goods – manufacturing, peat production, and mining – shot up by almost 61 per cent in five years, from 62,608 in 1931 to 100,575 in 1936. That productivity per employee fell is indicated by the fact that the value of net output went up by a smaller amount – 36.7 per cent – but this was largely because many of the new enterprises were 'screwdriver' operations, doing simple jobs requiring little capital equipment on imported parts. Even so, the rapid expansion of the industrial sector was a remarkable achievement.

Despite its success, the protectionist policy had its detractors, especially among the half-dozen or so academic economists Ireland supported at the time. Joseph Johnston of Trinity College, Dublin, reflected a widespread view in the Irish branch of the profession when he called[8] in 1935 for a return to 'a regime in which prices reflected not political ideals but economic realities.' Keynes, however, had no doubts that the country was on the right course and caused considerable embarrassment to his unsuspecting hosts by saying so in a lecture he gave at University College, Dublin, in April 1933. 'If I were an Irishman I should find much to attract me in the economic outlook of your present government towards self-sufficiency,' he said.[9]

Over an increasingly wide range of industrial products, and perhaps agricultural products also, I become doubtful whether the economic loss of national self-sufficiency is good enough to outweigh the other advantages of gradually bringing the producer and the consumer within the ambit of the same national, economic and financial organization. Experience accumulates to prove that most modern mass-production processes can be performed in most countries and climates with almost equal efficiency ... National self-sufficiency, in short, though it costs something, may be becoming a luxury which we can afford, if we happen to want it ... National self-sufficiency is to be considered, not as an ideal in itself but as directed to the creation of an environment in which other ideals can be safely and conveniently pursued.

Keynes also attacked the paying of too much attention to what today we would call the 'bottom line', powerfully yet succinctly anticipating some of the arguments in this book.

The nineteenth century carried to extravagant lengths the criterion of what one can call for short 'the financial results' as a test of the advisability of any course of action sponsored by private or collective action. This whole conduct of life was made into a sort of parody of an accountant's nightmare. Instead of using their vastly increased material and technical resources to build a wonder-city they built slums, and they thought it right and proper to build slums because slums, on the test of private enterprise, 'paid' whereas a wonder-city would, they thought, have been an act of foolish extravagance which would, in the imbecile idiom of the financial fashion, have 'mortgaged the future'; though how the construction today of great and glorious works can impoverish the future, no man can see until his mind is beset by false analogies from an irrelevant accountancy ... The nation as a whole will assuredly be richer if unemployed men and machines are used to build much-needed houses than if they are supported in idleness.

The minds of this generation are still so beclouded by bogus calculations that they distrust conclusions which should be obvious ... We have to remain poor because it does 'pay' to be rich. We have to live in hovels, not because we cannot build palaces but because we cannot 'afford' them.

The same rule of self-destructive financial calculation governs every walk of life. We destroy the beauty of the countryside because the unappropriated splendours of the countryside have no economic value ... London is one of the richest cities in the history of civilization but it cannot afford the highest standards of achievement of which its own living citizens are capable because they do not 'pay'.

If I had responsibility for the government of Ireland today I should most deliberately set out to make Dublin, within its appropriate limits of scale, a splendid city fully endowed with all the appurtenances of art and civilization on the highest standards of which its citizens were individually capable, convinced that what I could create I could afford, and believing that any money thus spent would not only be better than any dole but would make unnecessary any dole. For with what we have spent on the dole in England since the war we could have made our cities the greatest works of man in the world.

Although even de Valera lacked the nerve to go very far with Keynes, he went part of the journey, and an average of 12,000 houses were built with state aid each year between 1932 and 1942 compared with fewer than 2,000 a year between 1923 and 1931. It is hard to overestimate the difference these houses made to the families that built them. Hidden by the trees below me, not seventy metres from where I sit, is the roofless ruin of a stone cottage. It was abandoned in the thirties when the family that owns the fields at the foot of my hill moved to a new house beside a fresh-cut public road. The house they left had just two rooms: a bedroom and a big living-room, with the fireplace built into the dividing wall. The house was deliberately built on uneven land so that the floor in the living room sloped away from the fire, thus preventing animal urine flowing into the rest of the dwelling when the stock was brought inside during hard weather. Many cottages were once built that way, giving rise to the expression 'draw up to the fire.' Beside the new house, however, were separate cattle byres.

Although his industrial policy was an undoubted success, de Valera was unable to work a similar trick in agriculture. His strategy was to encourage farmers to supplement beef production with more labour-intensive activities, and he introduced subsidies to increase the production of wheat and sugarbeet. Unfortunately this did almost nothing to increase the total arable area of the country – farmers simply switched to subsidized wheat from unsubsidized barley and oats – and by 1939 only 4.7 per cent more acres were under the plough than in 1931. Yet all the while this attempt to create employment was going on, farmers were eliminating labour by steadily increasing the size of their farms and replacing horses with tractors. De Valera was therefore trying to climb an escalator that technological change was pushing steadily down. Unemployment rose to 100,000, and there was no fall in the number of people who felt it necessary to move overseas.

By 1951 the population of the state was 2.96 million, 11,000 less than at independence, a figure that inescapably means that all the natural increase, half a million people, had been forced to find places for themselves overseas. Agriculture provided incomes for 504,000 people, 40 per cent of all those 'gainfully occupied', compared with 655,000, exactly half of all workers, in 1926: the output of the sector, however, had gone up by 8.6 per cent in volume. A further 148,000 people were employed making transportable goods, a rise of around 100,000 over the twenty-five years. In other words, the growth of this category of industry had not even absorbed all those pushed out of farming. The service sector had taken up some of the slack but total employment was down by 33,000 on the 1926 figure at 1.27 million.

The best verdict we can give on this outcome is that de Valera, whose party was narrowly defeated in 1948, had come within a whisker of meeting his target of maintaining Ireland's population, which had fallen by very much more than 11,000 people in all previous quarter-centuries since the Famine. But why were the results of his experiment with self-sufficiency so much less spectacular than those Grattan's Parliament achieved in twenty years? Part of the answer has to be that his goals were different: he built dispersed cottages for the rural poor instead of prominent terraces for the urban rich. Another part of the answer is the Second World War, which disrupted the economy and limited what he was able to do.

But the ways in which the war restricted his freedom of action provide the clue to what was really wrong. During the war, farming was restricted by shortages of imported fertilizers, feedstuffs, machinery, and spare parts; industry by inadequate deliveries of raw materials, transport by a lack of petrol and steam-coal. Most of the items in short supply had not been invented 150 years before. Despite its attempt at self-sufficiency, Ireland was much more dependent on the outside world than it had been in 1800, because of the ways technologies had changed. Nor did supply restrictions apply only during wartime: in peace too the volume of goods Ireland could obtain from overseas was limited by the amount of foreign currency it could pay. The number of hands through which an expenditure of, say, £100 would pass before it had all leaked away abroad to pay for imports had been cut down significantly. As a result, in peace or war, de Valera's Ireland could build a far smaller edifice on the basis of its natural resources and labour than had been possible one-and-a-half centuries earlier when the country had been much more self-reliant.

However, there was an even more fundamental reason why less was accomplished during the de Valera years than during Grattan's Parliament. It was that the whole first generation of Irish political leaders was inherently conservative, de Valera included. In 1932, with the world in depression and Britain to fight economically, the creation of a self-sufficient society that could stand somewhat apart was by no means the radical step it seems today. Later, during the war itself, mere survival was enough and the frugal comforts about which de Valera dreamed seemed highly attractive. It was only when peace returned that the parties' aimlessness became apparent. One of the first of the next generation of politicians, Noël Browne, who was made Minister for Health on his first day in the Dáil after de Valera's election defeat in 1948, described[10] the public service of that time as 'a fossilized fly in amber' and the politicians as 'content to pester one another about each other's motives for the rest of their lives. They had no interest whatever in the outside world.'

As a result, Browne said, 'there was no serious mature informed debate on the causes for our chronic misuse of land, labour and capital in the creation of wealth, either in industry or agriculture. Nor [did] we seriously [attempt] to understand the causes or deal with the gross maldistribution of wealth and the mass suffering and chronic poverty of so many.' Moreover, when any proposals were made to assist the poor, they were squashed by the politicians who, as property-owners, would have had to pay increased taxes, or by the hierarchy of the Roman Catholic Church which was paranoid about anything remotely resembling communism. When Browne pointed out that only 10 per cent of children got any secondary education and that there were only thirty-five free scholarships to university, de Valera defended the system and denied that it needed to be improved.

Similarly, when Browne proposed a mother-and-child health service in 1950 that would have given all children free health care until they were sixteen and looked after mothers before, during and after childbirth, he was called before the archbishop and read a letter the bishops had sent to the Taoiseach that attacked his proposals on several grounds. Among the objections were that the scheme infringed the rights of the family and the individual to provide their own health care; that only the church was competent to give instruction about sexual relations, chastity, and marriage, and that if the state got involved, 'doctors trained in institutions in which we have no confidence ... may give gynaecological care not in accordance with Catholic principles,' leading to the introduction of abortion and contraception. When Browne tried to put his case, the Bishop of Galway told him it was unfair to tax the rest of the community to give the poor a free health service, a view most of the hierarchy held. Browne was later described from the pulpit of the church in the village where he spent his weekends as one of those people who 'come amongst us disguised as friends when meanwhile their real work is to poison the wells and so kill off our stock,' while the Bishop of Galway preached that the health scheme advocated euthanasia for the unfit and aged and that Browne's beliefs came from Nazi Germany. A Dominican magazine said it was a mortal sin to introduce a mother-and-child health service that was not means-tested; communist countries had a free health service, it carefully pointed out. All this was too much for the government whose members would never have dreamed of going against the church anyway. The mother-and-child scheme was dead and Browne's party forced him to resign as minister.

Browne did, however, manage to get an amazing number of things done during his three years in office, showing just how much more a self-reliant Ireland could have accomplished had it had the vision. He launched the blood transfusion service, which became one of the finest in the world. He started BCG inoculation against tuberculosis, copied a Danish system to control the disease, and raised the number of TB beds from 3,500 to 5,500 within two years; the result was that the TB death rate had fallen 40 per cent by the time he left office. But above all, he built a network of hospitals throughout the country with funds from the Irish Sweepstakes. Previous ministers had also had access to these funds but had just spent the interest from the capital sum that had been built up; Browne spent the capital, and even borrowed against the future income, with the result that by the mid-fifties the Irish hospital system was rated second only to that of Sweden.

With Browne banished to the back benches, the old-style politicians continued to bicker among themselves until a crisis brought them up sharp.

It was 1956 when the Fine Gael-Farmer-Labour coalition learnt one morning that it had run up a terrible balance of payments deficit the previous year: exports had been £107 million while imports had been £204 million. It panicked and immediately imposed swingeing import levies. Then, three months later, before the first set of taxes had a chance to work, it piled on a further set of import duties. Given that most of Ireland's imports were now raw materials for further processing, the result was to put thousands out of work. There were massive protest marches and 60,000 people emigrated within twelve months.

The incompetent handling of the crisis cost Ireland all the confidence in itself and the system it had built up since independence. Both government and opposition suggested solutions. The Taoiseach, John Costello, proposed tax incentives to encourage exports and grants for the building of factories. Fianna Fáil's idea was to mount a £67 million state investment programme to create 100,000 new jobs in the private sector. It took two years for the Secretary to the Department of Finance, T. K. Whitaker, to transform these ideas into a discussion document, *Economic Development*, and then into a White Paper, *Programme for Economic Expansion*, which was presented to the Dáil in November 1958. By this time the worst was over: the relative prices of imports and exports, which had caused the problem in the first place, had moved back in Ireland's favour, exports had increased, and payments were in surplus for the first time since the Second World War. However, this did not prevent Fianna Fáil, now back in power as a result of the coalition's panic, from abandoning de Valera's self-reliance policies in their entirety. It also abandoned the man, who was now seventy-five and almost blind, easing him out of politics and into the presidency as its candidate in the 1959 election.

The discussion paper that brought about this U-turn was by no means the neutral, dispassionate document most civil servants would have felt they ought to have produced in the circumstances. Whitaker abandoned the customary civil service anonymity and wrote out of personal conviction, clearly conveying the doomsday situation that he and many others had convinced themselves that Ireland faced. The next five or ten years, he wrote, 'will be critical for the country's survival as an economic entity,' omitting to spell out what that would mean, perhaps feeling that the threat of having to face the shame of begging to rejoin the United Kingdom was more powerful if left unspoken.

The policies hitherto followed, though given a fair trial, have not resulted in a viable economy. We have power, transport, factories, public services, houses, hospitals and a general 'infrastructure' on a scale which is reasonable by western European standards, yet large-scale emigration and unemployment still persist. The population is falling, the national income is rising more slowly than in the rest of Europe. A great and sustained effort to increase national production, employment and living standards is necessary to avert decadence.

His emphasis on production and living standards (consumption rates) is the parting of the ways. De Valera had set himself the target of maintaining Ireland's population and had come close to doing so. For him, consumption rates were a secondary consideration, and he had insisted that they should not be compared to those overseas. Even so, when Whitaker made the comparison in the passage above, he was forced to admit that Ireland did not come out too badly: things seemed 'reasonable by western European standards'. Yet because he wanted large-scale emigration and unemployment to end and the fall in population to cease, he thought that national income had to be made to rise as rapidly as elsewhere in Europe. Further, he argues that protection must be removed to bring this growth about, although he does not use the word itself:

Sooner or later protection will have to go and the challenge of free trade be accepted. There really is no choice for a country wishing to keep pace materially with the rest of Europe. It would be a policy of despair to accept that our costs of production must permanently be higher than those of other European countries. Our level of real incomes depends on our competitive efficiency. If that must be lower than the rest of Europe, we should have to be content with relatively low living standards … The effect of any policy entailing relatively low living standards here for all time would be to sustain and stimulate the outflow of emigrants and in the end jeopardise our economic independence. Any little benefit obtained in terms of employment would be outweighed by losses through emigration and general economic impoverishment.

Elsewhere in the document Whitaker made explicit what is implicit above: that growth must henceforward be the primary target, since it is the only way of stemming emigration. He also made it clear that government expenditure designed to improve living conditions directly must give way to that designed to raise output. 'It is most important to confine increases in national expenditure as far as possible to projects of a productive nature,' he wrote. 'A slowing down on housing and other forms of social investment must be faced from now on because of the virtual satisfaction of needs over wide areas.' What a tribute that last phrase is to a system he believed to have failed!

Whitaker's work led directly to the steady removal of protectionist tariffs, the lifting of the controls on foreign participation in Irish industry and the introduction of capital grants and export profits tax relief to encourage foreign firms to set up. He was also responsible for changing public attitudes to borrowing from overseas. External borrowing, he wrote, 'enables development to go ahead more rapidly. Countries with low incomes which have little margin for saving would be condemned perpetually to low standards of living in the absence of external borrowing,' and Ireland's savings had proved inadequate to enable investment to proceed at a rate sufficient for the country to keep up with the rest of Europe. Yet, as he himself made clear, there was no evidence that any really good project had been stifled for lack of funds and there was little demand for capital from the private sector. 'The real shortage is of ideas. These may have to come in part from external sources,' he was forced to conclude.

What has been the result of the thirty or so years in which, at Whitaker's urging, the pursuit of economic growth has been given priority above all else? The years immediately following his changes – the sixties – are now regarded as a golden age, and Whitaker himself referred to them as Paradise Lost in a radio lecture in 1986. Incomes rose quickly and emigrants began to return. In 1960, for example, unemployment dropped to 40,600, fully 20 per cent down on the previous year, while car sales reached 32,000, 40 per cent up on 1959. But these early gains cannot be attributed to Whitaker's policies – they came too soon. They were due instead to a further improvement in the terms of trade and to a boom in Britain. And the extent to which his strategy brought benefits later in the decade is doubtful too. As John Bradley of the Economic and Social Research Institute in Dublin points out in an assessment of Whitaker's impact that he contributed to a 1990 book, *Planning Ireland's Future: the Legacy of T. K. Whitaker*, other small countries – Denmark, Belgium, Norway, and Finland – did equally well, and Ireland did not narrow the gap between its level of consumption and those in the rest of Europe.

Whitakerism certainly produced nothing to feel happy about in the seventies and eighties, and Tim Pat Coogan, a former editor of the *Irish Press*, called his book about the period from 1966 to 1987, *The Lost Decades*. The opening of the Irish economy to foreign competition meant that indigenous industries declined while their foreign-owned replacements paid less in taxes, repatriated most of their profits, and bought a smaller proportion of their needs locally than those which had gone before. What's more, the total number employed in industry increased very little. In 1957, 162,000 people were employed in the transportable goods sector in predominantly Irish-owned firms. By 1990 the total had risen to 201,800, but only slightly more than half these people worked for Irish firms. True, industrial output had gone up very considerably but £1,500 million in state grants had been paid out over the three decades to achieve this, in effect lowering the cost of capital and making it cheaper to replace people with machines. Industry had also enjoyed very considerable tax reliefs – almost £1,500 million in 1987 alone. The official view is that these reliefs are at the expense of taxpayers overseas as far as foreign-owned, exporting firms are concerned, and that these firms' presence benefits the Irish exchequer, because they pay a 10 per cent tax on their profits and because their direct and indirect employees pay normal income taxes. However, because so large a part of the Irish economy is so lightly taxed and so generously aided, taxes on the rest of it, which is largely the labour-intensive part, have to be correspondingly higher.

In Westport, Irish Sewing Cotton closed down in 1984, and the shoe factory followed suit in 1990, while another firm that had been spawned by these pioneers, a weaving business called Westport Textiles (started jointly by English Sewing Cotton and Irish Sewing Cotton in the sixties and which wove and made up duvets under Danish ownership), went into receivership but was purchased by its local management in 1991. Fortunately the grand-mother of them all, Connaught Cosiwear, is still knitting on, albeit on a smaller scale and under another name, having been itself bought out of receivership in 1986. Mayo Workwear, an overall factory, is still trading too and is manufacturing in England as well as in Westport. It was set up by the Hughes family to make shirts when cloth became available immediately after the war and is still run by sons of the founder. But today the biggest employer in the town is Allergan, an American manufacturer of contact lens fluids, with 460 people on its payroll. 'It's the only factory in the town ever to have been set up without local money,' said Jeff O'Malley rue-fully.

The same story has been repeated across the country and whole indus-tries have almost completely disappeared. Whitaker mentions in *Economic Development* that 5,913 people were employed in shoe manufacturing in 1956. By 1988 the equivalent figure was 1,105, according to that year's Census of Industrial Production, and the total has fallen further since. The clothing trade was also badly hit, falling from around 23,000 workers in the late fifties to 10,792 in 1988. As a result, the proportion of the country's needs being supplied from overseas grew tremendously, as the chart on the next page shows.

Nevertheless, industrial employment can claim to have more than held its own since the mid-fifties. The agricultural sector, in contrast, has to hang its head in shame. 400,000 men were employed on farms on 1 June 1958, according to Whitaker's report. On 1 June 1989 the figure was put at 163,000, a 59 per cent fall. In *Farming Collapse: National Opportunity* (1990), Raymond Crotty, who gave up farming to become an economist and who has written extensively about the problems of Irish agriculture, shows that although output went up 83.5 per cent between 1929 and 1989 when measured in constant 1989 prices, once the cost of the extra inputs – the feeds, fertilizers and equipment – were taken away, the net output had changed scarcely at all, rising just 14.3 per cent in the sixty years.

The total number of people in employment in 1991 was just over one

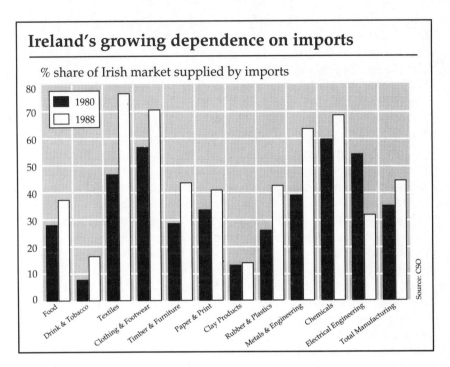

Ireland's growing dependence on imports

% share of Irish market supplied by imports

Source: CSO

Figure 14.3 In the eight years between 1980 and 1988, the proportion of Ireland's basic needs such as food and clothing made abroad shot up by between 50 and 100 per cent.

million, more than a fifth less than in 1951. The population, however, went up from 2.96 million in 1951 to 3.54 million in 1986, the most recent census year for which full results are available. Almost all the increase was attributable to the rise in the numbers of the young, of pensioners, and of the unemployed: between 1951 and 1986 the population under 24 rose by 300,000, that of people over 65 by 60,000 and the number of jobless by 170,000. Most of the young still try to emigrate as soon as their education is finished just as they did when Whitaker deplored their loss as a vicious circle that depleted the domestic market of initiative and skill and provided 'a reduced incentive for productive enterprise.' An estimated 46,000 people left Ireland in 1988, equivalent to three-quarters of those reaching the age of 21 that year, and losses were heaviest in the west. Only nine or ten of the fifty boys who sat their Leaving Certificate at the Christian Brothers' school in Westport in 1986 at the same time as my son are still living in the district.

Louisburgh, eighteen kilometres west along the coast of Clew Bay from my look-out place, is typical of hundreds of villages throughout Ireland. Apart from a newly opened museum about the life of Grace O'Malley, a piratical clan leader who met Elizabeth I, there is little to detain anyone driving through to catch the ferry to Clare Island or to visit one of Europe's finest beaches at Silver Strand. Scarcely more than two streets which meet near the former Protestant church, with pubs, a hotel, two schools, the Catholic church and several shops scattered along them, it seems to have little to detain the locals either, although there is a small factory that makes exhibition display equipment and a community-owned cluster of holiday homes. Its population has fallen by half since 1911, a more rapid fall than that for Co. Mayo as a whole, which is down by just over a third.

It looks as if the emigration will go on provided Louisburgh's people can continue to find countries to take them. Although the tide turned briefly between 1979 and 1981 and several emigrants came home, a survey of school-leavers in 1986 showed that 77 per cent wanted to leave. Less than a fifth of these said they would change their minds and stay even if they could find a job. And go they do; 3.2 per cent of the population of 2,260 – seventy-two people, mostly young – left in the 18 months between June 1984 and December 1986.

'All of last year's Leaving Certificate students have left,' Bill Farrell, a Louisburgh community development worker, told me in early 1991. 'We may have reached the point of terminal decline. I doubt if the flow can be stemmed. My job is to work with the women – they're the last resource in a way – to help them develop supplementary incomes. Farming itself has gone or will be going and the men are caught in the dole trap: they don't want to get involved in anything that would affect their dole. The women are less conservative.'

Once too many people leave an area, its economy collapses. Tom Boylan, who developed an input-output matrix of the Mayo-Galway economy at University College, Galway, estimates that for every four families that leave the area, a job is lost somewhere in the region because of the loss of spending power, thus accelerating the decline. In some communities, like Louisburgh, so many people have left and are leaving that many of the rest cannot afford to remain.

Pádraig Divilly, an official of the Irish Farmers' Association, described to Seán MacConnell of *The Irish Times* in January 1991 how this process had affected a Co. Galway village he knew well. First, he said, the local creamery closed down its milk collection station, putting two men out of work and taking away an important focal point for the farming community. Then the local Garda station closed when the single policeman was transferred to the nearest town. On the same day the mobile library announced that it would stop calling in the village because of insufficient demand. Then the local school, which once had enough children to warrant three teachers, closed when two families who had returned from England in the 1970s emigrated again, taking their seven children with them. Next, the postmistress died and the Post Office decided not to replace her. Letters and parcels are now delivered by a van from the town. One of the village's two pubs, which had been reduced to opening only in the evening, closed for good. The owner, a local man who had returned from Dublin, moved away with his four children. Most recently the local shop, which sold fertilizer, diesel fuel and some farm machinery got into financial difficulties and cut down its range, dismissing the man who worked in its yard. He moved to the town and lives on the dole while the shop now sells just a limited range of groceries.

On the basis of the evidence there is no doubt that the Whitaker experiment has been a disaster. The services that make rural life tolerable are being rapidly stripped away. There are 20 per cent fewer jobs and 400 per cent more unemployment than there were over thirty years ago when his strategy was proposed, and emigration rates are certainly no better, running at almost 45,000 in 1989. Total taxation, which Whitaker said was too high at 27 per cent of GNP in 1957, is now around 45 per cent. Worse still, over 40 per cent of the population depend on state welfare payments for the majority of their income, half as many again as the 27 per cent who 'could not live without public or private assistance' in Engels' day. In addition, Ireland has been turned from a country that was in credit internationally to the most seriously indebted in the EC apart from Belgium. Since 1958 it has also become more than twice as exposed to the fluctuations of the world economy and is much less economically independent than when the experiment began. The graph on the following page shows the growth in the trading risks the country is running: within the EC, only Belgium and Luxembourg are more at risk from an international downturn. The most powerful trading countries import and export an average of only 15 per cent of their production: the Irish figures are four times as great. Japan's exposure to foreign trade upheavals even declined slightly between 1960 and 1988, to reach just 8 per cent.

Whitakerism has amounted to no more than a variant of the development strategy followed since the Famine, that of banishing surplus people to improve the lot of those who remain. Modern Irish employers who cut their staffs by introducing new technology have the same effect as Lord Lucan had when he cleared his tenants to raise beef cattle: people have no option but to move away. Over the next few years, however, it is going to be difficult for Ireland to shed its redundant population, because of the depressed conditions overseas. Already, in fact, emigrants have had to return for lack of employment elsewhere, just as they did in the early thirties. According to a broadcast by the Archbishop of Tuam, Dr Joseph Cassidy, in February 1991, 7,000 people who had returned from Britain and the United States to spend Christmas with their families in his diocese, which

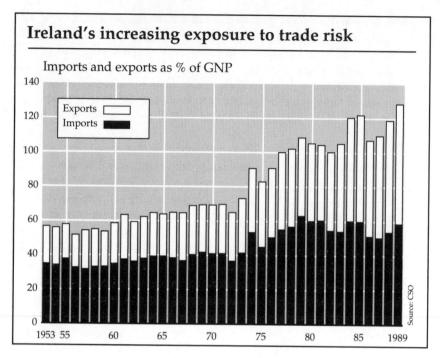

Figure 14.4 Ireland's dependence on imports and exports has rapidly increased since joining the EC, making the country one of the most exposed to foreign trade risks in the world.

covers Mayo and Galway, had not gone back overseas and were drawing the dole at home. Subsequent reports have confirmed this trend nationwide.

Yet against this background of increasing labour availability, employers were shedding jobs in response to a fall in export demand, and two state organizations, the Post Office and Irish Rail, put forward plans to create significant redundancies themselves. The Post Office plan, which has still to be implemented, involved shedding 1,500 people, almost a fifth of its staff, and cutting the heart out of 554 communities by closing their sub-post offices. However, the railway has already saved labour by closing down some of its smaller freight yards, including that in Westport. Since the surplus staff from both organizations is unlikely to find replacement jobs or to emigrate, the redundancies make no economic sense. All they mean is that taxpayers will have to support those 'let go' through the dole system rather than leaving the whole community to carry the burden through higher postal charges and rail fares. The latter course would at least allow the surplus workers to maintain their self-respect and give the community some prospect of better, rather than worse, postal and rail services in years to come. Only when Ireland develops a labour shortage – and unemployment

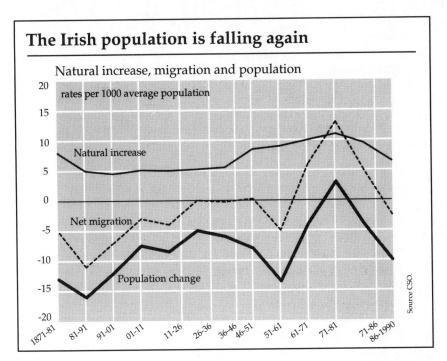

The Irish population is falling again

Natural increase, migration and population
rates per 1000 average population

Natural increase

Net migration

Population change

Source CSO.

1871-81, 81-91, 91-01, 01-11, 11-26, 26-36, 36-46, 46-51, 51-61, 61-71, 71-81, 71-86, 86-1990

Figure 14.5 Although Ireland is the only country in Western Europe where the birth rate is above replacement level, the population was falling in the late 1980s because so many young people were emigrating in search of work.

was over 20 per cent when these plans were published – will shedding labour by any organization, public or private, make sense at national level. Eliminating useful people who then have to be paid to do nothing makes a society less efficient rather than more so.

Unfortunately, neither state body's proposal was an isolated one. In 1990, so that the government could reduce the proportion of national income it was being forced to collect in taxes, hospitals were forced to cut back their nursing staffs to levels at which patients died from lack of care. Most of the nurses were able to emigrate, and as they did not draw the dole, the taxpayers were left better off – at least until they fell ill. Whitaker's system has made Ireland too poor to employ its own people to do the jobs it needs done.

How has this come about? In essence, for the same reason that de Valera found that he had less power than the members of Grattan's Parliament to feed, clothe and house his fellow countrymen: the limitations imposed by the availability of foreign exchange or foreign supplies. If the government allows as many Irish people as wish to work for each other actually to do so, there will be a balance of payments crisis, because a high proportion of any money circulated here leaks abroad. Only by holding the level of employment down can the current exchange rate be held, and if the currency is allowed to fall in value so that domestic production is better placed to displace that from overseas, why, that creates that Bad Thing, inflation. So long as it abides by the conventional wisdom, the government has no alternative but to do what it does.

RELIVING THE DREAM

Ireland does not need to grow any more. Although there is relative poverty, most of its people are well fed, well clothed and well housed by any objective standard. Because historical circumstances prevented industrialization, their countryside is the envy of most of Europe. In survey after survey they rate among the happiest humans in the world. Indeed, according to Richard Estes's Index of Social Progress,[11] the country ranks eighth in the world in economic development and social and political conditions, while Britain comes twelfth.*

If the Irish go for growth, the process will merely make agricultural and industrial goods, of which they have enough, relatively cheaper and threaten their countryside. On the other hand, those things they do need, like teachers and carers, will cost relatively more and will seem less affordable than they do at present. The needs of those Irish people who are poor are better met by redistributing the existing resources than by trying to get the system to generate higher incomes for everyone in the hope that the poor will somehow catch up; experience teaches they won't. Again, some people need better houses, but these can be built over the years at the current level of national income: there is no need to try to speed up the income flow. Indeed, trying to do so by endlessly striving to improve the country's position in the world innovation race by accelerating investment will probably waste more resources than it creates, as the Whitaker experiment has shown.

It does not take a high level of consumption to enable a country to be fed, clothed, housed, educated and entertained to an excellent standard – unless, that is, an extraordinarily wasteful system dictates otherwise. Ireland has all the land and renewable energy resources it needs to halt emigration and support its people well – but it must build a non-wasteful system to do

---

*The index, which assesses 124 countries, uses thirty-six different factors to reach its conclusions, and is based on data from 1970 to 1985. Its top ten countries were: Denmark, Italy, West Germany, Austria, Sweden, France, Norway, Ireland, the Netherlands and Belgium. The worst country was Angola, followed by Ethiopia, Chad, Guinea, Afghanistan, Somalia, Mali, Mozambique, Malawi and Mauritania in decreasing order of dreadfulness.

so. This probably means that the country will have to make its own way and control its foreign trade links because the growth imperative will otherwise destroy whatever it builds. Only if European energy policies impose a form of self-sufficiency might it escape having to take a course outside GATT and the EC.

The main mistake Ireland must avoid is to continue to think that its people will lead better lives if it increases labour productivity. Higher productivity destroys jobs, concentrates those that remain into fewer and fewer hands, and creates a much more stressful climate. What Ireland needs is not a cheaper mix of rather less labour and rather more capital – for this is all higher productivity means – but a greater range of jobs, from the very simple to the highly complex, within which people can fulfil themselves to the maximum extent. Creating these will mean, as de Valera insisted, that those living here must stop looking over their shoulders to see what their counterparts abroad are being paid; instead they must look at the richness of the lives they are able to make. It is a straight choice between a higher standard of living and a higher quality of life.

If one is an optimist, there are signs that people are beginning to realize that this is the choice to be made. Until the late 1980s, communities would welcome any project that promised employment, no matter what the environmental consequences might be. 'You can't eat the view,' was the prevailing attitude. Now, however, they have become cynical about the prospects of seeing long-term employment levels actually increase while they know only too well that the unfavourable environmental and quality-of-life consequences of such projects almost invariably come to pass. This new insight has led community groups to object to several schemes they would have welcomed previously, including pharmaceutical factories in Co. Cork, fish farms in Co. Galway, and an irradiation plant and talc mine in Westport, and sometimes they have won the day. A general recognition is dawning that economic development in other countries has had its drawbacks and Ireland will lose those things that make it special if it continues to 'hurry along after them'.

Another attitude has developed that may turn out to be the most positive gain from the Whitaker experiment: a feeling of national confidence and competence. On the day Ireland joined the European Monetary System, the Department of Finance file of correspondence with the British Treasury about the common currency, sterling, was sent down to the vaults and never called for again. The Irish pound was free. The last link with the United Kingdom had been broken, and in the years that have followed, Ireland has finally fought its way out of Britain's shadow, partly because of its equal standing with its former master within the EC but also because Irish people at all levels have dealt with their European counterparts and proved to themselves that they can operate at least as well. The former British politician and President of the European Commission, Roy Jenkins, once described the way that Ireland conducted its first European Presidency as 'a model of triumphing over the limitations of small-power resources to exercise skilled and authoritative diplomacy.' The Irish Foreign Minister, Garret FitzGerald, 'succeeded in making London look peripheral to Europe, while Dublin was metropolitan.'

Although almost everyone in Ireland realizes that continuing with current policies will exacerbate the country's severe and long-running problems, few outside the tiny Green Party believe there is any alternative way. However, during the spring of 1991 there was a hint that another strategy might emerge. As a result of an invitation from the Department of the Environment to submit its views on what the Irish position should be at the 1992 Earth Summit (the United Nations' conference on environment and development to be held in Brazil), the environmental organization Earthwatch prepared a paper it subsequently circulated to other organizations. This argued that the Irish countryside was the creation of the farming community and that if that community continued to be displaced by larger-scale, less labour-intensive methods, the consequences for the environment would be severe. The reason for the decline in rural populations, the paper said, was that high-labour, low-input Irish family farms could not compete with highly mechanized, energy-intensive farms elsewhere, particularly those on the prairies of the United States, and with large European livestock producers who imported most of their feedstuffs from outside the EC. However, if taxes on fossil fuels were imposed in response to the threat of global warming, small Irish farmers would become much more competitive again. The flight from the land, which had reduced the number of farmers by half over the previous fifteen years, would be stemmed, and traditional farming methods, and the countryside they created, might be retained.

In the autumn, there was another development. Two researchers at the Economic and Social Research Institute, John FitzGerald and Daniel McCoy, ran HERMES, the ESRI's computer model of the Irish economy, to see what would happen if energy taxes were imposed in Ireland independently of its European partners. On their first run, they assumed that the income from the tax was used to pay off the national debt and found that national income fell, while unemployment, prices and emigration rose.

However, if the tax was used to cut employees' social welfare contributions, thus lowering the cost of employing someone, unemployment levels and the rate of emigration fell and national income went up. In addition, the taxes had very little effect on the level of prices. 'The switch in the tax burden from labour to energy [would have] a positive impact on the Irish economy ... improving the competitiveness of the industrial sector,' the researchers told a conference in Dublin. Strangely, they also found that if the rest of the EC introduced the tax and used the proceeds to cut labour costs, Ireland would benefit less than if it acted alone. However, there was still likely to be an overall gain.

High taxes on energy could force countries and communities to become more self-sufficient, particularly as transport costs would rise sharply, while unemployment would fall as more labour-intensive methods of production began to be used. Indeed, energy taxes might deliver all the benefits of protectionism while avoiding its artificial, bureaucratic restrictions. My hope, certainly, is that restrictions on burning fossil fuel will enable Ireland to turn its back on policies which have made the country as helpless economically as it became after the Act of Union, and give it instead a basis from which it can work towards a society based on a vision, towards the modern equivalent of de Valera's dream.

15
The Myth of Sustainable Growth

As I pass through my incarnations in every age and place,
I make my proper prostrations to the Gods of the Market Place,
Peering through reverent fingers, I watch them flourish and fall,
And the Gods of the Copybook Headings, I notice, outlast them all.

We were living in trees when they met us. They showed us each in turn
That Water would certainly wet us as Fire would certainly burn,
But we found them lacking in Uplift, Vision and Breadth of Mind,
So we left them to teach the gorillas while we followed the March of Mankind.

We moved as the spirit listed. They never altered their pace,
Being neither cloud nor wind-borne like the Gods of the Market Place,
But they always caught up with our progress and presently word would come
That a tribe had been wiped off its icefield or the lights had gone out in Rome.
— Rudyard Kipling

In retrospect, it is not surprising that the idea that there are limits to growth disappeared almost without trace a few months after the publication of the book of that name in 1972, since our whole philosophy of life is based on the notion that there are no limits to anything at all. We accept no boundaries to what we can do in our private lives, refusing to regard even our wedding vows as limiting: the latest British surveys show that around two-thirds of men and up to half of women commit adultery at some stage during their married lives. Similarly, many pregnant women refuse to accept that their freedom to run their lives as they wish should be limited in the interests of their unborn children and seek abortions. Once, both sorts of behaviour would have been described as selfish, but the word has, significantly, largely gone out of use, replaced where necessary by 'self-centred', a term that is satisfactorily non-judgmental. The churches, which have tried continuously to insist that there are absolute standards of human conduct, have been increasingly regarded as irrelevant and out of touch.

Our overemphasis on personal freedom is a by-product of the quest for growth. 'I have a right to be myself' would have been a phrase without meaning in the late eighteenth century, even to most readers of Rousseau.

But as technology breached one limit after another, all limits came to be questioned, all authority suspect. 'Freedom' has been the recurrent cry of the growthmen in campaigns against regulations that restrict the power of the purse, and over the years they have successfully convinced us that the right to exploit and be exploited is an essential part of personal and political liberty. Indeed for many of us the ability to spend our money as we wish has become the most fundamental freedom of all. We forget that with all rights go responsibilities, in this case to those at whose expense our money was made and those affected by the way it is spent. But recognizing these responsibilities would impose limits on our behaviour, and these we have been conditioned to reject.

In view of our entrenched attitudes it is going to be as difficult in the nineties as it was in the seventies to get people to accept that limits to growth exist, that these have not just been reached but breached, that no more resources – of energy, forest, farmland, clean air, or water – are available and that the challenge now is to find a way to live happily on less. The first target has to be convincing ourselves, so deeply are expansionary attitudes ingrained. We also have to accept that limits to growth inescapably mean accepting limits to our behaviour. The problem is likely to be that even if, as a society, we are persuaded that limits to our behaviour and resources exist, we will deliberately and regularly break them because we no longer accept that any ban is absolute. Rather, we will try to escape the environmental and social consequences of our breaches, hoping that our technology will enable us to deal with the fall-out at not too great a cost.

Economists will dress environmental limit-breaking in jargon to make it respectable. They will talk about trade-offs and produce cost-benefit analyses showing that the consequences of exceeding limits are much less terrible than the cost of sticking to them, just as Professor Nordhaus did on the greenhouse effect. Unfortunately, however, these analyses will be what someone with considerable experience of them – John Adams of University College, London – calls 'horse and rabbit stew,' which can be given any flavour you like. While the rabbit (the quantifiable part of a cost-benefit analysis) is skinned and dressed with great care, the horse (all those factors whose size and condition are largely unknown) is tossed into the pot without any preparation at all beyond that which guarantees the outcome the analyst favours. Adams argues that as a result even the most careful economic calculations can do little more than provide a rabbit-sized part of any decision: a horse-sized judgment, based on firmly held moral principles rather than the pragmatism of the moment, is required to make up the rest. And it is just such principles that we either lack or are not prepared to adhere to.

One principle has to take precedence over any others in planning for the future: that of sustainability. Unfortunately, a lot of confusion has been created about what this actually means since the concept was introduced to the public in 1987 by the Brundtland Report*, *Our Common Future*. Most of the confusion has arisen out of attempts to make the principle less absolute, efforts that even Brundtland abets by advocating something which is itself unsustainable: sustainable development, a process it defines as follows:

> Sustainable development is development that meets the needs of the present without compromising the ability of future generations to meet their own needs ... Meeting essential needs depends in part on achieving full growth potential, and sustainable development clearly requires economic growth in places where such needs are not being met. Elsewhere it can be consistent with economic growth provided the content of the growth reflects the broad principles of sustainability and non-exploitation of others.

In other words, sustainable development is economic growth that has somehow been made more equitable and environmentally careful. However, since growth itself is not sustainable, the concept is a dangerous contradiction in terms. The only sustainable society is one in which all forces are in equilibrium and consequently, while there will be constant change as births replace deaths and buildings decay and are rebuilt, there will be no movement in any direction. If we wish to achieve sustainability therefore we have to follow a development path towards a stable state. Fortunately, as we noted in our discussion of energy, like St Augustine and chastity we don't have to accept stability just yet. Even so, a steady state rather than a growing economy must be our constant aim. Growth is a process – it produces something – and no process can be sustainable indefinitely unless a point is reached at which another process, decay, destroys what has been created at a sufficient rate to allow the two systems to come into balance. The sooner growth is dropped from our thinking and we revert to setting ourselves specific and finite objectives that lead towards our steady state the better our future will be.

Although the Brundtland Report accepts that this generation should not reduce the ability of future generations to meet their needs, it tries hard to blunt the cutting edge of its own position:

> As for non-renewable resources, like fossil fuels and minerals, their use reduces the stock available for future generations. But this does not mean that such resources should not be used. In general, the rate of depletion should take into account the criticality of that resource, the availability of technologies for minimizing depletion and the likelihood of substitutes being available. Thus land should not be degraded

*The Brundtland Report was prepared by the World Commission on Environment and Development under the chairmanship of the Prime Minister of Norway, Gro Harlem Brundtland. The WCED was set up by the UN in 1983 to 'propose long-term environmental strategies for achieving sustainable development by the year 2000'.

beyond reasonable recovery. With minerals and fossil fuels, the rate of depletion and the emphasis on recycling and economy of use should be calibrated to ensure that the resource does not run out before acceptable substitutes are available. Sustainable development requires that the rate of depletion of non-renewable resources should foreclose as few future options as possible.

Note the lack of absolute prohibitions. There is no ban on soil degradation, just the suggestion that we not take the process beyond the point of no return so that future generations – not us – can put the topsoil back if they have the need and the resources to do so. Instead of a clear statement that fossil fuels are part of humankind's capital stock that ought not to be spent as if they were income and whose only legitimate use is to provide the energy capital to develop renewable sources, we are told we ought not to use all the oil up before we can reasonably expect substitutes to have been found. The risk that alternatives do not emerge is left for our descendants. Nor does Brundtland ban our closing off options for future generations; instead, we get a weak request that we remove as few as possible, please.

A more extensive discussion of what sustainability means is found in David Pearce's report mentioned earlier, *Blueprint for a Green Economy*, which spends a whole chapter discussing sustainable development and devotes an appendix to a selection of different, though broadly similar, definitions of it. Strangely, while Pearce concedes that growth may not be sustainable indefinitely, he defines away the problem of the non-sustainability of sustainable development by stating that it is an increase in per capita well-being over time that 'is not threatened by "feedback" from either biophysical impacts (pollution, resource problems) or from social impacts (social disruption)'. Whether such a thing is possible, he does not stop to inquire. He suggests that the level of well-being be measured using a number of indicators including real national income per head and lays down the condition that the lot of the most disadvantaged people in society should not deteriorate as it went up. His other indicators would cover the quality of the environment and the level of the population's skills, knowledge, capability, choice, and self-esteem. Their health he unaccountably ignores.

Pearce then discusses whether sustainability means that each generation must inherit at least as great a stock of environmental assets as its parents did or whether human-made assets can be substituted for some environmental ones. In other words, can we trade off a deterioration in the natural environment for an improvement in, say, the housing stock, as Nordhaus was essentially urging us to do? Pearce's verdict is almost absolute. 'Each generation should inherit at least a similar natural environment,' he says, pointing out that no amount of human-made capital can re-create a species or provide a substitute for the ozone layer, for the oxygen released and the carbon dioxide absorbed by phytoplankton, or for the climate regulation function of the tropical forests. Moreover, while he concedes that one day it might be possible to invent artificial ways of doing all these things, 'if we do not know the outcome, it is hardly rational behaviour to act as if the outcome will be a good one,' and we must therefore protect the natural environment at least until we have a replacement. Finally, he argues that as it is more often the poor who are worst hit by environmental degradation, conserving or improving the natural resource base is in the best interests of both equity and future generations.

If applied generally, the effects of the principle that no further environmental degradation should be permitted – which is what Pearce is recommending – would be enormously far-reaching. The problem is, of course, that nobody will insist on the application of the no-further-inroads principle to a particular project unless it is very large. In Ireland, for example, I cannot see it affecting either the Minister for the Marine's decision to grant a licence for the expansion of a salmon farm or the Minister for Energy's view about a future gold mine. Consequently, if we liken the environment to a Roman mosaic, the danger is that we will sell off its tiles one by one rather than reaping the infinitely greater rewards of keeping it whole. The only solution, it seems to me, is that for every tile that is to be taken, at least one lost tile must be restored and replaced.

POPULATION AND PRINCIPLES

Although Pearce says that total environmental assets should not fall from generation to generation, he does not insist that everybody in each generation should inherit the same amount of natural capital as their parents did, a requirement that would either involve increasing the natural resources of the planet in line with population growth – which might be rather difficult to bring about – or stabilizing human numbers at their current level, an equally onerous task. The report does not mention population at all, an omission for which it has been widely criticized.[1]

A sustainable society must have a stable population, and yet, despite the best efforts of relatively well-funded bodies like the UN Fund for Population Activities or the International Planned Parenthood Federation, only once in the past quarter-century has the urgent need for population control become a matter of popular concern. This was in 1968, when the population biologist and ecologist Paul Ehrlich published *The Population Bomb*, whose stark yet obvious message was that the birth rate must be brought into balance with the death rate, by compulsion if necessary, or humanity would breed itself into oblivion. While Ehrlich succeeded in the short term by getting a worldwide debate running on the pros and cons of achieving 'zero population growth', in the longer term he failed. His book's message was so viciously attacked by a rainbow coalition of groups with vested interests in population growth that no-one has been able to raise the matter again until, perhaps, today.

Ehrlich was beaten because very few people are so badly affected by a growing population that they are roused to protest about it – on the contrary, many actually benefit. In *For the Common Good*, Herman Daly and John Cobb accuse upper-class Brazilians of welcoming the high birth rates in the lower classes since this provides them with cheap labour for their factories and farms. 'Foxes have always advocated high fertility for rabbits,' they comment acidly. In more advanced countries, much the same applies; more people means more demand and higher rates of economic growth, which in turn means higher rates of profit. In 1947, when it looked as though the population of Britain might be about to decline, one of Julian Simon's forerunners, Eva Habback, wrote a book, *The Population of Britain*, to alert the country to what she saw as the damaging economic, personal, social and political consequences.

Strangely, soft left intellectuals like Frances Moore Lappé, the co-author of *Food First*, Susan George, and Barry Commoner have not supported Ehrlich by attacking right-wing interests hoping to benefit from growing human numbers. Instead they have blamed world hunger on the policies of aid agencies and First World governments, on exploitation by multinational corporations, and on the use of inappropriate technology. Everything, in fact, except population growth. Their argument that if the earth's resources were better allocated there would be no need for anyone to starve was seized on with gratitude by the Vatican, which had resisted the 'no-limits' spirit of the age by reaffirming in its 1968 encyclical *Humanae Vitae* its absolute ban on interference with the reproduction process. What neither cleric nor campaigner considered in detail, however, was how long those resources would continue to be adequate, given the rate at which numbers were growing. Not that an investigation along these lines would have made any difference to the church's teaching – nor should it have done, because principles, however inconvenient, should not be diluted for reasons of expediency. In any case, there is no evidence that the Vatican ban counted for much. 'Catholic reproductive performance is much the same as that of non-Catholics in similar cultures and with similar economic status,' Paul and Anne Ehrlich say in their 1990 follow-up book, *The Population Explosion*. No, the real damage done by the Vatican's position, particularly when coupled with that taken by the soft left, was that it discouraged many people from stressing the importance of the population issue.

As a result, although Lester Brown of the Worldwatch Institute gets marks for a good try, no-one got the public to accept that, even if the First

World limited its consumption, there was scant possibility that the Third World would be able to conquer its poverty and thus slow population growth before human numbers grossly exceeded the maximum level compatible with the sustainable use of the earth's resources. 'With the population due to stabilize at *merely* [my emphasis] twice the current numbers, there would appear to be little cause for concern on a global level,' wrote the magazine *New Internationalist* in October 1987, demonstrating clearly how relaxed many people concerned about the need for a radical change in the relationship between the rich and poor worlds felt about the population question.

But perhaps the main explanation for our failure to limit population growth is that the poor, of whatever faith, have a vested interest in having large families. 'I need five children,' a Rajasthan villager told the magazine *India Today* in 1988. 'One to look after my goats. One to look after my cows. Another to tend my sheep. One to help me in the field and one to help my wife at home.' An official of the Family Planning Association of India commented: 'People are not breeding like rabbits. They have a rationale behind them. They still don't see how having less children would help them. For them, sons are like old age pensions. Does the Government offer any alternatives?' In democratic countries like India, politicians have had no incentive to try to change these attitudes. 'Democracy has become a game of numbers,' another Indian family planner complained. 'Castes and clans and groups are important. If you are in the position of fighting the establishment, the more hungry and dissatisfied people there are, the better off you are.'

In 1974 all these vested interests – politician, villager, intellectual and capitalist – trampled *The Population Bomb* underfoot. They did so at a UN conference on world population in Bucharest at which the United States tried to persuade the less developed countries to limit their numbers. Predictably, this approach was deeply resented: the Third World's response was that its population growth rates would fall of their own accord once poverty had been beaten. It was the excessive levels of consumption in the West that were the real problem.

The debate is still deadlocked although, ironically, the United States, influenced by Julian Simon, is now at best lukewarm about supporting overseas population control programmes (it cancelled its funding of the UN Population Fund and the International Planned Parenthood Federation in 1986 on the grounds that both were involved in abortions), while China and thirty-nine other nations representing half the world's population made an implicit appeal in 1985 for outside help. In 1984, at another World Population Conference, the United States even described population growth as a 'neutral phenomenon', an attitude still found in the World Bank's 1990 *World Development Report* on poverty. 'How does rapid population growth affect poverty?' the Bank asks. 'At the national level the relationship is not simple. In the short run, an increase in population will result, almost by definition, in lower per capita income growth but in the longer run, the larger number of productive workers may accelerate growth. It can even be argued that some countries – particularly in the West – need faster population growth even to sustain their current economic performance.'

Apart from the hesitation many people felt about getting involved in a campaign that could tread on religious toes, the reason so few attempts were made to alert the public was that almost everyone concerned with human numbers simultaneously accepted both the right-wing argument that technology would enable economic growth to put matters right and the left-wing one that the capitalist system was to blame. Activists failed to think deeply about the issue because, I suspect, in their hearts they knew that the position was so serious they did not want their heads to know, and in any case the only remedies they could propose were either physically disgusting or politically distasteful. But from this point on there can be no more pretence, no more self-delusion. Knowing that we have reached the limits of growth and that we have to share significantly fewer resources than we are consuming at present among a population growing faster than at any time since the world began – almost 100 million a year – should concentrate everyone's minds wonderfully.

Because of the belief that growth would solve the population-cum-poverty problem, the years since 1974 have been largely wasted. World population grew by 50 per cent in the twenty-two years between the Ehrlichs' two books: 'A largely prospective disaster has been turned into the real thing,' they say in the later one. As a result, we are getting perilously close to the maximum numbers the earth can support. The 1990 report of the World Hunger Programme at Brown University, Rhode Island, states:

In terms of aggregate food calories, some 5% fewer calories were produced in 1988 than in 1986 – and these calories were divided among a world population nearly 4% larger. If distributed according to need, the total primary food supply, consisting of vegetative food products and range-fed animal production, would have provided an adequate, principally vegetarian, diet for only about 5.5 billion people, or only 8% more than the 1988 world population.

For an average diet comparable to what many South Americans eat today with 15% of calories from animal products, this supply would have been adequate to feed only about 3.7 billion people, less than three quarters of the world's population. For a full-but-healthy diet that incorporates richer and more varied foods and 25% of calories from animal products, the 1988 production level would have fed only about 2.8 billion people or slightly more than half the world's population.

As the Ehrlichs point out, humankind is already using or has destroyed nearly 40 per cent of all the potential net primary production of the earth's land area. There is virtually no more unused land that we can take into cultivation on a sustainable basis. Indeed, as Lester Brown argues,[2] too much unsuitable land has already been put under the plough. The result is that during the 1980s more land went out of production throughout the world because of desertification, exhaustion, soil erosion or failed irrigation than was opened up. In 1990 there was only half as much cropland available per person as in 1950, and per capita food production seems to have peaked in 1986. Without a radical change in economic policies, hunger and malnutrition seem certain to increase.

LOSSES ON THE LAND

The effect of cuts in fossil fuel use on agricultural production and our consequent ability to feed ourselves is hard to predict. The use of artificial fertilizers and pesticides, both energy-intensive, will be sharply reduced but there is no clear evidence that this will lead to a fall in yields. A survey[3] of twenty farms in Colorado and Nebraska undertaken by Colorado State University in 1989 and 1990 showed that 'alternative' farms – which either used no synthetic inputs or did so only in response to specific pest, disease or fertility problems – did not produce significantly different yields than conventional ones, although a storm of criticism greeted these findings. Critics concentrated on the analytical methods employed and the validity of drawing conclusions from so small a sample of farms.

Whatever the effect on yields, cutting fossil fuel use in tractors and other farm machinery will certainly reduce the land area available for human food production. The reintroduction of horses would mean turning over a tenth of a typical arable farm's area to grazing. Growing rape for oil to power diesel engines is worse, since it takes about the same land area to grow the rape as it does to feed a horse, and tractors do not breed their own replacements. Only by making farming almost as labour-intensive as horticulture can we perhaps make up the lost output.

In any case, the continuation of conventional farming methods is unsustainable. The present dominant school of agricultural thought regards the soil as a rooting medium whose sole purpose is to enable the plant to stand up. Consequently, a soil's structure and organic and nutritional content has seemed of little relevance and has been neglected, with the result that millions of tonnes of topsoil has washed or blown away. Another American study, this time of two farms side by side in Washington state, one of which had been farmed organically since the land was first ploughed in 1909 and one of which had gone over to fertilizers in 1948, showed that the annual loss of soil on the conventional farm was four times that on the organic one.

'Organic farmers can, and generally do, achieve higher concentrations of organic matter in their soils than conventional farmers,' reported one of the scientists who studied the farms, John Reganold of Washington State University. He went on:

[This] has a profound impact on the quality of the soil; it encourages mineral particles to clump together to form granules, improving the structure of the soil; it increases the amount of water the soil will hold and the supply of nutrients; and the organisms in the soil are more active. All in all, organic material makes the soil more fertile and productive. In our experimental plots we found that the soil on the organic farm was well-granulated; the other soil was not. The organically-farmed soil also contained much more moisture; its cation-exchange capacity, a measure of the soil's capacity to store nutrients, was greater; the total amounts of nitrogen and available potassium were also much larger. Most of the extra organic matter came from green manure.

As microbes break down organic material they produce polysaccharides, gummy substances that can stabilize the soil by binding particles into aggregates. Aggregates are less vulnerable to breakdown and erosion. Soil organisms also break down polysaccharides, however, so farmers must continue to add organic matter to maintain a supply of these stabilizing substances.

The organic soil had a significantly lower 'modulus of rupture', an index related to the hardness of the crust that forms on the surface of the soil. In general, the lower the modulus of rupture, the easier it is for seedlings to emerge. The combination of all these factors gives the organically-farmed soil better tilth than the soil of the conventional farm. The better the tilth, the easier it is to till and the easier it is for plants to germinate and push out shoots and roots.

Forty years of fertilizer use had cost the conventional farm 160 mm of its topsoil in comparison with the organic farm on the other side of a string of barbed wire.

At this rate, all the topsoil will be lost in another fifty to 100 years. When this happens, wheat yields could drop by a third or more. Since the land [in the region around the farms] was first cultivated a century ago, 10% has lost all its original topsoil [and] between a quarter and threequarters of the topsoil has disappeared from 60% of the land. [However], the organic farmer should be able to maintain the topsoil for generations to come.

Was there a difference in yield between the two farms big enough to justify the soil loss? No: the organic farm's crop was just 8 per cent lower than that on the conventional one and 13 per cent higher than on another conventional one nearby. Its input costs, on the other hand, were significantly less. Studies on other matched pairs of farms in the Mid-West indicate that its fossil fuel consumption might have been 60 per cent less than that on the conventional farm.

Alternative systems have to be more diverse than conventional ones to prevent pests and diseases building up and to maintain soil fertility. The organic farm in Washington state grew either Austrian winter peas or alfalfa and grass as its manure crop, while the Colorado study found that most of its alternative farmers would have liked to use more animal manure but could not do so for lack of supplies. The Colorado study also found that the best farmers – whether conventional or alternative – were 'very aware of the nuances and fluctuations of their soils, crops and microclimate. The good farmers knew where their fields stayed wet and cool in the early spring, where an outbreak of root disease might occur because of the heavy soil in a particular spot, they knew the sandy patches that might need more water and the fields where compaction could be a problem during the drought days of summer.' As it is impossible to attend to this sort of detail and to handle diversity if one is farming on a large scale, we can look forward to a return to the small, family-run mixed farm as energy costs rise.

CONTROL BY COMPULSION?

Despite the lack of public awareness of the seriousness of the population problem, birth rates have been falling throughout the world, although at a rate rather slower than demographers expected. For example, while the UN Fund for Population Activities (UNFPA) predicted in 1984 that the world population would stabilize at about 10,200 million by the end of the next century, in 1990, only six years later, it said that it expected the total to be nearer 11,000 million. This was because some countries, including India, the Philippines and Morocco, which had steadily cut their birth rates by a point a year between 1960 and 1965 and between 1970 and 1975, only managed a tenth to a third of that rate over the following decade. For India this means that the population is likely to rise to 1,446 million instead of 1,229 million by 2025 or 217 million more than if the rate of reduction had been maintained. Of course there is nothing unusual in having to revise population estimates upwards: in the early forties, a leading American demographer predicted that world population would stabilize at 3,000 million.

One thing the population experts are sure about, however, is that the better educated women are the fewer children they tend to have. This is because they have increased options outside the home and they are better able to ensure that their children will survive to adulthood. The close correlation between the levels of female illiteracy in the various Indian states and their birth rates is striking. It is no accident that Kerala, where a record 66 per cent of women can read and write, has the lowest birth rate, although it is by no means a wealthy state. A child's chance of survival is also an important factor in determining the birth rate, because in countries without a social security system, couples rely on their children – particularly their sons – to look after them in old age. Consequently anything that helps a child survive – such as basic public health measures and a better diet – also helps bring down the birth rate. A state pension scheme for the elderly would help curb birth rates too, because it would lower the need for the traditional form of insurance.

A better diet, old-age pensions, longer schooling for girls, clean drinking water, adequate sanitation and other public health measures all require two things: a lot of labour, which is available in abundance in countries with a high birth rate, and a few resources. The latter will have to be released by richer countries, since, in a world already placing excessive pressure on its resource base, there is nowhere else they can come from. However, this would not be the obstacle it sounds if the rationing scheme for curbing fossil fuel use we discussed earlier were introduced, because it would automatically transfer resources to the poor: each person in the less energy-intensive areas of the world would, in effect, have an annual income as children and adults and a pension when they reached old age.

But, realistically, this transfer is most unlikely to take place. If it does not, and no other mechanism is introduced to transfer resources, the poorer countries could get stuck in the transition phase between the high rates of reproduction usual in poor societies and the lower rates found in more affluent ones. If this happens, world population will go on increasing until checked by famine, and women in the Third World will not reduce their current birth rate of 4.2 children each to replacement level within a foreseeable time.

Economists have of course come up with schemes for controlling the creation of children.[4] Kenneth Boulding put forward a 'transferable birth quota plan' in 1964, and Herman Daly produced a variant ten years later. Ingenious though these schemes are, they have more appeal to academics than to ordinary people. The basic principles are that each woman receives, as her birthright, permits to bear two live children. If she does not wish to become a mother, or only wants one child, she has the right to sell her surplus permits on the open market – but only within her country and to a member of her ethnic group. If the population of her nation or group was growing, child permits would quickly become a valuable commodity and many poorer couples might decide to sell their second permit, particularly if their first child was a boy, in order to obtain a capital sum that they might be unable to raise in any other way.

A problem with this plan arises when a penniless woman bears a child for which she has no permit, because unless she is able to get one from a relative, she has to be made to pay for one in some way. Should she or her husband be sent to a labour camp to work the debt off? Should an official come round to collect so much a week? Should she be made to have an abortion? Without some element of enforcement, the scheme would be ineffective, but whatever one proposes smells of fascism and is bound to be harmful to the new child.

The schemes' proponents admit this defect but argue that it is the Gods of the Copybook Headings, not them, who deny people the right to have as many children as they like, because unless humanity controls its numbers itself, the planet will do so in a much more unpleasant way. We have not got enough time left to stabilize population entirely voluntarily, they say, particularly if we continue to rely on world trade to raise Third World incomes and slow down population growth – in the past decade the flow of wealth has been entirely the wrong way. People are already dying of starvation as a result of laissez-faire, everything-will-be-all-right-in-the-end policies, and if limiting a woman's freedom to have more than two children unless she is wealthy enough to buy extra permits prevents even a few deaths, then, for them, the element of compulsion would be fully justified. 'By using a market mechanism to limit population, we are putting the decision-making power in the people's hands. We are giving women a valuable asset which will raise their status because they can sell it without reference to any man. On balance our proposal creates more freedom than it destroys,' is the essence of a baby-rationer's defence.

If we reject this and all other population control schemes involving compulsion – as I think we must – are we not continuing to indulge in patterns of thought that grew up during a period of unprecedented economic growth and which are unsupportable – indeed positively dangerous – in a stationary age? I think there is little doubt that we are. As we saw, the idea that social progress was possible first appeared in the second half of the nineteenth century and only then did anyone begin to feel a moral obligation to help the poor as a group. Previously, poverty and famine were simply the way things were. One did not even have to harden one's heart. Carlyle's comments on his visit to Westport were typical of his age; Marx showed the same spirit in his attack on Sismondi's 'hypochondriacal philanthropy' about land clearances.

The attitudes created by the feeling that social progress is possible – that individuals count, that their feelings matter, that one should do the best one can for anyone in hardship, and, of course, that one should not take legal sanctions against anyone having a child – are the most important gains the growth process has brought about. They are fundamental to popular democracy – indeed, universal suffrage can be regarded as a product of the growth process as well. They are some of the principles to which we must adhere in the years ahead even though doing so will jeopardize our survival. It will be hard to remain true. The 'compassion fatigue' that has developed about starvation in Africa shows how easily the battle may be lost.

We have to accept that, if we will the end – a stable population – and have no stomach for fascist means of bringing it about, we have to engineer the necessary redistribution of resources instead. Our obligation will be to work to ensure that economic and information barriers do not prevent people limiting their numbers if they wish to do so. Beyond that, we can do no more. It will be for couples and communities to decide how to respond.

MAKING THE FUTURE COUNT

While it will be difficult to create circumstances in which the poor receive their fair share of resources in a no-growth world, they are at least with us and can try to make their voices heard. Another group, the generations and generations of the yet-to-be-born, are in a worse situation, however, with no means at all to make their needs felt. As a result, we will be tempted to ignore their claims and continue to concentrate on maximizing immediate consumption, exactly as we do today. But if we are to build a sustainable world we have to change the way we think about the relationship between current costs and future benefits. We have to stop assuming that people in the future will be richer in material terms than we are and begin to feel that we will be doing rather well if we leave them the resources that we have today.

Even quite ordinary things appear differently once this mental switch has been made. One ceases to place any trust in life assurance companies' promises to beat inflation and pay back several times the total value of one's premiums at the end of an endowment policy's 25-year term. Instead, one wonders where the resources that such a payment represents would come from and at whose expense they would be paid (always assuming that they were) because very few new resources can be expected to be generated during the life of a policy in a slow-growth or no-growth world.

On another level, we have to look at the way we make our plans. When a property company plans an office block, it compares the costs of erecting a well-insulated, low-maintenance, long-life building against those of a cheaper one with higher running costs and, most likely, a shorter design life. If the comparison is done properly, the firm lists the costs of operating each design over perhaps fifty years, and estimates the value both buildings should have at the end of that time.

But how do the company's analysts compare, say, the cost of the major refurbishment the cheaper building can be expected to need after a number of years with the extra expenditure needed during construction to make that refurbishment unnecessary? The answer is that they bring all a project's costs and benefits back to their 'present value' by working out what sum of money placed on deposit today would grow to equal the sum needed to pay for the refurbishment when the expected number of years has passed. If the refurbishment will cost £2 million in twenty years' time, this is equivalent to just over £250,000 today if the interest rate used is 10 per cent, because that is the sum which, placed on deposit at that rate of interest, will grow to £2 million after two decades. Consequently, if the costs of avoiding the revamp are less than £250,000, the firm is likely to sanction the expenditure. If not, it won't.

The crucial figure in these calculations is obviously the rate of interest the analyst uses. If 7 per cent had been selected, the amount which could have been spent to avoid the repairs would have been £500,000, and if 3 per cent, the figure would have been £1 million. So what rate should the firm use in a no-growth world? The rationale behind discounting anticipated costs and benefits lies in the fact that the future is always uncertain, and any one of us – property company shareholders included – may not live to see next year. As a result, we would all like to have anything nice that is coming to us sooner rather than later and would gladly swap the promise of £5,000 next year for the certainty of a rather smaller sum, cash-in-hand, now. Our calculation of how much less than £5,000 we would accept means setting a discount rate. If we were entirely confident the promised payment would materialize on the due date, our discount rate might fall sufficiently to allow us to accept a sum which, placed in the bank, would grow to £5,000 next year. On the other hand, if there was a considerable risk of non-payment, we would grab whatever was offered and consider ourselves lucky to get it. Then again, if we were short of money at present and could not borrow from the bank, we would probably agree to a higher rate of discount than the rate of interest charged by the bank and allow an additional discount because we were not carrying the risk of non-payment.

As companies are usually short of money and all their projects carry a degree of risk, it is hard to imagine them ever using a discount rate lower than the real rate of interest at which they could borrow from the bank – that is, the actual rate of interest minus the expected rate of inflation. (Inflation is always ignored in discounting calculations: future prices are assumed to be the same as present-day ones. Consequently, interest rates also have to be made net of inflation.) In fact, according to James Winpenny, the author of *Values for the Environment* (1991), commercial firms are currently using real rates of between 6 and 10 per cent. 'At a discount rate of 10 per cent, benefits are reduced to below 10 per cent of their nominal value by year 25, and to less than 1 per cent by year 50,' he told me. 'The discount rate used by the government is 6 per cent because it is felt that public projects should not give a worse return than low-risk private-sector ones.'

These rates are very high in comparison with fifty or a hundred years ago, and as a result, buildings are built as cheaply as possible as the benefits of having low heating and maintenance bills stretching years into the future are of little interest to investors or to the government: the savings have too low a present value. Rob Harris of Stanhope Properties, a firm of developers, says that his company is now building offices to last twenty-five years instead of fifty or sixty. 'We're making them more disposable because of the massive rate of change in business technology. Offices quickly cease to be able to cope with new demands and a lot of those erected in the 1960s and 70s are being ripped down.'

Some property firms regard a building as having no value at the end of its initial lease because of the cost of refurbishment for a new tenant at that stage and some initial leases are now as short as fifteen years. However, David Fernbank, a member of the John Bonnington architectural partnership in St Albans, says that the British weather prevents very short-lived buildings being erected. 'The cladding and the windows we have to use will last sixty years.' In the United States, on the other hand, hotels in places like Miami Beach can last as little as seven years before being scrapped.

While the use of these high discount rates may be rational for firms and individuals, they are nonsense for society as a whole. Society, we hope, will endure indefinitely, and so the only basis on which it would prefer to have benefits now at the expense of reduced benefits later would be if it could safely assume that it was going to be so much richer in the future that the lost benefits would be unimportant. In an economy that was expected to grow indefinitely, this might have been a fair assumption to make. In a world of shrinking resources where the future may be darker than the past, it is folly. If a society has limitless resources and is changing rapidly as a result of innovation, tearing down buildings after fifteen years might not matter, because their replacements can be made to meet the new needs. But if resources are scarce, and society is technologically stable, the cost of heating and maintaining a stock of shoddily built and poorly insulated structures will represent an enormous burden.

It would be unrealistic to expect this generation to plan on the basis that things in the future will be worse and that, as a result, benefits that arise years hence ought to be valued above whatever price we would put on them today. However, we should at least assume that future benefits will matter as much to future populations as current benefits matter to us. In other words, we should cease to use any discount rate, and value future benefits as highly as any we are likely to enjoy ourselves.

If a zero discount rate had been used to compare the costs and benefits of a nuclear power station with those of other energy sources, the ridiculous course of building atomic plants that may consume more energy than they

Fig. 15.1 This office block, occupied by Shearson Lehman Hutton, is part of Stanhope Properties' major redevelopment in Broadgate in the City of London. It was designed by its architect, Grant Smith, to have an economic life of only twenty-five years.

produce would have been avoided. The mistake happened because the costs of dismantling the station and disposing of the radioactive waste are spread over hundreds of years and, as we have just seen, costs that arise more than a few years into the future have very little impact on a present-value calculation today. On the other hand, if an energy analysis of the nuclear plant had been undertaken rather than a monetary one, the kilocalories of energy involved from century to century in disposing of the waste would not have been discounted but added up as they stood. It would have been immediately apparent if less energy was going to come out than had been put in.

The principle of giving equal weight to the interests of future generations has a great deal wider import than the construction of longer-lasting, lower-maintenance buildings or truly productive power plants. It means, for example, that fossil fuels must not be used to satisfy our day-to-day needs directly, greenhouse effect or not. Oil and coal should be burned only to develop renewable energy sources or to increase the world's stock of metals extracted from their ores. Such fuels must not even turn bulk metal into useful goods. That is the job of renewables, which must also be used to replace metal stocks as they are lost or corroded. The principle also means that land should be farmed only by methods that maintain soil fertility.

Giving the future equal weight to the present is the first of the three key principles of the no-growth age. The second is valuing other people's interests equally with our own. If we acted on this principle we would not undertake projects that merely transferred resources from one group to another, as so many schemes have done in the past. If a project that produced an overall gain also involved a transfer of resources to those undertaking it or to another group, the beneficiaries would have to ensure that the losers were left no worse off, both at the time and in the future, and in relative rather than absolute terms. If the project could not afford this, it would not go ahead.

As we have seen, there are many ways in which development can make people worse off, but fortunately our second principle is very versatile and can cover most situations. Indeed, it is rapidly gaining support under the name 'the polluter pays', where it provides that if, say, a farmer contaminates a river with silage effluent, he pays the full cost of cleaning up and compensates anyone who suffered. Unfortunately, however, although most politicians claim to agree with this approach, they are still a long way from giving it full practical effect, particularly in relation to damage that might be discovered to have been done in the future. If makers of CFCs were now being obliged to compensate people who no longer felt it was safe to sunbathe – and Australians and New Zealanders have been advised officially not to do so – or the Chileans whose sheep are being blinded and who are having to send their children out of the Tierra del Fuego for safety, every company would become very much more cautious about launching new products. It is true that mere money can never make up for some forms of damage, but an attempt to make it do so would have a salutary effect. It is already recognized that an unlimited liability policy would impede the development of nuclear power. In 1991, a row broke out in the International Atomic Energy Agency because Germany and Switzerland wanted nuclear power plant operators to be forced to pay unlimited compensation for any damage they did. Britain, the United States and Belgium opposed this on the grounds that Chernobyl had done £10,000 million worth of damage within the Soviet Union alone, and such a provision would 'remove the incentive to develop the nuclear industry'. A £120 million compensation ceiling was suggested instead.

The third principle is that some things are simply not for sale and so cannot be traded off for money or increased production. Everybody has his or her own list of things whose destruction they would not permit no matter how much money was offered. It could be a wood, a bog, an animal species, the ozone layer or their lives. However, because a single person saying that something is of infinite value puts a veto on cost-benefit analysis, economists at present refuse to accept the position as valid. 'The equation of "priceless" with "infinite value" is illicit,' says David Pearce in *Blueprint for a Green Economy*, before going on to suggest that anyone who says that they cannot be compensated for a loss by money should be treated as irrational because it 'would seem to be inconsistent with the general view "that each man has his price."' He argues that even if someone insists on an infinite valuation, the analyst should just put an arbitrary value into the equation instead.

But John Adams, Pearce's colleague at University College, London, has no time for this position. 'It is an ethic that debases that which is important and disregards entirely that which is supremely important,' he says,[5] remembering how, by using the same lack of principles as the planners trying to find a site for London's third airport in the early seventies, he was able to show that Hyde Park was the most economic location, even though Westminster Abbey would have had to be demolished to make way.

Nor are compromises acceptable. 'Compromise *always* leads to environmental damage or loss,' says Tony Whilde of the Corrib Conservation Centre outside Galway, who has seen the way the system works in the west of Ireland. 'The developers gain something, even if only a proportion of their initial demand, and the conservationists lose something, even if only part of an important site or wildlife population. If the process is repeated several times, the conservation value of the shrinking remnants is eventually reduced to nothing – particularly where the criteria for conservation are large areas or large numbers.' The only basis on which it might be possible

to allow some developments to go ahead, in fact, is the way I suggested earlier: that the developers be required to restore an environmental fragment of
at least equivalent value to that which they are proposing to take away,
assuming the unlikely circumstance that their relative worths can be measured and compared.

Our job as citizens is to decide on the characteristics of the society we
wish to build, a process that is moral rather than economic, and to insist
that our politicians adhere to the three copybook principles. Then, and only
then, can we ask the cost-benefit boys to work out which of the myriad
roads before us is best for where we want to go: at present, they happily tell
us which road is fastest but give no idea at all of where it will lead.

In an editorial immediately before the Second World Climate Conference
in Geneva in November 1990, *The Economist* wrote that no country was
seriously contemplating committing itself to the 1988 Toronto conference's
20 per cent greenhouse gas cuts by signing an international convention to
that effect at the Earth Summit in Brazil in mid-1992: the economic cost
was too high. 'The convention will settle not for an informed guess of what
nature might bear but for what mankind thinks it worth paying to protect
her,' it said. It might have been right. It is up to us to convince our leaders
that we are prepared to pay the bill, whatever it is, and go through with the
other radical changes necessary to ensure a truly sustainable future for our
children and our children's children. It will always be easier for them, middle-aged men and women whose time horizons stretch no further than the
next election, to find people like Professors Nordhaus and Simon to tell
them that they need not worry too much. We need to counteract this tendency. Shortly before this book went to press, Maurice Strong, the Earth
Summit organizer, expressed the hope that the meeting would define goals
and get commitments from national leaders to enough measures to start
achieving them although specific agreements to reduce emissions of carbon
dioxide could take several years to work out. Our role is to see that any
pledges that are made are kept: what Strong wanted just as badly as signa-
tures to a treaty was a range of new mechanisms for holding leaders to their
promises.

The forces opposed to cutting fossil fuel consumption or accepting limits
of any other sort are so formidable that there is little chance of a favourable
outcome. Nevertheless, we have to try. A few years ago I was sitting outside
a hut in India, talking to Vilasrao Salunke, the owner of an engineering
company in Pune, who, with his wife, had helped fifty communities to
develop co-operative schemes for the management of irrigation water.
These had been so successful that families had even been able to return to
their villages from the big cities. Yet throughout most of the rest of India,
people were still being forced to migrate and forests and fertility were being

destroyed. Didn't he feel that his efforts were lost in view of the scale of his country's problems? Didn't he get depressed? I asked. 'The Gita tells us that we must not allow ourselves to be either optimistic or pessimistic but just to do the work which God has put before us,' was his reply. This is the spirit we must adopt. There is no more important nor urgent a cause than seeking the welfare of present and future generations.

16
Guiding the Invisible Hand

An American is probably the most unhappy citizen in the history of the world. He has not the power to provide himself with anything but money and his money is inflating like a balloon and drifting away subject to historical circumstances and the power of other people. From morning to night, he does not touch anything he has produced himself, in which he can take pride. For all his leisure and recreation, he feels bad, he looks bad, he is overweight, his health is poor. His air, water and food are all known to contain poisons. There is a fair chance he will die of suffocation. He suspects that his love life is not as fulfilling as other people's. He wishes that he had been born sooner, or later. He does not know why his children are the way they are. He does not understand what they say. He does not care much and does not know why he does not care. He does not know what his wife wants or what he wants. Certain advertisements and pictures in magazines make him suspect that he is basically unattractive. He feels that all his possessions are under the threat of pillage. He does not know what he would do if he lost his job, if the economy failed, if the utility companies failed, if the police went on strike, if the truckers went on strike, if his wife left him, if his children ran away, if he should be found to be incurably ill. And for these anxieties, of course, he consults certified experts who, in turn, consult certified experts about *their* anxieties. – Wendell Berry, *The Unsettling of America* (1977)

With every day that passes, the worldwide damage that economic growth is doing to levels of employment creeps closer to home. Only in highly favoured areas within a handful of industrialized countries can people now be sure of finding work, and as the waters of unemployment rise, these islands continually contract. No government has yet openly admitted that the rise in unemployment is a global consequence of economic growth. However, the fact that governments everywhere attempt to solve unemployment at home by raising national competitiveness in order to steal work from less competitive producers overseas proves that it is. In Britain, the Employment Institute's book, *Conquering Unemployment: the Case for Economic Growth* (1989), confines its analysis to achieving an advantage in national terms and completely ignores the effects that British job creation might have on employment overseas.

Our views about the desirability of growth will be forced to change fundamentally once we accept that the technologies that fuel the process lead to a net loss of jobs despite having favourable local effects. Once we have made this mental switch we will see that the law needs to be changed so that it makes innovations that displace labour illegal unless full employment exists before their introduction, and can be guaranteed to do so afterwards. It would rest with the entrepreneur to provide this guarantee, which might take the form of an undertaking backed by a financial institution to the effect that if anyone could show that they had suffered as a result of the project they would be fully compensated. The existence of such an undertaking would ensure that only those projects likely to produce a net gain, and not merely a redistribution of resources in favour of the entrepreneur, would actually go ahead.

The introduction of a new technology is as potentially destructive of the existing web of complex economic and social interrelationships that bind communities and nations as is the release of a genetically engineered organism to relationships within the natural world. For a generation that has grown up to be excited by and supportive of technological advance – even the term itself connotes progress – such a radical change in attitudes is a major step. Henceforward, before they are released into the world, new technologies will need to be put through searching safety procedures based on the assumption that they are guilty until proved innocent. Hitherto, our assumption has been entirely the other way.

Even old technologies can pose a serious threat if they are carried out in a new location. Alto is a village high in the hills behind the Algarve in Portugal, about ten kilometres from the warm springs at Monchique to which tourists drive from the coast. Until 1950, when a road to Alto was opened, its people were forced to live virtually self-sufficient lives because everything had to be carried in and out by donkey. Only cork, medronho (the local spirit, made from the berries of a tree that grows on the scrubby hillsides), sweet chestnuts, pigs and goats were sold to the outside world. With the proceeds the people purchased and carried in iron for tools and donkey shoes from the mines in Aljustrel, seven days' trek to the north, as Robin Jenkins tells us in his beautifully written and moving account, *The Road to Alto* (1979). Rice came from Saboia, two days away; almonds were brought up from the Algarve, a day or two away; cigarettes and other manufactured goods came from the railway town of San Marcos, three days there and back; salt came from Portimão, four days there and back. As a result,

life consisted of growing and making what you could from what was available locally. There is hardly a plant an old peasant cannot give you a use for. Grasses for making sacks and string and washing greasy dishes, willows for baskets, pine for chairs and tables, oak for doors, cork for a hundred and one odd tasks, including plates and cups, herbs for all manner of medicines. Local life was fashioned out of what happened to be available. It blended with the environment because it was almost totally a product of that environment. Of course, the peasants also acted upon the environment, day in, day out. In the end, the local landscape cannot be understood without the peasants and the peasants cannot be understood without the local landscape.

For a millennium, life in Alto was almost entirely the product of a limited technology working within a particular geology and micro-climate. People ate what they could grow at this altitude and latitude and they kept the animals which thrived under the same conditions. They worked to maintain the standard of subsistence living that their energies and their technology allowed. And experience over many years, handed down from generation to generation, told them how much energy it was worth putting into growing potatoes, or olives, or into keeping pigs. They never made any quick, intensive effort to grow a huge crop of something – what could they do with the surplus? It could not all be consumed. It could be stored for a limited period only and it could not be sold because the market was too far away. The environment and its isolation allowed a certain density of population and a certain standard of living and that is what the people worked to maintain over the centuries ...

Life under such conditions had its own stoic and simple grandeur but for all the fragrant scent of the mimosas and the fleshy succulence of the fruits that grow in abundance, it was no Garden of Eden. Subsistence living is dependent on the local geology and can, as it does in Alto, result in localized diseases caused by mineral deficiencies in the rocks and the soil. Until sardines became a regular part of local diet there was, for instance, a high incidence of goitre, especially amongst the poorer peasants who could not afford to buy the traditional salted cod that was eaten once a year to celebrate the pig-killing. Dietary deficiencies, in particular a shortage of protein, produced people rarely more than 1^{1}/$_{2}$ metres (5 ft) tall. And there were social problems too. There was a limit to the population that Alto could support but the population always tended to exceed this limit. The land inheritance laws determined the form of the solution to this problem. Poor peasants either without land or with insufficient land to make a living have left to work and live in the Alentejo or the Algarve and some have even gone to Brazil or Mozambique. Alto has probably been an exporter of people for centuries. Even today, there is pressure on the land.

Aware of these restrictions and hardships, officials doubtless believed that by pushing ahead with the construction of the road they were bringing a better life to the people of Alto. Instead the project put the community into a decline which may prove terminal.

Suddenly goods that had to be hauled by donkey for hours or days along the old Moorish track came speeding down the new road in fifteen minutes from Monchique. The trucks rolled in with fertilizer and the peasants found that they could increase their yields almost overnight. The effect was dramatic. They found that they were producing well in excess of their own needs. For the first time they had sizeable crops to sell from their terraces. In fact, they had to sell them to pay for the fertilizer so they quickly got bound into the wider economy. A new class of local entrepreneurs arose to exploit these new possibilities. Gradually, processes that had always been part of Alto's integrated existence were substituted by the 'higher technology' of Monchique.

Motorbikes were purchased – they could carry more than a donkey and did not need daily attention. Plastic buckets replaced locally made pots and baskets. Concrete replaced the earth of the cottage floors. The windmill above the village was closed down and wheat was sent to the electrically powered mill in Monchique. It all seemed like progress.

But fewer donkeys meant that less manure was available for the terraces and the people found that the chemical substitutes had to be applied in quantities that grew larger from year to year if they were to maintain crop yields. Moreover, fertilizers killed the worms, which had previously aerated the soil and brought up deep nutrients to within reach of plant roots. Without worms, the terraces became compacted and sterile, and with no humus to hold it, irrigation water quickly soaked away so that more had to be applied. Each application of water washed the fertilizer deeper into the soil away from plant roots. 'Now it is impossible to grow anything either as a cash crop or for home consumption without giving the plants liberal doses of fertilizer,' Jenkins says.

When potato prices failed to keep up with the price of fertilizer, the peasants found that there was no going back to their old ways, because unfertilized yields were too poor for them to subsist on and it would take years to restore the soil's fertility by natural means. As a result, many of them were forced to take up casual work to buy fertilizer to grow their own food. But then another effect of the road started to become apparent: the springs that provided irrigation water to the terraces for centuries began to dry up. The road had enabled outsiders to bring in bulldozers to clear the hillsides of their chestnuts, scrub and medronho trees in order to plant eucalyptus for paper pulp. A hectare of twelve-metre high eucalyptus transpires about a million litres of water a day and the new plantations were soaking up rainfall that had previously percolated through the earth to replenish the water table. By the time Jenkins left Alto in 1976, about 10 per cent of the terraces had lost their spring supply and the stable, sustainable way of life the water had made possible was dying. He mourns its loss:

If you sit by the windmill on the hill high above Alto and look down at the clusters of little cottages surrounded by their neat terraces far below, you have to marvel at what has been achieved here. This once-isolated hamlet has existed in a state of balance with its natural environment for centuries. The balance was not planned but came about through an odd assortment of factors, through trial and error. But once achieved, the knowledge of how to maintain it forever was laid down in the local customs and culture and passed on orally from generation to generation. There is a wealth of knowledge in those cottages down below and it will be lost forever in a few years. That knowledge arose out of the annual struggle to grow enough food and some extra for next year's seed. It is not just knowledge about a mode of production with very limited capital on a particular bit of mountain. It is also knowledge about the means of *perpetual reproduction* of that simple mode of production. It is a very sophisticated form of knowledge, lying deep in the local culture, almost inaccessible to an outsider because it is not part of conscious dialogue and will never be revealed in discussion. It can be deduced only by carefully watching and, above all, by copying local practices in great detail. Then, and only then, can one begin to understand the wisdom of simple peasants and the limits to that wisdom that makes it impossible for them to cope with the consequences of things like fertilizers and eucalyptus plantations.

FISH-FARMING FIASCO

If the construction of something as simple as a road can prove so destructive, the introduction of salmon farming to the west of Ireland gives some idea of the far-reaching and Hydra-headed consequences of introducing a complex technology. Two competent and well-motivated state agencies initiated this affair. One was Gaeltarra Éireann, the development body for the Irish-speaking areas of the country; the other was the Electricity Supply Board (ESB) which became involved because it knew something about salmon having been required to restock the River Shannon annually after its 1925 hydroelectric scheme there had destroyed the natural run by preventing fish returning to their spawning beds.

Gaeltarra had identified salmon farming and mussel cultivation as ideal activities for the people of its area because many of them had experience in handling both boats and livestock. Moreover the sea, rather than the rocky, infertile land, had to be the Gaeltacht's main physical resource. Accordingly, the two concerns set up a joint company in 1974, which began trying to rear salmon in floating cages in a sheltered inlet of the sea. The normal difficulties with any pioneering venture were encountered and overcome, and in 1980 the first sizeable sales of farmed fish – 18 tonnes, worth £69,000 – were made. Gradually a fully fledged industry began to develop, with specialist companies manufacturing feed, making salmon cages, and of course packing and exporting the resulting fish. By 1990 there were twenty-seven cage sites operated by a rather smaller number of companies along the west coast, producing some 6,500 tonnes of fish worth about £23 million. All told, 947 full-time and part-time workers were employed and life had returned to villages that had been dying.

On the face of it, a success story. Look more carefully and I fear it is not. The whole concept of salmon farming is fundamentally flawed, even for people who have no qualms about keeping a solitary fish in a crowded cage and thwarting its powerful urge to migrate. A salmon farm is basically a system for converting cheap fish such as herrings and mackerel, excellent eating just as they are, into about a tenth of the weight of another fish, but one with much more appeal to the palates of the rich. Why should anyone undertake such a wasteful conversion, especially as it involves the use of so much labour, equipment and energy? Because it is profitable, and growth is accomplished thereby. Just as capitalism concentrates wealth, fish farming concentrates food, removing the initial low-value fish from the reach of the poor.

Even if one is a realist and accepts that this is, unfortunately, the way the world works and that many other food businesses do exactly the same, one might still be worried by salmon farming's environmental impacts. One of the first indications of how harmful it could be came in the early eighties. Up to that time, Mulroy Bay on the coast of Co. Donegal was the most prolific site in Europe for scallop spat, the free-swimming stage in the life-cycle of that shellfish. Great hopes were held out that an industry could be built around this natural resource by collecting the spat and taking it to other parts of the coast where the shellfish could be grown to maturity. A multi-million pound business is run on these lines in Japan and a co-operative was set up by Mulroy people who hoped to be just as successful in Ireland.

In 1982, however, three years after salmon farming had started in the bay, spat production stopped, almost certainly as a result of a tributyl tin (TBT) anti-fouling that the salmon farms were using to stop weeds growing on the nets around their cages. One farm, Fanad Fisheries, stopped using TBT immediately the reports of the failure came through, but the ESB, by now involved in salmon farming in a big way, continued to use the treatment for another twenty months. By the time it stopped, the co-op had collapsed. Happily, spat production has since started again.

From the mid-eighties on, news of other environmental problems with salmon farming began to pour in. From the Shetlands came reports that the Arctic tern had failed to breed since 1983 and had started using earthworms instead of its main food, the sand-eel, in its courtship display. Kittiwakes had totally failed to breed as well, probably because the sand-eel had been grossly overfished by boats supplying plants making fishmeal for salmon food, among other uses. Catches had dropped from 52,600 tonnes in 1982 to 4,800 tonnes in 1988, and the fall had put some fishermen out of business. Then came reports from Norway, where salmon farming was much more advanced, that overfishing for capelin – itself, ironically, a fish in the salmon family that is regarded as a delicacy in Japan – had caused an environmental disaster in the Barents Sea. The problem was that so many capelin had been caught for fishmeal that sea urchins, on whose spat they had fed, had multiplied out of control and had eaten up the seaweed beds which cod and other fish used to spawn. As a result, the cod population had crashed and those that remained were starved because their food source, the capelin, had been taken away. 'The Faroese were unable to catch their cod quota this year,' Lars Petter Hansen of the Norwegian Directorate for Nature Management told me in 1988. 'Hundreds of seals have swum south from the Barents Sea looking for food. It will take twenty years for the capelin to recover, if they ever do.'

Two other worrying reports came out of Norway. One was that a parasite, *Gyrodactylus salaris*, had been accidentally introduced to thirty-three rivers there, possibly from the Baltic as the result of the transfer of young salmon from infected hatcheries for on-growing by the fish farms. Once the parasite is in a river it can only be removed by poisoning the entire wild salmon stock, and this has since been done. Hansen has estimated that the resulting loss of wild fish catches is 500 tonnes annually.

The second Norwegian report dealt with another effect that farmed fish were having on their wild cousins. Surveys by Harald Skjervold showed in 1987 that up to two-thirds of the fish in some rivers were farm escapes and that these were interbreeding with the native stocks. 'If genetic pollution continues at this rate, the hereditary variations of some of the river species will be halved within seven years,' he said, worried because the wild salmon in each river are a genetically unique stock that has evolved over thousands of years to suit the conditions there. If this evolutionary advantage is diluted by new blood, the resulting crosses may not survive. Certainly, when the Soviets transferred large numbers of wild salmon from a river on the north of an Aleutian island to a river on the south, neither native nor introduced stock survived and the entire salmon run in the southern river, on which a cannery depended, was wiped out.

Worries that salmon farming would destroy the wild salmon stocks in Irish rivers by introducing parasites and disease or by genetic pollution were not enough to halt the expansion of the industry, which by the late eighties had become big business and was competing fiercely with producers in Scotland and Norway for markets overseas. Since no-one had positive proof that salmon farming would be harmful, it had to be allowed to go ahead. Jobs and investment were at stake, profits were being made and the growth imperative was strongly at work. 'We need 10 per cent of the European salmon market if we are to get anywhere,' an official of Údarás na Gaeltachta, the successor body to Gaeltarra Éireann, told me when I asked him to explain why his organization had abandoned its policy of keeping foreign salmon farmers out of the bays of Connemara so that   cage sites would be available when local people wanted to take up fish farming.

The industry's growing economic importance meant that the Irish regulatory authorities had less and less power to control it. They took no action when it was found that the farms were adding a pigment to their fishes' food that was suspected of being a carcinogen: the colourant was necessary to stop the salmons' flesh staying a pasty white. They also did nothing to stop the use of antibiotics in lakes from which drinking water was drawn, although when a newspaper revealed in early 1990 that the ESB was using a potentially carcinogenic fungicide in Dublin's main reservoir, the junior minister responsible was out on the site the next day and the ESB was ordered to take its fish away. That incident struck just too close to home.

Late in 1990 it became known that ivermectin, which is widely used by cattle farmers to control parasites, was being added to salmon feed to kill parasitic sea lice that live on the caged salmon's skin. If left uncontrolled the lice eat so much skin away that the fish dies. The ivermectin treatment was to replace Nuvan, an organophosphorous pesticide that had previously been tipped into the cages to control the lice, an operation that endangered the farm workers and frequently stressed the fish so much that they developed pancreas disease and died anyway. When one well-respected farm, Camus Fisheries, was forced into receivership in autumn 1990 as a result of its pancreas disease losses, the survivors felt they had no alternative but to use the new – but illegal – ivermectin treatment and began buying it from local farmers' co-operatives to mix with their salmon feed.

Merck, the company that manufactures ivermectin, was appalled. 'It should not be used because we have no basis for recommending it. We don't know if it gets metabolized in fish or what the withdrawal period should be,' its spokesman told me. The National Drugs Advisory Board was even more upset. 'Who gave them the go-ahead?' a shocked official asked. 'It's clearly against the law. We cannot authorize this until we have assessed its effect on the target species and on the immediate environment. We don't know anything about the dose required or how long the withholding time needs to be before the salmon can be harvested. When used on cattle, the drug is excreted and delays the breakdown of the cowpat because it kills the insects which live on the dung. The drug may well be excreted by the salmon and could affect the creatures which break down fish droppings. However, what is even more worrying is what happens to the marine animals which consume any uneaten salmon food.' Yet, again, the regulatory authorities failed to act.

But perhaps the most serious charge against this well-meaning industry was made in February 1991 in a report from the Sea Trout Action Group, a body set up in 1988 by the owners of game fisheries in Mayo and Galway, the Department of the Marine, two regional fisheries boards, and the fish farmers themselves to investigate why sea-trout catches had collapsed after 1985: catches in 1990 were less than 2 per cent of their level five years before. The report said that sea-lice from fish farms were a major factor in the collapse, which largely affected fisheries on rivers flowing into the sea near where farms were placed. It proposed that any farm which could not control its lice be closed down. Unless action was taken immediately, sea-trout stocks might never recover because only one more run of fish – those which were to go to sea within two months of the report's publication – was left in the freshwater systems; the mature adults and younger generations of fish had almost completely disappeared. The minister, however, failed to act, claiming that the connection between the fish farms and the plague of sea-lice was still not proved. But even if he had removed the cages immediately it would probably have been too late, because lice numbers would not have dropped quickly enough to allow the young sea-trout safe passage.

In any case, by May 1991 most of the year's run of sea-trout smolts were back in fresh water. 'There was a lovely run of smolts this year. We monitored them very carefully,' the owner of the Delphi (Co. Mayo) fishery, Peter Mantle, told me. 'Everyone was hoping that the lice problem would not be as bad as in the past three years because of the cold winter and the cool spring. Unfortunately, this was not the case. More smolts returned to fresh water prematurely this year than in previous years and they have come back in worse condition and sooner than ever before. And they were absolutely heaving with sea lice.' As a result, Mantle thinks, sea-trout fishing – a tourist activity on which his and many other livelihoods depend – will have to be abandoned on many Irish rivers for far into the future.

And what of the wild salmon stocks? There are signs that the sea-lice are affecting the young wild salmon in the same way as they do the young sea-trout. If this is confirmed, then the wild salmon's survival is threatened. However, the effect of fish farm escapes on wild stocks might not be as bad as was once feared. 'Neither I nor anybody else knows what the effects of the escapes are,' says Tom Cross, a geneticist at University College, Cork, who is leading a two-year, EC-financed study involving Queen's University, Belfast, the Marine Laboratory, Aberdeen, and a Spanish university to try to find out. 'We do know that only about 10 per cent of escapees run up rivers but that they do spawn there, although later in the year and lower down the river than the wild fish, which probably reduces the survival chances of their offspring. We also know that they do interbreed with the wild fish. What we don't know is what happens to pure farmed-fish young or to hybrids. The purpose of our project is to see if we can find genetic markers which will tell us whether a wild-born fish is of wild, farmed or hybrid parentage so that we can find out.' Cross thinks that the more inbred the farmed fish, and consequently the more uniform the genetic make-up of the stock in a cage, the more damaging the impact of an escape is likely to be for the wild strain. 'Fortunately, the salmon kept on Irish fish farms are not highly inbred at this stage,' Cross says.

This sorry saga, which has close parallels with the regulatory authorities' behaviour in the salmonella and mad-cow disease episodes in Britain, shows just how radically our whole way of thinking has to change before we can have any confidence that humankind will not destroy the world. Here was an industry set up mainly to provide people in a relatively remote area with a livelihood. Most of the people who became involved, at least in the beginning, did so primarily out of idealism: they wanted to contribute to society far more strongly than they wanted to get rich. Moreover, most of them were, and are, biologists of one sort or another, supposedly familiar with the finely balanced systems that exist in the natural world. And yet their industry could scarcely have done more damage if it had been run by the crassest breed of road engineer. The regulatory bodies proved totally ineffective and yet there is no hint of inefficiency or corruption. Údarás na Gaeltachta forgot the people it was trying to serve when it came to a question of market share. The state company, the ESB, did no better than anyone else, although, if the Right are to be believed, its executives are under less pressure to produce a profit than their counterparts in private organizations.

I know many of the people involved in Irish fish farming, and without exception, they are people I respect. Although some environmentalists argued that salmon farming was inherently ecologically unsound when the first experiments were carried out, it was not the fish farmers' fault that things turned out so badly. Once the farms were established, those who ran them had no real option but to behave as they did if they wanted to stay in production. It was the system within which we all work that was mainly to blame. The same is true, I am sure, of all industries. Some environmental groups have done their cause a great disservice by painting industrialists, mining company bosses or South American ranchers as evil men, motivated mainly by greed. Most are not, and blaming them falsely only diverts our attention from the real enemy. Very few people are genuinely evil – far too few to bring about all the harm that gets done. People in business, however, are not *like* us: they *are* us, sharing all our values and aspirations. It is the capitalist system that forces us all to act as we do.

ECONOMIC TOTALITARIANISM

This is not to say that capitalism is an immoral system. It is, in fact, morally neutral. Our mistake has been to ascribe morality to it by accepting that we could behave as selfishly as we liked because the 'invisible hand' would turn everything to good. Then, in the 1950s, we compounded our error by making economic growth our primary social goal. Historically, a troika of competing influences has generally governed Western societies. The economic system was, of course, one influence, but it was constantly regulated and modified by the other two, the political system and the moral-cultural system, which is made up of diverse elements such as the press, the universities, writers and artists and, of course, the churches. Unfortunately, however, this latter group largely abdicated its moderating role in favour of the 'invisible hand' almost two centuries ago and then, when the politicians made increasing national income their paramount objective, the rule of economics became absolute. In short, we are all victims of an economic totalitarianism and have little freedom to determine what we think and do in the economic sphere.

Our immediate goal must be to break out of the processes of thought that imprison us. The first and most important step is to reject the notion that the achievement of economic growth is a fit, proper or desirable goal for any nation. Growth is like money in this respect. One is always unhappy about giving a relative money as a birthday or Christmas present, because to do so can appear to be an admission that one cares so little about them that one cannot be bothered to spend the time to think about a gift they would really appreciate. Yet in theory the money should be better than the gift because it enables them to buy exactly what they want. In practice, as we all know, presents of money are often used for everyday spending and so buy nothing in particular. So it is with growth. In theory, the resources it supposedly creates should allow us to achieve our objectives, whatever they may be. In practice, it either limits our choices by making some objectives unobtainable or it consumes the new resources itself or, since we have not identified our objectives, we fritter the resources away.

If we bothered to think about those things we might really like and, having identified them in hard, finite terms, set about achieving them directly, there is a much better chance that we would get them, and it would be possible to measure our progress towards our objectives. As things stand, with growth as the goal, few people have even attempted to discover if it is making us genuinely better off, as I remarked at the outset. Nor is that task easy: in chapters 7 to 9 I had to set the goals I thought Britain ought to have had between 1955 and 1988 before I could attempt to measure its success. Once we have destroyed the idea that growth is necessarily good, the political world will be able to retrieve its independence from the economic state and resume its monitoring function.

The second step must be to free the moral-cultural system. This can be done by establishing the principle that, just as the polluter should pay, the entrepreneur should be responsible for the consequences of his actions. Thus, if he puts someone out of work, at home or abroad, in his firm or another, he should support them until there is something else suitable for them to do. The taxpayer has no role in carrying this cost. Similarly, if the entrepreneur is involved in something like the destruction of the sea-trout, he should do the equivalent of compensating the game fishery owners for the loss of their fish. Naturally, these liabilities would compel caution, but that is the way it should be. The whole community should not have to suffer because someone takes risks trying to accomplish a personal goal that might not benefit everybody else as well. If the community is a formal partner in a venture, having assessed the risks and set them against its share of the potential gain, that is quite another thing, but we should no longer give new projects automatic economic and social approval, assuming that if the entrepreneur finds the venture worth while, the community will do so too. Henceforward, just as we insist on environmental impact assessments for new developments, we must demand economic and social impact assessments for projects and technologies. As the village of Alto showed, human communities can be as badly damaged by change as can the plant and animal communities of the natural world.

Of course there will be difficulties in making these assessments. It would not have been possible to have anticipated many, perhaps most, of the problems that came up with salmon farming. But if a project's speed and scale are kept down, the consequences of a faulty assessment are reduced. If salmon farming had had the freedom to develop more slowly because noone was worried about losing market share to the Norwegians or creating extra jobs this year rather than next, if it had been tried out over many years in just a few river systems rather than over a few years in many, it might have been possible to correct its problems or to abandon it before it led to disaster.

THE AMISH ANSWER

The best-known group of people who have successfully resisted the adoption of many new technologies and thus preserved important elements of their way of life are the Amish communities in North America. It would be wrong to pretend, however, that the Amish have a careful assessment procedure. Indeed in some cases, at least as far as the Amish in Lancaster County, Pennsylvania, are concerned, it appears that if a breakaway sect, the Peachey church, adopted something, the group from which they sprang did not, as happened with the telephone, which the Amish bishops outlawed immediately after the 1909 split. However, the underlying reasons for the ban have become apparent since. Although the telephone connects members of a highly mobile society over thousands of miles, for a close-knit localized community like the Amish it would have been a separator. 'If one can 'phone, why visit?' Donald Kraybill asks in his book *The Riddle of Amish Culture* (1989). 'The Amish never developed elaborate arguments against the 'phone but they understood that … [it] would eventually erode the core of Amish culture: face-to-face conversations.'

Since telephones are essential to modern American life, the ban does not apply to using a phone, just having one conveniently in the home. Farmers who must have one to summon the vet or to order supplies keep it in the barn. Amish-owned businesses can have them in their workshops or stores. And groups of families without a convenient non-Amish neighbour build a shed and install a community phone somewhere convenient for them all.

A similar ban has been applied to the car, which, although ideal for a complicated, individuated and mobile society was immediately recognized as a threat to a stable local community that cherished its high degree of independence from the outside world. Like the phone, to the Amish the car is a separator. Its use would enable young people to drive into the urban world of vice, adults to travel far afield on business. Vain people would use it to show off their status, and for others it would provide a means to escape social control. It would tear the community apart. But, again, the restriction is on ownership, not on use, and without the services of non-Amish taxi-drivers many Amish businesses would find it difficult to survive. Refusing to own vehicles and yet readily using them is not hypocrisy; it is a compromise which makes car travel much less convenient and thus maintains the slow pace of Amish life. When a journey too long for horse and buggy becomes really necessary, the Amish are able to travel and they frequently do so in groups, which also fosters community solidarity.

The most interesting technological compromise the Amish have had to make is over the tractor which, broadly speaking, is allowed in the farmyard but not in the field. The Amish bishops ruled that the land must be tilled with horses because they feared that their flock's horse culture might other-wise die and the car would find its way in to replace the buggy. In addition, horse-farming required more labour and it was necessary to maintain jobs for young men, who might otherwise seek factory work and be lost to the community. Perhaps worse, there might be more leisure and the Devil always found work for idle hands. As Kraybill says: 'The Amish have always welcomed work as the heart-beat of their community. The church was anchored on the farm, where work, like a magnet, pulled everyone together. A tractor might save labor but in Amish eyes that spelled trouble.'

Why are tractors permitted in the farmyard? Kraybill suggests that the answer is that the Amish were using stationary engines to power threshers and to blow silage into feed silos long before the tractor came along and that it would have been a difficult step for the bishops to have forbidden tractors to be used instead. What the church did do was to insist that tractors be fitted with steel wheels instead of rubber tyres so that they could not be used for trips to town. Fitting them with front-end loaders for moving muck was also forbidden, to preserve work to be done by hand. 'If we allowed tractors [to farm the land], we would be doing like the Mennonite people are doing, grabbing each other's farms up out there, mechanizing, and going off to the bank and loaning $500,000 and worrying later about paying it off, putting three other guys out of business and sending them to the town for work,' an Amish businessman explained to Kraybill.

Although the Amish can use powered balers in their hayfields so long as they are hauled by a horse, powered lifts to stack the bales in the barn are banned, to ensure that haymaking remains a labour-intensive event in the farm's year at which neighbouring families are brought together. Baling hay, in fact, only became necessary when Amish farmers increased their milk production to meet rising demand and needed to compress the extra hay required for their larger herds to get it into their barns. The bishops then became worried by the increasing herd sizes, and refused to allow machinery to be installed to clear dung from the byres, thus placing a natural limit on the number of cattle a family can handle. Milk pipelines were forbidden for the same reason.

Owning a car, using tractors in the field and installing a telephone in one's house are not considered evils in themselves. The evil lies in the effects a new invention might have on the community. Innovations the Amish have rejected include mains electricity and electric lights, radios, televisions, tape recorders, and computers. On the other hand, they have accepted electric cash registers, calculators, torches, twelve-volt motors, hearing aids, electric welders (one of the few acceptable uses for a motor generator), and electric fences. Freezers are also acceptable because they strengthen family life but, in view of the ban on mains power, they have to be kept in non-Amish homes. Jewellery, central heating, fitted carpets, flying by air, military service, secondary education, divorce and, indeed, any other lawsuit, are all banned.

These lists naturally strike the non-Amish as highly arbitrary. For me, however, the surprising thing is not that the Amish have had to compromise or that some of their compromises appear ridiculous but that they have been able to adhere to so many of their rules while living in the heart of the most consumerist, pro-technology society in the world. If they had their own country and did not live as a minority among people with an entirely different set of values, many of the compromises might be unnecessary. As things are, they have done remarkably well. This is Kraybill's assessment:

Here we have a social system without poverty. Widows, orphans and the destitute are all cared for by the church. The Amish are rarely imprisoned. Here is a society virtually without crime and violence. Amish youth are occasionally arrested for drunken driving [the Amish practise adult baptism and their young people are allowed considerable freedom, even to drink and drive, before they join the church as full members] and children are occasionally paddled [spanked] but incidents of violent crime and murder are conspicuously absent. Amish suicide and mental illness rates are substantially lower than those in the larger society. Alcohol abuse, while present among some youth, is practically nil in the adult population. Divorce is unheard of. Individuals are not warehoused in institutions – large schools, massive factories, retirement homes or psychiatric hospitals – but are cared for within the family. Recycling goods, frugal management, a thrifty lifestyle and a rejection of consumerism produce scant waste. Energy consumption per capita is remarkably low. Beyond exhaust fumes from diesel power plants and the contamination of streams by manure run-off, the Amish add little to environmental pollution. Personal alienation, loneliness and meaninglessness are for the most part absent. There are, of course, some unhappy marriages, lonely people, cantankerous personalities and family feuds. But, all things considered, the quality of life indicators for Amish society are remarkably robust. The Amish have created a humane and enviable social system.

GLOBAL ACTION, GLOBAL DISASTER

In an article in the *Atlantic Monthly* in February 1991, the Kentucky writer-farmer Wendell Berry attacked the popular slogan 'Think Globally, Act Locally.' It was not acting locally he was worried about – that's what he urged. It was the dangers of global thought. 'Global thinkers have been, and will be, dangerous people ... Global thinking can only be statistical. Its shallowness is exposed by the least intention to do something. Unless one is willing to be destructive on a very large scale, one cannot do something except locally, in a small place.' He suggests that our touchstone should be that of the Amish – 'What will this do to our community?' – rather than how will it affect the nation or the world. Had fish farming's effect on the local community and on the river system been, truly, the first consideration, far fewer disputes would have arisen between its promoters and those other groups – scallop fishermen, freshwater anglers, tourism promoters, members of local drinking water supply schemes – whose interests were also affected.

Capitalism has brought about the global concentration and use of economic power and it is this that has made it so damaging and dictated that local interests have to be largely ignored. How then can this global power be returned to the communities from which it was taken? Just because we have agreed that we have to work with capitalism because it is the only functioning economic system in the world does not mean we have to accept it warts and all. Indeed, the whole point of enabling the political and moral-cultural systems to act independently of the economic one is so that they can transform their current master. Changing the scale on which capitalism operates is just one of several major modifications the other parts of the troika have to make. Or rather *we* do, because we make them up. Wanting to change capitalism is not heresy. It has been constantly changing through the years. Thomas Jefferson urged that it should be revolutionized once a generation.

Capitalism, like a music enthusiast's sound system, is made up of several components, most of which can be tuned or modified. Its fundamental part is the payment of interest on borrowed money and it is this which has caused many of our problems, because it has created the system's need for growth. We can't remove this component, but we can cut the need for growth by turning the rate of interest knob steadily back so that, when we achieve our target stable state, it is down to the lowest setting: the individual's rate of time preference, the least rate of interest that makes it worth while for him not to spend all his income now. A stable world should have little risk and no inflation, so this rate could be in effect zero, since we all need to put money aside to see us through old age, whether we get interest on it or not.

Turning down the growth knob will remove the need for ever-bigger production units but it will not necessarily reduce the scale of those that already exist. One way of doing this would be to improve the functioning of another of the capitalist system's components, the free market, a feature for which it is widely admired. This fulsome paean of praise for the market came from Walter Wriston, a former president of Citibank, in an interview in *Harper's Magazine* in December 1986:

I happen to believe that the most important moral value is liberty. What social system produces more individual liberty than any other? The record of history is quite clear on this question. It is impossible for centralized economic planning, no matter how intelligently conceived, to produce rational choices over any period of time. Nobody is smart enough to guide an economy for the good of all. It's just not possible.

What we've developed instead of centralized planning is a price system that lets each individual communicate with hundreds of million other individuals in a way which, though imperfect, allows him to make sensible economic decisions about his own life. That increases freedom. When all is said and done, the maximizing of human liberty is the most important moral imperative, and it is democratic capitalism which is more congruent with human liberty than any other form of social organization.

Yet as the admiring Wriston admits, the market is imperfect. We have already seen how it fails to allocate resources fairly between this generation and future ones, since it permits us to use fossil fuels, erect short-life buildings, and open nuclear power stations with no regard for what happens beyond the next twenty-five years. In the same way, a market cannot operate

fairly when there is a grotesque imbalance between the wealth of the partici-
pants. Correcting both these failings would help put the size problem right:
if fossil fuels could not be used so lavishly, transport would be restricted, and
many large-scale, high-energy techniques would have to be given up.
Smaller, perhaps community-scale enterprises would be given their chance.
Also, the transfer of funds from rich to poor that a worldwide fuel rationing
system would entail would reduce the relative power of the world's well-off.
But there is a problem about all this: so ingrained is the importance of size
in our habits of thought that we are talking about worldwide action immediately after agreeing with Wendell Berry that global action is part of the
problem and that local action is what is required.

What's more, power is never given away by the powerful. It is taken
instead by the relatively powerless. It is most unlikely that the Earth
Summit in Brazil in 1992 will agree the radical measures that are needed, no
matter how much pressure we apply to our politicians beforehand. Too
many vested interests are at stake. As we cannot rely on the conference having a favourable outcome, we ought to prepare for direct action instead.
Such action would involve individual countries retrieving their autonomy
from the world system by setting their own targets for reducing fossil fuel
consumption and refusing imports made using more energy-intensive technologies than they themselves applied. They would also have to control the
flow of capital across their borders. As Keynes told his Irish audience in
1932 as they embarked on a similar course, 'ideas, knowledge, science,
hospitality, travel – these are the things which should of their nature be
international. But let goods be homespun whenever it is reasonably and
conveniently possible and, above all, let finance be primarily national.'

Such an independent path might seem harsh and painful but I believe it
will prove liberating and joyous instead. It is the only way to break out of a
system that continually impoverishes those at the periphery by taking
resources to the centre, wherever that centre might be. At present, rather
than fighting this process we help it along because all our thinking about
what constitutes development boils down to finding ways in which some of
the money circulating at the centre, in one or other of the remaining islands
of prosperity, can be returned to communities outside. We go into an Indian
village, see the underemployment and the grinding poverty, and immediately ask ourselves, 'What can these people make or grow that can be sold outside?' when a more appropriate question would be, 'What can these people
do to fill their own needs better from their own resources?' If the village sets
up a co-op and starts supplying, say, fresh vegetables to the nearest city, a
hundred or a thousand other villages will begin to do so too, forcing down
the prices that made the venture possible in the first place. The prime
beneficiaries of our mode of thought are the city folk who can now buy

cheaper and better vegetables while the people who supply them lose out.

Whenever a poorer country or region attempts to satisfy the needs of a wealthier one rather than attending to needs of its own, dependency and weakness are increased, not reduced. The World Bank's structural adjustment policies give clear evidence of this. They have had the effect of forcing many debt-laden primary producing nations to increase their exports to the wealthier world, and thus brought down the prices the importing countries have to pay. Naturally this has increased the prosperity of some groups in the wealthier countries, but has not reduced the indebtedness of the suppliers. Frequently both sides lose from these exchanges. The volume of tropical hardwood imported into Ireland rose by 64 per cent between 1977 and 1987, encouraged by a 20 per cent price fall. As a result the Ivory Coast, Ghana and Brazil were felling 4,000 hectares of forest a year at the end of the period to meet Irish demand, according to estimates prepared by Fergal Mulloy of the Forest Service.[1] Ireland, on the other hand, found it uneconomic to plant temperate species for the same uses, trees Mulloy would have dearly liked to|be asked to grow.

If the task of reducing the scale of things, of breaking out of unequal relationships, will not be done for us by international agencies, we will have to get our hands dirty and do it ourselves. There is a chance that our job might be eased by the worldwide economic collapse that seems to loom nearer each day as I write, although the crisis, when it breaks, will be a double-edged sword. One of its edges will be that, as people see banks and building societies crash and the numbers of unemployed grow, they will want to return to the relative security of what has gone before and, quite naturally, will set about trying to restore the system they have known. People are more ready to try something new when they are feeling rich and confident, and become rigid and conservative when life goes sour. The other edge, however, is that the crash will give to those who wish to take it the chance to convince others that repairing a system that has failed badly is to repeat a great mistake.

Will the hardships we are about to face force us to carry on as we are, or will they compel us, out of desperation, to accept the risk of the new? Will chaos provide the opportunity de Valera created when he took Ireland into the economic war? The future of humankind, and possibly the planet, depends on the answers.

Is capitalism's need for growth so powerful a force that it is beyond the capacity of democratic governments to control when once they have escaped from the grip of the 'invisible hand'? Will the high-powered car in which we are all passengers continue to increase its speed, doubling its output of carbon dioxide over the next quarter-century as it did in the last and, sooner rather than later, asphyxiate the planet with its fumes? Is trying to invent ourselves out of crisis after crisis the only course we can follow? Can we ever settle into a secure and stable state?

I like to think I would have written this book even if I thought there was no possibility that we could save ourselves. I hope I have given some idea of the ways in which the capitalist system can be brought to heel so that its formidable powers bring life instead of destruction. The system is not cast in stone: it can be changed. But have we left ourselves enough time to do so? The planet needs a pause. Humankind must cease its damage, its increasing. Then, after a generation or two of quiet, our successors can think again.

Epilogue
The Oak Beams of New College, Oxford

I owe this story to a man who was, I think, a New College student and was head of the Department of Medicine at the University of Hawaii, where he told it to me.

New College, Oxford, is of rather recent foundation, hence its name. It was probably founded around the late 16th century. It has, like other colleges, a great dining hall with big oak beams across the top, yes? These might be eighteen inches square, twenty feet long.

Some five or ten years ago, so I am told, some busy entomologist went up into the roof of the dining hall with a penknife, poked at the beams and found that they were full of beetles. This was reported to the College Council, who met in some dismay because where would they get beams of that calibre nowadays?

One of the Junior Fellows stuck his neck out and suggested that there might be some oak on college lands. These colleges are endowed with pieces of land scattered across the country. So they called the College Forester, who, of course, had not been near the college for some years, and asked him about oaks.

And he pulled his forelock and said, 'Well, sirs, we was wondering when you'd be askin'.'

Upon further enquiry it was discovered that when the College was founded, a grove of oaks had been planted to replace the beams in the dining hall when they became beetly, because oak beams always become beetly in the end. This plan had been passed down from one Forester to the next for four hundred years. 'You don't cut those oaks. Them's for the College Hall.'

A nice story. That's the way to run a culture.

– Gregory Bateson, *The Next Whole Earth Catalog* (1980)

Notes

The text, especially if used in conjunction with the bibliography, should provide enough details for readers to go to the source of most quotations and statistics. These notes provide additional information on sources it would have been cumbersome to have specified in the body of the book.

Introduction (pages 1-4)

1 Included in John Kenneth Galbraith, *Economics, Peace and Laughter* (1971).
2 E. J. Mishan, *The Costs of Economic Growth* (1967) and *The Economic Growth Debate, an Assessment* (1977). Also Wilfred Beckerman, *In Defence of Economic Growth* (1974), Fred Hirsch, *The Social Limits to Growth* (1977) and H. V. Hodson, *The Diseconomics of Growth* (1972).

Chapter 1 Quality or Quantity? (pages 5-17)

1 John F. Hall, 'Subjective measures of quality of life in Britain 1971–1975: some developments and trends', *Social Trends*, no. 7 (1976).
2 See R. Hueting, 'An economic scenario for a conserver-economy' in Paul Ekins's *The Living Economy* (1986), pp. 242-56. See also Hueting's *New Scarcity and Economic Growth: More Welfare through Less Production* (1980).
3 Earl E. Davis and Margret Fine-Davis, 'Predictors of satisfaction with environmental quality in eight European countries', *Social Indicators Research*, vol. 11 (1982), pp. 341-62.
4 See 'Whatever happened to social indicators? a symposium', *Journal of Public Policy*, vol. 9, 4, pp. 399-450.
5 William Nordhaus and James Tobin, ' Is growth obsolete?' in *Economic Growth* (1972).
6 Ibid.

Chapter 2 Why Capitalism Needs Growth (pages 18-32)

1 Quoted by Betsy Hartmann and James Boyce in *Needless Hunger* (1982), which provides a good account of how the British broke down the Indian economy. C. Edwards Lester, *The Glory and Shame of England* (1866), has some useful material but the fullest account of the downside of British involvement in India is probably Reginald Reynolds, *White Sahibs in India* (third edition, 1946). For the effect of imperialism on Africa, see Walter Rodney, *How Europe Underdeveloped Africa* (1972). Richard West's *Brazza of the Congo* (1972) tells a sickening story of how commercial interests beat an idealist.
2 Quoted in S. K. Srivastava, *History of Economic Thought* (1983).
3 Marc Ferro, *The Great War 1914-18* (1974).

Chapter 3 Ill Fares the Land (pages 33-50)

1 Quoted in C. Edwards Lester, *The Glory and Shame of England* (1866).
2 Arthur Young, *Travels in France,* ed. Maxwell (1929).
3 Lester, op. cit.
4 Eric Hobsbawm, *Industry and Empire* (1969).
5 See W. D. Rubinstein, *Wealth and Inequality in Britain* (1986), pp. 62-3, and Phyllis Deane, *The First Industrial Revolution* (1965) for details and a discussion of King's results.
6 B. R. Mitchell and Phyllis Deane, *Abstract of British Historical Statistics* (1962).
7 E. H. Phelps Brown and P. E. Hart, 'The share of wages in national income', *Economic Journal,* June 1952.
8 E. H. Phelps Brown and S. V. Hopkins, 'Seven centuries of the price of consumables, compared with builders' wages', *Economica,* vol. 23, November 1956, pp. 296-314.
9 T. B. Macaulay, review of Southey's *Colloquies on Society in Critical and Historical Essays* (1908 edition).

Chapter 4 The Benefits of War and Depression (pages 51-6)

1 E. H. Phelps Brown and P. E. Hart, op. cit.
2 A claim made by C. L. Mowat in *Britain Between the Wars* (1955).

Chapter 5 Mrs Thatcher and the Struggle Against Inflation (pages 57-76)

1 Lipsey's paper, 'After Monetarism', is included in *After Stagflation: Alternatives to Economic Decline* (1984), ed. John Cornwall, pp. 41-62.
2 The speeches were published under the title *Let Our Children Grow Tall.*
3 J. K. Galbraith, *Economics in Perspective* (1987).
4 Gordon Brown, *Where There Is Greed* (1989).
5 Reported in *The Economist*, 11 May 1991.

Chapter 6 Ned Ludd Was Right (pages 77-95)

1 Joseph Schumpeter, *History of Economic Analysis* (1974).
2 J. K. Galbraith, *The Age of Uncertainty* (1977).
3 Quoted from Johnson's paper, 'The criteria of economic advantage', *Bulletin of the Oxford University Institute of Statistics*, vol. 19 (1957). Johnson's estimate of the maximum gain from the EEC appeared in the *Journal of the Manchester School of Economic and Social Studies*, vol. 26 (1958). The figure was twenty times too high according to a Dutch economist, P. J. Verdoorn, quoted in Tibor de Scitovzsky's *Economic Theory and Western European Integration* (1958).
4 See Krugman's paper, 'Is free trade passé?', *Journal of Economic Perspectives*, vol. 1, no. 2, 1987.

Chapter 7 Growth and the National Health (pages 96-119)

1 Philip Evans and Nick Edgerton, 'Life events and mood as predictors of the common cold', *British Journal of Medical Psychology*, vol. 64, 1991, pp. 35-44.
2 See *Inequalities in Health* (1988) for the full text of both *The Black Report* (1982) edited by Peter Townsend and Nick Davidson, and *The Health Divide* (1988) by Margaret Whitehead. The government found Black so damning it made an unsuccessful attempt to limit its impact and circulation.
3 Elsie Pamuk, 'Social class inequality in mortality from 1921 to 1971 in England and Wales', *Population Studies*, 39, 1985, pp. 17-31.
4 See Richard Wilkinson's 'Class mortality differentials, income distribution and trends in poverty, 1921-1981', *Journal of Social Policy*, vol. 18 (3), pp. 307-35.
5 I. Knights, *The Heights and Weights of Adults in Britain* (1984).
6 Wilkinson's paper to the BSA was unpublished when this book went to

press. Much the same material was, however, included in 'Income distribution and mortality: a "natural" experiment', which appeared in *Sociology of Health & Illness*, vol. 12 (4), 1990, pp. 391-412. Wilkinson edited *Class and Health: Research and Longitudinal Data* (1986).

7 Yellowlees's paper to the RCGP, 'Ill fares the land', was published by the Wholefood Trust, London, in 1989.

8 Ministry of Agriculture, Fisheries and Food, *Pesticide Safety Precaution Scheme, Cleared Product List*, 1985.

9 Ronald Finn's talk, 'Nourishing the mind', was reprinted in the April 1989 issue of the newsletter of the McGarrison Society.

10 Department of the Environment, Digest of Environmental and Water Statistics, 1990.

11 Reported in *New Scientist*, 2 March 1991.

12 The widest-ranging paper on the effects of radiation and chemicals on male fertility I was able to trace was 'Occupational influence on male fertility and sexuality' by O. P. Steeno and A. Pangkahila, published in *Andrologia*, vol. 16 (1), 1984, pp. 5-22. J. Fisher-Fishbein's 'The effects of pharmaceutical, environmental and occupational agents on sperm motility' pp. 330-73 in Claude Gagnon's *Control of Sperm Motility: Biological and Clinical Aspects*, CRC Press, 1990, is more specific. Richard Levine covers seasonal variations in semen quality in *Temperature and Environmental Effects on the Testes*, Plenum Press, New York, 1991, pp. 89-96. Environmental risks to women are dealt with by Elizabeth C. McCloy in 'Work, environment and the fetus' which appeared in *Midwifery*, vol. 5 (1989), pp. 55–62.

13 *The Independent on Sunday*, 8 March 1992. The research was led by Professor Neils Skakkeback.

Chapter 8 How Growth Damaged Family and Community Life (pages 120-50)

1 Henley Centre for Forecasting, *Planning for Social Change, 1989-90*, vol. 1 (1989). A wide-ranging survey of social attitudes and aspirations.

2 David Appleyard, *Liveable Streets* (1981).

3 E. S. Paykel, 'Depression in women', *British Journal of Psychiatry*, vol. 158 (suppl. 10), 1991, pp. 22-9.

4 Robert Ornstein in *Psychology: the Study of Human Experience* (1988) cites an unpublished paper, 'Social networks in a vulnerable population: the separated and divorced' (1981) by N. Gerstel.

5 M. E. J. Wadsworth and M. Maclean, 'Parents' divorce and child's life chances', *Child and Youth Services Review*, vol. 8 (1986), pp. 145-59. For a wider glimpse of other factors which affect a child's development, see

Wadsworth's lecture 'The influence of childhood on later life: some evidence from the national birth cohort study' published by the University of Exeter in 1989.

6 See K. Roberts, 'Socioeconomic polarisation and the implications of leisure' in K. Roberts and Anna Olszewska (eds), *Leisure and Lifestyle* (1989).

7 A. W. Phillips, 'The relationship between unemployment and the rate of change of money wages in the United Kingdom, 1861-1957', *Economica*, vol. 25 (1958), pp. 283-99.

8 Studies which show a relationship between unemployment, sickness and premature death, including suicide, include K. A. Moser, A. J. Fox and D. R. Jones, 'Unemployment and mortality in the OPCS longitudinal study', *The Lancet*, vol. 2 (1984), pp. 1324-9, and the same authors' 'Unemployment and mortality' in *Class and Health* (1986), ed. R. G. Wilkinson. A deterioration in mental health has been shown by M. H. Banks and P. R. Jackson in 'Unemployment and the risk of minor psychiatric disorders in young people' in *Psychological Medicine*, vol. 12 (1982) pp. 789-98; A. G. Cook et al., 'Health of unemployed middle-aged men in Great Britain', *The Lancet*, vol. 2 (1982), pp. 1290-4; N. Beale and S. Nethercott, 'Job loss and family morbidity', *Journal of the Royal College of General Practitioners*, vol. 35 (1985), pp. 510-14. See also Mildred Blaxter, *Health and Lifestyles* (1990).

9 J. Jahoda, 'Work, employment and unemployment', *American Psychologist*, vol. 36 (1981), pp. 184-91.

10 Department of Education and Science, *Statistical Bulletin*, March 1990.

11 R. I. Nicolson and A. J. Fawcett, 'Automaticity: a new framework for dyslexia research', *Cognition*, vol. 35 (1990), pp. 159-82.

12 The Second Islington Crime Survey, Middlesex Polytechnic, 1990.

13 Gary Becker, *Essays in the Economics of Crime and Punishment* (1974).

14 Simon Field, *Trends in Crime and their Interpretation*, Home Office Research Study no. 119 (1990).

15 *Priorities for Health Promotion, an Economic Approach*, Discussion Paper 59, Centre for Health Economics, University of York.

16 *The Observer*, 6 August 1989.

17 *The Guardian*, 16 July 1991.

18 *The Daily Telegraph*, 15 September 1989.

19 Robin Page, *Decline of an English Village* (1975).

20 Statistics taken from Chris Rose, *The Dirty Man of Europe* (1990).

21 'Britain's filthy rivers', *The Observer Colour Magazine*, 21 July 1991.

Chapter 9 What Has All the Growth Done? (pages 151-71)

1 See John Adams, *The Transport Dilemma* (1991).
2 Mike Lake, 'Surveying all the factors', *Language and Learning*, June 1991, pp. 8-13.
3 The report *Youth Track* is available from Young Direction, 17-19, Bedford Street, London WC2E 9HP, price £850.
4 Among the publications which have reprinted Gatto's article are *Resurgence* 148, September 1991, and *Whole Earth Review* 72, fall 1991.
5 Jonathan Gershuny, 'Time budgets as social indicators', *Journal of Public Policy*, vol. 9, 4, pp. 419-24.
6 Bosquet's essay on Tristan da Cunha appears in a collection of his work, *Capitalism in Crisis and Everyday Life* (1977).

Chapter 10 Growth Must Have a Stop (pages 172-92)

1 The SPRU results were published as *Thinking about the Future: a Critique of 'The Limits to Growth'* in May 1973. The editors were H. S. D. Cole, Christopher Freeman, Marie Jahoda and K. L. R. Pavitt.
2 Lovelock's lecture, 'Stand up for Gaia', was printed in *The Biologist*, vol. 36 (1989), pp. 241-7.
3 A brief report of Barbara Prézelin's work appeared in *New Scientist*, 29 February 1992.

Chapter 11 Growth in the Greenhouse (pages 193-216)

1 See *Soil Remineralisation*, summer 1989.
2 These figures come from I. G. Simmons's wide-ranging study of the role of energy in human development, *Changing the Face of the Earth: Culture, Environment, History*, Blackwell, 1989. Another invaluable source is Juan Martinez-Alier, *Ecological Economics: Energy, Environment and Society* (1987).
3 'Greenhouse economics: count before you leap', *The Economist*, 7 July 1990.
4 The European Commission's scenarios were published as a edition of its magazine *Energy in Europe* in September 1989.
5 See *The Management of Greed* (1990), Slesser's introductory guide to the use of his ECCO simulation software for assessing national sustainable development. Available from the Resource Use Institute, Bonnethill Road, Pitlochry, Scotland. Slesser's estimate that investment caused 55 per cent of energy use was made in a letter to the author.

6 The results of the ECCO analysis of the EC's scenarios were published as *The Potential for Economic Growth in the European Community in the Context of Greenhouse Gas Constraints* by the Centre for Energy and Environmental Studies (IVEM) at the University of Groningen in March 1990.

7 The WRI estimates appeared as *World Resources 1990-91: a Guide to the Global Environment* (1990). They were severely criticized by Anil Agarwal and Sunita Narain in *Global Warming in an Unequal World: a Case of Environmental Colonialism* (1991).

Chapter 12 The Dutch Dilemma (pages 217-28)

1 V. N. de Jonge, K. Essink and R. Boddeke, 'The Dutch Wadden Sea: a changed ecosystem', *Hydrobiologia* (in press). See also R. Boddeke, 'Changes in the stock of brown shrimp in the coastal area of the Netherlands', *Rapp. P.-v. Réun., Cons. int. Explor. Mer*, vol. 172 (1978), pp. 239-49.

Chapter 13 The Mahatma's Message (pages 229-48)

1 Baba Amte, *Cry, the Beloved Narmada* (1989). See also *The Narmada Project: a Critique* by the environmental group Kalpavriksh, 1988.

Chapter 14 De Valera's Dream (pages 249-83)

1 This speech of de Valera's is known as his 'comely maidens' speech because that phrase appears in the official text. However, recordings show that he actually said 'happy maidens'.

2 Peter Flanagan.

3 All my material from Marx and Engels is drawn from Karl Marx and Frederick Engels, *Ireland and the Irish Question* (1971).

4 Henry D. Inglis, *A Journey Through Ireland During the Spring and Summer of 1834* (1835).

5 Thomas Carlyle, *Reminiscences of My Irish Journey in 1849* (1882).

6 Denis Browne, *Westport House and the Brownes* (1981).

7 See Kieran Kennedy, Thomas Giblin and Deirdre McHugh, *The Economic Development of Ireland in the Twentieth Century* (1988).

8 Johnston is quoted in Ronan Fanning, 'Economists and Government, Ireland 1922-52', a chapter in *Economists and the Irish Economy from the Eighteenth Century to the Present Day* (1984), ed. Antóin E. Murphy, pp. 138-56.

9 The full text of Keynes's lecture, 'National self-sufficiency', was reprinted in *Studies*, June 1933, pp. 177-93.
10 Noël Browne, *Against the Tide* (1986).
11 Richard Estes, *The Social Progress of Nations* (1989).

Chapter 15 The Myth of Sustainable Growth (pages 284-304)

1 Pearce replies to the criticisms that he ignored the population issue in the *Blueprint for a Green Economy* in the sequel, *Blueprint 2: Greening the World Economy* (1991), saying that as the first book was written as a report to the British government, a chapter on population control was unnecessary. However, he admits that he has no solutions. 'The "economic" approach offers few additional insights into practical policy for lowering population growth.'
2 See Lester Brown's Worldwatch Paper no. 85, *The Changing World Food Prospect: the Nineties and Beyond* (1988).
3 See 'Alternative farming: lower yields a myth' by Jack Fenwick and Pat Mielnick, *ILEIA Newsletter*, September 1990. Reganold's article appeared in *New Scientist*, 10 June 1989.
4 See Kenneth Boulding, *The Meaning of the Twentieth Century* (1964); Herman Daly, 'The economics of the steady state', *American Economic Review*, 1974; David M. Heer, 'Marketable licences for babies: Boulding's proposal revisited', *Social Biology*, spring 1975.
5 See John Adams, 'Unsustainable economics', *International Environmental Affairs*, vol. 2 (1), winter 1990, pp. 14-21.

Chapter 16 Guiding the Invisible Hand (pages 305-23)

1 Fergal Mulloy, 'Tropical deforestation: why bother?' in *Irish Forestry*, vol. 46 (2) (1989).

Bibliography

Abrams, M., *Condition of the British People, 1911-45* (Fabian Society, London, 1945).

Acton, Harold B., *The Morals of Markets* (Longman, London, 1971).

Adams, John, *Risk and Freedom* (Transport Publishing Projects, Cardiff, 1985).

Adams, John, 'Unsustainable economics', *International Environmental Affairs*, vol. 2 (1) (winter 1990).

Adams, John, *The Transport Dilemma* (Fabian Society, London, 1991).

Agarwal, Anil, and Narain, Sunita, *Towards Green Villages* (Centre for Science and Environment, New Delhi, 1989).

Agarwal, Anil, and Narain, Sunita, *Global Warming in an Unequal World: a Case of Environmental Colonialism* (Centre for Science and Environment, New Delhi, 1991).

Agrawal, A. N., Varma, H. O., and Gupta, R. C., *India: Basic Economic Information* (National, New Delhi, 1986).

Aldcroft, D. H., *The Inter-War Economy, Britain 1919-1939* (Columbia University Press, London, 1971).

Alderson, Stanley, *Britain in the Sixties: Housing* (Penguin, London, 1962).

Allaby, Michael, *Inventing Tomorrow: How to Live in a Changing World* (Hodder, London, 1976).

Amte, Baba, *Cry, the Beloved Narmada* (Maharogi Sewa Samiti, Anandwan, Warora, Maharashtra, 1989).

Anderson, Victor, *Alternative Economic Indicators* (Routledge, London, 1991).

Appleyard, David, *Liveable Streets* (University of California, Berkeley, 1981).

Arndt, H. W., *The Rise and Fall of Economic Growth* (University of Chicago Press, Chicago, 1978).

Ashworth, William, *An Economic History of England, 1870-1939* (Methuen, London, 1960).

Ayres, Jean, *Sensory Integration and Learning Disorders* (Western Psychological Services, Los Angeles, 1977).

Ayres, Jean, *Sensory Integration and the Child* (Western Psychological Services, Los Angeles, 1979).

Bach, G. L., *The New Inflation, its Causes and Effects* (Prentice-Hall, Englewood Cliffs, 1972).

Ball, R. J., and Doyle, Peter (eds), *Inflation* (Penguin, London, 1969).

Banks, M. H., and Jackson, P. R., 'Unemployment and the risk of minor psychiatric disorders in young people', *Psychological Medicine*, vol. 12 (1982).

Baran, Paul A., and Sweezy, Paul M., *Monopoly Capital* (Penguin, London, 1966).

Barber, William J., *A History of Economic Thought* (Penguin, London, 1967).

Barr, Pat, *The Coming of the Barbarians* (Macmillan, London, 1967).

Baster, A. S. J., *The Little Less: an Essay in the Political Economy of Restrictionism* (Methuen, London, 1947).

Beale, N., and Nethercott, S., 'Job loss and family morbidity', *Journal of the Royal College of General Practitioners*, vol. 35 (1985).

Becker, Gary, and Landes, William (eds), *Essays in the Economics of Crime and Punishment* (Social Behaviour and Social Institutions Series, no. 3, Books Demand UMI, 1974).

Beckerman, Wilfred, *In Defence of Economic Growth* (Cape, London, 1974).

Beckerman, Wilfred, *Pricing for Pollution: Market Pricing, Government Regulation, Environmental Policy* (Institute of Economic Affairs, London, 1990).

Beckerman, Wilfred, and Clark, Stephen (eds), *Poverty and Social Security in Britain since 1961* (Oxford University Press, Oxford, 1982).

Blaug, M., *The Economics of Education* (Penguin, London, 1968).

Blaxter, Mildred, *Health and Lifestyles* (Routledge, London, 1990).

Boddeke, R., 'Changes in the stock of brown shrimp in the coastal area of the Netherlands', Rapp. P.-v. Réun., *Cons. int. Explor. Mer*, vol. 172 (1978).

Boddy, Martin, *The Building Societies* (Macmillan, London, 1980).

Boissonnade, P., *Life and Work in Medieval Europe* (Dorset Press, New York, 1987).

Bosquet, Michel, *Capitalism in Crisis and Everyday Life* (Harvester Press, Sussex, 1977).

Boulding, Kenneth, *The Meaning of the Twentieth Century* (Harper and Row, New York, 1964).

Bowers, John, *Economics of the Environment: the Conservationists' Response to the Pearce Report* (British Association of Nature Conservationists, 1990).

Bowler, Peter, *The Invention of Progress* (Blackwell, Oxford, 1989).

Bowley, A. L., and Hogg, M. A., *Has Poverty Diminished?: English Workers and the Coming of the Welfare State* (1925) (Garland, New York, 1985).

Bradshaw, Jonathan, *Child Poverty and Deprivation in the UK* (National Children's Bureau, London, 1990).

Brand, Stewart (ed.), *The Next Whole Earth Catalog* (Random House, New York, 1980).

Braudel, Fernand, *Civilization and Capitalism: the Structures of Everyday Life* (Collins, London, 1981).

Braverman, H., *Labour and Monopoly Capital: the Degradation of Work in the Twentieth Century* (Monthly Review Press, London, 1976).

Brown, Gordon, *Where There is Greed* (Mainstream, Edinburgh, 1989).

Brown, Lester, *Building a Sustainable Society* (Norton, New York, 1981).

Brown, Lester, *The Changing World Food Prospect: the Nineties and Beyond* (Worldwatch paper no. 85, Worldwatch Institute, Washington, 1988).

Browne, Denis, *Westport House and the Brownes* (Moorland, Derbyshire, 1981).

Browne, Noël, *Against the Tide* (Gill and Macmillan, Dublin, 1986).

Brunt, Barry, *The Republic of Ireland* (Paul Chapman, London, 1988).

Butler, David, and Sloman, Anne, *British Political Facts, 1900-1975* (Macmillan, London, 1975).

Caldwell, Malcolm, *The Wealth of Some Nations* (Zed, London, 1977).

Cannon, Geoffrey, *The Politics of Food* (Century, London, 1987).

Capra, Fritjof, *The Turning Point* (Simon and Schuster, New York, 1982).

Carlyle, Thomas, *Reminiscences of My Irish Journey in 1849* (London, 1882).

Carson, Rachel, *Silent Spring* (Fawcett Crest, New York, 1962).

Carter, Charles, *Wealth: an Essay on the Purposes of Economics* (Penguin, London, 1968).

Cartter, Allan Murray, *Redistribution of Incomes in Post-War Britain* (Oxford University Press, Oxford, 1955).

Centre for Health Economics, *Priorities for Health Promotion: an Economic Approach* (University of York, York, n.d.).

Centre for Science and Environment, *The State of India's Environment, 1984-5* (New Delhi, 1985).

Centre for Science and Environment, *The Wrath of Nature: the Impact of Environmental Destruction on Floods and Droughts* (New Delhi, 1987).

Cipolla, Carlo, *The Economic History of World Population* (Penguin, London, 1962).

Clarke, John, *The Price of Progress: Cobbett's England, 1780-1835* (Granada, St Albans, 1977).

Cobbett, William, *Rural Rides* (Penguin, London, 1967).

Coghill, Roger, *Electropollution* (Thorsons, Wellingborough, 1990).

Commoner, Barry, *Science and Survival* (Ballantine, New York, 1970).

Commoner, Barry, *The Closing Circle* (Cape, London, 1971).

Congdon, Tim, *The Debt Trap* (Blackwell, Oxford, 1988).

Congdon, Tim, *Monetarism Lost* (Centre for Policy Studies, London, 1989).

Connery, Donald, *The Irish* (Eyre and Spottiswoode, London, 1969).

Cook, D. G., Cummins, R. O., Bartley, M. J., and Shaper, A. G., 'Health of unemployed middle-aged men in Great Britain', *The Lancet*, vol. 2 (1982).

Cooley, Mike, *Architect or Bee?: the Human Price of Technology* (Hogarth Press, London, 1987).

Crotty, Raymond, *Ireland in Crisis* (Brandon, Dingle, 1986).

Crotty, Raymond, *Farming Collapse: National Opportunity* (Amárach, Dublin, 1990).

Curwen, P. J., *Inflation* (Macmillan, London, 1976).

Daly, Herman, 'The economics of the steady state', *American Economic Review* (1974).

Daly, Herman, and Cobb, John, *For the Common Good* (Green Print, London, 1989).

Dammann, Eric, *The Future in Our Hands* (Pergamon, Oxford, 1979).

Darval, Frank, *Popular Disturbances and Public Order in Regency England: Being an Account of the Luddite and Other Disorders in England, 1811-17* (Oxford University Press, Oxford, 1969).

Das, Amritananda, *Foundations of Gandhian Economics* (Allied, Bombay, 1979).

Davidson, Frank, *Big is Beautiful* (Blond, London, 1986).

Davis, Earl, and Fine-Davis, Margret, 'Predictors of satisfaction with environmental quality in eight European countries', *Social Indicators Research* (11) (1982).

Davis, Lance, and Huttenback, Robert, *Mammon and the Pursuit of Empire: the Economics of British Imperialism* (Cambridge University Press, New York, 1986).

Deane, Phyllis, *The First Industrial Revolution* (Cambridge University Press, Cambridge, 1965).

de Groot, R. S., *A Functional Ecosystem Evaluation Method* (Agricultural University, Wageningen, 1986).

de Jonge, V. N., Essink, K., and Boddeke, R., 'The Dutch Wadden Sea: a changed ecosystem', *Hydrobiologia* (in press).

Department of Education and Science (Britain), *Statistical Bulletin* (March 1990).

Department of the Environment (Britain), *Digest of Environmental and Water Statistics* (HMSO, London, 1990).

Department of Foreign Affairs (Ireland), *Into Europe: Ireland and the EEC* (Stationery Office, Dublin, n.d.).

Department of Industry and Commerce (Ireland), *Review of Industrial Performance, 1986* (Stationery Office, Dublin, 1986).

Department of Industry and Commerce (Ireland), *Review of Industrial Performance, 1990* (Stationery Office, Dublin, 1990).

de Schweinitz, Karl, *England's Road to Social Security* (Barnes, New York, 1961).

de Scitovsky, Tibor, *Economic Theory and Western European Integration* (Greenwood Press, Westport [Connecticut], 1958).

Diwan, Romesh, and Lutz, Mark (eds), *Essays in Gandhian Economics* (Gandhi Peace Foundation, New Delhi, 1985).

Dobb, Maurice, *Capitalism Yesterday and Today* (Lawrence and Wishart, London, 1958).

Dobb, Maurice, *Economic Growth and Underdeveloped Countries* (Lawrence and Wishart, London, 1963).

Dobb, Maurice, *Studies in the Development of Capitalism* (Routledge, London, 1963).

Dunning, John, *The Role of American Investment in the British Economy* (PEP, London, 1969).

Ecologist, The, A Blueprint for Survival (Penguin, London, 1972).

Economic and Social Research Institute, *The Economics of 1992: a Symposium* (ESRI, Dublin, 1989).

Economic and Social Research Institute, *Poverty, Income and Welfare in Ireland* (ESRI, Dublin, 1989).

Edwardes, Michael, *The Myth of the Mahatma: Gandhi, the British and the Raj* (Constable, London, 1986).

Ehrlich, Paul, *The Population Bomb* (Ballantine, London, 1971).

Ehrlich, Paul, and Ehrlich, Anne, *The Population Explosion* (Hutchinson, London, 1990).

Ehrlich, Paul, and Harriman, Richard, *How to be a Survivor: a Plan to Save Spaceship Earth* (Pan, London, 1971).

Ekins, Paul (ed.), *The Living Economy: a New Economics in the Making* (Routledge, London, 1986).

Energy in Europe (September 1989).

Estes, Richard, *The Social Progress of Nations* (Praeger, New York, 1990).

Eurostat, *Basic Statistics of the Community* (Eurostat, Luxembourg, 1990).

Eurostat, *Environmental Statistics, 1989* (EC, Luxembourg, 1990).

Evans, Philip, and Edgerton, Nick, 'Life events and mood as predictors of the common cold', *British Journal of Medical Psychology*, vol. 64 (1991).

Fanning, Ronan, 'Economists and government, Ireland 1922-52' in A. E. Murphy (ed.), *Economists and the Irish Economy from the Eighteenth Century to the Present Day* (Irish Academic Press, Dublin, 1984).

Fenwick, Jack, and Mielnick, Pat, 'Alternative farming: lower yields a myth', *ILEIA Newsletter* (September 1990).

Ferro, Marc, *The Great War, 1914-1918* (Routledge, London, 1974).

Field, Simon, *Trends in Crime and Their Interpretation: a Study of Recorded Crime in Post-war England and Wales* (Home Office Research Study 119, HMSO, London, 1990).

Finn, Ronald, 'Nourishing the mind', *McGarrison Society Newsletter* (April 1989).

Fisher-Fishbein, J., 'The effects of pharmaceutical, environmental and occupational agents on sperm motility' in Claude Gagnon (ed.), *Control of Sperm Motility: Biological and Clinical Aspects* (CRC Press, New York, 1990).

Foley, Anthony, and Mulreany, Michael (eds), *The Single European Market and the Irish Economy* (Institute of Public Administration, Dublin, 1990).

Frank, André Gunder, *World Accumulation, 1492-1789* (Macmillan, London, 1978).

Fraser, Derek, *The Evolution of the British Welfare State* (Macmillan, London, 1984).

Frayman, Harold, *Breadline Britain, 1990s: the Findings of the Television Series* (London Weekend Television, London, 1991).

Fremlin, John, *Power Production: What Are the Risks?* (Oxford University Press, Oxford, 1987).

Friedman, Irving, *Inflation: a Worldwide Disaster* (Hamish Hamilton, London, 1973).

Fromm, Erich, *To Have or to Be?* (Abacus, London, 1979).

Galbraith, John Kenneth, *Economics, Peace and Laughter* (Deutsch, London, 1971).

Galbraith, John Kenneth, *Money: Whence it Came, Where it Went* (Penguin, London, 1976).

Galbraith, John Kenneth, *The Affluent Society* (third ed., Deutsch, London, 1977).

Galbraith, John Kenneth, *The Age of Uncertainty* (Deutsch, London, 1977).

Galbraith, John Kenneth, *The Nature of Mass Poverty* (Penguin, London, 1980).

Galbraith, John Kenneth, *Economics in Perspective* (Houghton Mifflin, Boston, 1987).

Gandhi, M. K., *Unto This Last: a Paraphrase* (Navajivan, Ahmedabad, 1956).

Gandhi, M. K., *Panchayat Raj* (Navajivan, Ahmedabad, 1959).

Gandhi, M. K., *Village Industries* (Navajivan, Ahmedabad, 1960).

Gatto, J. T., 'Confessions of a teacher', *Resurgence*, 148 (September 1991).

George, Dorothy, *England in Transition* (Penguin, London, 1953).

George, Susan, *How the Other Half Dies: the Real Reasons for World Hunger* (Penguin, London, 1977).

George, Susan, *A Fate Worse than Debt* (Penguin, London, 1988).

Gershuny, Jonathan, 'Time budgets as social indicators', *Journal of Public Policy*, vol. 9 (4).

Gever, John, Kaufman, Robert, Skole, David, and Vorosmarty, Charles, *Beyond Oil* (Ballinger, Cambridge [Massachusetts], 1987).

Giffen, Robert, *Economic Inquiries and Studies*, vol. 2 (Bell, London, 1904).

Gilder, George, *Wealth and Poverty* (Buchan and Enright, London, 1982).

Gimpel, Jean, *The Medieval Machine: the Industrial Revolution of the Middle Ages* (Gollancz, London, 1976).

Glyptis, Sue, *Leisure and Unemployment* (Open University, Milton Keynes, 1989).

Goldsmith, Edward, *The Stable Society* (Wadebridge Press, Cornwall, 1978).

Goldsmith, Edward, *The Great U-Turn: De-industrializing Society* (Green Books, Hartland, 1988).

Gough, Richard, *The History of Myddle* (Macdonald Futura, London, 1981).

Gould, J. D., *Economic Growth in History* (Methuen, London, 1972).

Government of India, *Economic Survey, 1987-88* (Ministry of Finance, New Delhi, 1988).

Graham, Frank, *Since Silent Spring* (Pan, London, 1972).

Gratton, Chris, and Taylor, Peter, *Leisure in Britain* (Leisure Publications, Letchworth, 1987).

Green, Francis, and Sutcliffe, Bob, *The Profit System: the Economics of Capitalism* (Penguin, London, 1987).

Greenpeace International, *The Failure of the Montreal Protocol* (Greenpeace International, Amsterdam, 1990).

Grierson, Edward, *The Imperial Dream: British Commonwealth and Empire, 1775-1969* (Collins, London, 1972).

Griffin, Keith, *Land Concentration and Rural Poverty* (Macmillan, London, 1976).

Griffith, Arthur, *The Resurrection of Hungary: a Parallel for Ireland* (Dublin, 1904).

Habback, Eva, *The Population of Britain* (Penguin, London, 1947).

Hall, John, 'Subjective measures of quality of life in Britain, 1971-1975: some developments and trends', *Social Trends*, no. 7 (1976).

Hansen, Stein, *India: Development and Aid: Norway's Contribution and Future Options* (Hansen, Bekkestua, 1987).

Harris, Kenneth, *Thatcher* (Fontana, London, 1989).

Harris, Marvin, *Cannibals and Kings: the Origins of Cultures* (Random House, New York, 1977).

Harrison, Bennett, and Bluestone, Barry, *The Great U-Turn: Corporate Restructuring and the Polarizing of America* (Basic, New York, 1990).

Hartman, Betsy, and Boyce, James, *Needless Hunger* (Institute for Food and Policy Development, San Francisco, 1982).

Hartman, Carolyn, *Du Pont Fiddles While the World Burns* (New York, 1989).

Hayter, Teresa, *Aid as Imperialism* (Penguin, London, 1971).

Hayter, Teresa, *The Creation of World Poverty* (Pluto, London, 1981).

Hazarika, Sanjoy, *Bhopal: the Lessons of a Tragedy* (Penguin, New Delhi, 1987).

Heer, David, 'Marketable licences for babies: Boulding's proposal revisited', *Social Biology* (spring 1975).

Henderson, Hazel, *Politics of the Solar Age: Alternatives to Economics* (Doubleday, New York, 1981).

Henley Centre for Forecasting, *Planning for Social Change, 1989-90* (1) (1989).

Henriksson, Benny, *Not for Sale: Young People in Society* (Aberdeen University Press, Aberdeen, 1983).

Hey, Christian, *Ecology and the Single Market* (European Environmental Bureau, Brussels, 1989).

Hibbert, Christopher, *The Dragon Wakes: China and the West, 1793-1911* (Longman, London, 1970).

Higgins, Benjamin, *Economic Development* (Norton, New York, 1959).

Hildyard, Nicholas, *Cover Up: the Facts They Don't Want You to Know* (NEL,

London, 1983).

Hillman, Meyer, Adams, John, and Whitelegg, John, *One False Move ...* (Policy Studies Institute, London, 1990).

Hillman, Meyer, and Whalley, Anne, *The Social Consequences of Rail Closures* (Policy Studies Institute, London, 1980).

Hillman, Meyer, and Whalley, Anne, *Energy and Personal Travel: Obstacles to Conservation* (Policy Studies Institute, London, 1983).

Hills, John, *Changing Tax* (Child Poverty Action Group, London, 1989).

Himmelfarb, Gertrude, *The Idea of Poverty: England in the Early Industrial Age* (Faber, London, 1984).

Hindess, Barry, and Hirst, Paul, *Pre-Capitalist Modes of Production* (Routledge, London, 1975).

Hirsch, Fred, *Social Limits to Growth* (Routledge, London, 1977).

Hobsbawm, E. J., *Industry and Empire* (Penguin, London, 1969).

Hodson, H. V., *The Diseconomics of Growth* (Pan, London, 1972).

Holt, John, *Freedom and Beyond* (Penguin, London, 1973).

Howard, Rhoda, *Colonialism and Underdevelopment in Ghana* (Croom Helm, London, 1978).

Hueting, Roefie, *New Scarcity and Economic Growth: More Welfare through Less Production?* (North-Holland, Amsterdam, 1980).

Hueting, Roefie, 'An economic scenario for a conserver-economy' in Paul Ekins (ed.), *The Living Economy* (Routledge, London, 1986).

Illich, Ivan, *Deschooling Society* (Harper and Row, New York, 1971).

Illich, Ivan, *Energy and Equity* (Marion Boyars, London, 1974).

Inglis, Brian, *The Story of Ireland* (Faber, London, 1964).

Inglis, Henry, *A Journey Through Ireland During the Spring and Summer of 1834* (London, 1835).

Ingrams, Richard, *Cobbett's Country Book* (David and Charles, Newton Abbot, 1974).

Jacobs, Jane, *The Economy of Cities* (Cape, London, 1970).

Jahoda, J., 'Work, employment and unemployment', *American Psychologist*, vol. 36 (1981).

Jalée, Pierre, *The Pillage of the Third World* (Monthly Review Press, New York, 1968).

Jayal, N. D., *Eliminating Poverty: an Ecological Response* (Intach, New Delhi, 1986).

Jefferson, Michael, *Inflation* (Calder, London, 1977).

Jenkins, Robin, *The Road to Alto* (Pluto, London, 1979).

Johnson, H. G., 'The criteria of economic advantage', *Bulletin of the Oxford University Institute of Statistics*, vol. 19 (1957).

Johnson, H. G., 'The gains from freer trade in Europe: an estimate', *Manchester School of Economic and Social Studies*, vol. 26 (1958).

Jones, Aubrey, *The New Inflation* (Penguin, London, 1973).

Jones, E. L., *Growth Recurring: Economic Change in World History* (Clarendon, Oxford, 1988).

Jones, Peter, *Energy and the Need for Nuclear Power* (UK Atomic Energy Authority, London, 1989).

Journal of Public Policy, 'Whatever happened to social indicators?: a symposium', vol. 9 (4).

Kalpavriksh, *The Narmada Valley Project: a Critique* (Ashish Kothari, Delhi, 1988).

Karas, J. H. W., and Kelly, P. M., *The Heat Trap: the Threat Posed by Rising Levels of Greenhouse Gases* (Friends of the Earth, London, 1989).

Kennedy, Kieran (ed.), *Ireland in Transition: Economic and Social Change since 1960* (Mercier, Cork, 1986).

Kennedy, Kieran, and Dowling, Brendan, *Economic Growth in Ireland* (Gill and Macmillan, Dublin, 1975).

Kennedy, Kieran, Giblin, Thomas, and McHugh, Deirdre, *The Economic Development of Ireland in the Twentieth Century* (Routledge, London, 1988).

Kennedy, Kieran, and Healy, Tom, *Small-Scale Manufacturing Industry in Ireland* (ESRI, Dublin, 1985).

Kennedy, Stanislaus, *One Million Poor?: the Challenge of Irish Inequality* (Turoe, Dublin, 1981).

Keynes, John Maynard, 'National self-sufficiency', *Studies* (June 1933).

Knight, Denis, *Cobbett in Ireland: a Warning to England* (Lawrence and Wishart, London, 1984).

Knights, I., *The Heights and Weights of Adults in Britain* (HMSO, London, 1984).

Kohr, Leopold, *The Overdeveloped Nations* (Davies, Swansea, 1977).

Kohr, Leopold, *The Breakdown of Nations* (Dutton, New York, 1978).

Kohr, Leopold, *Development without Aid: the Translucent Society* (Schocken, New York, 1979).

Krause, F., Bach, W., and Koomey, J., *Energy Policy in the Greenhouse* (European Environmental Bureau, Brussels, 1989).

Kraybill, Donald, *The Riddle of Amish Culture* (Johns Hopkins University Press, Baltimore, 1989).

Kriedte, Peter, *Peasants, Landlords and Merchant Capitalists* (Berg, Leamington Spa, 1983).

Krugman, Paul, 'Is free trade passé?', *Journal of Economic Perspectives*, vol. 1, no. 2 (1987).

Kumarappa, J. C., *The Economy of Permanence* (Akhil Bharat Sarva-Séva-Sangh, Wardha, 1958).

Lake, Mike, 'Surveying all the factors', *Language and Learning* (June 1991).

Lappé, Frances Moore, and Collins, Joseph, *Food First: the Myth of Scarcity* (Souvenir, London, 1980).

Lappé, Frances Moore, and Collins, Joseph, *World Hunger: Ten Myths* (Institute for Food and Development Policy, San Francisco, 1982).

Large, Martin, *Who's Bringing Who Up?: Television and Child Development* (Hawthorn Press, Stroud [Gloucestershire], 1990).

Lawson, Hilary, *The Greenhouse Conspiracy* (Channel 4 Television, London, 1990).

Lee, Joseph, *Ireland, 1912-1985* (Cambridge University Press, Cambridge, 1989).

Leggett, Jeremy (ed.), *Global Warming: the Greenpeace Report* (Oxford University Press, Oxford, 1990).

Lester, G. Edwards, *The Glory and Shame of England* (Bartram and Lester, New York, 1866).

Lever, Harold, and Huhne, Christopher, *Debt and Danger: the World Financial Crisis* (Penguin, London, 1985).

Levine, Richard, *Temperature and Environmental Effects on the Testes* (Plenum Press, New York, 1991).

Lewis, W. Arthur, *The Theory of Economic Growth* (Unwin, London, 1955).

Linder, Staffan, *The Harried Leisure Class* (Columbia University Press, New York, 1970).

Lipsey, Richard, 'After monetarism', in John Cornwall (ed.), *After Stagflation: Alternatives to Economic Decline* (Sharpe, London, 1984).

Litton, Frank (ed.), *Unequal Achievement: the Irish Experience, 1957-1982* (Institute of Public Administration, Dublin, 1982).

Liversidge, Douglas, *The Luddites: Machine Breakers of the Early Nineteenth Century* (Watts, London, 1972).

London Food Commission, *Food Adulteration and How to Beat It* (Unwin, London, 1988).

Lorenz, Konrad, *Civilized Man's Eight Deadly Sins* (Methuen, London, 1974).

Lovelock, James, 'Stand up for Gaia', *The Biologist*, vol. 36 (1989).

Lux, Kenneth, *Adam Smith's Mistake: How a Moral Philosopher Invented Economics and Ended Morality* (Shambhala, Boston, 1990).

McAleese, Dermot, *A Profile of Grant-Aided Industry in Ireland* (Industrial Development Authority, Dublin, 1977).

McCarthy, John (ed.), *Planning Ireland's Future: the Legacy of T. K. Whitaker* (Glendale, Dublin, 1990).

McCloy, Elizabeth C., 'Work, environment and the fetus', *Midwifery* (5) (1989).

McDonagh, Seán, *To Care for the Earth: a Call to a New Theology* (Chapman, London, 1986).

McGilvray, James, *Irish Economic Statistics* (IPA, Dublin, 1968).

McRobie, George, *Small is Possible* (Sphere, London, 1982).

Maddox, John, *The Doomsday Syndrome* (Macmillan, London, 1972).

Maddox, John, *Beyond the Energy Crisis* (Hutchinson, London, 1975).

Malthus, Thomas Robert, *An Essay on Population* (Dent, London, 1952).

Mankekar, D. R., *A Revolution of Rising Expectations* (Vikas, Delhi, 1975).

Map, Kurt, *The British Economy and the Working Class* (London Workers' League, London, 1959).

Marlow, Joyce, *The Peterloo Massacre* (Rapp and Whiting, London, 1969).

Martinez-Alier, Juan, *Ecological Economics: Energy, Environment and Society* (Blackwell, Oxford, 1987).

Marx, Karl, *Capital* (Dent, London, 1933).

Marx, Karl, and Engels, Frederick, *Ireland and the Irish Question* (Progress, Moscow, 1971).

Max-Neef, Manfred, *From the Outside Looking In: Experiences in Barefoot Economics* (Dag Hammarskjöld Foundation, Uppsala, 1982).

Maynard, Geoffrey, and van Ryckehem, W., *A World of Inflation* (Batsford, London, 1976).

Mayo, Katherine, *Mother India* (Cape, London, 1927).

Meadows, Donella, Meadows, Dennis, Randers, Jorgen, and Behrens, William, *The Limits to Growth* (Earth Island, London, 1972).

Meenan, James, *The Irish Economy Since 1922* (Liverpool University Press, Liverpool, 1970).

Merson, John, *Roads to Xanadu: East and West in the Making of the Modern World* (Weidenfeld, London, 1989).

Middlesex Polytechnic, *The Second Islington Crime Survey* (1990).

Millar, Susanna, *The Psychology of Play* (Penguin, London, 1968).

Millstone, Erik, and Abraham, John, *Additives: a Guide for Everyone* (Penguin, London, 1988).

Ministry of Agriculture, Fisheries and Food (Britain), *Pesticide Safety Precaution Scheme, Cleared Product List* (1985).

Mishan, E. J., *The Costs of Economic Growth* (Staples, London, 1967).

Mishan, E. J., *Twenty-One Popular Economic Fallacies* (Penguin, London, 1969).

Mishan, E. J., *Making the World Safe for Pornography* (Alcove, London, 1973).

Mishan, E. J., *The Economic Growth Debate: an Assessment* (London, 1977).

Mitchison, Naomi, *The Africans: a History* (Blond, London, 1987).

Morehouse, Ward, and Subramaniam, M. Arun, *The Bhopal Tragedy* (Council of International and Public Affairs, New York, 1986).

Morgan, Elaine, *Falling Apart: the Rise and Decline of Urban Civilisation* (Souvenir, London, 1976).

Morgan, Victor, *A History of Money* (Penguin, London, 1965).

Morris, James, *Pax Britannica: the Climax of Empire* (Faber, London, 1968).

Morton, W. Scott, *Japan, its History and Culture* (David and Charles, Newton Abbot, 1973).

Moser, K. A., Fox, A. J., and Jones, D. R., 'Unemployment and mortality in the OPCS Longitudinal Study', *The Lancet*, vol. 2 (1984).

Moser, K. A., Fox, A. J., and Jones, D. R., 'Unemployment and mortality' in R. G. Wilkinson (ed.), *Class and Health* (Tavistock, London, 1986).

Mowat, C. L., *Britain Between the Wars* (London, 1955).

Mulhall, Michael, *Fifty Years of National Progress, 1837-1887* (Routledge, London, 1887).

Mulloy, Fergal, 'Tropical deforestation: why bother?', *Irish Forestry*, vol. 46 (2) (1989).

Mumford, Lewis, *Technics and Civilization* (Routledge, London, 1934).

Mumford, Lewis, *The Pentagon of Power* (Secker, London, 1971).

Nadkarni, M. V., *Farmers' Movements in India* (Allied, Ahmedabad, 1987).

National Economic and Social Council, *A Review of Industrial Policy* (NESC, Dublin, 1982).

National Economic and Social Council, *An Analysis of Job Losses in Irish Manufacturing Industry* (NESC, Dublin, 1983).

National Environmental Policy Plan, *To Choose or to Lose* (SDU, The Hague, 1989).

National Research Council, *Alternative Agriculture* (National Academy Press, Washington, 1989).

New Socialist, Breaking the Nation: a Guide to Thatcher's Britain (Pluto, London, 1985).

Nicolson, R. I., and Fawcett, A. J., 'Automaticity: a new framework for dyslexia research', *Cognition*, vol. 35 (1990).

Nisbet, Robert, *History of the Idea of Progress* (Heinemann, London, 1980).

Nordhaus, William, 'Greenhouse economics: count before you leap', *The Economist*, 7 July 1990.

Nordhaus, William, 'To slow or not to slow: the economics of the greenhouse effect' (circulated privately, November 1990).

Nordhaus, William, and Tobin, James, *Economic Growth* (NBER/Columbus University Press, New York, 1972).

Nutting, Anthony, *Scramble for Africa* (Constable, London, 1970).

O'Day, Rosemary, *Economy and Community: Economic and Social History of Pre-Industrial England, 1500-1700* (Black, London, 1975).

OECD, *Historical Statistics 1960-1988* (OECD, Paris, 1990).

OECD, *The State of the Environment* (OECD, Paris, 1991).

One Plus One, *Marital Breakdown and the Health of the Nation* (One Plus One, London, 1991).

Ornstein, Robert, *Psychology: the Study of Human Experience* (Harcourt Brace, New York, 1988).

Packard, Vance, *The Waste Makers* (Penguin, London, 1963).

Page, Robin, *The Decline of an English Village* (Davis Poynter, London, 1975).

Pamuk, Elsie, 'Social class inequality in mortality from 1921 to 1971 in England and Wales', *Population Studies*, 39 (1985).

Panchmi, Basant, *The Seventh Five-Year Plan* (Good Companions, Baroda, India, 1986).

Pande, S. S. Pandhari, *Quest for a New Society* (Sarva-Seva-Sangh Prakashan, Varanasi, n.d.).

Payer, Cheryl, *The Debt Trap: the IMF and the Third World* (Penguin, London, 1975).

Paykel, E. S., 'Depression in women', *British Journal of Psychiatry*, vol. 158, supplement 10 (1991).

Pearce, David (ed.), *Blueprint 2: Greening the World Economy* (Earthscan, London, 1991).

Pearce, David, Markandya, Anil, and Barbier, Edward, *Blueprint for a Green Economy* (Earthscan, London, 1989).

Pearce, Fred, *Acid Rain* (Penguin, London, 1987).

Pearce, Fred, *Turning Up the Heat: Our Perilous Future in the Global Greenhouse* (Bodley Head, London, 1989).

Phelps, Edmund (ed.), *The Goal of Economic Growth* (Norton, New York, 1962).

Phelps Brown, E. H., and Hart, P. E., 'The share of wages in national income', *Economic Journal* (June 1952).

Phelps Brown, E. H., and Hopkins, S. V., 'Seven centuries of the price of consumables, compared with builders' wages', *Economica*, vol. 23 (1956).

Phillips, A. W., 'The relationship between unemployment and the rate of change of money wages in the United Kingdom, 1861-1957', *Economica* (25) (1958).

Pigou, A. C., *The Economics of Welfare* (4th ed., London, 1932).

Playfair, Guy Lyon, *The Evil Eye: the Unacceptable Face of Television* (Cape, London, 1990).

Plumb, J. H., *England in the Eighteenth Century (1714-1815)* (Penguin, London, 1963).

Pollard, Sidney, *The Development of the British Economy, 1914-1950* (Arnold, London, 1962).

Pollard, Sidney, *The Idea of Progress* (Watts, London, 1968).

Porritt, Jonathon, *Seeing Green: the Politics of Ecology Explained* (Blackwell, Oxford, 1984).

Porritt, Jonathon, and Winner, David, *The Coming of the Greens* (Collins, London, 1988).

Postman, Neil, *The Disappearance of Childhood* (W. H. Allen, London, 1983).

Prais, S. J., *The Evolution of Giant Firms in Great Britain, 1909-70* (Cambridge University Press, Cambridge, 1981).

Ramachandran, L., *India's Food Problem* (Allied, New Delhi, 1977).

Rees, Goronwy, *The Great Slump: Capitalism in Crisis, 1929-1933* (Harper and Row, New York, 1970).

Reganold, John, 'Farming's organic future', *New Scientist*, 10 June 1989.

Reich, Robert, *The Next American Frontier* (Penguin, London, 1984).

Reid, Robert, *The Land of Lost Content: the Luddite Revolt of 1812* (Heinemann, London, 1986).

Rentoul, John, *The Rich Get Richer: the Growth of Inequality in the Britain of the 1980s* (Unwin, London, 1987).

Reynolds, Brigid, and Healy, Seán (eds), *Work, Unemployment and Job-Creation Policy* (Conference of Major Religious Superiors, Dublin, 1990).

Reynolds, Brigid, and Healy, Seán (eds), *What Future for Rural Ireland?* (Conference of Major Religious Superiors, Dublin, 1991).

Reynolds, Reginald, *White Sahibs of India* (Secker, London, 1938).

Roberts, K., 'Socioeconomic polarisation and the implications of leisure' in K. Roberts and Anna Olszewska (eds), *Leisure and Lifestyle* (Sage, London, 1989).

Rodney, Walter, *How Europe Underdeveloped Africa* (Bogle-L'Ouverture, London, 1972).

Roebuck, Janet, *The Making of Modern English Society from 1850* (Routledge, London, 1973).

Roll, Eric, *A History of Economic Thought* (Faber, London, 1961).

Rolt, L. T. C., *High Horse Riderless* (Green Books, Hartland, 1988).

Rose, Chris, *The Dirty Man of Europe: the Great British Pollution Scandal* (Simon and Schuster, London, 1990).

Rothermund, Dietmar, *An Economic History of India* (Croom Helm, London, 1988).

Routh, Guy, *Occupation and Pay in Great Britain, 1906-1960* (Macmillan, London, 1968).

Roy, Ramashray, *Against the Current: Essays in Alternative Development* (Institute for Rural Development, Patna, 1981).

Rubinstein, W. D., *Wealth and the Wealthy in the Modern World* (Croom Helm, London, 1980).

Rubinstein, W. D., *Wealth and Inequality in Britain* (Faber, London, 1986).

Ryder, Judith, and Silver, Harold, *Modern English Society: History and Structure, 1850-1970* (Methuen, London, 1970).

Sale, Kirkpatrick, *Human Scale* (Secker, London, 1980).

Salunke, Vilasrao, *Pani Panchayat: Dividing Line Between Poverty and Prosperity* (Gram Gourav Pratishthan, Pune, 1983).

Sampson, Anthony, *The Money Lenders: Bankers in a Dangerous World* (Hodder, London, 1981).

Saorstát Éireann, *Official Handbook* (Stationery Office, Dublin, 1932).

Schultz, Theodore, *Transforming Traditional Agriculture* (Yale University Press, New Haven, 1964).

Schultz, Theodore, *Economic Crises in World Agriculture* (University of Michigan, Ann Arbor, 1965).

Schumacher, E. F., *Small Is Beautiful* (Sphere, London, 1974).

Schumpeter, Joseph, *History of Economic Analysis* (Oxford University Press, New York, 1954).

Schumpeter, Joseph, *The Theory of Economic Development* (Oxford University Press, New York, 1961).

Science Policy Research Unit, University of Sussex, *Thinking about the Future: a Critique of 'The Limits to Growth'* (Chatto, London, 1973).

Scientific American, Man and the Ecosphere (Freeman, San Francisco, 1971).

Scott, James, *Weapons of the Weak* (Yale University Press, London, 1987).

Seers, Dudley, *The Levelling of Incomes since 1938* (Oxford University Press, Oxford, 1951).

Shanks, Michael, *The Stagnant Society* (Penguin, London, 1961).

Shields, Jon (ed.), *Conquering Unemployment: the Case for Economic Growth* (Macmillan, London, 1989).

Simmons, I. G., *Changing the Face of the Earth: Culture, Environment, History* (Blackwell, Oxford, 1989).

Simon, Julian, *The Ultimate Resource* (Robertson, Oxford, 1981).

Simon, Julian, and Kahn, Herman, *The Resourceful Earth* (Blackwell, Oxford, 1984).

Singh, Chhatrapati, *Common Property and Common Poverty: India's Forests, Forest Dwellers and the Law* (Oxford University Press, Delhi, 1986).

Singh, Chhatrapati, *Forestry and the Law in India* (Indian Law Institute, New Delhi, 1987).

Singh, Narindar, *Economics and the Crisis of Ecology* (Oxford University Press, Delhi, 1976).

Sinha, Radha, *Food and Poverty* (Croom Helm, London, 1976).

Sked, Alan, *Britain's Decline: Problems and Perspectives* (Blackwell, Oxford, 1987).

Slesser, Malcolm, *The Management of Greed: ECCO – Introductory Guide* (Resource Use Institute, Pitlochry, 1990).

Slesser, Malcolm, and de Vries, Bert, *The Potential for Economic Growth in the European Community in the Context of Greenhouse Gas Constraints* (IVEM, University of Groningen, 1990).

Smith, Adam, *The Theory of Moral Sentiments* (1759) (Bell, London, 1907).

Smith, Adam, *The Wealth of Nations* (1776) (Dent, London, 1960).

Smith, Cyril, and Best, Simon, *Electromagnetic Man: Health and Hazard in the Electrical Environment* (Dent, London, 1989).

Smith, David, *The Rise and Fall of Monetarism* (Penguin, London, 1987).

Smith, J. W., *The World's Wasted Wealth: the Political Economy of Waste* (New World, Montana, 1989).

Soil Remineralization (summer 1989).

Sorel, Georges, *The Illusions of Progress* (University of California, Los Angeles, 1969).

South Commission, *The Challenge to the South* (Geneva, 1990).

Southampton Chamber of Commerce, *Report of the Economic Crisis Committee* (Southampton Chamber of Commerce, Southampton, 1933).

Southern, R. W., *The Making of the Middle Ages* (Hutchinson, London, 1953).

Srivastava, S. K., *History of Economic Thought* (Chand, New Delhi, 1983).

Stark, Thomas, *Income and Wealth in the 1980s* (Fabian Society, London, 1990).

Stassinopoulos, Arianna, *The Other Revolution* (Michael Joseph, London, 1978).

Steeno, O. P., and Pangkahila, A., 'Occupational influence on male fertility and sexuality', *Andrologia*, vol. 16 (1) (1984).

Stone, Richard, and Stone, Giovanna, *National Income and Expenditure* (Bowes, London, 1966).

Storry, Richard, *A History of Modern Japan* (Penguin, London, 1960).

Sturmey, S. G., *Income and Economic Welfare* (Longman, London, 1959).

Tawney, R. H., *The Acquisitive Society* (Bell, London, 1921).

Tawney, R. H., *Religion and the Rise of Capitalism* (Penguin, London, 1938).

Taylor, Gordon Rattray, *Rethink: a Paraprimitive Solution* (Secker, London, 1972).

Thatcher, Margaret, *Let Our Children Grow Tall* (Centre for Policy Studies, London, 1977).

Theobald, Robert, *An Alternative Future for America II* (Swallow, Chicago, 1971).

Thomas, Hugh, *An Unfinished History of the World* (London, 1979).

Thomson, David, *England in the Nineteenth Century (1815-1914)* (Penguin, London, 1950).

Thornton, Peter, *Decade of Decline: Civil Liberties in the Thatcher Years* (National Council for Civil Liberties, London, 1989).

Tobin, Fergal, *The Best of Decades: Ireland in the 1960s* (Gill and Macmillan, Dublin, 1984).

Toke, David, *Green Energy: a Non-Nuclear Response to the Greenhouse Effect* (Green Print, London, 1990).

Townsend, Peter, Davidson, Nick, and Whitehead, Margaret, *Inequalities in Health* (Penguin, London, 1988).

Trainer, Ted, *Developed to Death* (Green Print, London, 1989).

Treithick, J. A., *Inflation: a Guide to the Crisis in Economics* (Penguin, London, 1980).

Tsui Chi, *A Short History of Chinese Civilisation* (Gollancz, London, 1942).

Tudge, Colin, *The Famine Business* (Faber, London, 1977).

UNDP, *Human Development Report, 1990* (Oxford University Press, Oxford, 1990).

Unemployment Unit, *UK Unemployment Figures, 1980-91* (HMSO, London, 1991).

Utton, M. A., *The Political Economy of Big Business* (Martin Robertson, London, 1982).

van Dieren, W., and Hummelinck, M. G. W., *Nature's Price: the Economics of Mother Earth* (Marion Boyars, London, 1979).

Vohra, B. B., *The Greening of India* (Intach, New Delhi, 1985).

Wachtel, Paul, *The Poverty of Affluence: a Psychological Portrait of the American Way of Life* (New Society, Philadelphia, 1989).

Wadsworth, M. E. J., 'The influence of childhood on later life: some evidence from the national birth cohort study' (University of Exeter, 1989).

Wadsworth, M. E. J., and Maclean, M., 'Parents' divorce and child's life chances', *Child and Youth Services Review*, vol. 8 (1986).

Walker, Caroline, and Cannon, Geoffrey, *The Food Scandal* (Century, London, 1984).

Wallerstein, Judith, and Blakeslee, Sandra, *Second Chances* (Bantam, London, 1989).

Ward, Barbara, and Dubos, René, *Only One Earth: the Care and Maintenance of a Small Planet* (Penguin, London, 1972).

Warrick, R. A., Barrow, E. M., and Wigley, T. M. L., *The Greenhouse Effect and its Implications for the European Community* (European Commission, Luxembourg, 1990).

Weber, Max, *The Protestant Ethic and the Spirit of Capitalism* (1904) (Scribner's, New York, 1958).

Weir, David, *The Bhopal Syndrome: Pesticides, Environment and Health* (Earthscan, London, 1988).

West, Richard, *Brazza of the Congo* (Cape, London, 1972).

Westergaard, John, and Resler, Henrietta, *Class in a Capitalist Society: a Study of Contemporary Britain* (Penguin, London, 1976).

Whelan, Christopher, Hannan, Damien, and Creighton, Seán, *Unemployment, Poverty and Psychological Distress* (Economic and Social Research Institute, Dublin, 1991).

Whelan, Robert, *Mounting Greenery* (Institute of Economic Affairs, London, 1989).

Whitaker, T. K., *Economic Development* (Stationery Office, Dublin, 1958).

Wilkinson, Richard (ed.), *Class and Health: Research and Longitudinal Data* (Tavistock, London, 1986).

Wilkinson, Richard, 'Class mortality differentials, income distribution and trends in poverty, 1921-1981', *Journal of Social Policy*, vol. 18 (3) (1989).

Wilkinson, Richard, 'Income distribution and mortality: a "natural" experiment', *Sociology of Health and Illness*, vol. 12 (4) (1990).

Wilsher, Peter, *The Pound in Your Pocket, 1870-1970* (Cassell, London, 1970).

Winpenny, J. T., *Values for the Environment: a Guide to Economic Appraisal* (HMSO, London, 1991).

Wood, Anthony, *Nineteenth-Century Britain, 1815-1914* (Longman, London, 1960).

Woodham-Smith, Cecil, *The Great Hunger* (Harper and Row, New York, 1962).

World Bank, *World Development Report, 1990: Poverty* (Oxford University Press, Oxford, 1990).

World Commission on Environment and Development, *Our Common Future* (Oxford University Press, Oxford, 1987).

World Resources Institute, *World Resources, 1990-91: a Guide to the Global Environment* (Oxford University Press, New York, 1990).

Yellowlees, Walter, *Ill Fares the Land* (Wholefood Trust, London, 1989).

Young, John, *Post Environmentalism* (Belhaven, London, 1990).

Yudkin, John, *Pure, White and Deadly* (Penguin, London, 1988).

The following periodicals were also important sources of information and ideas: *The Aisling* (Inis Mór, Aran, Ireland), *Aquaculture Ireland* (Dublin), *Common Ground* (Boyle, Ireland), *The Courier* (Brussels), *Earthwatch* (Bantry, Ireland), *The Ecologist* (Sturminster Newton, England), *Economic and Political Weekly* (Bombay), *The Economist* (London), *Food Matters Worldwide* (Norwich, England), *Fourth World Review* (London), *ILEIA Newsletter* (Leusden, The Netherlands), *India Today* (New Delhi), *The Irish Banking Review* (Dublin), *New Economics* (London), *New Scientist* (London), *Resurgence* (Hartland, Devon, England), *South* (London), *Third World Now* (Dublin), *Third World Resurgence* (Penang, Malaysia), *Whole Earth Review* (Sausalito, California), *World Watch* (Washington DC).

Index